Contextual Embeddedness of Women's Entrepreneurship

Contextual Embeddedness of Women's Entrepreneurship brings together a range of research that provides powerful insights into the influences and restraints within a diverse set of gendered contexts including social, political, institutional, religious, patriarchal, cultural, family, and economic, in which female entrepreneurs around the world operate their businesses. In doing so, the contributing authors demonstrate not only the importance of studying the contexts in how they shape women's entrepreneurial activities, but also how female entrepreneurs through their endeavours modify these contexts.

Collectively, the edited collection's studies make a substantial contribution to the contextual embeddedness of women's entrepreneurial activity, provide numerous insights, and provoke fruitful directions for future research on the important role of the contexts in which women's entrepreneurial activities take place.

This innovative and wide-ranging research anthology seeks to reframe and redirect research on gender and entrepreneurship and will appeal to all those interested in learning more about female entrepreneurship.

Shumaila Yousafzai is Associate Professor at Cardiff University, UK. Her research focuses on the contextual embeddedness of entrepreneurship, institutional theory and entrepreneurial orientation. She has published in various international journals and has co-edited a special issue on Women's entrepreneurship for *Entrepreneurship & Regional Development*.

Adam Lindgreen is Professor of Marketing at Copenhagen Business School and Head of the Department of Marketing. He has published in *California Management Review*, *Journal of Business Ethics*, *Journal of Product and Innovation Management*, *Journal of the Academy of Marketing Science*, and *Journal of World Business*.

Saadat Saeed is Associate Professor in Entrepreneurship at the Durham University Business School, Durham University, UK. His past research efforts have included the global study of supportive institutions and women's entrepreneurship, entrepreneurship in adverse conditions, corporate entrepreneurship and firm performance in multi-county context.

Colette Henry, FRSA, is Head of School of Business & Humanities at Dundalk Institute of Technology, Ireland, and Adjunct Professor of Entrepreneurship at UiT-The Arctic University of Norway. Colette holds the Diana International Trailblazer award for female entrepreneurship, and the Sten K Johnson European Entrepreneurship Education Award.

Alain Fayolle is Professor of Entrepreneurship, and the founder and director of the entrepreneurship research centre at EM Lyon Business School, France. Alain has published thirty-five books and over one hundred articles. In 2013, Alain Fayolle got the 2013 European Entrepreneurship Education Award and has been elected Chair of the AOM Entrepreneurship Division for the 2016–2017 academic year. In 2015, he was awarded Wilford L. White Fellow by ICSB.

Contextual Embeddedness of Women's Entrepreneurship

Going beyond a Gender–Neutral Approach

Edited by Shumaila Yousafzai, Adam Lindgreen, Saadat Saeed, Colette Henry and Alain Fayolle

LONDON AND NEW YORK

First published 2018
by Routledge
2 Park Square, Milton Park, Abingdon, Oxon OX14 4RN

and by Routledge
711 Third Avenue, New York, NY 10017

Routledge is an imprint of the Taylor & Francis Group, an informa business

© 2018 selection and editorial matter, Shumaila Yousafzai, Adam Lindgreen, Saadat Saeed, Colette Henry and Alain Fayolle; individual chapters, the contributors

The right of Shumaila Yousafzai, Adam Lindgreen, Saadat Saeed, Colette Henry and Alain Fayolle to be identified as the authors of the editorial material, and of the authors for their individual chapters, has been asserted in accordance with sections 77 and 78 of the Copyright, Designs and Patents Act 1988.

All rights reserved. No part of this book may be reprinted or reproduced or utilised in any form or by any electronic, mechanical, or other means, now known or hereafter invented, including photocopying and recording, or in any information storage or retrieval system, without permission in writing from the publishers.

Trademark notice: Product or corporate names may be trademarks or registered trademarks, and are used only for identification and explanation without intent to infringe.

British Library Cataloguing-in-Publication Data
A catalogue record for this book is available from the British Library

Library of Congress Cataloging-in-Publication Data
A catalog record for this book has been requested

ISBN: 9781472483560 (hbk)
ISBN: 9781315574042 (ebk)

Typeset in Bembo
by Apex CoVantage, LLC

To the business acumen of Khadija bint Khuwaylid, a wealthy trader and a powerful businesswoman who operated her own very successful and highly esteemed caravan business in 7th century Mecca — Shumaila

For my friends Bente and Henrik, Franz and Birgitte, Peder and Camilla, and Tove, who always have been there for me — Adam

To all leading women of my family, without them life would not be as much joyful as it is now. A special thanks to Faiza, Nadia, Sidra and Sehrish — Saadat

To my mum, for bringing me up to be strong and hard-working! — Colette

To my family and to all women entrepreneurs who contribute towards changing the world for the better — Alain

Contents

Dedication	v
About the editors	xiii
About the contributors	xv
Introduction	xx

SECTION 1
Religious embeddedness of women entrepreneurship in the Islamic context   1

1 **Behind the green line: an examination of female entrepreneurial activity in the Muslim world**   3
BANU GOKTAN, VISHAL K. GUPTA, GÖNÜL BUDAK AND ERIK MARKIN

The Islamic context 4
Different implementations of Islam 4
Islam, women and entrepreneurship 5
Islam and female entrepreneurship 5
Female entrepreneurship and secularism 6
Female entrepreneurship in Turkey 7
Methods 9
Analyses and results 10
Discussion 11
Limitations and direction for future research 13

2 **If policy (half-heartedly) says 'yes', but patriarchy says 'no': how the gendered institutional context in Pakistan restricts women entrepreneurship**   18
KHIZRAN ZEHRA AND LEONA ACHTENHAGEN

Gender gap in entrepreneurship 18
Institutional theory as theoretical perspective 19
Critical analysis of the institutional environment in Pakistan 20
The emergence of gender-aware policy-making 21
Informal institutions and the role of patriarchy 26
Discussion 27

viii   *Contents*

Possible ways forward 28
Conclusion 29

3   Gendered expectations and ideologies of patriarchy: contextualizing Arab women's entrepreneurial leadership

33

HAYFAA TLAISS

Definitions of entrepreneurial leadership 34
Lebanon in the light of institutional theory 35
Methodology 36
Findings and discussion 38
Concluding remarks 42

4   'Pleasing the father': the impact of the political leader in shaping women's entrepreneurship in Oman

46

HADIL AL-MOOSA

Introduction 46
Women's entrepreneurship 46
Theoretical framework 47
Multi-level relational framework 48
Research context 50
Methodology 50
Findings 52
Discussion 55
Conclusion 57

5   Leveraging micro-level support factors to overcome macro-level challenges: Palestinian and Saudi Arabian female entrepreneurs

60

BEVERLEY MCNALLY AND GRACE KHOURY

The Palestinian and Saudi Arabian context 61
Methodology 63
Findings 63
Discussion and implications 70
Conclusion 71

6   Women's entrepreneurship in Turkey: promising initiatives and evidence for success in the face of culturally embedded barriers

74

CEYDA M. EYIUSTA

The institutional context of women entrepreneurship in Turkey 75
Key drivers and success factors for women's entrepreneurship in Turkey 79
Research methodology 80
Discussion 83

Contents ix

SECTION 2
Gendered embeddedness of women's entrepreneurial activity in the entrepreneurship ecosystem 89

7 **Developing gender-responsive trade ecosystems in the Asia–Pacific** 91
PATRICE BRAUN

Introduction 91
Positioning the research 92
Ecosystems 92
Trade and gender 94
Internationalization of women-led SME 95
Methodology 95
Survey findings 97
Gender-responsive trade practices framework 99
Discussion 100
Future directions 101

8 **Gender embeddedness in patriarchal contexts undergoing institutional change: evidence from Nepal** 106
MIRELA XHENETI AND SHOVA THAPA KARKI

(Women) Entrepreneurship and the institutional environment 107
The social context in Nepal 108
The formal institutional environment for (women) entrepreneurship
development in Nepal 109
Gendered institutions and women's entrepreneurship – Empirical evidence 110
Conclusions 115

9 **Opportunity creation for female entrepreneurs in the Welsh and Turkish entrepreneurial ecosystem: a social capital perspective** 119
SHANDANA SHEIKH, AYBENIZ AKDENIZ, FEDERICA SIST,
SHUMAILA YOUSAFZAI AND SAADAT SAEED

Women entrepreneurship in Wales and Turkey 120
Social capital and women entrepreneurship 121
Method 123
Findings 125
Conclusion 136

10 **Effectuation thinking and the manifestation of socio-cultural complexities in Sri Lankan female entrepreneurs' business decisions** 139
NADEERA RANABAHU AND MARY BARRETT

Effectuation and causation perspectives on entrepreneurship 140

x   Contents

Country context: Sri Lanka 141
Findings 142
Discussion 148
Implications for research and policy 149

**11   Cultural factors shaping women entrepreneurship in the
     Baltic Sea countries**   154

EWA LISOWSKA

Cultural factors and female entrepreneurship 155
Method 159
Findings 160
Conclusions 162

**12   The business life–cycle and entrepreneurial ecosystem study of women
     entrepreneurs in the Polish tourism industry**   167

ALINA ZAPALSKA AND ERIK WINGROVE-HAUGLAND

The context of women entrepreneurs in Poland 168
Methodology and conceptual framework 169
Findings 171
Analysis of the entrepreneurial ecosystem characteristics 173
Conclusions 177

**13   Women's entrepreneurial realities in the Czech Republic and the
     United States: gender gaps, racial/ethnic disadvantages, and
     emancipatory potential**   180

ALENA KŘÍZKOVÁ, MARIE POSPÍŠILOVÁ, NANCY JURIK AND GRAY CAVENDER

Theoretical Framing and study contexts 181
Methods 183
Findings I: Motivations for business 183
Findings II: Business approaches to disadvantage 187
Discussion and conclusion 190

**14   Women's entrepreneurship in Swedish forestry: a matter of adaptation
     or transformation?**   194

MARIE APPELSTRAND AND GUN LIDESTAV

Gender equality policies in the Swedish forestry sector 196
Gender and the process of modernization 198
Gender and identity 199
Gender and entrepreneurship 201
Concluding discussion 202

Contents xi

15 Women's business survival and the institutionalization of entrepreneurial support in the Malaysian handicraft industry 206

SALMAH TOPIMIN, CLARE BRINDLEY AND CARLEY FOSTER

Women entrepreneurs in the handicraft industry in Malaysia 206
Development of a conceptual framework for the survival of
*   women's businesses 208*
Business survival 209
Construct: business factors 210
Construct: The individual 210
Construct: The culture 211
Construct: GESPs 212
Construct: gender 213
Conclusion 214

16 Developing an understanding of entrepreneurship intertwined with motherhood: a career narrative of British Mumpreneurs 219

SHANDANA SHEIKH, FEDERICA SIST, AYBENIZ AKDENIZ AND
SHUMAILA YOUSAFZAI

Exploring mumpreneurship amidst institutional domain 220
Moving forward 229

17 An interdisciplinary framework to deconstruct second-generation gender bias 233

ETHNÉ SWARTZ AND FRANCES AMATUCCI

The gender-neutral paradox 233
Women entrepreneurs negotiating term sheets for equity funding 234
Social psychology, gender bias and negotiation 236
Labour market economics and gender bias 238
Contributions from law to second-generation gender bias 240
Conclusion 241

18 Entrepreneurial passion and social entrepreneurial self-efficacy among Spanish and Moroccan young females 247

JUAN DIEGO BORRERO

Women and social entrepreneurship in the contexts of Spain and Morocco 248
Conceptual development 249
Methodology 251
Results 253
Discussion and conclusions 254

xii *Contents*

SECTION 3
Moving forward   259

19 The lean scientific canvas method: a proposal to foster women's
    entrepreneurship in Mexico   261
    VERÓNICA ILIÁN BAÑOS MONROY, JOSÉ MANUEL SAIZ-ÁLVAREZ AND
    EDGAR ROGELIO RAMÍREZ SOLÍS

    A brief approach on the scientific method 262
    The lean canvas methodology 263
    The lean scientific canvas method 267
    Conclusion 268

20 Beyond the gender–neutral approach: gender and entrepreneurship
    as an intertwined social practice   272
    SILVIA GHERARDI AND BARBARA POGGIO

    A practice-based approach to gender and entrepreneurship 273
    Authoring as a material-discursive practice 275
    Gendering and entrepreneuring in the succession process 279
    Conclusion 282

    Index   285

About the editors

Shumaila Yousafzai is Associate Professor (Reader) at the Cardiff Business School, Cardiff University, UK where she teaches entrepreneurship, marketing and consumer behaviour. After her undergraduate studies in Physics and Mathematics (University of Balochistan), and an MSc in Electronic Commerce (Coventry University, UK), she finished her PG Diploma in Research Methods from Cardiff University. Shumaila received her doctoral degree in 2005 from Cardiff University. In her research, Shumaila focuses mainly on topics linked to contextual embeddedness of entrepreneurship, firm performance, institutional theory and entrepreneurial orientation. She has published articles in various international journals, such as *Entrepreneurship Theory and Practice*, *Journal of Small Business Management*, *Industrial Marketing Management*, *Technovation*, *Journal of Business Ethics*, *Psychology & Marketing*, *Journal of Applied Social Psychology*, *Computers in Human Behavior*. She has co-edited a special issue on Women's entrepreneurship for *Entrepreneurship & Regional Development*.

Adam Lindgreen. After studies in chemistry (Copenhagen University), engineering (the Engineering Academy of Denmark), and physics (Copenhagen University), Adam Lindgreen completed an MSc in food science and technology at the Technical University of Denmark. He also finished an MBA at the University of Leicester. Professor Lindgreen received his PhD in marketing from Cranfield University. Under his leadership, the Department of Marketing and Strategy at Cardiff Business School ranked first among all marketing departments in Australia, Canada, New Zealand, the United Kingdom and the United States, based upon the hg indices of senior faculty. Since 2016, he has been Professor of Marketing at Copenhagen Business School, where he also heads the Department of Marketing. From 2017, he is also a research associate with the University of Pretoria's Gordon Institute of Business Science. Professor Lindgreen's publications have appeared in *California Management Review*, *Journal of Business Ethics*, *Journal of the Academy of Marketing Science*, *Journal of Product Innovation Management*, and *Journal of World Business*, among others. The recipient of the 'Outstanding Article 2005' award from Industrial Marketing Management and the runner-up for the same award in 2016, Professor Lindgreen serves as co-editor-in-chief of *Industrial Marketing Management* and previously was the joint editor of the *Journal of Business Ethics'* section on corporate responsibility.

Saadat Saeed is Associate Professor (Senior Lecturer) in Entrepreneurship at the Durham University Business School, Durham University, UK. Previously he has worked for Essex Business School (University of Essex). Saadat received his doctoral degree from the xiv *About the editors*

University of Padova, Italy in Entrepreneurship, where he is part of the Global Entrepreneurship Monitor Team. Saadat's past research efforts have included, but are not limited to, the global study of supportive institutions and women's entrepreneurship, entrepreneurship in adverse conditions, corporate entrepreneurship and firm performance in multi-country context, cross-cultural comparison of corporate support programmes on employees' innovative behaviour, all targeted for premier and high-quality journals, such as *Journal of Product Innovation Management, Entrepreneurship Theory and Practice, Journal of Small Business Management,* and *Industrial Marketing Management.* He has also co-edited a special issue on Women's entrepreneurship for *Entrepreneurship & Regional Development.*

Colette Henry is Head of School of Business and Humanities at Dundalk Institute of Technology, Ireland, and Adjunct Professor of Entrepreneurship at UiT-The Arctic University of Norway. She is also a Fellow of the Royal Society, and Visiting Fellow at CIMR, Birkbeck, London. In 2015, Colette was awarded the prestigious Diana International Trailblazer award for her research on female entrepreneurship, and in 2017 became the first Irish recipient of the Sten K Johnson European Entrepreneurship Education Award. She is the founding and current Editor-in-Chief of the *International Journal of Gender and Entrepreneurship.* Her research interests include women's entrepreneurship, entrepreneurship education and training, the creative industries, social enterprise and veterinary business.

Alain Fayolle is a full-time professor of entrepreneurship, the founder and director of the entrepreneurship research centre at EM Lyon Business School, a leading European institution. He is also visiting professor at Ecole Hôtelière de Lausanne (Switzerland). He has been visiting professor, for a five-year period, at Solvay Brussels School of Economics and Management (Belgium) and is regularly invited by international universities and institutions. Professor Fayolle has several interests and topics in research: entrepreneurial processes, entrepreneurship education, corporate entrepreneurship, social entrepreneurship, necessity entrepreneurship, critical studies in entrepreneurship, family entrepreneurship. Alain has published over twenty books and over one hundred articles in leading international and French-speaking scientific journals. Among his editorial positions, he is an Associate Editor of *JSBM* and the Editor of *Revue de l'Entrepreneuriat* and *Entreprendre & Innover,* two leading French-speaking journals in entrepreneurship. Alain is also a board member of eight entrepreneurship and small-business journals. Professor Fayolle has served as ICSB (International Council for Small Business and Entrepreneurship) Board of Directors as Director-At-Large for the year 2013–2014. He has also been elected as a member of the Executive Board of the Entrepreneurship Division of the Academy of Management and is now Chair of the Entrepreneurship Division during the academic year 2015–2016.

About the contributors

Alena Křížková is a senior researcher and head of the Gender & Sociology Department in the Czech Academy of Sciences. She is conducting research on economic justice, gender in entrepreneurship and management, and gender wage gap. She is a country expert for the European Commission in the network of experts on Scientific Analysis and Advice on Gender Equality (SAAGE). She was awarded a Fulbright Fellowship to conduct research on the entrepreneurship environment for disadvantaged populations at Arizona State University.

Alina Zapalska is Professor at the US Coast Guard Academy. She holds a PhD in Economics from the University of Kentucky, Lexington, USA. Professor Zapalska's extensive and varied teaching experience spans over thirty years in the US and abroad. Her research is in areas of economics, international business, entrepreneurship and pedagogy.

Aybeniz Akdeniz is Assistant Professor at Onyedi Eylul University, Turkey. She obtained her PhD in Marketing from Uludag University, Turkey and MBA from University of Balikesir. She was also a visiting academic at Cardiff University, UK, doing research on women entrepreneurship. Her research interest areas include consumer behaviour, brand management, social marketing and women entrepreneurship.

Banu Goktan is Associate Professor of Management at the University of North Texas at Dallas. Her research interests are in the areas of entrepreneurship, innovation, national cultural values and gender issues.

Barbara Poggio is Vice-Rector for Equality and Diversity Policies at the University of Trento, where she also coordinates the Centre for Interdisciplinary Gender Studies. Her research interests mainly deal with social construction of gender in organizations and qualitative research on work and organization. She has published several articles and books on gender and entrepreneurship, gender and science, work–life balance and on narrative analysis in social sciences.

Beverley McNally is Assistant Professor in Prince Mohammad Bin Fahd University, Saudi Arabia. She obtained her PhD from Victoria University, Wellington, New Zealand. Beverley's research interests include Strategic Leadership, Human Resource Development, Organization Behaviour and special issues such as youth unemployment and women and entrepreneurship.

xvi *About the contributors*

Carley Foster is Professor and Head of the Centre for Business Improvement at the University of Derby, UK. Her research interests concern diversity issues in the service sector. She has published widely in journals such as the *Services Industries Journal*, the *International Journal of Retail & Distribution Management* and the *Journal of Marketing Management*.

Ceyda M. Eyiusta is Assistant Professor in Kadir Has University, Istanbul, Turkey. She obtained her PhD from Bogazici University in 2010. Her research interests include Women's Entrepreneurship, Women in Management, and work engagement and proactivity in organizational life.

Clare Brindley is Professor at the University of Derby, UK. Her research has two central themes: the small-business sector and supply chain risk. She has published widely in journals such as the *International Journal of Operations and Production Management*, *International Journal Agile Supply Management*, *International Journal of Operations and Production Management*, *European Journal of Innovation Management* and *Journal of Small Business Management*.

Edgar Rogelio Ramírez Solís is Professor of Management and is family business consultant at Tecnológico de Monterrey, Guadalajara (Mexico). He obtained his first PhD in Administrative Science from UNAM, México and a second PhD in International Business from the Autonomous University of Madrid, Spain. His research interests include family firms with a special interest in strategy and corporate governance practices.

Erik Markin is a doctoral student of Management at the University of Mississippi, in Oxford, Mississippi, USA. His research interests centre on entrepreneurship and strategy. Recent publications focus on author and institutional contributions to the entrepreneurship literature, entrepreneurial orientation and family business.

Erik Wingrove-Haugland has been Professor of Philosophy and Ethics at the U.S. Coast Guard Academy since he received his PhD from Vanderbilt University in 1996. He regularly presents papers at the Society for Ethics Across the Curriculum and serves as a member of their Executive Committee.

Ethné Swartz is Professor of Entrepreneurship in the Silberman College of Business at Fairleigh Dickinson University, USA. She obtained her PhD from Manchester University, UK. Her research interests include Gender and Management, Innovation Management and Technology Management.

Ewa Lisowska is Professor of Warsaw School of Economics, Institute of International Management and Marketing, Poland. She obtained her PhD in economics from Warsaw School of Economics in 1986. Her research interests include women's entrepreneurship, women in management and equality between women and men in the labour market.

Federica Sist is Assistant Professor at LUMSA University, Italy. She obtained her PhD in Banking and Finance from Tor Vergata University Her research interests include internationalization of firms, gender impact, social entrepreneurship and sustainable markets.

Frances Amatucci is Associate Professor at the School of Business at Slippery Rock University of Pennsylvania in the United States. She obtained her PhD in from the University of Pittsburgh. Her research interests include gender issues in the workplace and sustainability entrepreneurship.

Gönül Budak is Full Professor of Management at Dokuz Eylul University in Izmir, Turkey.

Grace Khoury is Associate Professor of Management and the Dean of the Faculty of Business and Economics at Birzeit University, Palestine. She obtained her PhD from Bradford University, UK, in 2000 and is an author, co-author and editor of a number of books and journal articles. Her research interests include entrepreneurship, leadership, organizational behaviour and management.

Gray Cavender is Professor of Justice & Social Inquiry in Arizona State University. His interests focus on corporate crime and regulation, punishment, gender and media studies. He is a member of the international advisory board for Crime Media Culture and is an associate editor and board member of the *Oxford Research Encyclopedia on Crime, Media, and Popular Culture.*

Gun Lidestav is Associate Professor in the Swedish University of Agricultural Sciences, Sweden. She obtained her Doctoral degree in Forest Technology in 1994. Her research interests include various aspects of gender in relation to forest ownership and management as well as forestry as business sector and an arena of policy-making and implementation.

Hadil Al-Moosa is a PhD candidate at the University of Bedfordshire, UK. Her PhD thesis is about women's entrepreneurship in Oman. She obtained her MSc in HRM from the University of Stirling in 2007. Her research interest is in women entrepreneurship, gender, entrepreneurial culture and mid-set, and meaning making process across contexts.

Hayfaa Tlaiss is Associate Professor in Alfaisal University, Saudi Arabia. She obtained her PhD in Business Studies from Manchester Business School in 2009. She has published in the *Journal of Business Ethics, Journal of Small Business Management, International Small Business Journal* and the *International Journal of Human Resource Management.* Her research interests include diversity in entrepreneurship, employment and management and career studies.

José Manuel Saiz-Álvarez is Research Professor in Tecnológico de Monterrey, Mexico. He obtained his PhD in Economics and Business Administration from the Autonomous University of Madrid (Spain) in 1998 and a second PhD in Sociology from the Pontifical University of Salamanca (Spain) in 2002. His research interests include entrepreneurship, labour market, women studies and family business.

Juan Diego Borrero is Associated Professor, the Director of the Social Entrepreneurship Laboratory (SimpleLab) and Director of the Agricultural Economics research Group in Huelva University, Spain. He obtained his PhD in Economics from Huelva University in 2002. His research interests include entrepreneurship, social entrepreneurship, social networks, Big Data and Internet of Things.

Khizran Zehra is a PhD student in business administration at Jönköping International Business School, Sweden. Her research interests include women's entrepreneurship, the informal economy and resourceful behaviours.

xviii *About the contributors*

Leona Achtenhagen is Professor of Entrepreneurship and Business Development at Jönköping International Business School, Sweden, and the Director of its Media, Management and Transformation Centre. She is interested in (women's) entrepreneurship in different contexts. Her research results have been published in journals such as *Entrepreneurship Theory & Practice*, *Entrepreneurship & Regional Development*, *Journal of Small Business Management* and *Long Range Planning*.

Marie Appelstrand is Senior Lecturer and researcher at the Department of Business Law, Lund University, Sweden. She obtained her PhD in Sociology of Law from Lund University in 2007. Her research is concentrated on the field of environmental law with special focus on forest policy and law from international to local level. Research themes of particular interest are policy analysis and implementation studies, governmental guidance and the potential for soft-law instruments and processes in implementing gender equality in entrepreneurship in forestry.

Marie Pospíšilová is a research assistant in the Academy of Sciences of the Czech Republic and a doctoral student of Sociology at the Faculty of Social Sciences at Charles University in Prague. She is interested in qualitative research, gender and entrepreneurship issues, and more specifically in work-life balance within copreneurial couples.

Mary Barrett is Professor of Management at the School of Management, Operations and Marketing at the University of Wollongong, Australia where she teaches general management, human resource management, business communication and business research methods. Her research interests include business communication, family business, gender in management and entrepreneurship.

Mirela Xheneti is Senior Lecturer in University of Sussex. Mirela holds a PhD from the University of Bristol, UK. Prior to joining Sussex, Mirela worked as a researcher at the Small Business Research Centre, Kingston University. Mirela has a special and long-standing interest in how institutional change and enterprise policies affect entrepreneurial behaviour. Mirela's work has appeared in the *Entrepreneurship and Regional Development Journal* and the *Strategic Entrepreneurship Journal*.

Nadeera Ranabahu is a PhD candidate at the University of Wollongong, Australia. Her thesis examines effectual and causal decision-making among microfinance borrowers in Sri Lanka. Her other research interests include micro-businesses and SMEs, returnee and migrant entrepreneurs, agro-industries and human resource management.

Nancy Jurik is Professor of Justice & Social Inquiry in the School of Social Transformation, Arizona State University. Her interests focus on gender, occupations, entrepreneurship, and media constructions of gender and work. She is a distinguished faculty in ASU's College of Liberal Arts and Sciences, recipient of the 2014 Feminist Mentor Award from the Sociologists for Women in Society, and of the 2015 Lee Founder's Award for Lifetime Achievement from the Society for the Study of Social Problems.

Patrice Braun is Adjunct Professor at Federation University Australia. She is an Action Researcher with a PhD in regional small-business network development underpinned by ICT. Her global research and consultancy work focuses on women's entrepreneurship and gender integration in institutions, labour markets and standards.

Salmah Topimin is Senior Lecturer in Universiti Malaysia Sabah, Malaysia. She obtained her PhD from Nottingham Trent University, UK, in 2015. Her research interests include women's business survival and indigenous women's entrepreneurship in Malaysia.

Shandana Sheikh is Doctoral Researcher at Cardiff Business School, Cardiff University, UK. Her research area particularly focuses on women entrepreneurship, their challenges and public value amidst an entrepreneurial ecosystem. Prior to her doctoral studies, Shandana received her MBA in Marketing from Lahore School of Economics, Lahore, Pakistan and an MSc in Marketing and Strategy from Warwick Business School, University of Warwick, UK. Shandana has also worked in the capacity of a Teaching fellow at the Lahore School of Economics where she was teaching undergraduate and graduate level courses.

Shova Thapa Karki obtained her PhD from and is a Lecturer at the University of Sussex. Her research interests lie in the nexus of sustainability and entrepreneurship. This interest originated from her previous work on women entrepreneurs and micro-credit programmes for biodiversity conservation in protected areas of Nepal.

Silvia Gherardi is Senior Professor of sociology organization at University of Trento, Italy. She received the degree of Doctor Honoris Causa from the following Universities: Roskilde (DK) in 2005; Kuopio (FI) in 2010; St Andrews (UK) in 2014. Her research interests include feminist gender studies, entrepreneurship, epistemology of practice and qualitative methodologies in organization studies.

Verónica Ilián Baños Monroy is Professor of Entrepreneurship and is family business consultant at Tecnológico de Monterrey, Mexico. She obtained her PhD in Administrative Science from UNAM, Mexico, and a second PhD in International Business from the Autonomous University of Madrid, Spain. Her research interest is the succession process and innovation in family firms. She has been Visiting Professor at University of San Diego, USA.

Vishal K. Gupta is Associate Professor at The University of Alabama. He has previously served on the faculty of University of Mississippi and Binghamton University. He has also been a guest faculty at b-schools in India and Bahrain. His research interests are in the area of women's entrepreneurship, corporate governance, and entrepreneurial orientation.

Introduction

Female entrepreneurs are the new engines of inclusive and sustainable growth. By 2020, 870 million women will have entered the economic mainstream for the first time, increasing GDP growth rates and productivity by as much as 34 per cent and 25 per cent, respectively, in some countries (World Economic Forum, 2012). Therefore, it is becoming ever more certain that women's entrepreneurship is and will continue to be a formidable force of socio-economic development (Minniti & Naudé, 2010).

Although women make up 48 per cent of all entrepreneurial activity globally, men overwhelmingly outnumber women in high-tech industries (GEM, 2012; World Economic Forum, 2012), which receive the most attention from media and the public sector (Marlow, 2002). Women's entrepreneurial activity is clustered in low-growth and low-skilled business sectors 'which are pejoratively labelled as *mice*, *failure*, and *plodder* [businesses,] compared with high-growth *gazelle* businesses that are commonly associated with men' (Gupta et al., 2009). The entrepreneurial gender gap varies widely from country to country, and in some countries female entrepreneurs are a substantial yet unrecognized source of socio-economic development (Marlow & McAdam 2013; Henry & Kennedy, 2003; Vossenberg, 2013).

Although the impressive expansion of scholarly interest and activity in the field of women's entrepreneurship has done much to correct the historical inattention to female entrepreneurs and their initiatives, the literature on women's entrepreneurship tends to focus on a direct relationship between the overall entrepreneurial environment (for both male and female entrepreneurs) and women's entrepreneurial activity (Ahl, 2006; Brush et al., 2009; Hughes et al., 2012; Tedmanson et al., 2012). This approach ignores research that suggests that gender differences should be conceptualized as fluid processes that are rooted in a historical context that informs and sustains the normative, hierarchical subordination that shapes women's lives (Marlow & McAdam, 2013). As the field continues to develop and mature, it is increasingly characterized by calls for scholars to take their research in new directions, to 'contextualize' and enrich the 'vastly understudied' field of women's entrepreneurship (De Bruin et al., 2006, p. 585) by going beyond biologically determined identities to question the gendered hierarchies and structural constructions that are embedded in highly informed conceptual frameworks (Ahl, 2006; Ahl & Marlow, 2012; Brush, de Bruin, & Welter, 2009; De Bruin, Brush, & Welter, 2007), thus shifting the focus to the 'more silent feminine personal end' of entrepreneurial process (Bird & Brush, 2002, p. 57).

A major criticism of women's entrepreneurship research is that most has been devoid of context. The dominant discussions in entrepreneurship research focus on individual factors instead of taking into account the institutional and social factors that shape the entrepreneurial environment and influence women's entrepreneurial activity. Scholars focus on the individual entrepreneur as the unit of analysis, thereby disregarding the interaction of the multiple actors that constitute the entrepreneurial environment. Because of the lack of interaction between individuals or organizations and their environment in the systems approach to entrepreneurship, many of the contributions of entrepreneurs and organizations are under-recognized. Consequently, what we know about how the entrepreneurial gender gap is developed, measured, and evaluated in terms of how women entrepreneurs deviate from the yardstick of the male norm (Ahl, 2006; Bird & Brush, 2002; Mirchandani, 1999). Thus, patriarchal economies and societies and their gendered power structures that shape the context of entrepreneurs (men and women alike) but that favour men over women remain unchallenged (Vossenberg, 2013). This bias has consequences for research and policy-making and may explain why the gender gap continues and why real reform for the development of women entrepreneurs has not yet taken place (Ahl, 2006; Calas et al., 2009).

The chapters in this volume

This volume of chapters seeks to clarify the contextual embeddedness of women's entrepreneurship. Our goal is to co-create expertise that can feed joint learning, innovative practices and evidence-based policy-making for the gender-just promotion of women's entrepreneurship promotion and inclusive growth around the globe. In doing, so we highlight what influences and restrains the growth of women's entrepreneurship and offer useful insights into women's entrepreneurship within as they apply to specific contexts.

We sought contributions that reflect a variety of perspectives and methodological approaches and that explore women's entrepreneurship at the macro-, meso- or micro-level of analysis and across a range of international economic and cultural contexts and industry sectors. In particular, contributions were sought from researchers in geographic regions that are not sufficiently represented in the women's entrepreneurship literature. We received chapters based on data from Baltic Sea countries, Czech Republic, Italy, Lebanon, Malaysia, Mexico, Morocco, Nepal, Oman, Pakistan, Palestine, Poland, Saudi Arabia, Sri Lanka, Spain, Sweden, Turkey, USA and Wales and multi-country studies based on the Global Entrepreneurship Monitor (GEM) dataset. Collectively, these studies make a substantial contribution to the contextual embeddedness of women's entrepreneurial activity, provide numerous insights and provoke fruitful directions for future research on the important role of the context in which women's entrepreneurial activity takes place.

Section 1: Religious embeddedness of women's entrepreneurship in the Islamic context

Despite the proliferation of research on women's entrepreneurship, few studies have focused on it in the Islamic context. The six chapters that make up Section 1 extend what we know about women's entrepreneurship by delving into the institutional and social factors that shape the entrepreneurial environment for women in the context of Muslim societies. While Islam is often seen as a rigid, homogeneous faith, it is actually a complex religion with considerable variations across the areas where Muslims live. Academic discourse often paints Islam as incompatible with business and commerce, although trading was a common vocation among the Arab tribes to which Islam was initially introduced. Although Islam is viewed as authoritarian, androcentric and especially limiting for women, a closer look at Islam and its core values challenges that view and sheds light on the nature of the relationship between Islam and women's entrepreneurship. In Chapter 1 *Banu Goktan, Vishal K. Gupta, Gönül Budak and Erik Markin* examine the links among Islam, gender and entrepreneurship and whether women's entrepreneurship varies systematically across Muslim-majority and non-Muslim societies. The authors' investigation uses GEM survey data to raise questions about the assumption that Islamic societies present unique obstacles to women's entrepreneurship. Despite the need for in-depth qualitative work that examines the hurdles that confront female entrepreneurs in Muslim countries, the authors find that the overall rate of female entrepreneurs does not vary markedly between Muslim and non-Muslim nations, rejecting the hypothesis that Islam and women's entrepreneurship are incompatible.

In Chapter 2, *Khizran Zehra and Leona Achtenhagen* explore the institutional system of Pakistan as a highly gendered context for women's entrepreneurship. Consistently ranking low regarding gender equality, Pakistan has ratified an impressive number of policies and measures that promote the role of women and women entrepreneurs. Nonetheless, the country scored 144 out of 145 countries in the 2015 Global Gender Gap Report. In this chapter, the authors seek to explain this apparent contradiction between Pakistan's efforts and its reality for women. Their findings show that, although many institutional measures have been authorized to improve the situation of women and women entrepreneurs, these measures have been implemented half-heartedly at best. Thus, despite formal institutional measures taken to provide female entrepreneurs the opportunity to participate in entrepreneurship, the failure to enact these policies meaningfully and the largely negative societal attitude toward women entrepreneurs restrict their entrepreneurial endeavours.

Aware of the embeddedness of entrepreneurship in the contexts where it unfolds, Chapter 3 by *Hayfaa Tlaiss* explores Arab women's experiences as entrepreneurial leaders and the role of gendered expectations and patriarchal ideologies. Applying a poststructuralist feminist approach to in-depth, face-to face interviews, Tlaiss explores the meaning of entrepreneurial leadership to women in Lebanon and the reasoning that underlies their definitions and conceptualizations of entrepreneurship. Tlaiss also employs an intersectionality lens to investigate how these women's understanding of entrepreneurial leadership is related to and influenced by the normative expectations of the Arab patriarchal culture that associates women only with motherhood and domesticity and only men with entrepreneurship. Tlaiss' findings highlight the influence of institutional cultural and normative elements on Arab women entrepreneurs' career choices, their pursuit of legitimacy, and their understanding and attribution of meaning to entrepreneurial leadership.

Chapter 4 by *Hadil Al-Moosa* explores the role of political leaders in shaping the experience of Arab women's entrepreneurship in the context of Oman. Oman is characterized by a traditional paternalistic leadership style, and although Omani women are exposed to Western-style education, they do not challenge the male tribal leaders' authority because their behaviour is rooted in the tribal and familial system. In the Arab culture the *Sheikhs*, the male tribal leaders, embody power in the social structure and take responsibility for the needs of the tribes' members. Hence, this relationship is viewed as a paternalistic, rather than autocratic. Al-Moosa concludes that, under a tribal social structure, a patriarchal society and a paternalistic leadership style, the leadership must take a strong and active role in women's issues in order to encourage women's entrepreneurs and other inputs into a strong economic structure.

Although the traditional view of women's roles in Arab societies influence women's attitudes, intentions and self-perceptions with respect to their career choices, there is evidence of a change taking place in these societies, including a shift from the male as the sole breadwinner to both husbands and wives working and husbands supporting their wives in their business endeavours. Chapter 5, by *Beverley McNally and Grace Khoury*, examines how successful female entrepreneurs in Palestine and Saudi Arabia use the micro-level support factors of family support, education, opportunity, motivation, financing and performance to overcome macro-level regulatory, socio-cultural and economic challenges.

Chapter 6, the final chapter in Section 1, by *Ceyda M. Eyiusta*, explores women's entrepreneurship in Turkey through the lens of promising initiatives. This chapter explores the current position of Turkish women in the overall entrepreneurial landscape and the features of the institutional context and the major support mechanisms that influence women's entrepreneurship in Turkey, Eyiusta also identifies the problems and challenges Turkish female entrepreneurs face when they initiate and run their businesses and the key drivers and success factors for women's entrepreneurship in Turkey.

Section 2: The gendered embeddedness of women's entrepreneurship in the entrepreneurship ecosystem

Section 2 features a collection of studies that provide an in-depth examination of the key components of the Entrepreneurship ecosystem and their gendered influences on women's entrepreneurial activity. Entrepreneurship ecosystems refer to the interactions between entrepreneurial firms and the context within which such enterprises operate, with the central focus the entrepreneurs, rather than their enterprises (Stam, 2015). Isenberg (2011) identifies six interdependent components within the Entrepreneurship ecosystem: a conducive culture supportive policies and leadership, the availability of appropriate financing, quality human capital, market demand, and a range of institutional supports (Figure 0.1).

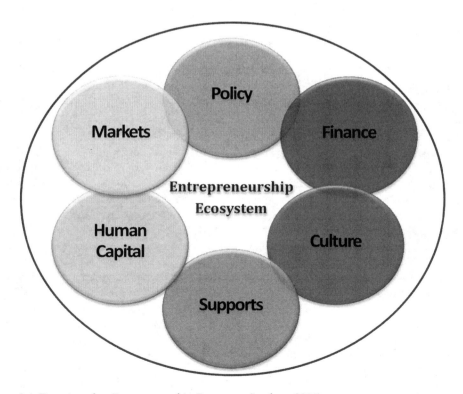

Figure 0.1 Domains of an Entrepreneurship Ecosystem (Isenberg 2011)

xxiv *Introduction*

The studies in Section 2 highlight the complex interplay between the informal socio-cultural aspects of the entrepreneurial ecosystem and the formal institutions, such as regulatory bodies, public policy and government. These studies make way for future research to explore the nature and effect of this interplay between the factors in the ecosystem and how it affects the viability and performance of women's entrepreneurial activity. In Chapter 7 *Patrice Braun* argues that an enabling ecosystem is a shared responsibility of the public and private sectors whereby policy inputs are interwoven with socially embedded factors to nurture entrepreneurship and growth. Few studies have considered the Entrepreneurship ecosystem from a trade-support perspective, as they often ignore potential institutional shortcomings in this area. Patrice fills this gap by arguing that gender inequality is not only a pressing moral and social issue but a critical economic challenge as well, and that a favourable enabling Entrepreneurship ecosystem and targeted government intervention are pivotal to helping women entrepreneurs to access markets, as without paying heed to gender, Entrepreneurship ecosystems may well perpetuate systemic discrimination in favour of male-led enterprises.

Chapter 8 by *Mirella Xheneti and Shova Thapa Karki* draws on evidence from policy documents of the Government of Nepal and a qualitative project on women's entrepreneurship in the informal economy to show how socio-cultural gender embeddedness plays out in patriarchal contexts that are undergoing institutional change. More specifically, the authors focus on gendered institutions like caste, marriage, family and rights to property and education and their influence on women's entrepreneurship. These issues are particularly relevant in the highly patriarchal and caste-based stratified societal context of Nepal, where power relationships are not equal and the roles, behaviours and expectations for men and women are socially prescribed. The authors highlight that, despite the provisions made in the formal institutional environment that discourage caste and gender discrimination, these social institutions have long-lasting effects in prescribing the behaviour and attitudes of those in the society.

Although women entrepreneurs may face considerable challenges from their entrepreneurial environments and ecosystems, leveraging their formal and informal social networks can help them to be successful in their businesses and to create opportunities within it. In Chapter 9, *Shandanan Sheikh, Aybniz Akdeniz, Shumaila Yousafzai, Federica Sist* and *Saadat Saeed* explore how, midst the perceived weaknesses and strengths of the entrepreneurial ecosystem, the three dimensions of social capital – relational, cognitive and structural social capital – impact opportunity creation for female entrepreneurs in Wales and Turkey. Following a qualitative case study methodology, they find that, while Welsh and Turkish women entrepreneurs' perceptions about their Entrepreneurship ecosystems and their individual components differ, these ecosystems create opportunities for their businesses through the women's social capital. Specifically, women use both formal and informal social capital to create opportunities in multiple ecosystems' contexts, including the *business, financial, human capital* and *social contexts*. The authors find that, while relational and structural social capital positively affect the extent of opportunity creation for women's businesses, cognitive social capital restricts opportunity creation and negatively impacts their business performance.

Female entrepreneurs in developing countries, including Sri Lanka, face severe cultural and social restraints in managing their businesses. In Chapter 10 *Nadeera Ranabahu and Mary Barrett* explore the entrepreneurial thinking and behaviour of Sri Lankan female entrepreneurs who use micro-credit in their businesses, especially in terms of how they mobilize aspects of their social and cultural context in their businesses. Drawing on the framework of effectuation and causation thinking, the authors explain how female entrepreneurs' business decisions and reasoning are influenced by effectual (means-driven) and causal (predictive) logics. Their findings suggest that cultural and societal norms heighten women micro-entrepreneurs' effectuation thinking during the business start-up phase, when they use their knowledge and experience, rely on family support, use inexpensive ways to open a business, form agreements with customers, and convert socio-cultural challenges into opportunities. The study also highlights the unexpected business opportunities that can arise from the lack of long-term institutional commitments and the risks associated with those opportunities.

In the World Bank's Doing Business 2015 ranking of the Baltic Sea countries, Sweden was ranked 8th, Estonia 16th, Lithuania 20th, Latvia 22nd and Poland 25th position. Sweden has the most advanced equal-treatment policy, the highest employment rate and the highest gender-equality index. However, women's entrepreneurship rate in Poland is twice as high as it is in Sweden, and it is also higher than that in Estonia, Lithuania and Latvia. To explain this apparent contradiction, in Chapter 11 *Ewa Lisowska* explores whether factors other than economic and administrative factors are included in the Doing Business ranking that can explain the disparity in women's entrepreneurship rates in the Baltic Sea countries. Lisowska's findings suggest that cultural factors (e.g., tradition, history, norms, values, prejudices, stereotypes and the laws and institutions that combat prejudices and stereotypes) have a significant impact on the level of entrepreneurship and attitudes toward entrepreneurship.

Chapter 12, by *Alina Zapalska and Erik Wingrove-Haugland*, identifies the major characteristics of women's entrepreneurial businesses in the Polish tourism industry and the factors that have promoted or inhibited the growth of those businesses. The success of female entrepreneurs in the tourism industry in Poland has resulted from their ability to recognize and take advantage of the opportunities presented by the country's natural resource base, socio-cultural traditions, and ecological characteristics by creating distinctive products that have a positive impact on economic growth and employment development. By analysing female entrepreneurship within the life-cycle model of an entrepreneurial firm's growth and development, the authors provide recommendations for policy-makers to foster and encourage female entrepreneurship through targeted policy initiatives that reflect an understanding of the factors that contribute to the success of women's entrepreneurial activity.

In Chapter 13, *Alena Křížková, Marie Pospíšilová, Nancy Jurik and Gray Cavender* use data from interviews with women entrepreneurs in the Czech Republic and the United States to determine how the institutional context of each nation converges with multiple dimensions of social identities to shape women's entrepreneurial motivations and strategies. Their study draws attention to the need to combine contextual and intersectional theories of entrepreneurship to understand women's varied experiences of the gender gap. Their study also finds issues that relate to emancipatory struggles, as some of their respondents use businesses to challenge race/ethnic and gender hierarchies.

In Chapter 14 *Marie Appelstrand and Gun Lidestav* study women's entrepreneurship in the context of the Swedish forestry sector. Although 38 per cent of Swedish forest owners are women, forestry is still one of the most gender-segregated sectors in Sweden. The gendering of the sector as a distinct male arena has led to a number of negative outcomes for gender equality as well as economic stability and ecosystem vitality. The authors write that gender inequality indicates a policy failure, so to address these concerns, the government has introduced various soft governance action programmes and strategies. Appelstrand and Lidestav examine the potential for altering gendered norms in a sector that is under change and ask whether a transformation requires that the practices of the forestry sector

xxvi   *Introduction*

be 'encoded' in feminine terms women should 'act like men' in order to claim their place in the forestry sector, thereby reinforcing the male experience as a preferred norm.

The complexity of women's social environments affects their activities in the public sphere, but this reality cannot be revealed without acknowledging the importance of using a gender lens in researching women's entrepreneurial activities. Chapter 15 by *Salmah Topimin, Clare Brindley and Carley Foster* explores the context of business survival and the institutionalization of entrepreneurial support for the Bumiputera women entrepreneurs in the Malaysian handicraft industry. The authors' proposed framework for women's business survival takes into account the significant influence of the context in which the female entrepreneur is positioned. The authors acknowledge the strong patriarchal social customs and traditions that exist in the cultural landscape of Malaysia that have caused women to struggle in managing their multiple roles and has put them in a difficult position in their efforts to maximize their business potential, particularly in ensuring that their efforts are consistent with the demands of the social order.

In Chapter 16, *Shandana Sheikh, Federica Sist, Aybeniz Akdeniz and Shumaila Yousafzai* employ a career narrative approach to tell the stories of a group of British 'mumpreneurs'. The authors' findings suggest that, perhaps because of their dual responsibility for children and business ownership, mumpreneurs work particularly hard to achieve their aspirations and career objectives. However, their ability to do so is severely constrained by the lack of institutional support, particularly in terms of the availability of child care, business training and financial support.

A recent report from Kauffman Foundation suggests that the gender gap in financing is persistent and that women receive only 3 per cent of the equity financing that is available through angel investments and venture capital (Krause, 2016). Similarly, women start their new ventures with half as much capital as their male counterparts do (Brush et al., 2014). Taking a multi-disciplinary view of the contextual embededdness of women's entrepreneurship research, in Chapter 17 *Ethné Swartz and Frances Amatucci* study second-generation gender bias as a barrier to success in women's entrepreneurship. They contend that the empirical nature of labour economics can help to illustrate the unequal odds that women face in labour markets and entrepreneurship.

In Chapter 18 *Juan Diego Borrero* contends that, although socially constructed and historically attributed responsibilities for child care and housework have a negative effect on women entrepreneurs' performance, they are still an integral part of the complex social identity of contemporary women. As a result, women who operate part-time or home-based businesses are not making a choice that reflects restricted entrepreneurial ambitions or limited capital but are responding to social imperatives and ascribed roles. He argues that, in evaluating their firms' performance, women pay attention to factors such as personal fulfilment, flexibility and the desire to serve the community. Acknowledging the socially constructed expectations from women and challenging the label of underperformance, Juan presents a view of performance for Spanish and Moroccan female entrepreneurs that aligns with the entrepreneurs' preferences, instead of those of society.

Section 3: Moving forward

The traditional business model canvas (BMC), a powerful tool that creates a shared language when businesses are defined, is an instrument for creating hypotheses using brainstorming and an informal way of testing. The BMC is a gender-neutral conceptual approach, as it does not discriminate between men and women. Chapter 19, by *Verónica Ilián Baños Monroy,*

José Manuel Saiz-Álvarez, and Edgar Rogelio Ramírez Solís, presents a female-oriented, non-gender-neutral, lean scientific method canvas (LSMC) as a framework with which to identify problems and solutions that are focused on better business strategies and market research proposals that foster women's entrepreneurship. The authors argue that higher educational levels achieved by women and improvements in women's integration into the labour market have already helped to reduce both job and educational gender gaps. The authors contend that the application of the LSCM methodology can accelerate this enriching process.

In the final chapter, Chapter 20, *Silvia Gherardi and Barbara Poggio* consider the relationship between gender and entrepreneurship, going beyond a gender-neutral view in favour of a practice-based approach to gender and entrepreneurship as intertwined practices. They argue that from the 'gendering of the entrepreneurship' perspective, the social practice of co-producing gender and entrepreneurship are seen as both a material and a semantic space in which meaningful collective actions are carried out and contextually organized. Based on empirical examples from two qualitative studies conducted in Northern Italy with women entrepreneurs who work in several sectors, they analyse two particularly significant practices: the authoring of the process of becoming a female entrepreneur, and the succession of the firm from one generation to the next. They conclude by proposing a framework with which to grasp the situated, fluid and fragmented nature of gender and entrepreneurship practices and processes.

Closing remarks

We extend a special thanks to Routledge and its staff, who have been most helpful throughout this entire process. We also warmly thank all of the authors who submitted their manuscripts for consideration for this book. They showed their desire to share their knowledge and experience with the book's readers and a willingness to present their research and their views for possible challenge by their peers. We also thank the reviewers, who provided excellent independent and incisive consideration of the anonymous submissions.

We hope that this compendium of chapters and themes stimulates and contributes to the ongoing debate surrounding the contextual embeddedness of women-owned enterprises. The chapters in this book can help to fill some gaps in what we know while stimulating further thought and action.

Shumaila Yousafzai, *Cardiff University, UK*
Adam Lindgreen, *Copenhagen Business School, Denmark*
Saadat Saeed, *Durham University, UK*

Colette Henry, *Dundalk Institute of Technology, Ireland*
Alain Fayolle, *EM Lyon Business School, France*
14 August, 2017

References

Ahl, H. (2006). Why research on women entrepreneurs needs new directions. *Entrepreneurship Theory and Practice, 30*(5), 595–621.

Ahl, H., & Marlow, S. (2012). Exploring the dynamics of gender, feminism and entrepreneurship: Advancing debate to escape a dead end? *Organization, 19*(5), 543–562.

Bird, B., & Brush, C. (2002). A gendered perspective on organizational creation. *Entrepreneurship Theory and Practice, 26*(3), 41–65.

xxviii   *Introduction*

Brush, C. G., de Bruin, A., & Welter, F. (2009). A gender–aware framework for women's entrepreneurship. *International Journal of Gender and Entrepreneurship, 1*(1), 8–24.

de Bruin, A., Brush, C. G., & Welter, F. (2006). Introduction to the special issue: Towards building cumulative knowledge on women's entrepreneurship. *Entrepreneurship Theory and Practice, 30*(5), 585.

de Bruin, A., Brush, C. G., & Welter, F. (2007). Advancing a framework for coherent research on women's entrepreneurship. *Entrepreneurship Theory and Practice, 31*(3), 323–339.

Calás, M. B., Smircich, L., & Bourne, K. A. (2009). Extending the boundaries: Reframing entrepreneurship as social change through feminist perspectives. *Academy of Management Review, 34*(3), 552–569.

Global Entrepreneurship Monitor (GEM) (2012) *2011. Global Report.* Available online at www.gem consortium.org.

Gupta, V., Turban, D., Wasti, S., & Sikdar, A. (2009). The role of gender stereotypes in perceptions of entrepreneurs and intentions to become an entrepreneur. *Entrepreneurship Theory & Practice, 33*(2), 397–417.

Henry, C., & Kennedy, S. (2003). Female entrepreneurship: In search of a new Celtic tiger. In J. Butler (Ed.), *New Perspectives on Women Entrepreneurs,* Vol. 3 in Research in Entrepreneurship and Management (pp. 203–224). Hong Kong: Information Age Publishing.

Hughes, K. D., Jennings, J., Carter, S., & Brush, C. (2012). Extending women's entrepreneurship research in new directions. *Entrepreneurship Theory and Practice, 36*(3), 429–442.

Isenberg, D. J. (2011). *Introducing the Entrepreneurship Ecosystem: Four Defining Characteristics.* Available online at www.forbes.com/sites/danisenberg/2011/05/25/introducing-the-entrepreneurship-eco system-four-defining-characteristics/.

Marlow, S. (2002). Women and self-employment: A part of or apart from theoretical construct? *Entrepreneurship and Innovation, 3*(2), 83–91.

Marlow, S., & McAdam, M. (2013). Gender and entrepreneurship: Advancing debate and challenging myths; Exploring the mystery of the under-performing female entrepreneur. *International Journal of Entrepreneurial Behaviour and Research, 19*(1), 114–124.

Marlow, S., & Swail, J. (2014). Gender, risk and finance: Why can't a woman be more like a man? *Entrepreneurship & Regional Development: An International Journal, 26*(1–2), 80–96.

Minniti, M., & Naudé, W. A. (2010). What do we know about the patterns and determinants of female entrepreneurship across countries? *European Journal of Development Research, 22*(3), 1–17.

Mirchandani, K. (1999). Feminist insight on gendered work: New directions in research on women and entrepreneurship. *Gender, Work and Organization, 6*(4), 224–235.

Stam, E. (2015). Entrepreneurial ecosystems and regional policy: A sympathetic critique. *European Planning Studies, 23*(9), 1759–1769.

Tedmanson, D., Verduyn, K., Essers, C., & Gartner, W. (2012). Critical perspectives in entrepreneurship research. *Organization, 19*(5), 531–541.

Vossenberg, S. (2013). Women entrepreneurship promotion in developing countries: What explains the gender gap in entrepreneurship and how to close it? *Maastricht School of Management.* Available online at www.msm.nl/resources/uploads/2014/02/MSM-WP2013–08.pdf.

World Economic Forum (2012). *Women as the Way Forward. Annual Meeting.* Available online at www. weforum.org/videos/women-way-forward-annual- meeting-2012.

Section 1

Religious embeddedness of women entrepreneurship in the Islamic context

1 Behind the green line

An examination of female entrepreneurial activity in the Muslim world

Banu Goktan, Vishal K. Gupta, Gönül Budak and Erik Markin

Recent years have seen organizations, governments and institutions around the world promote entrepreneurship as a means to economic growth, job creation and social development. A significant part of these efforts focus on women-owned businesses (Brush & Cooper, 2012; Sullivan & Meek, 2012). Despite the widely accepted belief that women's ability to freely start and grow their business is beneficial for gender equality and economic empowerment (Jennings & Brush, 2013), the gender gap in entrepreneurship – in terms of both the rate of business start-up and venture performance – persists. Individual differences have attracted attention from researchers in explaining the performance gap; however, contextual factors have not. In addition, although existing studies cast light on various aspect of female entrepreneurial activity (Ahl & Marlow, 2012; Elam, 2014; Marlow & McAdam, 2013), it is mostly in the context of Western nations rooted in Judeo-Christian values and beliefs (e.g., United States and United Kingdom). The purpose of the present study is to extend our understanding of female entrepreneurship by delving into institutional and social factors that shape the entrepreneurial environment for women within the context of Muslim societies.

Religion, as a value system, forms a crucial basis for human behaviour (Boutroux, 1980). It is a major force in shaping beliefs and attitudes of individuals and plays a vital role in the entrepreneurial as well as personal lives of members of the society (Hafsi, 1987; Patai, 1976). While existing research suggests a relationship between national culture and entrepreneurship (Hayton et al., 2002), very few studies have actually examined the role of religious affiliation in entrepreneurship (Gümüşay, 2015). Islam in particular is an 'under-researched' area in entrepreneurship studies (Essers & Benschop, 2009). Academic discourse and popular discussions often paint Islam as incompatible with business and commerce although trading was a common vocation among the Arab tribes to which Islam was initially introduced (Ahmed, 1992; Essers & Benschop, 2009). Furthermore, Islam is considered especially limiting to women. Although, Islam is viewed as authoritarian, androcentric and hostile to women as exercised today, a closer look at Islam and its core values challenges that view and sheds much needed light on the nature of the relationship between Islam and female entrepreneurship (Ahmed, 1992).

This study considers the interplay between gender and religious affiliation in shaping female entrepreneurship. We help extend the knowledge frontier in entrepreneurship beyond its traditional focus on Western countries with predominantly Christian populations. Specifically, we examine whether Islamic affiliation has a depressing effect on entrepreneurship at the country level. Finally, delving deeper into the Republic of Turkey, we examine whether the rate of entrepreneurial activity is boosted in a constitutionally secular Muslim-majority country like Turkey as compared to other Islamic countries.

The Islamic context

With more than 1.5 billion followers worldwide (23.2% of the global population), Islam is the second largest religion in the world today with Muslims (as the followers of Islam are generally called) present in nearly every country (Johnson & Grim, 2013; Richardson, 2015). The largest Muslim population resides in Southern Asia (25%), 20 per cent or Muslims live in the Middle East and 15 per cent in Sub-Saharan Africa. Islam was founded in the seventh century in the Arabian Peninsula when Prophet Muhammad (p)[1] (who the Muslims revere as the last messenger of God), delivered a monotheistic message to the local tribes. 'Allah' is an Arabic word for God and the religion is based on the reading and understanding of Qur'an, the holy book that is based on the revelations to Muhammad (p) by Angel Gabriel. According to Islam, all of God's prophets and messengers (Noah, Abraham, Moses, Jesus and Muhammad (p)) bring monotheism and Muhammad (p) is the final messenger of God (Richardson, 2015).

While Islam is similar to other Abrahamic religions (Jewish and Christian faiths) in terms of monotheism, there are also key differences. Islam is not only a set of beliefs and ceremonies but also a social system that has a substantial influence on the life styles of its followers (Weir, 2000). From the beginning, Islam is meant to be a comprehensive religion that governs all aspects of life including social, political, and military as well as spiritual. It plays a major role in shaping personal, family and business values of its followers (Tlaiss, 2015). In order to understand Islam and its essence, one needs to understand the time at which and the society to which it was introduced, as well as its core values.

Not all Arabs are Muslims and not all Muslims are Arabs (Sidani, 2005), however, the Arab world is significant in Islam. Prophet Muhammad (p) was born in ad 570 in Mecca, which was strategically located close to the west coast of the Arabian Peninsula, midway between the north and south of the Arab world and close to the Mediterranean. As trade grew in the region, Mecca benefited significantly from the development and became a prosperous area where people enjoyed wealth and luxury. This lifestyle was in contrast with Muhammad (p)'s belief in a simple life. Muhammad (p) would spend time in solitude, meditating in a cave in the hill of Hira and living the simple life he desired (Ahmed, 1980). When he was about 40, he started receiving revelations, which marks the beginning of Islam. These revelations were gathered after his death and constitute what is now the Qur'an.

Different implementations of Islam

While Islam tends to be usually discussed (and often caricatured) as a rigid homogeneous faith, it is actually a complex religion with considerable variations across the different areas where Muslims live. While some Islamic societies moved towards secularism (e.g. Persian, Turkish, Egyptian), there have also been Islamic revivalist movements (e.g. Iran, Saudi Arabia) hence adding to differences across societies. Islam's norms and teachings are not consistently followed by all believers (Syed 2008, 2009, 2010). The teachings of Islam have three main sources: 1) the Qur'an, 2) Hadiths (the teachings of Muhammad (p)) and 3) derivations from several Muslim cults and schools. Hadiths, Qur'an and cultural norms form the basis of Sharia law, which governs all aspects of life for orthodox Muslims (Ahmed, 1980). Hadiths refer to a body of literature consisting of short stories and narratives based on the Prophet's sayings and actions that were collected into written form in the three or four centuries after his death (Ahmed, 1992).

Some sects accept Islam's ethical teachings as the fundamental rules to follow and Muhammad's (p) practices as relevant to the social context of the time and not necessarily binding today. While Islam was progressive for its time, there are challenges to its literary implementation today. For example, the Quran limits the number of wives to four which was 'severely restrictive' to the polygamous society of Pre-Islamic Arabia (Ahmed, 1980), however, seems unacceptable by many today. Orthodox Islam, on the other hand, focuses on the practices rather than the ethical teachings. For the Islamic literalists, Qur'an is not culture or society bound and should be closely followed. According to Ahmed (1992), Islamic law would have been more humane and egalitarian regarding women if the essence of the religion had been followed. In sum, varying views regarding women's role and place in society are present in Islam and there is not a complete consensus on how Islam should be practised.

Islam, women and entrepreneurship

While Islam has similarities to other monotheistic religions, a differentiating aspect of Islam is its focus on the governance of relationships between men and women. Islam considers family the pillar of Islamic faith and defines roles, rights, and responsibilities for men and women to properly conduct themselves in their everyday lives. While some scholars view the Islamic family law as restricting women (McIntosh & Islam, 2010), Mernissi (2011) claims that in pre-Islamic Mecca, most children had no identifiable genetic father and wearing clothes had been a privilege of the aristocrats. With Islam, individuals gained the right to body privacy. Many researchers view Islam as bringing clarity to the roles and responsibilities of men and women as a way to structure order and harmony in the Arabian society of the time (Irigaray, 1993).

Despite claims that Islam limited the power of women, there are various accounts of equal treatment of men and women during early Islam. Men and women prayed together with Prophet Muhammad (p) and he stipulated that women were not to be restricted from going to the mosque (Ates, 2006). Women and men had comparable rights in terms of place in the family and society, as well as legal, financial and property rights (Yildirim, 2014). In early Islamic period, women occupied respectable professional positions such as being judge and being involved in politics and public service. Women were free to study medicine, literature and science, and some women were indeed more proficient than men in these fields (Savas, 1991). They took active part during wars by providing logistical help to the army (Gurhan, 2010, p. 65). They engaged in discussions, and debates regarding the contours of the emergent religious order with Prophet Muhammad (p), and held the caliphate accountable.

Islam and female entrepreneurship

Studies that focus on women in Islam tend to portray women as being systematically subordinated in patriarchal Islamic societies although female entrepreneurship in Islam is neither forbidden nor frowned upon (Roomi, 2013; Tlaiss, 2015). A close look at Islam through the centuries reveals many successful female entrepreneurs (Hamdan, 2005), most prominently Khadija, first wife of Prophet Muhammad (p), who was a successful business owner herself (Cetindamar, Gupta, Karadeniz, & Egrican, 2012). Although Islam emphasized respect for both sexes and equal rights, the Arab tribes preserved their autocratic system and patriarchal family order (Arab Human Development Report, 2005). According to Mernissi (1991), women rights is an issue not because of Qur'an, Prophet Muhammad (p) or the Islamist tradition, but because the existing institutions prior to Islam suppressed women's power and male elite didn't want to give up power and maintained the order. Sidani (2005) believes that prevailing strict religious interpretation by some scholars is an 'unconscious attempt to provide religious justification for various cultural norms and practices' (508). In the Middle East, traditional restrictions (Ilhaamie, Arni, Rosmawani, Al-Banna, 2014), negative stereotypes of women (Grey and Findely Hervey, 2005), lack of finance, restrictive mobility, government rules and regulations, social issues, lack of education and training in business (Ahmad, 2011; Shmailan, 2014) have been cited as important barriers for female entrepreneurs. Therefore, the way Islam is implemented in certain areas is not true to the essence of Islam. According to the Arab Human Development Report (2005), the religious culture that places men in a higher place within the society is not built on sacred text but rather on interpretations based on customs and traditions which are geared towards preserving the order of the family and society.

Female entrepreneurship in MENA countries is seen among the educated, wealthy families. Although globally women start businesses mostly out of necessity, women in MENA region are more likely to be opportunity motivated. Opportunity motivated individuals perceive, evaluate and act upon opportunities because they have access to resources such as education, networks, and family support and they are less likely to face social obstacles. Constraints are fewer and pressures are less on women among educated groups (Roomi & Harrison, 2011). Females who come from lower strata of the society face disadvantages in terms of education, access to networks and legal or social rights such as restrictions on their activities outside the home or their ability to travel (Terjesen & Lloyd, 2015). The obstacles female entrepreneurs face result mostly from 'deeply rooted discriminatory socio-cultural values and traditions, embedded particularly in the policy and legal environment and in institutional support mechanisms' which are less common among educated groups (Ilhaamie, Arni, Rosmawani, & Al-Banna, 2014, p. 429). Considering that entrepreneurship is an option for only a limited group of educated women of high social status in Muslim societies, we expect to see lower levels of female entrepreneurship in countries where the majority of the population is Muslim compared to other groups. Thus, we hypothesize:

> H1: Rates of female entrepreneurship will be lower in societies where the majority of the population is Muslim.

Female entrepreneurship and secularism

Secularism is the separation of religion from politics, where each one is defined as distinct spheres (Arik, 2016). There are differences in how secularism is implemented across societies. According to Kuru (2009), the dominant ideology in the United States is passive secularism where the state allows individuals to live their religion according to their beliefs, but does not disrupt religious practices observed in public sphere (e.g., the use of the phrase 'In God We Trust' on currency bills in the US and the celebration of Christmas at the White House). In Turkey and France, on the other hand, the dominant ideology is assertive secularism where the state actively excludes religion from the public sphere. However, in either case, despite the fact that individuals live and express their religion differently, religion is separated from the state in secular societies. Therefore, it is expected that in secular societies religion will not be as overarching and will be confined to certain, private aspects of life.

MENA is dominated by Muslim-majority societies; however, it consists of many independent nations. Although there are commonalities due to religion (Bhagat & McQuaid, 1982; Farid, 2005; Yasin et al., 1989), there are also differences in how religion is practised across these countries. Power and Nadine (1998) argued that influences and superstitions, as well as the political and economic structures that have crept into Islam mask the essence of Islam which is tolerance, social justice, and human rights. In most secular countries, 'active secularism' is implemented where the 'state itself actively embraced and fostered a nonreligious worldview in the public realms' (Warhola & Bezci, 2010, p. 428). Societies based on secularism try to enforce these values and remind people that democracy and free market economy are not incompatible with Islam (Farid, 2007). Secularism brings with it an emphasis on notions of gender equality and human rights. In secular societies, active policies are implemented to promote women's empowerment and to challenge patriarchal cultural norms and structures (Özkazanç-Pan, 2015). Therefore, in secular societies where majority of the population is Muslim, we expect the rate of female entrepreneurship to be higher than in societies that tend to be more religiously Islamic. We hypothesize:

> H2: Rate of female entrepreneurship will be higher in secular societies where the majority of the population is Muslim compared to societies where Sharia law or a mixed system is enforced.

Female entrepreneurship in Turkey

Turkey is unique among MENA countries in the sense that it has long had a leadership position in the region for industrialization, economic growth, democratization, and women's rights (Yetim, 2008). Unlike most other MENA countries, Turkey is not a resource-based economy reliant on revenue generated by natural resources. Turkish history exemplifies the implementation of active secularism and also, the secular and gender egalitarian nature of the 1937 family law make Turkey unique in the context of the MENA region (İlkkaracan, 2012). In the next section, we provide a historic perspective of Islam's evolution within the Turkish society, explaining how Turkey went from being heir to the Ottoman Empire, which was the historical seat of the Caliphate, to a modern secular country. We also discuss how the role of women changed over time in Turkey.

Islam and women in Turkey

Turkey has long been a melting pot of cultures and societies over centuries due to its geographic location. Although Turkey is a secular country without an official religion, its population is predominantly Muslim. Long before the birth of Islam near Mecca, there was the land of Anatolia to the east. The Anatolian plateau – the westernmost part of Asia – witnessed the rise and fall of several kingdoms over hundreds of years due to its geographic position as a gateway between Europe and Asia, 'leaving behind an impressively diverse patchwork of cultures' (Yardumian & Schurr, 2011, p. 7). After the split in the Roman Empire, Anatolia became part of the East Roman Byzantine Empire. Christianity spread early in Anatolia, so that the local population was overwhelmingly Christian by the end of the seventh century. Anatolia, also called Asia Minor, is the peninsula of land that constitutes the Asian portion of Turkey today, where the continents of Asia and Europe meet. Human habitation in Anatolia dates back to the Paleolithic period. During the tenth century, groups of Turkmen warriors, originally from Central Asia, began to move into Anatolia through Azerbaijan (Çalen, 2013). The Ottoman Empire was founded by Turkish tribes in Anatolia in the late thirteenth century under the rule of Osman Gazi who overthrew the Seljuk, and his tribe ruled the land for 600 years until its dissolution in 1918 (Ottoman Empire, 2016). Thus, Seljuk Turks and the Ottoman Empire are the ancestors of the Turks living in the region today.

Women enjoyed a place of respect and reverence in Anatolian history. Patrilineal and matrilineal principles were equally emphasized in family structures, so that children belonged to both parents, women-owned independent property, and were also regarded as capable warriors (Anadolu-Okur, 2005). After Ottoman Turks took over Constantinople in 1453, traditional Ottoman social life came under the influence of Byzantin and Persian state structure. Turkish women's status declined sharply (Anadolu-Okur, 2005). The fifteenth century brought with it the establishment of the *harem* in the Ottoman palace where women were permanently segregated from men, polygamy was introduced as a new system, and Sharia law came into effect. During Sultan Abdulhamit Second's autocratic regime (1876–1909), women came under strict control for 32 years.

After this significant decline, women's status saw an improvement in 1923 with the reform-oriented *Tanzimat* era directed at 'modernization and westernization' of certain aspects of Ottoman social and political life (Anadolu-Okur, 2005). The Ottoman Empire spanned 600 years and covered North Africa, East and Central Europe, and the Middle East (Kabasakal & Bodur, 2002). By the nineteenth century, various religious and/or ethnic groups had sought to establish their own independent political entities. So, the Ottoman Empire could not support a uniform faith and practice. One way for the Ottomans to hold the empire together was by implementing secularism in the Ottoman Empire (Heper & Toktas, 2003), which separated religion and state (Tank, 2005). Secularization efforts had started during the Ottoman Empire and were enforced by Ataturk and his democratic government after the founding of the Turkish Republic.

By most accounts, 1923 was the year the modern Turkish republic was founded (Kurtulus 1987). Under Mustafa Kemal Ataturk's leadership European forces were ousted from Turkish territory, Ottoman Empire ended and Turkey became a democracy. Ottoman Empire had been centre of the Islamic seat of power – the Caliphate – which was abolished overnight by Ataturk on 3 March 1924 (Kabasakal & Bodur, 2002). At this time, educational reforms were prioritized and the former system of religious education (known as the *medrese* system) was terminated. In April 1924, religious courts were closed and Sharia law was abolished. Family names, an old Anatolian tradition which had been eliminated under Sharia rule, were adopted in 1934. 'Active secularism' became the credo of the new Turkish government so that the 'state itself actively embraced and fostered a nonreligious worldview in the public realms' (Warhola and Bezci, 2010, p. 428).

Ataturk launched profound social, political, linguistic and economic reforms based on the principles of secularism, nationalism and modernization (Aycan & Eskin, 2005). He introduced several radically new ideas to this predominantly Muslim country (e.g. women's right to vote before women in many Western democracies had this right) in an attempt to bring Turkey into the modern world (Özkazanç-Pan, 2015). Women were granted the right to vote in local elections in 1930 and at the national level in 1934 together with the right to be elected, earlier than their European counterparts (Anadolu-Okur, 2005). Founding politicians of the Turkish republic formed a society upon a broader and contemporary nationalism idea. The idea behind secularism introduced by Ataturk was to embrace all citizens regardless of their religion, sect, ethnic background and personal appearances. The founders thought that the Turkish republic, as the successor of a multi-religious and multi-nationalist empire, would best be founded upon secular ideas and modern nationalism (Akkaya, 2012, p. 227).

The constitution of Turkey guarantees equality between women and men. Turkey has taken action to assure equality by putting laws into practice in accordance with international agreements and institutions such as the United Nations Convention on the Elimination of All Forms of Discrimination Against Women (CEDAW), International Labor Organization (ILO), the Organization for Economic Cooperation and Development (OECD), the Organization for Security and Co-operation in Europe (OSCE), the Cairo Conference on World Population, United Nations Millennium Development Declaration and national action plan (Turkish Statistics Institute). Given Turkey's long history of active secularism and the emphasis on gender equality in the Turkish constitution, we expect that:

H3: Rates of female entrepreneurship will be higher in Turkey than in non-secular countries where majority of the population is Muslim.

Methods

Data for this study were obtained from the Global Entrepreneurship Monitor (GEM), the largest international study of entrepreneurial activity worldwide. GEM considers new venture creation as the quintessential feature of entrepreneurship (Gartner, 1989; Sternberg & Wennekers, 2005) and those who are taking active steps towards starting a new venture are considered nascent entrepreneurs. We focused our inquiry on Global Entrepreneurship Monitor's 'adult population survey' data for 'total early-stage entrepreneurial activity for female working age population (18 to 64)' which is a part of the Global Key Indicators for years 2001 to 2015. While it would be ideal to examine data collected every year, we decided to take the following approach: We randomly selected years 2006, 2008, 2010 and 2015 from GEM data to conduct our analyses. The use of data collected over time to validate our findings has the rare benefit of demonstrating temporal stability. Selecting GEM data from more years, instead of the ones we used, would not have made substantive differences to our inquiry (as discussed later).

We used The World Factbook published by U.S. Central Intelligence Agency to identify countries with more than 50 per cent of the population considering themselves Muslim. We also used Pew Research Center's Religious Landscape Study and popular press (Tatchell, 2015; Sacirbey, 2012; Brooks-Pollock, 2015) to identify Muslim-majority countries as secular, ruled by Sharia law or mixed. In mixed systems, Sharia law and secular law co-exist, with each one governing different aspects of life. Muslim countries were further categorized as secular and non-secular.

Analyses and results

To test hypotheses, we conducted t-tests on one variable of interest (Female Total Entrepreneurial Activity (FTEA)). According to De Winter (2013), a regular t-test can be used with sample sizes of as few as two data-points without concern. Results of the t-tests comparing Muslim and non-Muslim countries in terms of FTEA for each year included in the study are displayed in Table 1.1. We find no significant difference between mean entrepreneurial activity in Muslim and non-Muslim countries for years shown. Thus, H1 is not supported.

Testing H2 posed substantial data challenges. The GEM data provides little coverage of secular Muslim countries (except Turkey). We find no significant difference between mean entrepreneurial activity in secular Muslim and non-secular Muslim countries and the lack of support for H2 seems consistent over time. Thus, H2 is not supported. Likewise, we find no significant difference between mean entrepreneurial activity in Turkey compared to non-secular Muslim countries across years. Thus, H3 is not supported.

A glance at our numbers suggest that the variances among our groups are not equal, neither are the sample sizes. We were able to conduct Welch's t-test when comparing Muslim versus non-Muslim countries and secular versus non-secular countries for years 2010 and 2015 because this analysis can only be run with groups having two or more data-points. However, this analysis was not useful when comparing Turkey with non-secular Muslim countries or comparing secular versus non-secular Muslim since there was only one secular country in the group.

Table 1.1 Results of t-test and Descriptive Statistics for TEA by Religion, Secular vs. Non-secular, and Turkey vs. Other

	TEA 2006	*TEA 2008*	*TEA 2010*	*TEA 2013*	*TEA 2015*
Muslim					
Mean	8.42	4.27	4.34	8.98	13.92
SD	8.24	1.73	0.81	7.99	11.92
n	4	3	7	6	10
Non-Muslim					
Mean	7.36	8.3	10.33	11.61	10.53
SD	7.22	6.63	10.46	9.22	7.31
n	38	40	53	64	50
95% CI	−6.70, 8.82	−11.86, 3.80	−13.97, 1.98	−10.41, 5.15	−2.29, 9.08
t	0.275	−1.04	−1.5	−0.67	1.2
df	40	41	58	68	58
Secular					
Mean	3.53	2.44	3.87	6.33	17.4
SD			0.29		16.94
n	1	1	2	1	3

	TEA 2006	TEA 2008	TEA 2010	TEA 2013	TEA 2015
Non-Secular					
Mean	10.05	5.19	4.53	9.51	10.05
SD	9.27	0.96	0.9	8.81	9.12
n	3	2	5	5	6
95% CI	−52.56, 39.52	−17.71, 12.21	−2.41, 1.10	−29.98, 23.61	−12.54, 27.23
t	−0.61	−2.34	−0.96	−0.33	0.87
df	2	1	5	4	7
Turkey					
Mean	3.53	2.44	3.67	6.33	−
SD					−
n	1	1	1	1	−
Non-Secular					−
Mean	10.05	5.19	4.53	9.51	−
SD	9.27	0.96	0.9	8.81	−
n	3	2	5	5	−
95% CI	−52.56, 39.52	−17.71, 12.21	−3.60, 1.88	−29.98, 23.61	−
t	−0.61	−2.34	−0.87	−0.33	−
df	2	1	4	4	−

$\star p < .05$

Welch's t-test suggests no significant differences among means for the years of 2010 and 2015 for secular and non-secular countries (other years had a sample of 1 for the secular group, therefore, analysis could not be conducted). When it comes to Muslim versus non-Muslim societies, although we did not find significant differences when comparing FTEA for Muslim versus non-Muslim countries for years 2006, 2013 and 2015, we found significant differences for years 2008 and 2010. For 2008, Welch's $F (1, 8.34) = 7.751$, $p < .05$ and for 2010 Welch's $F(1, 56,94) = 14.18$, $p < .001$.

Discussion

Over the years, Islam has often been accused of suppressing entrepreneurial inclinations (Turner, 2010), particularly among women (Hamdan, 2005). The present study sought to delve deeper into the link between Islam, gender and entrepreneurship by examining whether female entrepreneurship showed any systematic variations across Muslim majority and non-Muslim societies. We generated three specific predictions, which were tested using

GEM data as it is the largest international dataset of nascent entrepreneurial activity in the world. It is also the only dataset that focuses on female entrepreneurship to our knowledge. Predictions were validated at multiple points in time, which strengthened confidence in the validity of our findings and boosted the validity of our research, providing a solid empirical base for further theoretical development.

Our inquiry revealed mixed evidence for significant differences between Muslim and non-Muslim nations on the rate of female entrepreneurial activity in the country. Our investigation, though somewhat coarse-grained, raises questions about the almost taken-for-granted assumption that Islamic societies present unique obstacles to female entrepreneurship (Welter & Smallbone, 2008). Despite the need for in-depth qualitative work to closely examine the hurdles confronting female entrepreneurs in Muslim countries, it seems evident from our finding that the overall rate of female entrepreneurship does not consistently vary between Muslim and non-Muslim nations. These findings are in line with Essers and Benschop's (2009) findings rejecting incompatibility of Islam and female entrepreneurship. While not significant, in some years FTEA was higher in Muslim countries compared to non-Muslim countries (e.g. 2006, 2015). We accept that our findings do not offer a direct test of the Weberian thesis that inherent features within Islam discourage the development of a capitalistic work ethic, but it does call into question the implications of Weber's work for entrepreneurship scholars interested in studying the link between religious beliefs and female entrepreneurial activity.

Contrary to our expectations, we found that the rate of female entrepreneurship does not vary significantly between Muslim countries that are constitutionally secular versus those that are under Sharia law or mixed system. It has generally been assumed that women enjoy more freedom of choice in secular Muslim countries than they do under Sharia law or mixed system governance. While we may have some knowledge about the differences between Sharia and secular governance in Islamic societies, there has been little systematic research on how different governance systems shape the working lives of enterprising women in Muslim countries. We believe our results offer an intriguing starting point from which to delve deeper into the environment for female entrepreneurship in Muslim societies.

The influence of religion on entrepreneurship is not well understood because the relationship is complex and indirect. Studies in the field are limited and data is scarce (Zelekha, Avnimelech and Sharabi, 2014). More importantly, the relationship between religion and entrepreneurship is affected by many factors such as personality, ethnicity, access to networks, education and risk attitude among other individual level factors (Carswell & Rolland, 2004; Caliendo et al., 2009). At the macro level, political system and cultural factors have significant impact on entrepreneurship as well (Zelekha, Avnimelech, & Sharabi, 2014). Studies by Dana (2010) and Zelekha, Avnimelech, and Sharabi (2014) suggest that religion affects entrepreneurship indirectly through its effect on cultural values. They add that regardless of whether a person is religious, one is affected by the cultural values promoted through religion. Future research should take a closer look at the mediating effect of culture and values on the relationship between religion and female entrepreneurship.

Entrepreneurship is generally perceived as a stereotypically masculine endeavour around the world (Gupta, Turban, Wasti, & Sikdar, 2009) and society attaches lower value to female entrepreneurship compared to male entrepreneurship in Turkey (Karatas-Ozkan et al., 2010).

Patriarchal social values, traditional gender roles along with limited access to education and training opportunities, lack of experience in business life, lack of role models and limited access to networks have been listed as factors that deter women from entrepreneurship in Turkey (Karatas-Ozkan et al., 2010). Work–family conflict is a major obstacle faced by Turkish women (Shelton, 2006; Ufuk & Ozgen, 2001a; Winn, 2004; Koyuncu et al., 2012). Having children between the ages of 0 to 11 decreases the odds of being an employer for women because women are expected to be the main childcare providers in the home. Gender norms appear to be the main factor affecting women's economic participation in Turkey (Boudet & Agar, 2014; Ufuk & Ozgen, 2001b). Future research should look examine the mediating role of gender role expectations on the relationship between religion and female entrepreneurship.

Limitations and direction for future research

Our findings about the (lack of) differences in the rate of female entrepreneurship across different groupings of countries (Muslim vs non-Muslim, secular vs non-secular, and Turkey vs non-secular) should be interpreted in light of its limitations. First, under the best circumstances, our sample comprised less than a third of the countries in the world. GEM is the largest available international dataset on entrepreneurial activity worldwide, but it samples a minority of the countries recognized worldwide. Especially the number of secular countries included in the databases was sparse. Availability of larger dataset, encompassing more countries than currently included in GEM, should enhance the validity of our research. It would also be beneficial for research if databases other than GEM (e.g. World Bank Entrepreneurship Data) had female entrepreneurship as a unit of analysis.

Our study was a comparative study that contrasted the rate of female entrepreneurship across countries. Another possible option to better understand the link between Islamic values and female entrepreneurship is to conduct within-country studies that focus on population clusters in specific nations. The salience of within-country studies increases when one considers that many countries with different levels of wealth, industrialization and education besides MENA countries (e.g., United States, Germany, France, India and Denmark, to name a few) have Muslim populations. In addition, our study examines religion at the macro level focusing on religious affiliation rather than examining how religious individuals within these societies are and how their interpretation of Islam varies. Future studies should focus on religiosity and individual religious beliefs in relation to entrepreneurship in general, female entrepreneurship in particular.

Finally, we looked at only the rate of female entrepreneurship but not its structure. It is possible that Muslim and non-Muslim, secular and Sharia countries differ on types of businesses females engage in and goals they set for their businesses (e.g. macro versus micro entrepreneurship), even though they do not differ significantly on the absolute quantity of entrepreneurial activity among women.

Note

1 (p) is an abbreviation of 'peace be upon him', an honorific that Muslims use when the name of the Prophet Muhammad is mentioned (Beekun, 2012).

References

Ahl, H., & Marlow, S. (2012). Exploring the dynamics of gender, feminism and entrepreneurship: Advancing debate to escape a dead end? *Organization, 19*(5), 543–562.

Ahmad, S. Z. (2011). Evidence of the characteristics of women entrepreneurs in the Kingdom of Saudi Arabia: An empirical investigation. *International Journal of Gender and Entrepreneurship, 3*(2), 123–143.

Ahmed, L. (1980). The resurgence of Islam: 2: The return to the source. *History Today, 30*(2), 23.

Ahmed, L. (1992). *Women and gender in Islam: Historical roots of a modern debate.* New Haven, CT: Yale University Press.

Akkaya, S. (2012). Rise of political Islam in Turkey and its effects on Turkish-Syrian relations. *Contemporary Readings in Law & Social Justice, 4*(2), 226–237.

Anadolu-Okur, N. (2005). The demise of the great mother: Islam, reform, and women's emancipation in Turkey. *Gender Issues, 22*(4), 6–28.

Arik, H. (2016). Security, secularism and gender: The Turkish military's security discourse in relation to political Islam. *Gender, Place & Culture: A Journal of Feminist Geography, 23*(5), 641–658.

Ates, A. O. (2006). *Hadis temelli Kalip Yargilarinda Kadin.* Beyan yayini, 2. Baski, Istanbul.

Aycan, Z., & Eskin, M. (2005). Relative contributions of childcare, spousal support, and organizational support in reducing work–family conflict for men and women: The case of Turkey. *Sex Roles, 53*(7–8), 453–471.

Beekun, R. I. (2012). Character centered leadership: Muhammad (p) as an ethical role model for CEOs. *Journal of Management Development, 31*(10), 1003–1020.

Bhagat, R. S., & McQuaid, S. J. (1982). Role of subjective culture in organizations: A review and directions for future research. *Journal of Applied Psychology, 67*(5), 653–685.

Boudet, A. M. M., & Agar, M. (2014). *Female entrepreneurship in Turkey.* The World Bank Report.

Boutroux, É. (1980). *Science et religion dans la philosophie contemporaine.* New York: E. Flammarion.

Brooks-Pollock, T. (2015). 'Yes, we have joined ISIS' say missing British family of 12 who fled to Syria. Retrieved 3 September 2016, from www.independent.co.uk/news/uk/home-news/yes-we-have-joined-isis-say-missing-british-family-of-12-who-fled-to-syria-luton-islamic-state-isis-10365915.html.

Brush, C. G., & Cooper, S. Y. (2012). Female entrepreneurship and economic development: An international perspective. *Entrepreneurship & Regional Development, 24*(1/2), 1–6.

Çalen, M. K. (2013). Celâl Nuri'ye göre muhit, irk, zaman teorisi bağlaminda eski Türkler ile Osmanli Türkleri arasindaki münasebetler. *Trakya University Journal of Social Science, 15*(1), 279–296.

Caliendo, M., Fossen, F. M., & Kritikos, A. S. (2009). Risk attitudes of nascent entrepreneurs: New evidence from an experimentally validated survey. *Small Business Economics, 32*(2), 153–167.

Carswell, P., & Rolland, D. (2004). The role of religion in entrepreneurship participation and perception. *International Journal of Entrepreneurship and Small Business, 1*(3/4), 280–286.

Cetindamar, D., Gupta, V. K., Karadeniz, E. E., & Egrican, N. (2012). What the numbers tell: The impact of human, family and financial capital on women and men's entry into entrepreneurship in Turkey. *Entrepreneurship & Regional Development, 24* (1–2), 29–51.

Dana, L. P. (Ed.) (2010). *Entrepreneurship and religion.* Cheltenham: Edward Elgar.

De Winter, J. C. F. (2013). Using the student's t-test with extremely small sample sizes. *Practical Assessment, Research & Evaluation, 18*(10), 1–12.

Elam, A. B. (2014). *Gender and entrepreneurship.* Cheltenham: Edward Elgar.

Essers, C., & Benschop, Y. (2009). Muslim businesswomen doing boundary work: The negotiation of Islam, gender and ethnicity within entrepreneurial contexts. *Human Relations, 62*(3), 403–423.

Farid, M. (2005). Organizational environment for nonprofit entrepreneurship development. *Academy of Entrepreneurship Journal, 11*(1), 59–78.

Farid, M. (2007). The relevance of transition to free market, attitude towards money, locus of control, and attitude towards risk to entrepreneurs: A cross-cultural empirical comparison. *International Journal of Entrepreneurship, 11*, 75.

Gartner, W. C. (1989). Tourism image: Attribute measurement of state tourism products using multidimensional scaling techniques. *Journal of Travel Research, 28*(2), 16–20.

Grey, K. R., & Finley-Hervey, J. (2005). Women and entrepreneurship in Morocco: Debunking stereotypes and discerning strategies. *International Entrepreneurship and Management Journal, 1*, 203–217.

Gupta, V. K., Turban, D., Wasti, S. A., & Sikdar, A. (2009). The role of gender stereotypes in perceptions of entrepreneurs and intentions to become an entrepreneur. *Entrepreneurship Theory & Practice, 33*(2), 397–417.

Gümüsay, A. A. (2015). Entrepreneurship from an Islamic perspective. *Journal of Business Ethics, 130*(1), 199–208.

Gurhan, N. (2010). Toplumsal Cinsiyet ve Din. *Journal of Oriental Scientific Research / E-Sarkiyat Ilmi Arastirmalar Dergis, 4*, 58–80.

Hafsi, M. (1987). The effect of religious involvement on work centrality. *Psychologia, 30*, 258–266.

Hamdan, A. (2005). Women and education in Saudi Arabia: Challenges and achievements. *International Education Journal, 6*(1), 42–64.

Hayton, J. C., George, G., & Zahra, S. A. (2002). National culture and entrepreneurship: A review of behavioral research. *Entrepreneurship: Theory & Practice, 26*(4), 33.

Heper, M., & Toktas, S. (2003). Islam, modernity, and democracy in contemporary Turkey: The case of Recep Tayyip Erdogan. *Muslim World, 93*(2), 157.

Ilhaamie, A. G. A, Siti Arni, B., Rosmawani, C. H. M., & Hassan Al-Banna, M. (2014). Challenges of Muslim women entrepreneurs in Malaysian SMEs. *International Journal of Innovation, Management and Technology, 5*(6).

İlkkaracan, İ. (2012). Why so few women in the labor market in Turkey? *Feminist Economics, 18*(1), 1–37.

Irigaray, L. (1993). *Je, tu, nous: Toward a culture of difference (thinking gender)*. Abingdon: Routledge.

Jennings, J. E., & Brush, C. G. (2013). Research on women entrepreneurs: Challenges to (and from) the broader entrepreneurship literature? *Academy of Management Annals, 7*(1), 663–715.

Johnson, T. M., & Grim, B. J. (2013). *The world's religions in figures: An introduction to international religious demography*. Chichester: John Wiley & Sons.

Kabasakal, H., & Bodur, M. (2002). Arabic cluster: A bridge between East and West. *Journal of World Business, 37*(1), 40–54.

Karatas-Ozkan, M., Inal, G., & Özbilgin, M. (2010). Turkey, in S. Fielden and M. Davidson (Eds), *International handbook of successful women entrepreneurs* (pp. 175–188). Cheltenham and New York: Edward Elgar Press.

Koyuncu, M., Burke, R. J., & Wolpin, J. (2012). Work-family conflict, satisfactions and psychological well-being among women managers and professionals in Turkey. *Gender in Management, 27*(3), 202–213.

Kurtulus, K. (1987). Entrepreneurship in Turkey. *Journal of Small Business Management, 25*(4), 66.

Kuru, A. T. (2009). *Secularism and state policies toward religion: The United States, France, and Turkey*. Cambridge: Cambridge University Press.

McIntosh, J. C., & Islam, S. (2010). Beyond the veil: The influence of Islam on female entrepreneurship in a conservative Muslim context. *International Management Review, 6*(1), 102–108.

Marlow, S., & McAdam, M. (2013). Gender and entrepreneurship: Advancing debate and challenging myths; Exploring the mystery of the under-performing female entrepreneur. *International Journal of Entrepreneurial Behavior & Research, 19*(1), 114–124.

Mernissi, F. (1991). *The veil and the male elite: A feminist interpretation of women's rights in Islam*. New York: Basic Books.

Mernissi, F. (2011). *Beyond the veil: Male-female dynamics in a Muslim society*. London: Saqi Books.

Ottoman Empire (2016). *Colombia electronic encyclopedia*. 6th edition, 1–3.

Özkazanç-Pan, B. (2015). Secular and Islamic feminist entrepreneurship in Turkey. *International Journal of Gender and Entrepreneurship, 7*(1), 45–65.

Patai, R. (1976). *The Arab mind*. New York: Scribner's.

Power, C. & Nadine, A. (1998). The new Islam, *Newsweek*, 131, no. 11, pp. 34–37.

Richardson, E. (2015). *Islam for beginners: Basics of Islam and Muslim customs*. Amazon digital services.

Roomi, M. A. (2013). Entrepreneurial capital, social values and Islamic traditions: Exploring the growth of women-owned enterprises in Pakistan. *International Small Business Journal, 31*(2), 175–191.

Roomi, M. A., & Harrison, P. (2011). Entrepreneurial leadership: What is it and how should it be taught? *International Review of Entrepreneurship, 9*(3), 1–44.

Sacirbey, O. (2012). World's '500 most influential Muslims'. *US Huffington Post*. www.huffingtonpost.com/2012/11/29/worlds-500-most-influential-muslims-2012_n_2208667.html.

Savas, R. (1991). *Hz. Muhammed Devrinde Kadin*, Farkli yayinevi, 1. baski, Izmir.

Shelton, L. M. (2006). Female entrepreneurs, work–family conflict, and venture performance: New insights in the work–family interface. *Journal of Small Business Management, 44*(2), 285–297.

Shmailan, A. (2014). Female entrepreneurs in Saudi Arabia: A comparison of barriers and motivations: moving from disenfranchisement to empowerment. *Elite Research Journal of Education and Review, 2*(2), 6–21.

Sidani, Y. (2005). Women, work, and Islam in Arab societies. *Women in Management Review, 20*(7), 498–512.

Sternberg, R., & Wennekers, S. (2005). Determinants and effects of new business creation using Global Entrepreneurship Monitor data. *Small Business Economics, 24*(3), 193–203.

Sullivan, D. M., & Meek, W. R. (2012). Gender and entrepreneurship: A review and process model. *Journal of Managerial Psychology, 27*(5), 428–458.

Syed, J. (2008). A context-specific perspective of equal employment opportunity in Islamic societies. *Asia Pacific Journal of Management, 25*(1), 135–151.

Syed, J. (2009). Reconstruction of gender in Islamic thought: Iqbal's vision of equal opportunity. *Women's Studies International Forum, 32*(6), 435–444.

Syed, J. (2010). An historical perspective on Islamic modesty and its implications for female employment. *Equality, Diversity and Inclusion, 29*(2), 150–166.

Tank, P. (2005). Political Islam in Turkey: A state of controlled secularity. *Turkish Studies, 6*(1), 3–19.

Tatchell, P. (2015). Sharia Law versus secular democracy. *The Huffington Post*, n.p., 2015. Web. 2 February 2017.

Terjesen, S., & Lloyd, A. (2015). *The 2015 Female Entrepreneurship Index*.

Tlaiss, H. A. (2015). How Islamic business ethics impact women entrepreneurs: Insights from four Arab Middle Eastern countries. *Journal of Business Ethics, 129*(4), 859–877.

Turner, B. S. (2010). Islam, capitalism and the Weber theses. *British Journal of Sociology, 61*, 147–160.

Ufuk, H., & Özgen, Ö. (2001a). Interaction between the business and family lives of women entrepreneurs in Turkey. *Journal of Business Ethics, 31*(2), 95–106.

Ufuk, H., & Özgen, Ö. (2001b). The profile of women entrepreneurs: A sample from Turkey. *International Journal of Consumer Studies, 25*(4), 299–308.

United Nations Development Programme, Regional Bureau for Arab States (RBAS) (2006). *The Arab Human Development Report: Towards the Rise of Women in the Arab World*. New York. http://hdr.undp.org/sites/default/files/rbas_ahdr2005_en.pdf.

Warhola, J. W., & Bezci, E. B. (2010). Religion and state in contemporary Turkey: Recent developments in Laiklik. *Journal of Church & State, 52*(3), 427–453.

Weir, D. (2000). Management in the Arab world. In M. Warner (Ed.), *Management in the emerging countries* (pp. 291–300). London: Business Press-Thomson Learning.

Welter, F. and Smallbone, D. (2008). Women's entrepreneurship from an institutional perspective: The case of Uzbekistan. *International Entrepreneurship and Management Journal, 4*(4), 505–520.

Winn, J. (2004). Entrepreneurship: Not an easy path to top management for women. *Women in Management Review, 19*(3), 143–153.

Yardumian, A., & Schurr, T. G. (2011). Who are the Anatolian Turks? *Anthropology & Archeology of Eurasia, 50*(1), 6–42.

Yasin, M., Zimmerer, T. & Green, R. (1989). Cultural values as determinants of executive attitude. *International Journal of Value-Based Management, 2*(2), 33–47.

Yetim, N. (2008). Social capital in female entrepreneurship. *International Sociology, 23*(6), 864–885.

Yildirim, E. (2014). Social sex issue in terms of the Quran sociology. *AIBU Journal of Social Sciences, 14*(1), 437–460.

Zelekha, Y., Avnimelech, G., & Sharabi, E. (2014). Religious institutions and entrepreneurship. *Small Business Economics, 42*(4), 747–767.

2 If policy (half-heartedly) says 'yes', but patriarchy says 'no'

How the gendered institutional context in Pakistan restricts women entrepreneurship

Khizran Zehra and Leona Achtenhagen

Many governments around the world aim to enhance entrepreneurship through different policy measures (Easterly, 2005). Empowering women to participate in entrepreneurship might help in reducing poverty (Hausmann et al., 2009). Also the Government of Pakistan (GoP) has recognized the importance of involving women into the country's economic development. It claims to be positively committed to fostering women's entrepreneurship and has taken various actions to promote it. While many studies have assessed measures to enhance women's entrepreneurship in emerging economies, e.g. regarding training or financing, little attention has been paid so far to assessing the situation in Pakistan (Rehman & Azam Roomi, 2012). Evidence for how policy programmes influence entrepreneurial activities in Pakistan is also missing, as the country has a history of lacking reliable data (e.g., Ali, 2006). Yet, institutional analyses of gender-related policies are important, as institutional contexts can be a liability or asset (Welter, 2011).

The aim of this chapter is to critically assess the Pakistani context for women's entrepreneurship, including its policies. We draw on extensive secondary materials from different public and policy sources in Pakistan, published in Urdu or English, and other internationally published references. The chapter starts with an overview of how the current formal institutional context in Pakistan emerged in relation to entrepreneurship and gender issues. Thereafter it presents measures taken to support women entrepreneurs. Then it explains some core characteristics of the country's patriarchy which as informal institution constrains women entrepreneurs in practice. The concluding section discusses the findings and their implications and outlines some suggestions as to how the situation of women entrepreneurs in Pakistan could be improved. This chapter contributes to the emerging research agenda calling for a systematic analysis of women's entrepreneurship and gendered policies (Lundstrom & Stevenson, 2006). We conclude that it is not enough to ratify institutional measures promoting women and women entrepreneurs, but that commitment and resources for implementing these in practice are needed – combined with a focus on bringing about the social change needed to reduce barriers created through informal, often patriarchal, institutions in Pakistan.

Gender gap in entrepreneurship

The gender gap in entrepreneurship refers to the difference between men and women in terms of numbers engaged in entrepreneurial activity, motives to start or run a business, industry choice and business performance and growth (Vossenberg, 2013, p. 2). The Global

Entrepreneurship Monitor (GEM) finds that globally women make up for 39% of all entrepreneurial activity (Kelley, Singer, & Herrington, 2012). However, at the level of individual countries the gender gap is much more pronounced and some countries only have few women entrepreneurs (Minniti, 2009). Pakistan is the country that exhibits the lowest level of women's entrepreneurial activity in the world, and this gender gap is alarming, as the total entrepreneurial activity (TEA) in Pakistan already is rather low. GEM data shows that male TEA in Pakistan is 21.27, and thus 17 times higher than the female TEA of 1.21 (Mian & Qureshi, 2014). Pakistan joined the GEM survey in 2010, and the 2014 survey indicates that the gender gap in entrepreneurship not only persists, but increases (Mian & Qureshi, 2014) – requiring attention towards explaining the determinants of this gap. Yet, these numbers are a clear indicator for the failure of the country's general institutional set-up to promote entrepreneurial activities.

Institutional theory as theoretical perspective

There still is a lack of reliable data on women's entrepreneurship that would capture the complexity of their entrepreneurial endeavours, limiting the development of an in-depth understanding of the gender gap in entrepreneurship across the globe. Early research aiming to understand differences in male and female entrepreneurial activity focused on micro-economic factors (Ahl & Marlow, 2012; Minniti, 2009). Some also believed that women lacked certain skills needed to be entrepreneurial (Jamali, 2009). However, Brush, De Bruin, and Welter (2009) suggest that the gender gap in entrepreneurship cannot be explained on its own, but needs to take into account contextual factors and other macro-level explanations. Institutional theory can explain context at three different levels by focusing on formal rules, regulations and informal norms (Scott, 1995). Institutions are multifaceted, durable social structures made up of regulative, normative and cognitive elements (Scott, 2005). The regulative pillar refers to formal institutions and is about establishing rules, policy-making and monitoring. The normative pillar refers to values and expectations that set the standards for legitimate behaviour in a society. The cognitive pillar constitutes the social reality and refers to the shared conception and meaning making. Cognitions precede behaviours and provide inputs to persons' information processing and problem solving. Cognition is culturally supported and culture is the main frame for and source of shared knowledge and meaning making. While the regulative pillar is formal, the normative and cognitive pillars represent informal expectations in which entrepreneurial behaviours of individuals are embedded (Baughn, Chua, & Neupert, 2006). Formal institutions such as policies and politics can improve or diminish entrepreneurial activity (Brush et al., 2009). But also informal institutions, through their attitudes towards gender and entrepreneurship, can impact women's entrepreneurship (Baughn et al., 2006). Indeed, a lack of acceptance or social legitimacy for women to be entrepreneurs may constrain women's entrepreneurship and result in a wider gender gap (Amine & Staub, 2009; Kalantaridis & Fletcher, 2012).

That Pakistan ranks lowest in the GEM survey suggests that its gender gap in entrepreneurship is due to a seriously constrained institutional system (Klapper & Parker, 2011; Waylen, 2014). Therefore, using the institutional context to explain the gender gap in entrepreneurship presents a relevant theoretical ground (De Bruin, Brush, & Welter, 2007).

Critical analysis of the institutional environment in Pakistan

While women entrepreneurs are playing a key role for the development of economies around the globe, this pattern does not reappear in Pakistan. Almost 70 years after the country gained independence, female labour-force participation, including women entrepreneurs, is still only 22% (Pakistan Bureau of Statistics, 2016). A common explanation for this low rate of women's labour-force participation relates to Pakistan's very poor rural areas (Rehman & Azam Roomi, 2012; Tambunan, 2009). Yet, as explanation for the low entrepreneurial activity this remains inadequate – after all, poverty could just as well act as a push factor into entrepreneurship. The low rate of women's entrepreneurship in Pakistan rather appears to be a consequence of two phenomena, namely the formal institutional environment regarding gender equality and entrepreneurship as well as the informal institutional set-up restricting the role of women in Pakistani society. Such mixed embeddedness of women entrepreneurship embraces different structural and agency factors and is the result of an interplay of cultural, social, economic factors (Welter, 2011).

Next, we will discuss the formal (i.e., regulative) institutional set-up in Pakistan, before presenting informal (i.e. normative and cognitive) institutional hindrances for women entrepreneurs in that country. However, it needs to be kept in mind that for the sake of readability this differentiation into formal and informal institutions is simplifying a much more complex reality. For decades, policies and development planning for women in Pakistan have been influenced by the social and cultural factors that are deeply rooted in its patriarchal structure, implying that formal and informal institutions are much more entangled than presented below.

Formal institutional set-up

The formal institutional set-up refers to the governmental actions and their rules and policy-making to facilitate entrepreneurial activity in Pakistan (cf. Scott, 2005).

Historically grown scepticism towards entrepreneurship

Pakistan has always been controlled by feudal elites, bureaucratic and military structures which have followed a 'the government knows best' approach (Ul Haque, 2007). The result of such government-led economy was that government policies were supportive of the manufacturing and industrial sectors (Goheer, 2003), while remaining sceptical of small-business opportunities. The development of entrepreneurship in Pakistan has been seriously affected by the resource distribution among government's favoured through which wealth remained concentrated in the hands of bureaucrats and elites (Ul Haque, 2007).

SMEs in Pakistan contribute around 30% to the GDP and generate 25% of exports (Economic Census of Pakistan, 2005). There were 2.96 million business enterprises in Pakistan in 2005 (SMEDA, 2007). Among these were 70,658 women-owned businesses, representing less than 3% of total enterprises (Economic Census of Pakistan, 2005). In Pakistan, women-owned and managed SMEs remain mostly concentrated in low-threshold, traditional business sectors. These are often extensions of women's domestic tasks, such as managing livestock and poultry, or based on skills that are passed on from one generation to the next, such as embroidery and craftsmanship (Safavian & Haq, 2013). Women remain in these business sectors due to restrictions regarding their mobility, a lack of access to financial capital as well as patriarchal constraints (Aslam et al., 2013). Even in urban areas, women's businesses tend to be in sectors like fashion-designing, home textiles, dress making, knitting, food retailing and health (Mizlink, 2016).

The emergence of gender-aware policy-making

Policy-making in Pakistan was gender insensitive until 1983, when international pressure during Zia-ul Haq's regime (in power between 1977 and 1988) officially shifted policies towards a positive stance on women-development planning. In result, the GoP proclaimed a positive commitment to women development by signing numerous international conventions as well as deciding on various policies to promote women. However, these policies were in stark contrast to ul Haq's commitment to establish Pakistan as an Islamic state and to enforce Shariah law, which in effect harshly restricted the freedom, mobility and safety of women. For example, he introduced the *Hudood Ordinance* which prescribed the use of the *purdah*, a type of clothing similar to a burqa which was created to isolate women from their surroundings and which had to be worn in public (Baig, 2012). Yet, theoretically the possibilities for women to become entrepreneurially active improved as a result of the official policy shift. The 6th Five-Year Plan (1983–1988) represented the first time that an official chapter explicitly emphasized the importance of improving the status of women. Even the subsequent 7th (1988–93) and 8th (1993–98) Five-Year Plans explicitly addressed the integration of women in society.

The regime of Benazir Bhutto, as the 11th and 13th Prime Minister of Pakistan and in power during most years of the 7th and 8th plan, was more committed to bringing about positive change for women, for example by setting up women police stations and implementing the Ministry of Women Development (MoWD). These measures were important, as they promoted women empowerment through the possibility of reporting domestic violence and through policies aimed at gender development. Her main legacy may be the Benazir Income Support Programme (BISP), which distributes cash, without conditions, to very poor families throughout Pakistan. In 2013, 5.5 million families received 1,200 Pakistani rupees (about 12 USD) twice a month to spend on food. Bhutto had developed this programme, which after her death was enacted by Prime Minister Gilani, but named after Bhutto as a tribute to her. Gilani was aware that '[g]ender inequality remains a big challenge to socio-economic development in Pakistan' and stated that BISP 'is the bedrock of initiatives' that can help to empower women. (*Daily Times*, 2011/03/09). BISP transfers cash into the bank account of a woman in the family, not a man. This aims to empower poor Pakistani women by placing spending power directly into their hands, making them decision-makers within the family, in result increasing their respect in the community (Shah, 2014).

However, Bhutto was also criticized for not using her position as first female Prime Minister more actively to improve the situation of women in Pakistan. While she is accredited to having reduced the invisibility of women resulting from Zia-ul Haq's regime, e.g. by lifting press censorship that marked a change in the media's portrayal of women, her election as Prime Minister had been so controversial that she largely tried to function within the given Islamist framework (Khan, 2010). Governing through a fragile coalition, her focus was on sustaining her government and appeasing the opposition and Islamist lobbyists, rendering it difficult for her to revoke the previous government's policies, especially regarding women. As Khan (2010) states: 'Many state policies on gender remained within the aegis of Islamic law or were of symbolic rather than lasting significance. Thus, Benazir's policies on gender are ambivalently received'.

Starting during the 1990s, Pakistan became signatory of different international conventions aiming to promote gender equality, such as the Convention on Elimination of All Forms of Discrimination Against Women (CEDAW; signed in 1995) and the Millennium Development Goals (MDGs; signed in 2000 and running until 2015) – their scope included empowering women to participate in entrepreneurship (Montgomery & Weiss, 2011). While on a worldwide level, the MDGs have been very successful, especially in reducing poverty, 'Pakistan failed terribly to achieve the MDGs' (Shahid, 2015). The United Nations Development Group (UNDG, 2016) ascribes this failure 'in part to a lack of awareness and [provincial] ownership early on in the process'.

Pakistan has also committed to the MDGs' successor, the Sustainable Development Goals (SDGs) that run between 2015 and 2030. It is still unclear whether the GoP will succeed better this time. Sheikh (2016) comments on the challenge of implementing the SGDs: 'Pakistan is needlessly struck with an archaic method of budgetary planning. Over the years, the state has developed a notoriously weak reputation when developing, implementing or monitoring social sector projects, resulting in globally dismal and embarrassingly poor indicators'. The SDGs have been aligned with the country's own 'Vision 2025'. Its 120-page document treats gender-equality issues on half a page only, and the lack of women empowerment is not mentioned as one of the country's challenges: While the criticism regarding the MDGs' lack of provincial ownership is met in this document by including introductory statements by all Chief Ministers of the Pakistani regions, none of these express their commitment to women or gender issues. Thus, it appears doubtful whether the SGDs will lead to an empowered role of women in society.

Even other formal activities aimed at promoting gender equality have largely been failures. The MoWD was established in 1989 to bring positive changes to the lives of Pakistani women in line with the constitution. The Ministry had four wings, including 'Development' and 'Gender-inequality', which were to focus on including women in mainstream development – dealing with capacity building, trainings, gender-issue assessments and awareness among various stakeholders. A National Plan of Action was issued in 1998 by the MoWD, which detailed the strategic objectives and plans of 12 targeted areas. The military government under General Pervez Musharraf (in power between 1999 and 2008) formulated the first ever National Policy for Development and Empowerment of Women (NPDEW), which was ratified in 2002. This policy was a statement of intent of the GoP to specify its measures for the development and empowerment of women. With this policy providing the guidelines, the MoWD had the task to ensure a gender perspective in all national policies and plans. However, the NPDEW never became a success, as Ahmad et al.'s (2010) evaluation clearly demonstrates.

Another big policy failure under the patronage of the MoWD was the Gender Reform Action Plan (GRAP). In February 2000, the GoP approached the Asian Development Bank for technical assistance in preparing a gender-reform programme to improve the framework of gender policies and to develop institutional-reform proposals outlining interventions at the federal, provincial and district level, for a proactive approach to include a gender perspective in public-sector policies, programmes and projects. In result, the GRAP was launched in 2002 (www.grap.gop.pk). In a formal evaluation of this policy measure, Yazdani and Jawad (2010) conclude i.a. that its goals were unrealistic, that important concepts such as gender equality and women empowerment were never defined, and that a lack of ownership, institutional weaknesses, systemic gaps and a 'goldfish syndrome' hampered the design and implementation of GRAP. In 2012, in response to the lack of impact achieved by the MoWD, its devolution to the provinces took place, making lower levels of government fully responsible for policy, financing and execution of women-development issues (Citizens' Commission for Human Development, 2014).

A National Commission on Status of Women (NCSW) was set up by the GoP in July 2000. The main purpose of this commission was to examine policy measures taken by the GoP for women development and to recommend necessary remedial measures. It was also to review laws, rules and regulations that affect the rights and status of women and monitored institutional mechanisms for their effective implementation. Other tasks included to encourage research generating women-related data and to develop dialogues with NGOs regarding policies and strategic actions for promoting gender equality. It appears to be here that the commission has delivered relatively substantial output, and some research reports can be found on the commission's website (www.ncsw.gov.pk). Also, the NCSW developed and distributed information materials, such as posters and brochures, to inform women how and where they can get help in case of rape, child marriages and other forms of violence. However, the commission appears to be riddled by struggles related to defining its tasks (e.g. in relation to the GRAP and MoWD) and leadership, leaving its current status difficult to fully assess (see Yazdani & Jawad, 2010).

The Constitution of Pakistan realizes the importance of gender equality in its articles 25, 27, 34, 35 and 37, which grant women equal rights as men and provide for affirmative action against gender discrimination (Constitution of Pakistan, 1973). However, the aftermath of ul Haq's oppression was only somewhat reduced in 2006, when the Pakistani parliament under the leadership of General Musharraf passed the Women's Protection Bill, which was supposed to repeal some of the Hudood Ordinance (Weiss, 2012). In 2011, a Thomson Reuters Foundation poll ranked Pakistan the third most dangerous country in the world for women (Reuters, 2011), indicating that '[t]he unfair treatment of women in Pakistan is also due to the country's legislation, which, throughout the years, has greatly restricted the rights of women' (Baig, 2012). Conservative Islamist forces maintain a strong grip on the power granted to them during ul Haq's regime and fiercely oppose changes in the legislation that would improve the situation of women (see Reuters, 2016).

Given this legal framework and policy situation regarding women in Pakistan, we will next turn to an analysis of policies and initiatives that were introduced over the years to promote entrepreneurship in general and women entrepreneurs in particular.

Formal measures to support SMEs and entrepreneurs

Chambers of commerce and business associations

Already in 1972, the GoP established specific units to facilitate SMEs in four provinces of Pakistan. These units have never targeted women entrepreneurs in specific (Goheer, 2002). In 1998, a Small and Medium Enterprise Development Authority (SMEDA) was established to make the business environment more favourable to SMEs. SMEDA has also realized that research could play a role in improving the context for SMEs, and the first edition of their research journal was launched in December 2010. However, so far it has only published six papers, and none addressing a gender issue. Yet, it could have the potential to become an outlet for gender research related to entrepreneurship in the future. Nonetheless, SMEDA explicitly aims to promote women's empowerment, as stated on its webpage:

> The women economic development in Pakistan has been quite ignored . . . Despite governmental commitment and donors' efforts to reduce gender inequalities, nothing has been done with regards to developing proper women economic action plan to uplift women socio-economic status. On an ad hoc basis, some common facility centres and vocational/technical training institutes to enhance female participation rate have been established which provide traditional skills. On the other hand, to mobilize youth energy into economic sectors, government has launched internship programmes and other incentives yet its impact on the grass-root level is not visible due to lack of information and knowledge to young females regarding these facilities. The result is that many girls become confined to their homes.
>
> (SMEDA, 2016)

In 2007, SMEDA initiated the first women business-incubation centre (WBIC) in Lahore, and has since opened similar centres in other provinces (Quetta, Karachi and Swat). The centres provide business counselling, training, furnished offices, marketing services and exhibition facilities to women entrepreneurs.

The Trade Development Authority of Pakistan (TDAP) was established in November 2006 as a successor to the Export Promotion Bureau (EPB), with the aim of promoting Pakistani trade holistically rather than just focusing on export promotion, as its predecessor EPB had done. Within its facilitation division, the TDAP has one section for women entrepreneurs that stresses the role of innovation and quality in exports, e.g. by organizing seminars related to best business practices for exports or how to start businesses. Since 2001, a network for women exporters, WEXNET, has been developed, and exhibitions arranged in Lahore – the 9th exhibition took place in December 2015. WEXNET serves as a platform for women entrepreneurs from all over Pakistan to interact as well as promote and exhibit their products for exports. In the 2014 exhibition, over 300 women entrepreneurs presented their products for around 25,000 visitors. The same section of TDAP also maintains a directory of the women entrepreneurs connected to WEXNET to promote accessibility and facilitate interaction (www.tdap.gov.pk/wexnet-directory.php).

Business-women associations

The Pakistan Association of Women Entrepreneurs (PAWE) was registered as a nongovernmental organization (NGO) in 1985, and has since been led by well-known female entrepreneurs. PAWE is a member of the governing body of the World Assembly of Small and Medium Enterprises (WASME) and is affiliated to the Economic and Social Council of the UN (ECOSOC). It has carried out various activities in urban areas, especially in Karachi, and mainly focuses on representing the interests of women entrepreneurs at international forums.

The Association of Business, Professional and Agricultural Women is another organization in Karachi that engages in multiple activities to facilitate social harmony, and to promote an exchange of views and greater interaction among women. It has also identified business areas and prepared some pre-feasibility reports for enterprise creation.

The Pakistan Federation of Business and Professional Women is another organization in Karachi engaged in similar activities. The Women Entrepreneurs Society (WES) in Lahore shows no significant activity. The women entrepreneurs' committee of the Lahore Chamber of Commerce and Industry (LCCI) has various collaborations with Australian, Dutch and US American delegates and is partnering with the World Bank regarding business development training for women entrepreneurs (www.lcci.com.pk). The labour union Pakistan Worker Federation (PWF) is also conscious of its responsibilities to encourage women to partake in economic activities to enable them to contribute to national economic development (www.pwf.org.pk). Part of this responsibility has been addressed through various project initiatives with the aim of supporting women's entrepreneurship development activities.

Banks and micro-finance

The Small Medium Enterprise Bank began its operation in January 2002, by merging the Small Business Finance Corporation (SBFC) and the Regional Development Finance Corporation (RDFC). One proclaimed intention was to focus on women entrepreneurs (Goheer, 2002). Until today, no women-specific activity associated with the SME Bank can be identified (on www.smebank.org; as of February 2017). More successful in supporting women entrepreneurs is the First Women Bank Limited (FWBL), established in 1989 by Benazir Bhutto to cater for the financial needs of (business) women (www.fwbl.com.pk). On its homepage, the bank states as its charter: 'Undertaking the conduct of all forms of business of Banking Company in a manner designed to meet the special needs of women and to encourage and assist them in promotion and running of trade and industry and practice of profession.' The bank offers loans on easy terms for women entrepreneurs, but also consultancy for investments, identification of agricultural and industrial projects for women entrepreneurs, and trainings in managerial skills. It has 42 branches all over Pakistan. The main impact of the bank on women entrepreneurs is its small-loan facility for women from low-income groups with an initial allocation of Rs.35 million from the MoWD. Under this scheme, women could borrow up to Rs.25,000 (approximately US$ 400) by using a group guarantee, NGO warranty or personal surety from two government officials. By the bank's 25-year anniversary in 2014, more than 50,000 women had benefited from these schemes. In addition, the FWBL set up Business Development and Training Centres to inspire the economic empowerment of women, and have so far trained more than 6,500 women in different trades (www.fwbl.com.pk).

The last decade has seen additional micro-credit initiatives as a tool for poverty alleviation, e.g. the Pakistan Poverty Alleviation Fund (PPAF), the National Rural Support Program (NRSP), other Rural Support Programs (RSPs), and the Khushali Bank. These programmes target women for two reasons: firstly, the success of micro-credits in Bangladesh is partly built on lending to women due to their conservative and trustworthy behaviour. Second, the rising levels of poverty in Pakistan and the preponderance of poor women have forced policy-makers to support women in starting micro-business activities. However, Safavian and Haq (2013) question the success of Pakistani micro-financing initiatives in reaching women entrepreneurs. Their study shows that while 59% of micro-finance clients were women, the majority of these loans were passed on to male members of the household – husbands, fathers and sons. They find that business women often are restricted to group-lending schemes and rarely given the opportunity to access individual loan products, which the banks tend to offer exclusively to male borrowers. They conclude that lending practices often are discriminatory, requiring husbands' permission and male guarantors, while unmarried women are rarely considered as potential clients.

Next, we will turn to an analysis of the impact of informal institutions on women entrepreneurs in Pakistan.

Informal institutions and the role of patriarchy

Normative forces

Normative factors enable or constrain social behaviours and actions, and provide rights as well as obligations. Norms and values provide social standards to judge evil and good and define socially acceptable patterns of behaviours.

Patriarchy

Although women in Pakistan often participate in family and farm affairs, their work is considered to be a social duty rather than appreciated for its economic contribution (Kamal, 1997). A recent study concludes that 'women in Pakistan do not take up paid employment because of mobility restrictions resulting from both cultural and social norms and security concerns. Almost 40% of women who are not working report that the main reason for this is that male family members do not permit them to work outside the home' (ADB, 2016, p. 2).

The systematic subordination of women in Pakistan continues to be determined by two patriarchal forces enforced during ul Haq's Islamization regime: the first one is that of *purdah* ('veil'), which no longer refers to a burqa-type veil (covering head and face), but to the continuing demand on women to dress 'properly' by covering their bodies and the physical segregation of the sexes, demanding from women to avoid contact with men who are not their close relatives. This force still makes it uncommon for women to naturally interact with men, thereby restricting the freedom and mobility of women, as well as their possibilities to conduct business activities. Shaheed (2010) discusses purdah as an institution that controls and governs women's lives in Pakistan, both as an ideology that, through internalized behaviour codes, predetermines a woman's options and actions, and as externally enforced gender segregation and female seclusion.

> For most women the long drawn 'curtain' of Purdah, is much more like a steel wall which seals them indoors for most of their natural lives. Mobility is considered shameful. Segregation is enforced, primarily by shaming, and women willingly participate in this segregation as culturally encouraged, as much by tradition, as by religious law.
> (Pitlane Magazine, 2017)

The second patriarchal force restricting women entrepreneurs is that of *izzat* ('honour') (see Roomi & Parrott, 2008) – viewing it as a woman's main task to maintain her family's 'honour'. 'Izzat is based upon control, the ability to control key social and economic groups and persons in the society. Almost all the things that directly affect izzat are instances of success or failure to control these social elements. The most fundamental level of control is that of women' (Fischer, 1991, p. 108).

These two patriarchal influences have contributed to gender-role stereotypes, where women are confined to the boundaries of the home to be considered honourable (Rehman & Azam Roomi, 2012), leading to additional subordination through limiting the mobility of women (Azam Roomi & Harrison, 2010; Shabbir & Di Gregorio, 1996). Mobility is restricted by the socio-cultural expectation that women either be chaperoned by a man or take transportation which is for women only, such as special buses which do not run frequently. At the same time, these social and cultural factors affect the personal goals of women themselves, as many wish to adhere to what society expects of them. Women interested in entrepreneurial activities need to find ways to deal with these institutionalized socio-cultural constraints. Yet, not only tradition, culture and fundamentalist interpretations of the Quran and Shariah constrain women – safety concerns in view of recent terrorist attacks and the general lack of safety of women in society contribute to serious worries about female family members, even in families generally supportive of entrepreneurial endeavours.

The social norm regarding the handling of finances being the responsibility of male family members in most households of Pakistan is another constraint for women entrepreneurs. As pointed out in the discussion of micro-financing in Pakistan above, women entrepreneurs typically lack control not only regarding their ventures' finances, but also regarding core decisions around how to develop the business activities by taking in external sources of financing.

Finally, women entrepreneurs do not have equal access to social networks, because of their restricted mobility and demands regarding acceptable behaviours. All these patriarchal norms constrain overall women empowerment and their entrepreneurship.

Cognitive forces

The cognitive pillar of institutional theory is embedded in culture and related to people's lives and the interaction with their environment.

Education is a crucial cognitive factor in that a lack of business and market knowledge is posing a serious constraint on women's entrepreneurial endeavours and business development. Given these cognitive constraints, many women do not dare to pursue entrepreneurial activities. According to the GEM study, 27.7% of potential business activities worldwide do not get started because of a fear of failure (Mian & Qureshi, 2014). Some grass-root activities have emerged, such as the network of women entrepreneurs and executives *mizlink* (www.mizlink-pakistan.com), offering network links and knowledge resources. Such resources can play an important role for women entrepreneurs in the country, as to date women largely remain passive recipients of various programmes regarding their business development (Goheer, 2003; Roomi & Parrott, 2008). Most trainings organized by the associations presented above are targeted at improving the domestic role of women, rather than giving them knowledge about markets, business and entrepreneurship.

Discussion

We started our analysis by outlining how Pakistan has promoted rent-seeking behaviour – instead of entrepreneurship – through favouring a small segment of society, i.e. feudals and elites (Ul Haque, 2007). These path-dependent policies allowed industrialists to maintain their firm grip on the allocation of resources in the market – at the expense of entrepreneurship, and especially women's entrepreneurship, thereby hampering the development of free and flexible markets. Moreover, favouritism fosters corruption, which impedes law enforcement. According to Transparency International's annual Corruptions Perception Index survey, Pakistan is currently placed on rank 115 out of 176 countries assessed (Transparency, 2016). However, the country has managed to slightly improve its position for each of the past five years, indicating that the GoP's recent commitment to take policy implementation more seriously is beginning to show some effect. Similarly encouraging is that new documents, such as 'Vision 2025', tend to contain a critical reflection about the country's history of failed policy implementation as well as a discussion of how this will be improved.

Less encouraging are the signs that gender-related measures which could lead to an improvement of women's role in society are hindered by conservative Islamic forces. Thus, the aftermath of ul Haq's regime remains. As Majid Siddiqui, a Karachi-based journalist, tells in a recent newspaper article: 'Today's Pakistan is a reflection of Zia-ul Haq's policies, and it is becoming increasingly difficult to get rid of it' (Shams, 2016).

It is striking to note that although many different initiatives have been implemented to enhance women's entrepreneurship, little change has happened. One additional reason for this limited impact can be seen in the disconnectedness of the different change initiatives, which were implemented in a piecemeal fashion by different governmental agencies without a clear understanding of what kind of entrepreneurship policies could work for women entrepreneurs in the specific context of Pakistan. The low level of entrepreneurial activities in Pakistan can thus be partly attributed to the mismanaged institutional-policy set-up that is embedded in its socio-cultural, economic and political context. While the institutional context in practice regulates women's entrepreneurship, this is hardly acknowledged in the policy measures.

Possible ways forward

What could be possible approaches for the GoP to improve the situation of women entrepreneurs? An important starting point to nurture the demand of more justice towards women is education. However, education policies suffer from a similar lack of coordination and commitment to implementation as the gender-oriented policies introduced above (Ali, 2006). In fact, illiteracy remains a main problem in developing countries and is at the root of (reproductive) health, poverty and empowerment among women (UN Women, 2017). Here, quality education for both genders, which includes legal rights, health awareness, gender issues and empowerment, could lead to a changing role of women in society and sustainable economic development.

But education is not only important on this rudimentary level. It is also important to support the business development of women entrepreneurs. To date, knowledge accumulation is hardly addressed in the different measures, and an educational system that provides entrepreneurial skills to women could help to bring new ideas to the market. Expanding access to individual-based loans (rather than group lending) and strengthening property rights could be additional initiatives to foster women's economic involvement (Giné & Mansuri, 2014) in Pakistan.

Most non-financial support interventions aiming at business development (such as skill enhancement) are directed to urban rather than rural women, which might explain why a higher percentage of rural than urban women end up in the informal sector (Giné & Mansuri, 2014). The ratio of women participating in the informal sector is 73.1% compared to

26.9% in the formal sector (Mumtaz et al., 2010). As the informal sector is not regulated, women entrepreneurs – who often contribute to the informal sector through products manufactured in the confines of their homes – are currently exploited through middle-men who bring the products to the markets and retain most of the profits. Due to their lack of education as well as societal restrictions, these women cannot raise their voice or market their products effectively themselves. The resulting non-branding of their products increases the uncertainty of their future (Webb et al., 2013). Thus, it could be considered whether legalization of the informal sector could boost women's entrepreneurship in Pakistan, not least by granting the right to wages and controlled working hours.

Despite the history of poor policy implementation, the GoP should make sure to take on a gender-sensitive and gender-neutral approach for developing its policies and support programmes. From a policy perspective, it is important to leverage the growth potential of women entrepreneurs in Pakistan and not to confine women to traditional skills and business endeavours. Current policies are typically aimed at poor and rural women and lack perspective for urban and growth-oriented women entrepreneurs. Researchers and mass media also need to actively contribute to creating awareness for gender issues among men and women in the country to allow for more modern gender roles, adapted to the local context, to emerge.

Conclusion

In conclusion, the current underprivileged status of women's entrepreneurship and the widening entrepreneurial gender gap can be largely attributed to the unfriendly institutional environment. The GoP is clearly aware of the potential benefits of women's entrepreneurship, reflected by the different policy initiatives presented above. However, the historic lack of commitment to making these policies work illustrates the tendency in Pakistan to avoid addressing women in general, and especially as entrepreneurs in their own right. Recent statistics, as those provided by the GEM, witness the poor gender-equality ratio and confirm these policy failures. Current interventions are aiming and performing low, and policies targeting SMEs and the empowerment of women do not even use words like woman entrepreneur, business woman or similar.[1] This contradictory situation, where on the one side Pakistan is signatory of international conventions for gender mainstreaming and empowerment and on the other side there is a lack of gender focus even in gender-aware policies, demonstrates the flawed institutional set-up.

Gender equality needs to be approached more holistically, developing future entrepreneurship policies without traditional role-stereotyping which confines women largely to their traditional gender roles. Then, women can become empowered regarding the kind of entrepreneurial activity they could perform. Opportunity-based women's entrepreneurship, which could enhance the innovativeness of the Pakistani economy, is largely lacking attention, as such entrepreneurial endeavours are even more difficult to align with socio-cultural expectations. To help women unleash their full entrepreneurial potential, development platforms, e.g. in form of research centres, entrepreneurship institutes and business incubators – at national, regional and local level – could be added to the current focus.

To sum up, this chapter aims at contributing to a better understanding of women entrepreneurs in Pakistan from an institutional perspective. The findings reveal that the formal institutional set-up is embedded in informal patriarchal structures that largely confine women entrepreneurs. The GoP needs to make more concerted efforts to pursue the implementation of its policies – currently hindered not only by the patriarchal structures,

Khizran Zehra and Leona Achtenhagen

but also the level of corruption characterizing the country's elite. Last but not least, a modernization of gender roles, initiated, for example, through adjusted public discourses, could help Pakistani women entrepreneurs to redefine their family roles and responsibilities to enhance their possibilities of combining these with their professional development and advancement (Ali & Knox, 2008; Rehman & Azam Roomi, 2012).

Note

1 For example, the core SME Policy document in Pakistan published by SMEDA, 2007.

References

ADB (2016). Policy briefs on female labour force participation in Pakistan. Retrieved from https://www.adb.org/sites/default/files/publication/209661/female-labor-force-participation-pakistan.pdf.

Ahl, H., & Marlow, S. (2012). Exploring the dynamics of gender, feminism and entrepreneurship: Advancing debate to escape a dead end? *Organization, 19*(5), 543–562.

Ahmad, B., Khan, A., & Saeed, M. (2010). *National policy for development and empowerment of women.* Saarbrücken: VDM Verlag.

Ali, S. (2006). Why does policy fail? Understanding the problems of policy implementation in Pakistan – a neuro-cognitive perspective. *International Studies in Educational Administration, 34*(1).

Ali, F., & Knox, A. (2008). Pakistan's commitment to equal employment opportunity for women: A toothless tiger? *International Journal of Employment Studies, 16*(1), 39.

Amine, L. S., & Staub, K. M. (2009). Women entrepreneurs in sub-Saharan Africa: An institutional theory analysis from a social marketing point of view. *Entrepreneurship and Regional Development, 21*(2), 183–211.

Aslam, M., Bari, F., & Kingdon, G. (2012). Returns to schooling, ability and cognitive skills in Pakistan. *Education Economics, 20*(2), 139.

Azam Roomi, M., & Harrison, P. (2010). Behind the veil: Women-only entrepreneurship training in Pakistan. *International Journal of Gender and Entrepreneurship, 2*(2), 150–172.

Baig, Y. R. (2012). Pakistani women continue to fight gender equality. *DW Akademie.* Retrieved from www.dw.com/en/pakistani-women-continue-to-fight-gender-inequality/a-16264593.

Baughn, C. C., Chua, B. L., & Neupert, K. E. (2006). The normative context for women's participation in entrepreneurship: A multicountry study. *Entrepreneurship Theory and Practice, 30*(5), 687–708.

Brush, C. G., De Bruin, A., & Welter, F. (2009). A gender-aware framework for women's entrepreneurship. *International Journal of Gender and Entrepreneurship, 1*(1), 8–24.

Daily Times (2011). Bhutto's Dream of empowering women. *Daily Times.* Retrieved from www.sify.com/news/pak-govt-determined-to-fulfil-benazir-bhuttosdreamofempoweringwomen.gilani-news-international.html.

De Bruin, A., Brush, C. G., & Welter, F. (2007). Advancing a framework for coherent research on women's entrepreneurship. *Entrepreneurship Theory and Practice, 31*(3), 323–339.

Easterly, W. (2005). National policies and economic growth: A reappraisal. *Handbook of Economic Growth, 1*, 1015–1059.

Economic Census (2005). External Trade. Pakistan Bureau of Statistics. Retrieved from www.pbs.gov.pk/trade-tables.

Fischer, D. M. (1991). Marriage and power: Tradition and transition in urban Punjabi community. In H. Donnan & P. Werbner (Eds), *Ecoomy and culture in Pakistan migrants and cities in a Muslim society.* Basingstoke: Palgrave Macmillan.

Giné, X., & Mansuri, G. (2014). Money or ideas? A field experiment on constraints to entrepreneurship in rural Pakistan. A field experiment on constraints to entrepreneurship in rural Pakistan (June 1, 2014). World Bank Policy Research Working Paper (6959).

Goheer, N. A. (2003). *Women entrepreneurs in Pakistan*: International Labour Organization.

Hausmann, R., Zahidi, S., Tyson, L., Hausmann, R., Schwab, K., & Tyson, L. D. A. (2009). *The global gender gap report 2009.*

Jamali, D. (2009). Constraints and opportunities facing women entrepreneurs in developing countries: A relational perspective. *Gender in Management: An International Journal, 24*(4), 232–251.

Kalantaridis, C., & Fletcher, D. (2012). Entrepreneurship and institutional change: A research agenda. *Entrepreneurship & Regional Development, 24*(3–4), 199–214.

Kamal, S. (1997). Women empowerment and poverty alleviation in South Asia: The dual benefits of microcredit. *South Asia Poverty Alleviation Program, 114.*

Kelley, D. J., Singer, S., & Herrington, M. (2012). *Global entrepreneurship monitor 2011 global report.* London: Global Entrepreneurship Research Association, London Business School.

Khan, K. (2010). What Benazir did (not do) for women. *The Express Tribune.* Retrieved from https://tribune.com.pk/story/24581/what-benazir-did-not-do-for-women/.

Klapper, L. F., & Parker, S. C. (2011). Gender and the business environment for new firm creation. *The World Bank Research Observer, 26*(2), 237–257.

Lundstrom, A., & Stevenson, L. A. (2006). *Entrepreneurship policy: Theory and practice* (Vol. 9). Berlin: Springer.

Mian, S., & Qureshi, M. S. (2014). Social network structures of nascent entrepreneurs: A study of adviser networks in GEM cross-country data. *Frontiers of Entrepreneurship Research, 34*(7), 4.

Minniti, M. (2009). *Gender issues in entrepreneurship.* Boston, MA: Now Publishers Inc.

Montgomery, H., & Weiss, J. (2011). Can commercially oriented microfinance help meet the millennium development goals? Evidence from Pakistan. *World Development, 39*(1), 87–109.

Mumtaz, K., Saleem, N., Shujat, S., & Qureshi, J. (2010). Informal economy budget analysis in Pakistan and Ravi Town, Lahore. *Women in Informal Employment: Globalizing and Organizing (WIEGO).* Retrieved from www. wiego. org/publications/urban_policies_rr3_mumtaz_saleem. pdf.

Pakistan Bureau of Statistics. (2016). Labour Force Survey. Retrieved from www.pbs.gov.pk/content/labour-force-survey-2014–15-annual-report.

Pitlane Magazine (2017). Women rights in Pakistan: Pakistani purdah and human rights crimes against women. *Pitlane Magazine.* Retrieved from www.pitlanemagazine.com/cultures/womens-rights-in-pakistan-pakistani-purdah-pakistan-and-human-rights-crimes-against-women-islam.html.

Rehman, S., & Azam Roomi, M. (2012). Gender and work-life balance: A phenomenological study of women entrepreneurs in Pakistan. *Journal of Small Business and Enterprise Development, 19*(2), 209–228.

Roomi, M. A., & Parrott, G. (2008). Barriers to development and progression of women entrepreneurs in Pakistan. *Journal of Entrepreneurship, 17*(1), 59–72.

Safavian, M., & Haq, A. (2013). Are Pakistan's women entrepreneurs being served by microfinance sector: Directories in development. Washington, DC: World Bank.

Scott, W. R. (1995). *Institutions and organizations: Foundations for organizational science.* London: Sage.

Scott, W. R. (2005). Institutional theory: Contributing to a theoretical research program. In Ken G. Smith and Michael A. Hitt (Eds), *Great minds in management: The process of theory development* (pp. 460–485). Oxford: Oxford University Press.

Shabbir, A., & Di Gregorio, S. (1996). An examination of the relationship between women's personal goals and structural factors influencing their decision to start a business: The case of Pakistan. *Journal of Business Venturing, 11*(6), 507–529.

Shaheed, F. (2010). Contested identities: Gendered politics, gendered religion in Pakistan. *Third World Quarterly, 31*(6), 851–867.

Shahid, J. (2015). Pakistan fails to achieve most MDG's. *Dawn News.* https://www.dawn.com/news/1190124.

Shams (2016). Pakistan's Islamization – before and after dictator Zia-ul Haq. Retrieved from www.dw.com/en/19480315.

Sheikh, T. A. (2016). Pakistan's challenges: Sustainable development goals, 2015–2030. *Dawn News.* Retrieved from https://www.dawn.com/news/1284960.

SMEDA (2007). SME Policy 2007: SME led growth – creating jobs and reducing poverty. Ministry of Industries and Production, Lahore, Pakistan.

Tambunan, T. (2009). Women entrepreneurship in Asian developing countries: Their development and main constraints. *Journal of Development and Agricultural Economics*, *1*(2), 27–40.

Transparency (2016). https://www.transparency.org/country/PAK.

Ul Haque, I. (2007). Rethinking industrial policy. Retrieved from http://unctad.org/en/docs/osgdp 20072_en.pdf.

UN Women (2007). SDG 5: Achieve gender equality and empower all women and girls. Retrieved from www.unwomen.org/en/news/in-focus/women-and-the-sdgs/sdg-5-gender-equality.

Vision 2025. Planning Commission. Pakistan. Retrieved from http://fics.seecs.edu.pk/Vision/Vision-2025/Pakistan-Vision-2025.pdf.

Vossenberg, S. (2013). Women entrepreneurship promotion in developing countries: What explains the gender gap in entrepreneurship and how to close it. *Maastricht School of Management*, 1–27.

Waylen, G. (2014). Informal institutions, institutional change, and gender equality. *Political Research Quarterly*, *67*(1), 212–223.

Webb, J. W., Bruton, G. D., Tihanyi, L., & Ireland, R. D. (2013). Research on entrepreneurship in the informal economy: Framing a research agenda. *Journal of Business Venturing*, *28*(5), 598–614.

Weiss, M. A. (2012). Moving forward with the legal empowerment of women in Pakistan. *United States Institute of Peace*. Retrieved from https://www.usip.org/sites/default/files/resources/SR305.pdf.

Welter, F. (2011). Contextualizing entrepreneurship: Conceptual challenges and ways forward. *Entrepreneurship Theory and Practice*, *35*(1), 165–184.

Yazdani, F., & Jawad, S. (2010). Review of the implementation of Gender Reform Action Plan (GRAP) Phase I. *Japan International Cooperation Agency (JICA)*.

3 Gendered expectations and ideologies of patriarchy

Contextualizing Arab women's entrepreneurial leadership

Hayfaa Tlaiss

Despite the recent growth of the literature on entrepreneurial leadership, the subject remains a theoretical in nature and lacks definitional clarity (Harrison, Leitch, & McAdam, 2015). The currently available body of work draws on entrepreneurship and leadership literature but does not clearly articulate a theory of entrepreneurial leadership (Leitch, McMullan, & Harrison, 2013). Furthermore, when entrepreneurship studies mention *gender*, it is synonymous with women (Marlow & Swail, 2014) and is applied as a generic and static concept in women's entrepreneurship studies. Gender is simply another variable that women introduce into entrepreneurship, which itself is gender-neutral or non-gendered in nature (Marlow & McAdam, 2013; Lewis, 2006). Collectively, these studies promote the image of the entrepreneur as a Western white male (Lewis, 2006; Ahl, 2006), problematize the feminine, categorize women entrepreneurs as lacking and deficient (Marlow & McAdam, 2013; Marlow & Swail, 2014) and position women as, at best, the Other (Verduijn & Essers, 2013; Ahl & Marlow, 2012; Lewis, 2006). Women's entrepreneurial leadership is mainly explored in comparison to the male normative discourse (Galloway, Kapasi & Sang, 2015; Yousufazi, Saeed, & Muffatto, 2015), with the objective of explaining the 'under-performance' of women-owned enterprises in the context of masculinized normativity (Marlow & McAdam, 2013).

Given that 'mainstream entrepreneurship literature implicitly prescribe[s] masculinity and Westerness for successful entrepreneurship' (Verduijn & Essers, 2013, 615) and that 83% of research on women's entrepreneurship comes from the Anglo-Saxon world (Ahl, 2006), knowledge of the experiences of women entrepreneurs in developing countries, especially in the Arab Middle East (AME), is limited (Al-Dajani & Marlow, 2010; Tlaiss, 2015a). This geographic focus and cultural bias, along with a widespread decontextualization of entrepreneurship studies (Welter, 2011; Zahra, Wright, & Abdelgawad, 2014), create a significant gap in the understanding of the embedded nature of entrepreneurship and the influence of AME cultural practices and gender ideologies on women's experiences of entrepreneurship and entrepreneurial leadership.

To attend to these shortcomings and knowledge gap, this chapter explores the experiences of Arab women in Lebanon with entrepreneurial leadership. To give voice to these historically marginalized women, face-to-face, in-depth interviews with Lebanese women entrepreneurs were conducted and analysed from a post-structuralist feminist approach to better understand the contextual embeddedness of their entrepreneurship (Ahl, 2006; Ahl & Marlow, 2012). This feminist theorizing enables exploring gender as socially constructed, created, maintained and negotiated within Arab patriarchal socio-cultural contexts. It also permits analysing entrepreneurship as a gendered process built around the normalization of the masculine discourse. An intersectionality lens (Essers & Benschop, 2009; Verduijn & Essers, 2013) is also adopted to investigate how these women's understanding of entrepreneurial leadership is related to and influenced by the normative expectations of the Arab patriarchal culture that associates women with motherhood and domesticity and men with entrepreneurship. The findings demonstrate how difficult it is to discuss Arab women's entrepreneurial leadership without contextualizing the findings within country-specific institutional cognitive-cultural, normative and regulative constraints.

To achieve these objectives, this chapter starts with a brief overview of the contemporary debate on the meaning and definitions of entrepreneurial leadership. Next, Lebanon is examined using the pillars of institutional theory (Scott, 2014), and the impacts of these cognitive, normative and regulative pillars and elements on women's entrepreneurship are assessed. Then, the research methodology and the results are discussed. The last section presents the conclusions and suggestions for future gendered analysis of women's entrepreneurship in the Arab world.

Definitions of entrepreneurial leadership

Studies (Harrison et al., 2015; Renko et al., 2015) suggest that the rising interest in entrepreneurial leadership is fuelled by the growing recognition that while leadership plays an important role in the growth of entrepreneurial ventures, entrepreneurial leaders also promote creativity and entrepreneurial thinking that make large established organizations more adaptable and resilient to uncertainty and change. However, entrepreneurial leadership remains a vague concept, constructed on scant theoretical foundations (Leitch et al., 2013; Harrison et al., 2015; Renko et al., 2015) and supported by even fewer empirical investigations (Yousufazi et al., 2015). This lack of definitional clarity (Vecchio, 2003; Antonakis & Autio, 2007; Kuratko, 2007) also arises from the 'definitional challenge of the construct itself' (Roomi & Harrison, 2011, p. 4) as a new paradigm (Fernald & Solomon, 1996).

To further explain, the origins of entrepreneurial leadership studies in both the entrepreneurship and the leadership literatures divide the relevant research into two camps. The first camp focuses on business owners, founders and entrepreneurs and entrepreneurial leadership behaviour in start-ups (Antonakis & Autio, 2007), while the second camp focuses on the entrepreneurial leadership behaviour of corporate executives (Kuratko, 2007). Consequently, entrepreneurial leadership has been defined, first, as a leadership role performed in entrepreneurial ventures rather than in the more general sense of an entrepreneurial style of leadership. Second, it has been defined as the direction and influence of group members' performance to achieve organizational goals that involve exploring and recognizing entrepreneurial opportunities (Renko et al., 2015). Entrepreneurial leadership has also been defined as leadership that creates visionary scenarios used to assemble and mobilise a supporting cast of participants committed to the vision of discovery and the exploitation of strategic value creation (Gupta, MacMillan, & Surie, 2004).

To better understand these varied definitions of entrepreneurial leadership, recent studies (Roomi & Harrison, 2011; Harrison et al., 2015) have categorized the various approaches to defining entrepreneurial leadership. The psychological approach defines entrepreneurial leadership by identifying the innate traits or behaviours of entrepreneurial leaders, while the contextual approach examines the environmental factors (e.g. type of firm and organizational culture or climate) that favour specific modes of entrepreneurial leadership. The holistic approach focuses on leadership style and proposes that transformational leadership

(Bass, 1985; Avolio & Bass, 2002) is the most appropriate style of entrepreneurial leadership due to its focus on corporate vision and the engagement of followers in realizing this vision. A fourth approach treats entrepreneurship and leadership as two separate constructs and attempts to demonstrate or identify commonalities between them. For instance, Cogliser and Brigham (2004) identify common areas relevant to leaders and entrepreneurs, and Fernald et al. (2005) derive a set of similar characteristics common to both. Despite the proliferation of studies focusing on the common ground between entrepreneurship and leadership, more recent studies refuse this approach (e.g., Harrison et al., 2015; Roomi & Harrison, 2011). For example, from the perspective of leadership studies, Vecchio (2003) argues that nothing is distinctive about entrepreneurial leadership; everything known about leadership can be extended into entrepreneurship research, rendering entrepreneurship a sub-domain of leadership. However, from the entrepreneurship perspective, Kuratko (2007) considers leadership to be constituent of entrepreneurship as an entrepreneurial mind-set and behaviour are essential for effective leadership; accordingly, entrepreneurship becomes the essence of leadership, and today's leaders must be effective entrepreneurs to succeed.

Although these various perspectives are useful, 'they do not help to define entrepreneurial leadership conclusively, and in fact offer essentially conflicting models' (Roomi & Harrison, 2011, p. 9). The absolute accuracy of any of the views and definitions reviewed, therefore, is rejected. Instead, this study instead explores the definitions of women entrepreneurs in Lebanon. The analysis focuses on these women's understanding of entrepreneurial leadership as it unfolds within the institutional cultural, normative and regulative mandates of Lebanon and the salient gender ideology and the masculinized discourse of entrepreneurship in the Arab world, as explained in the following section. (For a thorough overview of the various definitions of entrepreneurial leadership and the most contemporary debates on this issue, see Gupta et al., 2004, and Renko et al., 2015).

Lebanon in the light of institutional theory

To better understand the embedded nature of women's entrepreneurship in developing countries including the AME region (Tlaiss, 2015a; Yousufaz et al., 2015), we apply institutional theory (hereafter, IT) (Scott, 2014). According to IT, institutions are multifaceted, durable social structures and comprise of cultural-cognitive, normative and regulative pillars. By defining these pillars or boundaries, institutions constrain individual behaviour, distinguishing between what is and is not acceptable and providing meaning and stability to social life (Scott, 2014). In the broadest sense, the cultural-cognitive pillar refers to the understandings and taken-for-granted meanings shared at a national level. The normative pillar concerns notions of appropriateness and socially binding expectations which set the standards of preferred behaviour and appropriate ways to conform. In the regulative pillar, rules and laws impose legal and social sanctions, such as punishments and rewards, to ensure individuals' conformity to social expectations and behavioural standards (Scott, 2014).

Despite the global increase in women entrepreneurs (Ahl, 2006; Marlow & Swail, 2014), Arab Middle Eastern women have the lowest participation rates in economic activity in the world and own only 13% of businesses in the region. Consequently, most research on Arab women's entrepreneurship published to date has been preoccupied with exploring the challenges and barriers that hinder women's entrepreneurial activities (for example, Al-Dajani & Marlow, 2010; Itani, Sidani, & Baalbaki, 2011; Tlaiss, 2015b). Notwithstanding the cultural diversity in the Arab world (Tlaiss, 2015a), the common thread running through-out this research is the negative impact of socio-cultural values and traditional gender ideologies on women's entrepreneurship. To further explain, from the perspective of the cultural-cognitive pillar, the Arab culture is highly patriarchal, collectivist and masculine, with a traditional gender ideology that strictly defines gender roles (Al-Dajani & Marlow, 2010; Itani et al., 2011; Tlaiss, 2015a, b). Although Lebanese women are known as pioneers in educational attainment and workforce participation, Lebanese culture commonly sets gendered expectations for what women may and may not do. To ensure its survival, Arab culture promotes norms determining the appropriateness of behaviour (the normative pil-lar). From childhood, men are socialized to be independent and decisive, and women to be communal and build relationships. According to these social rules of conduct (Tlaiss, 2015b), women should prioritize their families' needs and their roles as wives and mothers over their own personal career aspirations. Moreover, they are expected to pursue socially acceptable career choices (Itani et al., 2011) and not entrepreneurship, which is associated with masculinity (Tlaiss, 2015a, 2015b). Under the regulative pillar demanding obedi-ence to rules (Scott, 2014) and avoidance of social scorn, women are expected to adhere to prescribed gender ideologies, fulfilling their familial obligations and expected roles and responsibilities. Those who challenge this ideology are sanctioned with unfavourable social attitudes (Itani et al., 2011).

Despite this body of knowledge, understanding of the impact of hindering institutional cultural, normative and regulative systems on conceptualizations and definitions of entre-preneurial leadership is limited. Filling that gap is the objective and intended contribution of this study. To achieve these goals, this study adopts a post-structuralist feminist approach that posits that gender is not static but socially constructed across time and context (Ahl, 2006; Lewis, 2006; Galloway et al., 2015). This approach allows challenging the assumed gender neutrality of the entrepreneurship discourse (Marlow & McAdam, 2013; for details about feminist theory and its divisions, see Ahl, 2006) and grants women's entrepreneurial experiences more legitimacy (Ahl & Marlow, 2012). This research focuses on understanding how Lebanese women entrepreneurs perform gender and entrepreneurship at the intersec-tion with other aspects of society, such as culture.

Methodology

Conducting academic research in the AME is challenging and often encounters a low response rate to mail surveys. Furthermore, the available archival data are often of ques-tionable quality (Tlaiss, 2015a). To overcome these barriers, qualitative research using in-depth, face-to-face interviews with eight Lebanese women entrepreneurs was conducted. Along with other entrepreneurship studies (e.g. Essers & Benschop, 2009; Verduijn & Essers, 2013), the objective of this research is not to generalize but to provide insights into the entrepreneurial experiences of Lebanese women and to improve our understanding of the contextual factors influencing their conceptualizations of entrepreneurial leadership. The interviews enabled a progressive approach to data analysis, capturing the complexity of normative institutions in a national context and their impact on the women's entrepre-neurial experiences. This approach also enabled us to describe the richness of the local context, generate, insightful results and give the Lebanese Arab women a voice to express their ideas and experiences.

Data sample

The interviewees ranged from 30 to 60 years old, with an average of 45 years old; similar to recent global and regional trends in the age of women entrepreneurs (Tlaiss, 2015b). The majority of the interviewees had masters' degrees, indicative of the Lebanese women's high educational attainments. The majority were married and had three children on average, reflecting the collective culture of Lebanon and the importance of the women's roles as wives and mothers. Although this study did not deliberately focus on women entrepreneurs in the services sector, all of the interviewees had businesses in the services sector, including hair salons, event planning, travel agencies, marketing research, drug distribution, clothing boutiques and even a furniture boutique. The concentration of women's enterprises in the services sector is typical of female enterprises as reported in cross-cultural studies (GEM, 2011) and research on the AME region (e.g. Al-Dajani & Marlow, 2010; Itani et al., 2011; Tlaiss, 2015b).

Data collection

In the absence of accurate information on the number of entrepreneurs in the AME (Tlaiss, 2015a), a purposeful sampling strategy that capitalised on the author's personal connections and networks to identify entrepreneurs willing to participate was suitable for this study. In the snowballing approach, the participants were asked to identify other entrepreneurs interested in participating in this study. Data collection consisted of the semi-structured, in-depth interviews, which were **audio**-recorded. Most interviews were conducted in English. Those conducted in Arabic were translated into English and then back-translated by the researcher and later cross-validated by an academic fluent in both languages.

Data analysis

This study employed a phenomenological approach focusing on the entrepreneurs' lived experience within their situational, social and cultural contexts. The interviews were analysed thematically and interpretively, focusing on understanding the social action as perceived by the agents rather than the external forces that could be interpreted differently by various agents. First, an initial codebook based on the major themes identified in the literature was developed (Glaser & Strauss, 1967; Strauss & Corbin, 1990). For example, the initial codebook included the main schools of thought defining entrepreneurial leadership as leadership performed in entrepreneurial ventures; as the direction and guidance of group members' performance to achieve goals; as the exploration and recognition of entrepreneurial opportunities; and as the creation of visionary scenarios to support employees who become committed by the vision of discovering and exploiting strategic value creation. The codebook was adjusted as new themes emerged during the analysis, comparing the initial list of themes and those expressed by the interviewees. For example, although the codebook included the various definitions of entrepreneurial leadership, the interviewees' definitions of entrepreneurial leadership evolved in a complex manner due to socio-cultural values and gender-role stereotypes. Axial coding was performed until a final coding template emerged (Strauss & Corbin, 1990).

Findings and discussion

This section explains the results of the data analysis and discusses them in relation to the entrepreneurship literature. Quotations that best represent the responses of our interviewees are presented. Analysis of the conceptualizations of entrepreneurial leadership identified one major common theme expressed by all the interviewees: entrepreneurial leadership starts with being an entrepreneur. In other words, the starting point for most of the conceptualizations discussed is that to be an entrepreneurial leader, one first has to be an entrepreneur. This idea in clearly demonstrated in the following excerpts:

> An entrepreneurial leader is an entrepreneur who . . .
>
> (Zeina)

> To me entrepreneurial leadership refers to an entrepreneur who . . .
>
> (Hala)

These findings, therefore, concur with Kuratko (2007) but do not provide support to Vecchio's (2003) argument that entrepreneurship is merely a sub-domain of leadership. According to the interviewees, being an entrepreneur and having an entrepreneurial mindset are necessary requirements for effective entrepreneurial leadership. Additional analysis highlights three prominent definitions or ways of understanding entrepreneurial leadership: survival, transformational and value-based leadership.

Survival leadership performed by entrepreneurs

The interviewees perceived entrepreneurial leadership as leadership assumed by entrepreneurs to ensure the survival of their businesses. They conceptualized entrepreneurial leaders primarily as entrepreneurs who had ideas for new businesses and took the risk of leaving secure jobs to start their own businesses. To move beyond being entrepreneurs or businesspersons, entrepreneurial leaders had to demonstrate leadership by ensuring the survival of their businesses amid uncertainty and then outperform other firms by assuming market leadership or community leadership.

> To be an entrepreneurial leader, you have to have an idea for a new business and to start or create this business, and this is not easy. It requires taking risks and putting your life and that of your family at stake. Then you have to work hard to establish it. And the most important part is that you have to make sure it survives the economic conditions of Lebanon.
>
> (Zeina)

> An entrepreneurial leader is an entrepreneur who is capable of going through the ups and downs of the business and who perseveres in making their business a success. Opening your own business is a fantasy for a lot of people, and a lot of them think that it is easy, but it is not . . . It, therefore, it takes an entrepreneur with a survival spirit to make a business grow and survive before being called an entrepreneurial leader.
>
> (Ruba)

In these conceptualizations, the women framed entrepreneurs as 'creative individuals with ideas for new businesses' and 'risk takers' who act on their ideas and start their own businesses. Assuming leadership takes the entrepreneur to the next level, from merely owning a business to achieving market leadership or playing an active role in their local community. In contrast to Fernald et al. (2005) who considered risk-taking and problem solving to be areas of conceptual overlap between the entrepreneurship and the leadership literatures, the interviewees limited these characteristics to leaders. The interviewees' conceptualizations, therefore, aligned more with Kuratko's (2007, p. 8) definition of entrepreneurial leadership as 'a unique concept combining the identification of opportunities, risk taking beyond security, and being resolute enough to follow through'.

In their conceptualizations, the women also reflected on their own entrepreneurial careers and the impact of local institutional mandates. Their families and male competitors resisted their choice to be entrepreneurs and questioned their ability to be both mothers and entrepreneurs based on the gendered expectations limiting women to domestic chores and motherhood. The following quotations elaborate:

> Achieving entrepreneurial leadership for women is even more difficult and requires a lot more effort . . . In addition to my family, who refused to let me have my own business and said that I should focus on my children, my male competitors made me even feel worse . . . They always laughed at me and reminded me that I am a woman and having an event planning business was not for me . . . I was always told to go home and look after my children.
>
> (Rana)

> Entrepreneurial leadership for women is even more difficult because everyone is against them . . . Society criticises you because you are not working in a company or teaching like other women . . . Having your own business is not acceptable in Lebanon . . . We [women] have come a long way, but this still is a masculine society, and you are expected to focus only on your family and husband . . . To succeed and be an entrepreneurial leader as a woman, I had to fight and work really hard to prove myself.
>
> (Ghida)

As Arab women entrepreneurs, the interviewees conceptualized entrepreneurial leadership at the intersection of the salient gender ideology, institutional barriers and their own agency. The Lebanese women participating in this study experienced their culture and its normative systems as barriers questioning the legitimacy of their career choices. The normative elements of the Lebanese society view entrepreneurship as inappropriate for women, so the interviewees experienced negative sanctions from the regulative elements of their society and received no support from their families. Ridicule by male competitors served as another regulative sanction for the Lebanese women entrepreneurs for not abiding by their society's ascribed norms and gendered roles. These findings demonstrate that the women's conceptualizations of entrepreneurial leadership as an act of survival arose not only from the overall difficulty of starting and sustaining businesses in the politically unstable Lebanon, but also from their own struggles against societal gender inequality and discrimination. The findings also support previous claims emphasizing the salience of the masculine entrepreneurship discourse in Lebanon and the wider Arab world.

Transformational leadership performed by entrepreneurs

The Lebanese women entrepreneurs also emphasized the role of entrepreneurial leaders as a source of motivation for employees. They stressed out the requirement for entrepreneurial leaders to have a vision and good communication skills to be able to ensure employees' commitment to the vision and to gain the support of other stakeholders. The following quotations describe this conceptualization:

> Entrepreneurial leaders are entrepreneurs who have a vision and are flexible . . . They should also be good communicators . . . They have to sell themselves to the employees and the bank funding their business, the business itself and the vision and the growth potential . . . They also have to positively influence their employees by motivating them to be better and to work harder.
>
> (Rola)

> Then you have to communicate your vision to others and to be able to get others on board with your ideas, see things from your perspective and eventually have them work on your vision . . . Entrepreneurial leaders should set the example for the rest of their employees. They should work hard to encourage their employees to work hard for them.
>
> (Fida)

These conceptualizations strongly resonate with the evolving definitions of entrepreneurial leadership (e.g. Cogliser & Brigham, 2004; Gupta et al., 2004), especially in terms of the significance accorded to having and communicating a vision to secure buy-in from stakeholders and to persuade them to realize the vision. The interviewees' emphasis on the leader's relationship with the followers as their role models (idealized influence), source of inspiration (inspirational motivation), and source of motivation (intellectual stimulation) also concurs with the transformational leadership approach (Bass, 1985; Avolio & Bass, 2002). In other words, the interviewees conceptualized entrepreneurial leadership as the entrepreneurs' ability to communicate their vision to their followers and encourage them to achieve it by acting as role models, providing motivation and leading by example – the building blocks of transformational leadership (Avolio & Bass, 2002). These behaviours also strongly resemble those featured in the definition of entrepreneurial leadership by Gupta et al. (2004). In short, entrepreneurial leadership was conceptualized as transformational leadership performed in entrepreneurial ventures. Along with the holistic approach to entrepreneurial leadership (Roomi & Harrison, 2011; Harrison et al., 2015), these findings suggest the suitability and feasibility of transformational leadership in entrepreneurial contexts.

The women entrepreneurs also highlighted the barriers imposed by their society, requiring women to work hard to prove themselves and realize their vision. They described how overstretched they were as they attempt to balance the feminine and masculine characteristics to avoid appearing too masculine, to be role models and to lead by example. Interview excerpts further explain these findings:

> As a woman, you are still expected to look after your home and children . . . To set a good example means that you have to wake up early, finish the cooking, attend to

all your duties at home and then be there on time, so no one will say that you are not paying attention to your business.

(Fida)

When I communicate with my employees or when we have a staff meeting, I have to be firm and decisive . . . This is a masculine culture, and I don't want them to take me lightly if I speak nicely or softly . . . I do not want to act like a man, but I will when I need to . . . With the bank, for example, I need to be firm and aggressive to be taken seriously . . . The same with my clients, I have to be serious and decisive, so they don't think that I don't know my business.

(Rola)

These findings highlight that normative institutional boundaries associated masculinity with decisiveness and good entrepreneurship and leadership. Accordingly, to be taken seriously as entrepreneurial leaders, these women had to balance their feminine and masculine characteristics. Although the dominant norms of behaviour in Lebanon and the Arab world might view adopting masculine characteristics as challenging gendered expectations (Al-Dajani & Marlow, 2010; Itani et al., 2011), the women deemed it to be necessary and did so accordingly. In short, the Lebanese women entrepreneurs in this study believed that women can find agency through resorting to some masculine characteristics on an ad-hoc basis to validate their entrepreneurial leadership.

Value-based leadership performed by entrepreneurs

The interviewees' conceptualizations of entrepreneurial leadership also concentrated on the role of entrepreneurs' values, morals and ethics. According to them, entrepreneurial leaders must be highly ethical persons who model moral behaviour to their employees and promote the values of ethicality, honesty, trustworthiness in their dealings with stakeholders. These findings resonate with value-based leadership (House & Aditya, 1997, in Gupta et al., 2004), in which leaders articulate a vision or mission grounded in and derived from superordinate values and behave in a highly value-based, ethical manner that inspires emulation in followers. The following quotations further explain this idea:

Entrepreneurial leaders are also entrepreneurs who are honest and ethical. They treat their employees fairly, and their employees are loyal to them because they know they are treated fairly . . . Their employees like them and are committed to them and to their business and vision.

(Hala)

Entrepreneurial leaders are those entrepreneurs who care for their followers and their well-being. They ask them about their families and treat them well and fairly.

(Maha)

The interviewees built their conceptualizations of entrepreneurial leadership amid a pull–push relationship with their society and its institutional, cultural and normative elements. While emphasizing the need to portray masculine traits, the women also expressed the need to adhere to social norms to reduce questioning of the suitability of women entrepreneurs. These women felt that by caring about their employees' well-being and building relationships with them, they conformed to societal gendered expectations of women as communal, thus diminishing societal rejection of women entrepreneurs. The interviewees also believed that providing fair treatment and acting ethically could validate their status as entrepreneurial leaders and their possession of characteristics suitable for entrepreneurship. While these findings confirm the salience of normative and gendered expectations (Itani et al., 2011; Tlaiss, 2015a,b), they also clearly demonstrate that the women's conceptualizations and understanding of entrepreneurial leadership unfolded in a complex manner, resisting and complying with socio-cultural constraints at various times.

> It is very important for me to be known as fair and honest . . . I don't want them [male competitors] saying that I don't know how to manage my employees.
>
> (Hala)

> As a woman, I think women are more sympathetic . . . I know that I care about my people. I mean, I am expected to be like that as I am a mother, so I do not mind . . . Plus, I think it makes them [employees] like me more as they know that I care about them. And for me, they are humans, not only people that work for me . . . I think that makes them accept me more.
>
> (Maha)

Concluding remarks

This chapter explores how Arab women entrepreneurs in Lebanon perceive and define entrepreneurial leadership and how institutional, patriarchal cultural and normative systems, along with the salient gender ideology and the masculinization of entrepreneurship, influence these women's definitions and conceptualizations. The interviewees' definitions of entrepreneurial leadership evolved in a complex manner, as the women's entrepreneurial experiences, career choices and struggles to gain legitimacy as entrepreneurs intersected with their understanding of entrepreneurial leadership. These definitions support the multi-fold contributions of this study.

First, the current study's findings highlight the contextual embeddedness of women's entrepreneurship and the need to understand the contextual specificities to advance entrepreneurship research as a field, particularly in the area of women's entrepreneurship. The Arab women in this study understood entrepreneurial leadership by reflecting on their entrepreneurial careers and the resistance to legitimizing their career choices amidst the institutional barriers in their context. Accordingly, the results indicate that women entrepreneurs in Lebanon and, by extension, in the AME, contextualize their understanding of entrepreneurial leadership based on the Arab culture and norms that subordinate women and gender the entrepreneurship career. The findings concerning the influence of local contexts, particularly cultural institutions, on the women's overall experiences of entrepreneurship and definitions of entrepreneurial leadership reflect and are reflected in the broader AME region to a certain extent. At the same time, a multitude of differences exist across the AME region in terms of national education levels, average income, civil laws and regulations, and human development which influence the entrepreneurial experiences of Arab women. In other words, despite the evidence that local socio-cultural values negatively influence women's entrepreneurial careers, the current study warns against assuming the homogeneity of Arab women and their entrepreneurial experiences. Nevertheless, looking at Lebanese women entrepreneurs sheds light on Arab women, a group of entrepreneurs neglected in mainstream studies.

Second, adopting a post-structuralist feminist approach introduces the notions of feminism and intersectionality into entrepreneurship research on Lebanon and the Arab world. This study contributes to feminist theorizing in entrepreneurship by demonstrating how the Arab women's understanding of entrepreneurial leadership is shaped by the cultural reproduction of gender and their entrepreneurial experiences within the normative expectations of their context. Exploring the contextual embeddedness of Arab women's understandings of entrepreneurial leadership and gender through their intersection with culture and their own agency responds to growing scholarly calls to apply the notions of intersectionality in women's entrepreneurship studies. Thus, this study not only puts Lebanese and Arab women entrepreneurs on the map in entrepreneurship research but also advances entrepreneurship research, intersectionality research, women's entrepreneurship and feminism.

Third, this study advances the small but growing research stream on women and entrepreneurial leadership. The interviewees perceived entrepreneurial leadership as leadership demonstrated by entrepreneurs. In other words, entrepreneurship comes first, and leadership second as a means to advance the entrepreneur's business. The women's understanding and definitions reflect a salient understanding of entrepreneurial leadership as survival, transformational and value-oriented, based on contextual experiences that result in a specific mode of leadership called entrepreneurial. Although this understanding of entrepreneurial leadership affirms some of the available literature, the women also offer new perspectives, reinforcing the need for studies aimed at better understanding what entrepreneurial leadership is and stands for. The lack of agreement among the entrepreneurship scholars on the definition of entrepreneurial leadership highlights the importance of context. This study demonstrates that it is virtually impossible to separate individuals and their entrepreneurial experiences from their contexts. The interviewees' entrepreneurial experiences as Arab women in Lebanon and its institutional cultural, normative and regulative contexts affect their understanding of the concept of entrepreneurial leadership. As contemporary research (e.g. Harrison et al., 2015) argues against applying leadership theories from the organizational domain to the entrepreneurial domain, the current study's findings push against applying entrepreneurial leadership frameworks developed in Western contexts to the Arab world. Improving our understanding of entrepreneurial leadership thus demands conducting contextually based studies to explore the meaning of entrepreneurial leadership and how and why it develops in different contexts. These studies are important given the well-known influence of context on not only the traits and personality of entrepreneurs and leaders but also on the act of entrepreneurship and its attendant risks, ambiguities, opportunities and constraints.

The present study has limitations. First, the sample was small and focused on women entrepreneurs in the services sector in one Arab country. Future studies could compare entrepreneurial leadership in a larger sample of Arab women across a wider range of sectors and countries to better understand the extent to which socio-cultural values and other national factors (e.g. national human development) influence the entrepreneurial experiences of women in the Arab region. Second, this research focused on definitions of entrepreneurial leadership and did not explore the impact of the participants' demographic

44 Hayfaa Tlaiss

characteristics on their definitions. Future studies could be aimed at understanding the influence of personal demographics (e.g. age, marital status and education level) on women's entrepreneurial experiences. Research could also go beyond exploring Arab women's definitions of entrepreneurial leadership to consider the impact of context on their identity, confidence and success.

Accordingly, more studies exploring women's entrepreneurship and entrepreneurial leadership in the developing contexts of the Arab world are needed. Although gender discrimination is universal, it is more pronounced in the AME than most Western contexts, and the governments in this region have made minimal efforts to improve women's overall status, promote gender equality or counter the strong role that Arab patriarchal cultural values and traditions continue to play. Hence, this research calls for more empirical studies that focus on specific cultures in the Arab countries and their impact on women's entrepreneurship. Researchers are strongly encouraged to consider the political, economic and demographic diversity of the region against a backdrop of historical and cultural commonalities.

References

Ahl, H. (2006). Why research on women entrepreneurs needs new directions. *Entrepreneurship Theory and Practice, 30*(5), 595–621.

Ahl, H., & Marlow, S. (2012). Exploring the dynamics of gender, feminism and entrepreneurship: Advancing debate to escape a dead end? *Organization, 19*(5), 543–562.

Al-Dajani, H., & Marlow, S. (2010). Impact of women's home-based enterprise on family dynamics: Evidence from Jordan. *International Small Business Journal, 28*(5), 470–486.

Antonakis, J., & Autio, S. (2007). Entrepreneurship and leadership. In J. R. Baum, M. Frese & R. Baron (Eds), *The psychology of entrepreneurship* (pp. 189–207). Abingdon: Routledge.

Avolio, B. J., & Bass, B. M. (2002). *Manual for the multifactor leadership questionnaire (Form 5X)*. Redwood City, CA: Mindgarden.

Bass, B. M. (1985). *Leadership and performance beyond expectations*. New York: The Free Press.

Cogliser, C. C., & Brigham, K. H. (2004). The intersection of leadership and entrepreneurship: Mutual lessons to be learned. *Leadership Quarterly, 15*(6), 771–799.

Essers, C., & Benschop, Y. (2009). Muslim businesswomen doing boundary work: The negotiation of Islam, gender and ethnicity within entrepreneurial contexts. *Human Relations, 62*(3), 403–423.

Fernald, L. W., & Solomon, G. T. (1996). Entrepreneurial leadership: Oxymoron or new paradigm. *Journal of Management Systems, 8*, 2–16.

Fernald, L. W., Solomon, G. T., & Tarabishy, A. (2005). A new paradigm: Entrepreneurial leadership. *Southern Business Review, 30*(2), 1–10.

Galloway, L., Kapasi, I., & Sang, K. (2015). Entrepreneurship, leadership, and the value of feminist approaches to understanding them. *Journal of Small Business Management, 53*(3), 683–692.

Gender Entrepreneurship Monitor (GEM) (2011). *2010 Report: Women's entrepreneurship worldwide*. Babson College and Global Entrepreneurship Association. Retrieved from www.gemconsortium.org/docs/download/768.

Glaser, B., & Strauss, A. (1967). *The discovery of grounded theory*. Chicago, IL: Aldine.

Gupta, V., MacMillan, I. C., & Surie, G. (2004). Entrepreneurial leadership: Developing and measuring a cross-cultural construct. *Journal of Business Venturing, 19*(2), 241–260.

Harrison, R., C. Leitch, & McAdam, M. (2015). Breaking glass: Toward a gendered analysis of entrepreneurial leadership. *Journal of Small Business Management, 53*(3), 693–713.

Itani, H., Sidani, Y. M., & Baalbaki, I. (2011). United Arab Emirates female entrepreneurs: Motivations and frustrations. *Equality, Diversity and Inclusion: An International Journal, 30*(5), 409–424.

Kuratko, D. F. (2007). Entrepreneurial leadership in the twenty-first century. *Journal of Leadership & Organizational Studies, 13*(4), 1–11.

Leitch, C. M., McMullan, C., & Harrison, R. T. (2013). The development of entrepreneurial leadership: The role of human, social and institutional capital. *British Journal of Management*, *24*(3), 347–366.

Lewis, P. (2006). The quest for invisibility: Female entrepreneurs and the masculine norm of entrepreneurship. *Gender, Work and Organization*, *13*(5), 453–469.

Marlow, S., & McAdam, M. (2013). Gender and entrepreneurship: Advancing debate and challenging myths; exploring the mystery of the under-performing female entrepreneur. *International Journal of Entrepreneurial Behavior & Research*, *19*(1), 114–124.

Marlow, S., & Swail, J. (2014). Gender, risk and finance: why can't a woman be more like a man? *Entrepreneurship and Regional Development*, *26*(1–2), 80–96.

Renko, M., El Tarabishy, A., Carsrud, A. L., & Brännback, M. (2015). Understanding and measuring entrepreneurial leadership style. *Journal of Small Business Management*, *53*(1), 54–74.

Roomi, M. A., & Harrison, P. (2011). Entrepreneurial leadership: What is it and how should it be taught? *International Review of Entrepreneurship*, *9*(3), 1–44.

Scott, W. R. (2014). *Institutions and organizations: Ideas, interests, and identities* (4th ed.). Thousand Oaks, CA: Sage.

Strauss, A., & Corbin, J. (1990). *Basics of qualitative research: Grounded theory procedures and techniques*. Newbury Park, CA: Sage.

Tlaiss, H. (2015a). Islamic work-related values and entrepreneurship: Evidence from the Middle East. *Journal of Business Ethics*, *129*(4), 859–877.

Tlaiss, H. (2015b). Women entrepreneur motivation: Evidence from the United Arab Emirates. *International Small Business Journal*, *33*(5), 562–581.

Vecchio, R. P. (2003). Entrepreneurship and leadership: Common trends and common threads. *Human Resource Management Review*, *13*(2), 303–327.

Verduijn, K., & Essers, C. (2013). Questioning dominant entrepreneurship assumptions: The case of female ethnic minority entrepreneurs. *Entrepreneurship and Regional Development*, *25*(7–8), 612–630.

Welter, F. (2011). Contextualizing entrepreneurship: Conceptual challenges and ways forward. *Entrepreneurship Theory and Practice*, *35*(1), 165–178.

Yousufazi, S. Y., Saeed, S., & Muffatto, M. (2015). Institutional theory and contextual embeddedness of women's entrepreneurial leadership: Evidence from 92 countries. *Journal of Small Business Management*, *53*(3), 587–604.

Zahra, S. A., Wright, M. and Abdelgawad, S. G. (2014). Contextualization and the advancement of entrepreneurship research. *International Small Business Journal*, *32*(5), 479–500.

4 'Pleasing the father'

The impact of the political leader in shaping women's entrepreneurship in Oman

Hadil Al-Moosa

Introduction

Scholars studying women in the Arab Gulf countries highlight the role of political leaders in shaping women's positions in the economic, social and political spheres (Al-Awadhi, 2005; Fakhro, 2005). Given the limited studies in this region (Jamali, 2009), the existing literature on Arab women's entrepreneurship is yet to recognize the political leader's role in shaping women's entrepreneurship. The results of this study demonstrate this important role.

Initially, the aim of this study was to explore the dominant contextual factors that shape women's entrepreneurship in the context of Oman. However, based on the preliminary data, the study shifts focus and pays special attention to unexpected factors that dominate the entrepreneurial experience. A qualitative approach adopts a narrative analysis of twenty-nine Omani women entrepreneurs. This research draws on the thesis of entrepreneurial embeddedness in the specific context of women's entrepreneurship (De Bruin et al., 2007) to propose a theoretical framework that integrates the normative institution (Scott, 1995) with a multi- level relational framework (Syed & Özbilgin, 2009) to clarify the normative embeddedness of women's entrepreneurship in Oman.

Women's entrepreneurship

The traditional theory of entrepreneurship promotes entrepreneurship as a fixed and discrete concept that is universal and context-free (Ogbor, 2000). However, the 'context-free' notion of entrepreneurship is itself built and developed in the context of a middle-class white male, written by white male thinkers, and represents an individualistic culture in a capitalist economy (Ahl, 2006).

Contemporary studies on women entrepreneurship highlight the importance of contextual factors in shaping entrepreneurship, which has been widely neglected in mainstream entrepreneurship literature. The mainstream literature also failed to represent the wider racial, ethnic and gender groups (Ogbor, 2000). Hence, contemporary scholars on women's entrepreneurship assert that 'women' is not a homogeneous group (Marlow & Patton, 2005).

In response to these calls, a new trend in contemporary women's entrepreneurship research is paying attention to the role of context in the experience on non-Western women (Al-Dajani & Marlow, 2010). Based on the premise of entrepreneurial embeddedness (De Bruin et al., 2007), the results of these studies provide new insights on women's entrepreneurship knowledge (Naguib & Jamali, 2015)

However, recent criticism raised in contemporary research in entrepreneurship studies is challenging how contextual factors are defined and analysed (Davidsson & Wiklund, 2001). The oversimplification in how contextual factors are treated has resulted in a shallow picture of women's entrepreneurial experience, especially that of women in the Middle East (Al-Dajani and Marlow, 2010). Contemporary scholars on women's entrepreneurship call for the development of integrated frameworks that reflect the embeddedness of women's entrepreneurship at the macro, meso and micro levels in order to clarify the experience of women entrepreneurs (De Bruin et al., 2007).

Moreover, contemporary scholars argue that the cultural context play a stronger role in the experience of women's entrepreneurship (Baughn et al., 2006). Scholars call for special attention to be paid to the cultural context in research on women's entrepreneurship (Baughn et al., 2006; De Bruin et al., 2007).

Theoretical framework

In support of the thesis of the embeddedness and context specificity of women's entrepreneurship, and responding to the need to pay special attention to the cultural setting, De Bruin, Brush, and Welter (2007) suggest adopting multi-level institutional and integrated frameworks. Also, Madichie and Gallant (2012) suggest that cultural context can be approached through institutional frameworks. In order to do so, this study explores the contextual factors in Oman by using the normative pillar of institutional theory as a frame of reference and integrating a relational framework that is based on multiple levels of analysis.

Institutional theory has three pillars: the normative, the regulative and the cognitive. The regulative pillar refers to formal laws, while the cognitive pillar represents the set of skills and shared knowledge among individuals. The normative pillar refers to the uncodified rules that shape individuals' attitudes and behaviour; it defines the roles and relationships in the social system and provides social meaning. It is when individuals normalize and internalize meaning, understanding and behaviour. Therefore, individuals' actions and behaviour conform to socially and culturally shared meanings and practices. The logic behind is the logic of appropriateness (Scott, 1995).

Contemporary entrepreneurship research investigates the impact of the normative institution on entrepreneurial behaviour. For example, Baughn, Chua, and Neupert (2006) state that normative institutions play a stronger role in women's entrepreneurship, so normative institutions can have a significant impact in supporting or discouraging women's entrepreneurship. Based on Global Entrepreneurship Monitor research, this study examines the impact of normative institutions on women's entrepreneurial activities across countries and shows that women are more responsive to the support of normative institutions. They also suggest that women entrepreneurs' activity can be predicted through the level of normative support a given country. Therefore, the present study focuses on the normative institutions in women's entrepreneurial experiences in Oman.

Contemporary scholars call for research on normative behaviour in women's entrepreneurship research (De Bruin et al., 2007). Hence, scholars on Arab women's entrepreneurship state that culture is underestimated in the existing studies. For example, in reviewing the limited extant studies on Arab women entrepreneurs, Naguib and Jamali (2015) find that phrases like 'unique social norms', 'traditional practices', 'social constraints', 'unique socio-cultural' and 'social behaviour' are frequent and interchangeable, but without further

48 *Hadil Al-Moosa*

investigation it results in an oversimplified image of social reality in shaping the entrepreneurial experience (Tlaiss, 2014).

In order for the present study to address the complexity of a normative behaviour, it uses a multiple analysis model outlined in the relational model Syed and Özbilgin (2009) propose under the normative pillar of institutional theory that is proposed by Scott (1995).

Multi-level relational framework

Institutional and multi-level are contextual approaches that are considered holistic perspectives in the study of entrepreneurship. The directions of these approaches are both top-down and bottom-up, where the top-down refers to the influence of higher-level contexts on the social setting, group dynamics and individuals behaviour, and the bottom-up refers to individuals' responses and actions (Welter, 2011). These multiple perspectives use a multiple unit of analysis rather than a single level of conceptualization, resulting in a comprehensive clarification of the social structure and agency in a particular context (Syed & Özbilgin, 2009).

Applying these analytical frameworks enables the researcher to identify the significance of the factors that constitute a lived experience in their broader context. These factors also facilitate and capture the complexity and the dynamics of the social life that shape an individual's experience (Welter, 2011).

Under the normative pillar of institutional theory (Scott, 1995), this study uses the multi-level relational approach first proposed by Syed and Özbilgin (2009) in the field of diversity management practices and recommended by Jamali (2009) after applying it in exploring the constraints faced by women entrepreneurs in Lebanon. Syed and Özbilgin (2009) suggest that the multiple level of analysis allows examining a notion historically and culturally in a given context. Such analysis takes the historical roots of the phenomenon as a backdrop and captures the interplay of a notion on three levels: macro, meso and micro. The macro, or national, level includes the societal and structural patterns that are represented in the culture and political economy and that affect laws and regulations, along with the role individuals play in creating and re-enforcing them. The macro-level influences the meso, or organizational, level, which is group-based. It is represented in the relationships and practices within the hierarchy of the organizational context that are embedded within broader social relationships. The micro, or individual, level refers to individuals' agency and identity. It refers to how individuals react to the issues and challenges around them and is based on the premise that individuals' behaviour is an outcome of the interplay between structure and agency.

Hence, this model represents an overlapping of the micro level on the meso level, so despite the interplay between the macro and the meso levels in shaping individuals' behaviour, this model suggests that the individual has a level of agency that enables him/her to form an appropriate behaviour in relation to the wider context.

In order to address the underestimation of culture in Arab women's entrepreneurial experience, and to handle the complexity and the uniqueness of the normative context in the Middle Eastern Arab countries, this study develops a normative relational framework (Figure 4.1) that builds a theoretical foundation for the normative institution (Scott, 1995). This foundation is framed as an overarching category and is integrated into a multi-level relational framework (Syed & Özbilgin, 2009). This framework allows a given normative behaviour that interplays in multiple levels in the society and shapes individuals' experience to be captured and analysed. This normative relational framework offers the chance to clarify a certain normative behaviour by delving deeply into its underlying meaning and the logic of appropriateness.

Only the relevant elements from the relational framework are included under the overarching normative pillar, as shown in Table 4.1. Analysing a normative behaviour within the multiple levels will help to clarify the experience of entrepreneurial Omani women in the Omani culture. Table 4.1 shows the relevant dimensions of each level (Syed & Özbilgin, 2009) and describes them based on the literature that also guided the interviews and the data analysis.

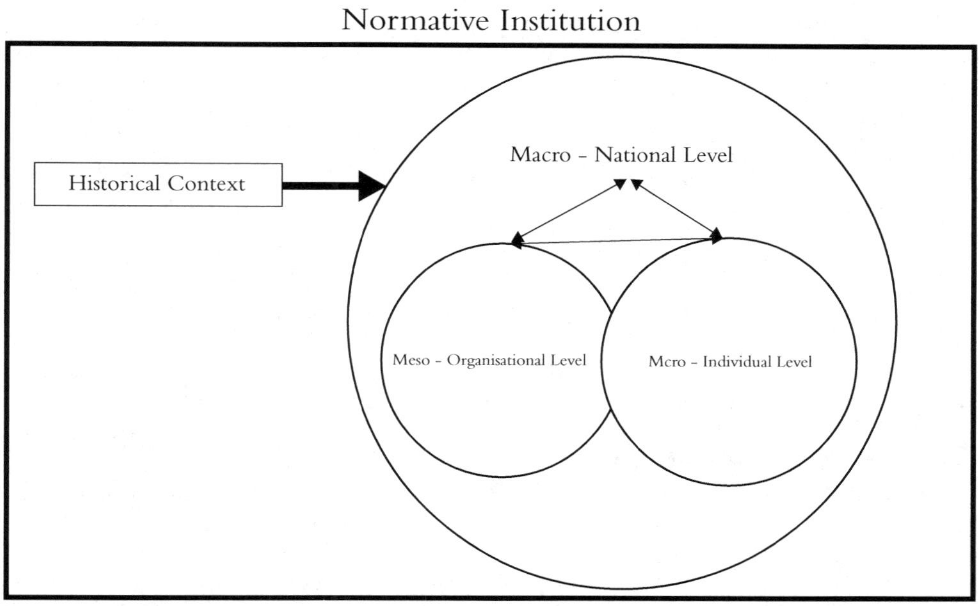

Normative Institution

Figure 4.1 A relational perspective framework (adapted from Syed & Özbilgin, 2009)

Table 4.1 Interview guide addressing macro-, meso- and micro-level factors

	Normative institution		
	Level	*Dimension*	*Description*
Macro	National	Societal and structural patterns	The most dominant contextual factors in shaping the notion
Meso	Groups and organizations	Relationships and practices within the hierarchy of an organizational context, between individuals and between groups	Society's perceptions and reactions and the dynamics of social practices
Micro	Individuals	Motivation, agency	The reason behind the decision and the form of agency exhibited

Research context

The Sultanate of Oman is one of the Gulf Cooperate Council (GCC) countries. Since the 1970s, these countries have witnessed tremendous political, economic and social changes because of oil exports, resulting in high demand for foreign labour to support the ambitious economic investments and to develop these countries (Forstenlechner & Rutledge, 2011).

The labour market is characterized by increasing numbers of expatriates in parallel with increasing national unemployment rates. To reduce unemployment rates and to diversify the economy, governments initiated entrepreneurship-support programmes for nationals (Ennis, 2015). The economic necessity and shortage of labour pushed authorities to encourage women's participation as a potential economic force. However, women's issues are highly sensitive because of the patriarchal culture and social norms, so the government's attempts to improve women's conditions often meet obstacles (Al-Awadhi, 2005).

Since His Majesty Sultan Qaboos bin Said (HM) came to power in Oman in the 1970s, progress has been made in involving women in various aspects of the economic, social and political spheres. Women are granted equal rights to education, employment opportunities and political rights. With the support of HM, women have been appointed to senior political positions and serve as ministers and ambassadors (Al-Lamky, 2007). Oman is the first in the Arab region to appoint women in such positions. However, patriarchy culture and conservative resist women's actual participation in these opportunities (Al-Talei, 2010).

Women's entrepreneurship in Oman

The unemployment rate in Oman is increasing, reaching approximately 15 per cent in 2011 (Ennis, 2015). Despite the progress Oman has made in women's condition, their representation in the labour market remains low (Al-Talei, 2010).

The Omani government has initiated and promoted entrepreneurship for both genders to reduce unemployment (Ennis, 2015). This promotion started after HM Sultan Qaboos' speech during the SME Development Symposium in 2013. PASMED was established in 2013 by Royal Decree No. 36/ 2013 by HM Sultan Qaboos bin Said (Times of Oman, 2013). PASMED is the result of the SME Development Symposium (21–23 January 2013), the primary objective of which was to create employment opportunities for nationals (Al Sanfari et al., 2013).

Methodology

This study uses qualitative research to explore the contextual factors that shape the experience of women entrepreneurs in Oman. Based on the interpretive paradigm, this research examines individuals' perceptions of and meanings ascribed to their experiences (Gephart, 2004). Life-story narrative interviews and a mode of analysis proposed by Lieblich, Tuval-Mashiach, and Zilber (1998) are applied in order to delve into the experience researched and allow new insights to emerge.

Narratives are forms of reality that explain how individuals construct reality in their own contexts (Bruner, 1991), and they are localized within their broader cultural setting (Holstein & Gubrium, 2012). Therefore, narrative approaches to research are recommended to explore the embeddedness and the shared experience of entrepreneurship (De Bruin et al., 2007).

The life-story method clarifies the sequence of incidents within a broader context according to participants' understanding. It also allows participants to explain the meanings they ascribe to their experiences and to explain the local cultural setting (Lieblich et al., 1998).

Purposeful sampling techniques are applied in which a small number of participants rich in experience are selected (Patton, 2002). Only women who were registered as entrepreneurs with PASMED were selected, as Oman's regulatory system sets 'entrepreneur' as an official category for nationals. This category has been recognized officially since 2013, but the traditional form of registration for businesswomen with the Ministry of Commerce and Industry remains an option. The difference between the two is that entrepreneurs registered with PASMED must be nationals are entitled to government support, while those registered with Ministry of Commerce are not entitle for government support, but allowed to partner with non-nationals with 30 per cent ownership for Omani nationals. Oman has very strict regulation for foreign partnership and ownership (PWC, 2017).

The sample comprises twenty-nine women, among which twenty-three once had respected jobs in the government, quasi- government, international organizations, or private sector, while six had never worked before. Seventeen of the women started their businesses before 2013 as side businesses but quit their jobs after the government began offering support for small businesses, while twelve started after 2013 as a result of the support offered.

The participants' educational background varied, with twelve holding bachelor's degrees, mostly from local universities, six holding master's degrees from Western universities, eight having diplomas from local colleges, and the rest holding high school certificates, with one dropout. Ages ranged between 22 and 55 years, while twenty were married with children, two were divorced with children, and seven had never married. Eighteen of the participants were from the capital, eight were originally from rural villages but had moved to the capital, and three were from the rural areas and remained there.

A semi-structured interview guide was prepared based on a combination of the life-story narrative structure and the multi-level dimensions reflected in Table 4.1. The interview started by asking the participant to 'tell me your story', which allowed the participants to take the lead in the interview. The researcher then chose topics of particular interest, guided by Table 4.1, to ask further questions. The interviews lasted an average of two hours, were conducted in Arabic and were audio-taped. Analysis was based on verbatim transcriptions of the interviews done by the researcher.

The data are categorized based on a categorical content mode of narrative analysis suggested by Lieblich et al. (1998) which is recommended when the research explores a shared experience among group of people. This mode of analysis extracts sections and words from the participants' stories and classifies them into categories that are either pre-defined or developed either through reading the text thematically. In this sense, the frequency of the words, phrases and incidents are taken into consideration.

This mode of analysis was used to analyse all the stories and to find patterns and themes of a shared experience among participants. Categories were developed based on the frequency. Sub-categories were developed based on the explicit meaning of the stories told that were associated with the main category. The researcher analysed the data based on the frequency with which certain topics and incidents appeared across all the stories and developed categories based on this frequency and the weight the participants ascribed to an incident or an issue. Then the categories were analysed based on the levels outlined in Table 4.1 in order to capture the multiple impacts of the identified categories. Because of

52 *Hadil Al-Moosa*

the findings from this analysis, this study turned its attention to focus on a single category that dominated the participants' experiences.

The challenge in qualitative data is to determine the substantive significance of the categories developed; this significance is judged based on the solidarity, coherence and consistency of the evidence, by the degree to which the results help to clarify the topic researched, and whether the results found contribute to or add new perspectives to the body of knowledge (Patton, 2002). In the present study, the main categories are based on the frequency of shared incidents across all stories and are considered the dominant factors based on the subjective interpretation of the participants.

This study is qualitative in nature, and the quality of the research is based on its trustworthiness. Qualitative research uses trustworthiness to ensure the value and the quality of the research equivalent to the validity and reliability of quantitative research (Marshall & Rossman, 2010). In the case of this study, trustworthiness is accomplished by credibility, which refers to a 'member check' for confirmation and validation (Lincoln & Guba, 1985). A member check involves sharing the written transcripts with participants so they can confirm their validity. Most of these member checks were carried out through field trips since email is used infrequently in the Omani culture, but a few of the participants were unreachable for member checks because of logistics and time constraints.

Findings

The research findings revealed some contextual factors that play significant roles in shaping women's entrepreneurship in Oman. Some, such as the family role, were expected, as they were identified in the literature; some were unexpected, such as the role of a woman's age in gaining authority over one's career choices; and some were surprising, such as the role of political leadership in shaping the notion of entrepreneurship. Based on the significance of the findings, and in order to delve as deeply as possible into the most useful findings, the study turned its focus to the most unexpected factor, that of the role of political leadership, and analysed it against the normative relational model to explore how it is shaping the experience of Omani women entrepreneurs.

Considering first the macro-level factors, the findings suggest that the role of political leaders was first reinforced not so long ago. The participants stated that their knowledge of the term and the notion of entrepreneurship is due to the HM's acknowledgement during his speech at the SME Development Symposium in early 2013. This view was expressed by all of the participants, who emphasized that HM is the reason for the existence and the legitimacy of the notion. For example:

> The whole wave of entrepreneurship happened only when HM spoke about it . . . I just hope it's not just a wave . . .
>
> (BH)

> If HM had not conducted the symposium, if there had been no royal decree, no one would ever care . . . We [as Omani] always wait for something, anything from HM. We never initiate . . . We have to wait for something, and then we move . . .
>
> (IA)

These quotations describe how the notion of entrepreneurship was introduced and legitimized through HM's recognition and encouragement describes the society's response and reaction. The society refers to the people and the government, as participants highlighted that both share the same mentality in dealing with women and entrepreneurship.

These macro-level insights lead to the meso level, which is reflected in the response of the society, the government, and some parties in the society, such as banks and companies. While the leadership is expected to choose and address the important issues, society is expected to react positively to the leadership's choices. Although there were some critical views, the participants highlighted the underpinning model of this relationship. For example:

> We are grateful that HM held the symposium and brought [entrepreneurship] to light . . . but, HM needs to appear in public and tell people what to do. He needs to come out and say 'drink water because water is healthful,' and he needs to say that we shouldn't be driving too fast on the roads . . .

(SW)

Several participants shared this view of society's comparatively submissive stance, where the emphasis is placed on the leadership role in setting priorities. SW's comment, above, provides fictional examples of the leadership's advising the public to drink water and drive slowly, but these examples indicate the role and the level of the leadership's influence on shaping the society's behaviours and focus, so they emphasize the dynamic of the relationship between the leadership and the nation. Some of the participants normalized this leadership model. For example:

> In our country, the instructions must come from the leader; in our case, HM is the leader.

(ZR)

As result of the political leader's actions, the government launched supportive programmes for entrepreneurs that included funding, training and mentoring, among others. Other parties, such as private organizations, also came on board (Ennis, 2015). Not all of the participants were aware of the range of supportive programmes available to them, but the participants believed that they are supported more than their male entrepreneur counterparts are. For example:

> What I have noticed, being female, is that I'm treated very differently from males. I get, you know, special attention . . . I'm supported more . . . and we are spoiled like children . . . For example, I have been hearing my male colleagues say that it takes ages to get your business registered. I got it in half an hour . . .

(SI)

This favouritism might be explained in light of HM's historical support of Omani women, as rights have been given equally to women since HM came to power in the 1970s, and he has appointed women to many political positions (Al-Lamky, 2007). This support of women is also reflected in the right to entrepreneurship, as the following quotation describes:

> The government created an authority to formulate, organise and legalise the entrepreneurship sector . . . By legitimising the entrepreneurship sector, women came into the

light . . . They became visible in society through the support of the government. The term 'entrepreneur' was not recognised until HM brought it to light . . .

(HL)

Women interpreted the government's encouragement and society's reaction as a way to please HM. For example:

Look, when you have a father who's very loving, you want to please this father . . . and you want to show him your best . . . So, for us, HM is our father and we want to show him we are doing very well . . .

(BS)

BS's quotation reflects how the political leader is framed and perceived, which in turn reflects how the society is positioned in this power hierarchy. The dynamic of the relationship plays on both sides, the authority and the society, where each has roles to play and expectations to meet. The 'pleasing' aspect of this relationship's dynamic reflects the expected behaviour of the society in return for the political leader's 'loving' behaviour.

The dynamic interplay on the macro and meso level shapes the micro-level individual's behaviour, as reflected in her agency and identity. The political leader's acknowledgement, which led to the strong support offered by the government, encouraged women to become full-time entrepreneurs. Twenty-three of the twenty-nine participants in the present study once had full-time jobs, most in respected positions in organizations, and seventeen of the twenty-three employed women had businesses on the side. They all quit their jobs and became full-time entrepreneurs after HM's acknowledgement in 2013 and the establishment of PASMED. This is not to say that HM's impact and the government support are the only motivations for the participants' entrepreneurship, as many had already begun before 2013 because of the desire to pursue hobbies and interests, create change, and to contribute to society or because of family reasons or limited career prospects in their jobs, but they were encouraged to take the pledge of becoming a full-time entrepreneur.

Agency refers to the business orientation most of the participants exhibited. For example:

Youth today are interested in this combination [traditionalism and modernism] and they care about Omani stuff that makes proud. I feel that this is the payoff of HM's efforts: he was the first to call for us to pay attention to our heritage . . . The most important things is our heritage and identity. Now the youth are embodying the Omani identity in their products and services . . . and so do I . . . As I told you, our path in the business is toward nationalism . . .

(RH)

My work [in business] relates to HM . . . We do things in the business that are related to his appearance . . . This is what HM taught us to do, to include Oman in everything we do . . . I adopted that national direction . . .

(RM)

RH's and RM's views are two examples from many stories that show the strong influence of HM and national identity in their businesses. Most of the participants shared that their businesses stand out as Omani businesses because of the national and heritage symbols

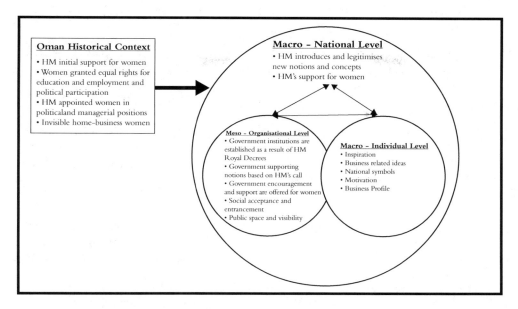

Figure 4.2 A relational perspective of the political leader impact on Women's entrepreneurship in Oman

they embody. While these women are registered and supported by the government, perhaps the government supports businesses with national symbols and discourages others, but such a universal expression of this common thread would be unlikely in such a case. The participants chose this national path for their businesses, which the researcher interpreted as a form of agency in the decision made. It could also be seen as an identity formation, and the interplay between the agency, identity formation within the Omani society them that is reflected in their businesses' orientation. The findings are illustrated in Figure 4.2.

Discussion

This study's findings emphasize the significant role of the normative institution in shaping the experience of women entrepreneurs in Oman and clearly illustrate the interplay of the macro, meso and micro levels in shaping the experience. The findings support the thesis of the embeddedness of women's entrepreneurship and context specificity (De Bruin et al., 2007) and point out the usefulness of integrating the normative institution as overarching pillar into a relational framework in order to enable an in-depth analysis of a factor – in this case, one that dominated the experience of women entrepreneurs.

On the macro level, the father metaphor shows how HM is framed and perceived in Oman and how those in the society perceive their positions in its hierarchy. Given the importance of the family in the Arab and Omani society (Barakat, 2005), and the importance of a father's role in women's career choices in the Gulf countries (Madichie & Gallant, 2012), this metaphor reflects the relationship of the political leader to society in general and to women in particular. Oman is characterized by a traditional paternalistic leadership style, and although Omani women are exposed to Western-style education, they do not challenge the traditional style of authority because their behaviour is rooted in the tribal and familial system in the Arab context (Neal et al., 2007). The concept of 'Sheikh' in the tribal system has influenced the leadership style in the contemporary Arab world; the Sheikh is the male tribal leader who embodies power in the social structure and takes responsibility for the needs of the tribe's members, in exchange of their loyalty. Hence, this relationship is viewed as a paternalistic, rather than an autocratic model (Finlay et al., 2003).

Normalizing this leadership style and the behaviours practised in the nation can be understood in the light of the normative institution (Peters, 1999). In this context, the paternalistic leadership style is depicted strongly in the findings of this study, where HM is perceived as the 'father of the nation'. The notion of 'father of the nation' has formed a shared perception among the Omani people (Valeri, 2015, p. 3), which is represented in the case of entrepreneurship in Oman.

While this case might be unique to Oman, lack of research on the political leaders' effect on Arab women's entrepreneurship means that the claim of exclusivity to Oman cannot be made. It is possible, or even likely, that the experiences of women entrepreneurs in countries with similar cultural and social values, such as a tribalism pattern and paternalistic leadership style, are also similar to those of Omani women.

In the case of Oman, backing up the paternalistic leadership style with the historical condition of 'given' rights to women draws attention to the assumption that women's issues are addressed by the political leader, so entrepreneurship is similar to the 'given' rights.

Official institutions are formed and regulations are established on the meso-organizational level, which includes the government and the society. Government officials support and encourage women's entrepreneurship. The participants indicated that the support offered motivated women to reach out and become visible, as they believed that Omani women entrepreneurs are favoured by the government. The visibility of women entrepreneurs is increasing and encouraged, and the government support was evident across all of the participants' stories. Social resistance did not appear overtly in their experiences, which might indicate that there is a social acceptance for women's entrepreneurship because of the political leader's encouragement.

The notion of working women is a new concept in the Arab world (Itani et al., 2011), but what about entrepreneurship? Research has done little to investigate the social or personal perceptions of entrepreneurship in the Arab world, and based on the findings of this study, entrepreneurship does not stand as a new concept, but it is legitimized and supported by the political leader.

The participants did not mention the political leadership's impact on their families. Drawing on the importance of families in shaping women's career choices and entrepreneurship in the Gulf countries, it is possible that Arab women who face family resistance will choose alternative career options (Tlaiss, 2014). It is also possible that entrepreneurship is not a new phenomenon but has historical, cultural and religious roots that are yet to be explored. In any case, the leader's encouragement may have enhanced social acceptance, making entrepreneurship a more desirable choice. In addition, the older generation of Omani families have exhibited full loyalty to and trust of HM (Valeri, 2015), so the participants in this study are likely to have come from those families.

The findings show the interplay between the macro and meso levels that offer what women perceive as an opportunity to become entrepreneurs. The macro (national) level formed a new and legitimized public space for Omani women and created social acceptance across the society at the meso level. On the micro level, women practise agency by associating their businesses with HM by using national symbols in the product or the service. This behaviour might reflect the common interests of the society, or it might represent the type of business that the government is most likely to support, that which reflects 'appropriate' behaviour in the Omani context in relation to entrepreneurship. However, the question here is whether this situation is related only to women's entrepreneurship. HM introduced the notion of entrepreneurship for both genders and support is offered to both, albeit with some favouritism toward women.

The representation of national symbolism in businesses might create the need to symbolize national identity in businesses profiles. According to Gunz and Heslin (2005, entrepreneurial careers characterize individual self-expansion, but the 'self' in Arab Middle Eastern societies exists only within one's social group (Sidani & Thornberry, 2012). Women may have conformed to this expectation of shared behaviour by identifying their business with the common and supported national identity. This behaviour also reflects how women entrepreneurs respond in choosing the behaviour that is most suitable to their context (Syed & Özbilgin, 2009).

The results of this study emphasizes on the political leader's effect as part of the normative institution in Oman, which had an immediate effect on women's entrepreneurship. This study supports the embeddedness and context specificity of entrepreneurship and the salience of the normative institution on women's entrepreneurship (De Bruin et al., 2007). The study is unique, however, in that the findings are captured through multiple lenses through the relational and dynamic process of lived experience. The depth of analysis is achieved through a model that integrates the normative institution with multiple levels (macro, meso and micro). The findings contribute to the usefulness of these integrated and contextual models in capturing an experience within the complexity of a context. The findings of the present study provide a portrait of one contextual factor that is considered to be dominant in the context researched. The findings endorse the salience of the normative institution on women's entrepreneurship generally, and on Arab women in the Gulf countries in particular.

Conclusion

This study started out to explore the dominant contextual factors that shape the experience of Omani women entrepreneurs, but preliminary findings highlighted the importance of the political leader, so that became the study's focus.

To our knowledge, this study is the first to explore and investigate in depth the role of the political leader in women's entrepreneurship in an Arab country. Despite the importance of the political leader's role in women's experience in the Arab context (Al-Awadhi, 2005; Fakhro, 2005), research on Arab women entrepreneurs has been neglected. Because of the paucity of such research and the oversimplification of culture in the existing literature on shaping Arab women's experience (Tlaiss, 2014), this study supports the thesis of entrepreneurial embeddedness by recommending the adoption of institutional perspectives and integrative frameworks in the search to clarify the experience of women entrepreneurs in the Arab context.

The key contribution of this study is its highlighting of the importance of the political leader as a dominant contextual factor in shaping Arab women's entrepreneurship. Under a tribal social structure, a patriarchal society and a paternalistic leadership style, the leadership must take a strong and active role in Arab women's issues in order to encourage entrepreneurship and other inputs into a strong economic structure.

58 *Hadil Al-Moosa*

Although this study adopts one pillar of the institutional perspective, the normative pillar, it offers rich insights that can be used as a foundation for further research, further research is needed to integrate the other pillars into the topic in order to provide a comprehensive overview of the contextual factors.

References

Ahl, H. (2006). Why research on women entrepreneurs needs new directions. *Entrepreneurship Theory and Practice, 30*(5), 595–621.

Al-Awadhi, B. A. (2005). Women in the Gulf and globalization: Challenges and opportunities. In *The Gulf: Challenges of the future* (pp. 423–440). Abu Dhabi: United Arab Emirates The Emirates Center for Strategic Studies and Research.

Al-Dajani, H., & Marlow, S. (2010). Impact of women's home-based enterprise on family dynamics: Evidence from Jordan. *International Small Business Journal, 28*, 470–486.

Al-Lamky, A. (2007). Feminizing leadership in Arab societies: The perspectives of Omani female leaders. *Women in Management Review, 22*(1), 49–67.

Al Sanfari, D., Al Said, A., Al Said, F., & Al Busaidi, S. (2013). *SME development symposium: The main report.* Unpublished. Sultan Qaboos University.

Al-Talei, R. (2010). *Women's rights in the Middle East and North Africa: Progress amid resistance.* New York: Freedom House; Lanham, MD: Rowman & Littlefield.

Barakat, H. (2005). The Arab family and the challenge of social transformation. *Women and Islam: Social Conditions, Obstacles and Prospects, 2*, 145–165.

Baughn, C. C., Chua, B. L., & Neupert, K. E. (2006). The normative context for women's participation in entrepreneurship: A multicountry study. *Entrepreneurship Theory and Practice, 30*(5), 687–708.

Bruner, J. (1991). The narrative construction of reality. *Critical Inquiry, 18*(1), 1–21.

Davidsson, P., & Wiklund, J. (2001). Levels of analysis in entrepreneurship research: Current research practice and suggestions for the future. *Entrepreneurship Theory and Practice, 25*(4), 81–100.

De Bruin, A., Brush, C. G., & Welter, F. (2007). Advancing a framework for coherent research on women's entrepreneurship. *Entrepreneurship Theory and Practice, 31*(3), 323–339.

Ennis, C. A. (2015). Between trend and necessity: Top-down entrepreneurship promotion in Oman and Qatar. *The Muslim World, 105*(1), 116–138.

Fakhro, M. A. (2005). The changing role of women in the Gulf region. In *The Gulf: Challenges of the Future* (pp. 391–422). Abu Dhabi, United Arab Emirates The Emirates Center for Strategic Studies and Research.

Finlay, J. L., Neal, M., Catana, G. A., & Catana, D. (2003). Anticipated management styles: Viewpoints of potential women employees from selected evolving economies. *Economic and Business Review for Central and South-Eastern Europe, 5*(4), 285.

Forstenlechner, I., & Rutledge, E. J. (2011). The GCC's 'Demographic imbalance': Perceptions, realities and policy options. *Middle East Policy, 18*(4), 25–43.

Gephart, R. P. (2004). Qualitative research and the *Academy of Management Journal. Academy of Management Journal, 47*(4), 454–462.

Gunz, H. P., & Heslin, P. A. (2005). Reconceptualizing career success. *Journal of Organizational Behavior, 26*(2), 105–111.

Holstein, J. A., & Gubrium, J. F. (Eds) (2012). *Varieties of narrative analysis.* Thousand Oaks, CA: Sage.

Itani, H., Sidani, Y. M., & Baalbaki, I. (2011). United Arab Emirates female entrepreneurs: Motivations and frustrations. *Equality, Diversity and Inclusion: An International Journal, 30*(5), 409–424.

Jamali, D. (2009). Constraints and opportunities facing women entrepreneurs in developing countries: A relational perspective. *Gender in Management: An International Journal, 24*(4), 232–251.

Lieblich, A., Tuval-Mashiach, & Zilber, T. (1998). *Narrative research: Reading, analysis, and interpretation.* London: Sage.

Lincoln, Y. S., & Guba, E. G. (1985). *Naturalistic inquiry.* Newbury Park, CA: Sage.

Madichie, N. O., & Gallant, M. (2012). Broken silence: A commentary on women's entrepreneurship in the United Arab Emirates. *The International Journal of Entrepreneurship and Innovation, 13*(2), 81–92.

Marlow, S., & Patton, D. (2005). All credit to men? Entrepreneurship, finance, and gender. *Entrepreneurship Theory and Practice, 29*(6), 717–735.

Marshall, C., & Rossman, G. (2010). *Designing Qualitative Research.* Thousand Oaks, CA: Sage.

Naguib, R., & Jamali, D. (2015). Female entrepreneurship in the UAE: A multi-level integrative lens. *Gender in Management: An International Journal, 30*(2), 135–161.

Neal, M., Finlay, J. L., Catana, G. A., & Catana, D. (2007). A comparison of leadership prototypes of Arab and European females. *International Journal of Cross Cultural Management, 7*(3), 291–316.

Ogbor, J. O. (2000). Mythicizing and reification in entrepreneurial discourse: Ideology-critique of entrepreneurial studies. *Journal of Management Studies, 37*(5), 605–635.

Patton, M. (2002). *Qualitative research & education methods* (3rd ed.). London: Sage.

Peters, B. (1999). *Institutional theory: The 'New institutionalism' in political science.* London: Cassells.

Public Authority for Development of SMEs set up (2013). *Times of Oman* (Online). Retrieved from www. timesofoman.com/News/Article-16829.aspx.

PWC (2017). *Doing business in Oman: A tax and legal guide.* [PDF document] Retrieved from https://www. pwc.de/de/internationale-maerkte/assets/doing-business-in-oman-2017.pdf.

Scott, W. (1995). *Institutions and organizations.* Thousand Oaks, CA: Sage.

Sidani, Y. M., & Thornberry, J. (2012). Nepotism in the Arab world. *Business Ethics Quarterly, 23*(1), 69–96.

Syed, J., & Özbilgin, M. (2009). A relational framework for international transfer of diversity management practices. *The International Journal of Human Resource Management, 20*(12), 2435–2453.

Tlaiss, H. A. (2014). Women's entrepreneurship, barriers and culture: Insights from the United Arab Emirates. *Journal of Entrepreneurship, 23*(2), 289–320.

Valeri, M. (2015). *Simmering unrest and succession challenges in Oman.* Washington DC: Carnegie Endowment for International Peace.

Welter, F. (2011). Contextualizing entrepreneurship: Conceptual challenges and ways forward. *Entrepreneurship Theory and Practice, 35*(1), 165–184.

5 Leveraging micro-level support factors to overcome macro-level challenges

Palestinian and Saudi Arabian female entrepreneurs

Beverley McNally and Grace Khoury

Entrepreneurship is the consequence of the interplay between the individual and their environment (Solesvik, Westhead, & Matlay, 2014). Specifically, female entrepreneurial activity is deeply embedded in the structural and institutional characteristics of the country in which it is situated. Therefore, it is important that any examination of female entrepreneurship must include consideration of the institutional structures of the context in which it is situated. This includes how entrepreneurship is influenced by the norms, values and principles of the social context and the priority ascribed to the employment of women (Welter, 2004).

The traditional view of women's roles within Arab societies influences women's attitudes, intentions and self-perceptions with respect to their career choices and their role is connected to household, caregiving and family responsibilities (Jamali, 2009). These social values can have a detrimental influence as positive self-perception and strong self-efficacy are critical to successful entrepreneurial activity (Arenius & Minniti, 2005). Nevertheless, successful entrepreneurship is not only an outcome of individual characteristics, it is also an outcome of a supportive and vibrant social and institutional contexts (Jamali, 2009). Furthermore, it is important to incorporate multiple units of analysis if we are to better understand the complexities of female entrepreneurship across a diversity of environments (Naguib & Jamali, 2015).

Much of the empirical research ignores the mediating role of context on female entrepreneurship (Jamali, 2009). For the purpose of this study, context is defined as a temporal construct in that it is bound by time and place (Al-Rasheed, 2015). Consequently, a myth has arisen around female entrepreneurial underperformance 'in the context of masculine normativity' (Marlow & McAdam, 2013, p. 114). Thus, context and its influence must be acknowledged to better understand female entrepreneurial behaviour and success (Pathak, Goltz, & Buche, 2013). Often, prior research examining female entrepreneurship has assumed an individual centric approach at a micro-level (Jamali, 2009). The macro-level factors influencing and supporting successful female entrepreneurship have been confined to research conducted in developed Western countries and somewhat neglected in the literature of female entrepreneurship in the Middle East (Naguib & Jamali, 2015). To enrich the discussion on the contextual embeddedness of female entrepreneurship, in this chapter we explore the key challenges confronting female entrepreneur in the Palestinian and Saudi Arabian context. In doing so, we move past the gender debate and focus on the social and institutional structures that influence entrepreneurial performance and provide a signpost for future empirical work and contributes to the growing body of entrepreneurial literature situated in the Middle East, North African (MENA) region.

We situate this study within the frameworks of the institutional theory (Scott, 1995) and the social–cultural theory and thus acknowledged that the success of female entrepreneurship can be considerably enhanced by recognizing the formal and informal institutional factors within a context that impact upon and constrain female entrepreneurial performance (Sheriff & Muffatto, 2015; Yousafzai et al., 2015). This includes the institutional and structural characteristics of a country, for example, the economic, socio–cultural, political, religious and legal environments (Yousafzai et al., 2015). Consequently, the presence of unique social norms, such as, gender–segregated social relations, or a patriarchal society all serve to impact on women's entrepreneurial performance (Ahmad, 2011). Informal institutions may also create restrictive societal norms and attitudes to female entrepreneurs which may, with the passage of time, have become normalized and are not viewed as discriminatory (Blanchard & Warnecke, 2010). Therefore, it is vital to be responsive and understand local cultures in order to find solutions from within the context to support female entrepreneurs (Warnecke, 2013). Failure to take into account the social, cultural, political, legal, technological and institutional variables within a specific context may lead to female entrepreneurs being deemed to be underperforming.

We conclude that the development of self-esteem and confidence, along with changes to policy and regulatory institutions and providing support to work within the cultural norms of the specific environment are all considered vital to successful entrepreneurship (Yousafzai et al., 2015). As suggested by Ahl (2006) and Sheriff and Muffatto (2015), entrepreneurial research in the future should focus on the macro environment and how it constrains performance for female entrepreneurs. Marlow and McAdam (2013) contend that the myth of underperformance has its origins in the historical socio-economic context, which informs and sustains the social and institutional structures that shape women's life choices. These institutional and social structures include restrictions on mobility, working outside the home, discrimination in accessing venture capital and the inability to easily access networks of knowledge and business information (Jones & LeFort, 2014).

The Palestinian and Saudi Arabian context

Saudi Arabia and Palestine were selected as two transitioning Arab societies, as they are deemed to be engaged in the management of planned change, with many commonalities, yet the business and social environments are very different (Sparkman, 2015). Palestine can be characterized as a transitioning society because it is moving from a high dependency on international aid to one of development and self-reliance (Paprock, 2006). However, Saudi Arabia is considered a transitioning society as it is moving from a high dependence on expatriate labour to a society reliant on its own people to make up the majority of the workforce (Vision-2030, 2016). As these transitional changes take place, it is important to add to the body of knowledge of the macro environment in the MENA region, an element that is currently under-researched.

Every country in the MENA region has different historical and cultural traditions, which contribute to a diversity of social contexts. There are social norms within each country in the MENA region that may serve to constrain or challenge female entrepreneurial activities (Ahmad, 2011). For example, in Saudi Arabia, female entrepreneurs have to navigate a very careful course between their ambitions, the sensitivities of different groups and the wider social mores, all while trying to function within the commercial realities required of entrepreneurial businesses (Danish & Lawton-Smith, 2012). The World Bank (2016) rankings for the ease of doing business, Saudi Arabia ranked at 94 of a 190 countries while Palestine ranked at 129 of 189 (GEM, 2012). Similarly, for the ease of facilitating new business ventures, Saudi Arabia ranked at 130 and Palestine at 170. Nevertheless, both countries have accomplished female entrepreneurs who have succeeded in non-traditional businesses, for example, trade, finance and construction (Elmuti, Khoury, & Omran, 2012). Yet, there is limited empirical literature in Arab countries examining these women and their education, training and learning experiences (Elmuti et al., 2012).

Palestine

Palestine's population is reported as 4.48 million, of which 49.2% are women (Palestinian-Central-Bureau-of-Statistics, 2016). The reported literacy rate among females in Palestine in 2014 was 94.4%, one of the highest rates in the Middle East. Palestinian women have a 59.3% participation in higher education. Yet, despite this high education participation, female involvement in the workforce is relatively lower (PASSIA, 2015). The labour force participation rate of Palestinian's adult population aged 15 years and over, is 45.8%. Of this 45.8%, male participation was recorded at 71.6% as compared with 19.4% for females (Palestinian-Central-Bureau-of-Statistics, 2016). Additionally, the unemployment rate in Palestine is high. However, there is a significant difference between the two geographic areas of Palestine, with 41.2% in the Gaza Strip and 18% in the West Bank. Despite numerous capacity building programmes and efforts made by aid donors, governmental agencies and NGO's advocating for female economic empowerment, the female unemployment rate in 2016 was 48.1% with thirteen-plus years of schooling (Palestinian-Central-Bureau-of-Statistics, 2016). Al-Botmeh (2013) found that 65% of Palestinian women expressed a willingness to engage in start-up business ventures. However, the primary reasoning provided for an individual not becoming involved in entrepreneurial activity was because of the prolonged occupation of the Palestinian State and the ongoing conflict and destruction of infrastructure (Sadeq, Mamed, & Glover, 2011). Consequently, the resultant weak economy, social fragmentation and resource constraints were perceived to create unacceptably high levels of risk for women (PASSIA, 2015). Al-Botmeh (2013) also identified a high level of gender bias and discrimination impacting on women who apply for commercial credit or venture finance. The existing legislation is not sensitive to gender and does not take account of the different needs and risk profiles of women in business, creating challenges for women when attempting to access venture capital (Jones & LeFort, 2014).

Saudi Arabia

As is the case in traditional Arab communities, Saudi Arabian women have domestic duties as their primary focus (Harvard-Kennedy-School, 2015). However, from the beginning of the twenty-first century this situation has begun to change (Le-Renard, 2014). Saudi Arabia has introduced two key strategic initiatives, the Saudization programme, aimed at addressing the high levels of unemployment amongst its people and the Vision 2030 initiative, which has the strategic intent of reducing the country's dependence on oil as the primary source of income. This requires diversification, development and creation of alternative sources of income, thus placing a greater emphasis on the development of a vibrant private sector, including entrepreneurial endeavours (Vision-2030, 2016). Nevertheless, in 2013 the unemployment rate for Saudi nationals was at 12.2% (7.6% for men and

33.4% for women). It is suggested the higher level of women may be due to the willingness of younger women to register with the appropriate government agencies as 'looking for work' (Le-Renard, 2014). Le-Renard (2014) goes on to state that this willingness may indicate increasing aspirations of Saudi women to become part of the workforce. Moreover, Saudi Arabian legislation protects women in employment, reserving jobs in the retail sector in areas that deal with women's products, check out operators in supermarkets, and women's branches in banks.

Among the proactive attempts to encourage entrepreneurial activity are programmes created by the government to encourage more women to join the workforce as business owners. However, the involvement in such programmes may be constrained by social mores such as gender segregation and family influence placing limitations on the fields entrepreneurial woman are able to enter (Basaffar, 2012). Therefore, those women who elect to enter the workforce choose careers such as doctors or teachers where they interact with women and children. As a result, there is an excess of eligible teachers and a paucity of women in the business and entrepreneurship fields (Al-Munajjed, 2010; Yamani, 1996) as cited (Basaffar, 2012).

Methodology

A qualitative research approach was selected as it is more appropriate for inductive studies dealing with people's lived experiences, behaviours, emotions, feelings, organizational functioning and cultural phenomena where the bulk of analysis is interpretive (Bhattacherjee, 2012; Strauss & Corbin, 1990). Both purposive and snowball sampling were used to build the sample. This resulted in a sample of seven women entrepreneurs in Saudi Arabia and nine in Palestine.

Five of the Palestinian participants had Masters Degrees, previous business experience and had travelled outside Palestine. The participants from Saudi Arabia all possessed university qualifications at Bachelors level. Two had attended executive development programmes at European and US business schools. All had travelled outside Saudi Arabia. The Palestinian interviewees were older in age and have had longer work experience than the Saudi interviewees and work in non-traditional businesses for women. This is not surprising as the societal changes in Saudi encouraging female entrepreneurship are relatively recent.

Findings

Our findings are divided into two main sections based on the analysis of the data. The first are the micro-level factors; opportunity, motivations, financing and performance. The second are the macro-level challenging factors; political, government and economic, regulatory, normative and financial institutions.

Micro-level factors

Opportunity factors

Palestinian and Saudi women who had the opportunity to engage in higher education or had travelled gaining exposure to other cultures were likely to have a greater awareness of opportunities for women. In addition, as Saudi society is changing as part of the Vision-2030 strategic plan, entrepreneurial women are more likely to identify new opportunities, developing products and services to specifically meet women's needs. There was also evidence that women from higher socio-economic backgrounds having a greater ease of access into the entrepreneurial field. Palestinian participants mentioned self-development and hard work as important for success and did not consider their journey to success as easy.

Motivation

Similar motivators were identified in both Palestine and Saudi Arabia. There were two main reasons. First, the ability to provide financial security for themselves and their children. That is push or necessity factors. The second was for the women to fulfil their personal growth needs, which indicates pull or opportunity factors (Jones & LeFort, 2014). In Palestine and Saudi Arabia the majority of participants had motivational pull factors. One interviewee stated:

> successful people are always perceived as a threat to their colleagues, in my previous work my male colleagues tried to oppress me and put barriers in front of me at work to stop my ambition and development. I quit and established my own company.
>
> (PA4)

> I wanted it for my own sense of satisfaction be able to provide opportunities for other young women.
>
> (SA 3)

Both groups of participants recognized that what is most important is the ability to persevere 'no-one is going to do it for you' (SA1). The ability to be self-motivated was paramount. Experiencing situations that built self-discipline, business skills, people and teamwork skills, professional business behaviour and personality in general were deemed vital.

Financing

Three Palestinian participants, PA 6, 7&9, emphasized the encouragement and financial support they received from their fathers. In Saudi and Palestine there are different funding mechanisms available. However, what emerged was that often the women were reluctant to ask for money. The ability to do so depended very much on each woman's personal circumstances, for example, supportive fathers or husbands who encouraged them to ask. Underlying the issues regarding the sourcing of funding is a fear of failure. 'If I get this money and I fail then I will embarrass my family and possibly deprive my children' (SA5). There were many variables that acted to constrain Saudi women from accessing venture capital, not all of them extrinsic e.g. a deep sense of shame felt about the possibility of failure and the potential loss of money, particularly family money.

Performance

As new areas of business are opening up to women, the drive to achieve in these new endeavours lead to high levels of self-esteem and satisfaction thereby increasing the individual's determination to succeed. Prior research has shown that one of the most positive influences on entrepreneurial success and performance has been the presence of positive role models and mentors who encourage women become involved in starting their own businesses (Breen, 2010). This extends to the ability to develop strong personal networks supporting the findings of McGregor and Tweed (2002), who argue that well networked women with higher level educational qualifications and strong family and tribal affiliations tend to be more successful.

Both groups of women spoke of the increased self-confidence gained from having strong role models. However, these were primarily male and usually a previous boss or a father – a business man. For those who were married, a supportive husband was considered vital for success. This supports the assertion of Verheul, Stel, and Thurik (2006), who suggested that one of the most constant positive influences on entrepreneurship was a strong supportive family. One Palestinian woman stated 'when my daughter was sick my husband was there to take care of the business' (PA5). Strong female role models were not common. One woman spoke of her mother:

> She encouraged me to try new things and experience different activities. My family travelled extensively in the west and my mother had made sure I experienced many different activities.
>
> (SA 4)

Another woman who had worked in a large finance company in the west had a male mentor who 'I learned a great deal from and I still refer back to that learning' (PA1). All the interviewees spoke about their personal responsibility to help create and support an entrepreneurial community for women. This included their role as a mentor for young women.

Additional factors contributing to performance and success was the experience gained from working in a family business 'My brothers and I used to help during summer breaks in my father's pharmaceutical factory' (PA 7) or being the elder daughter in the family 'We were a large family of thirteen and I'm the eldest so I had early responsibility in helping my parents' (PA3). However, these were not factors for Saudi Arabian women, as the social mores spoken of earlier precluded them from easily gaining such experiences.

Macro-level factors

The political context

The findings of this study support the findings of Sadeq et al. (2011) who found the most significant challenge facing the majority of women entrepreneurs and entrepreneurial activity in Palestine arises from the current political situation. The Palestinian context is considered a high risk, high conflict environment in which to do business and this in turn discourages investors. This high risk environment also increases the cost of doing business. The Israeli authorities control the borders, thus increasing the costs for supplies that must cross those borders. There is no freedom of movement, borders are commonly closed and there are frequent high-level security checks. Moreover, the Palestinian Authority is dependent on the Israeli authorities reimbursing them the taxes and surcharges. These are frequently delayed, creating cash flow issues for businesses. The political situation is a general challenge facing all businesses in Palestine (Muna & Khoury, 2012). However, it creates extra burdens for female entrepreneurs as a result of the constraints presented by the social norms within a patriarchal society. One participant commented:

> I had to work for late hour and go home at night to be able to finish the work that was delayed because of security curfews in our city.
>
> (PA9)

One Palestinian woman in the construction industry and heavily reliant on NGO funded projects stated: 'meeting deadlines and finishing projects on time under these conditions is a big challenge' (PA9).

> Warehousing and distribution are costly and suffer from a lack of cohesion with some facilities under the control of the Israeli and other under the control of the Palestinian authority which creates extra distribution cost and burden for our company.
>
> (PA6)

Political agreements between different Gulf States also influenced the motivation of Saudi women to undertake new ventures because there were no other options available. One young Saudi woman talked about her experience:

> I was not able to obtain a work visa while living in Kuwait with my husband. Consequently, I turned to the learning I gained from my entrepreneurial course which I completed at a Saudi university. Subsequent to developing a business plan I'm now working on the implementation in Saudi Arabia.
>
> (SA7)

Overall, the political situation in Saudi Arabia was viewed as being more supportive of entrepreneurship. The Vision-2030 programme having as a key strategy the encouragement of women into entrepreneurial endeavours in order to encourage more women into the workforce and lessening the reliance on oil revenue.

Government and economic support

Both countries had challenges with respect to government and economic support. However, these challenges were different for each. In Palestine it is considered important to provide economic support for entrepreneurial endeavours. This ensures that Palestinian's are able to enter the business sector, thereby creating jobs for the Palestinian people. There is an awareness that it is not possible for the country to rely on foreign labour, as is the case in much of the MENA region. Therefore, 'the economic support may be in the form of taxation relief during the early years of a venture' (PA 3 & 4). Another alternative may include targeted venture capital assistance for women. In addition there was a lack of policy to protect new ventures from unfair competition, illegal or unsafe practices and price wars.

> There are no restrictions or policies to ensure that companies entering the industry sector meet industry standards especially with regard to safety, so we are not protected although we've been in the market for a longer period.
>
> (PA4)

Much of the funding in Palestine is dependent on donor funding from aid agencies. If this funding ceases, then some entrepreneurial ventures may be unsustainable, as was confirmed by PA2, PA4 and PA9 who operated in the consultancy, elevator and construction, and contracting industry sectors respectively. Palestine does not have its own currency and the economy is reliant on the US dollar, Israeli shekels and the Jordanian dinar. Consequently, entrepreneurial ventures are dependent on international currency rates. In contrast, the Saudi Riyal is 'pegged' to the US dollar providing greater currency stability. Raw materials and supplies have to be sourced outside Palestine, as the country does not have the natural resources or manufacturing base to supply these.

> there is a risk of currency devaluation, our material are bought and paid for in advance in US dollars and customers of the business pay for the final product or service in Israeli shekels.

> (PA9)

The lack of political stability in Palestine translates into a lack of economic stability. Consequently, the delay in the peace process has resulted in a decline in GDP per capita growth rate from 8.8% in 2011 to 2.4% in 2012 (Palestinian-Central-Bureau-of-Statistics, 2016). Accordingly, this situation has a negative impact on profitability and creates challenges in obtaining venture finance. This in turn dissuades many women from engaging in entrepreneurial activities (GEM, 2012).

In both countries, often the structures are not in place to support entrepreneurial activities. In addition, there is not a clear understanding of risk-taking, therefore it is difficult to put a case for permissions as officials do not understand. 'Sometimes when you go to the Ministry with a new venture there is not the policies or permissions in place to help set up your business' (SA7). Moreover, in Saudi Arabia the bureaucracy is relatively young and when new ventures are initiated, often barriers arise as it takes time to implement the necessary policies and procedures.

The regulatory environment

As transitioning societies, often legislation is not keeping pace with societal changes and new innovative ideas that entrepreneurs wish to develop. Within Saudi Arabia, legislation does exist for many ventures. However, this legislation covers ventures typical of those found in traditional patriarchal societies. 'I found that because I knew the right people to ask I was able get information more quickly than some others' (SA3). Comments were made about how the different ministries had made substantial efforts to facilitate access electronically.

> Yes it is good to find out things on-line – then when you go into the office the official does not know what you are talking about – there is a mismatch between what is on-line and the level of knowledge of the officials.

> (SA3)

Conflicting advice was the norm.

> I found that often the officials did not know the answer and I had to visit many times before I found the correct answer – often I was told different things by different officials.

> (SA 4)

A similar situation faced the Palestinian women. Comments were received about the lack of awareness of services available via different government and NGO sources. There was also a perceived lack of co-ordination between the processes of different ministries, which were considered complex and not user friendly. The research participants expressed the desire to have a 'one-stop-shop' which would assist them in navigating the process, paperwork and registration processes in order to facilitate the starting of new business ventures. There was a concern expressed,

> I'm a member of a women's forum and I notice young female entrepreneurs are not aware of which ministry they should approach first and what they could do in preparation to ensure they minimise both time and effort.
>
> (PA3)

Within the Saudi environment, legal obligations create a need for substantial levels of start-up funding. This is particularly applicable where there is a reliance on expatriate labour for example, retail and hospitality ventures. These expatriates require visas, yet it is not possible to apply for a visa until the business is completed and ready to commence trading.

> That is – the establishment must be completed; chairs and tables in place, kitchen ready for preparation and only then can the owner apply for work visas. You must have sufficient capital to sustain you until the visa is approved.
>
> (SA3)

The visa process could take up to six months.

> This means that I am paying rent and also paying invoices for capital equipment but I have no money coming in because I am waiting for visas to be approved.
>
> (SA3)

This was deemed to impact more on women because of difficulties in accessing funding. Also, it did constrain small individual ventures. Companies with high levels of capital, e.g. international franchises, were more able to meet this challenge. This is critical to ensuring a robust immigration process. Mention was made of how the legal system still had many weaknesses. While the situation is improving (Al-Botmeh, 2013; Sadeq et al., 2011), Palestine in particular still has discriminatory practices governing property rights, labour laws and investment practices, specifically concerning how long it took for a resolution to be achieved for legal cases. 'It took more than six years to prosecute an employee that stole from my company' (PA7). This can result in considerable costs to new ventures, costs that they may not be able to absorb.

The normative institutions

Almost half of the Palestinian and all the Saudi interviewees mentioned the difficulty of work-life balance and its effect on them. However the micro-level factor related to performance through finding family support and role models allowed these women to overcome the challenge of work-life balance. Several mentioned how 'stereotypes predominate of women as secretaries and housewives rather than handling major business and household financial responsibilities' (PA4).

The Saudi focus group spoke of international entrepreneurial forums where work-life balance was identified. However, there was an acknowledgement that in Saudi Arabia with the tribal and family obligations there was an increased pressure on women and high levels of guilt about the perceived neglecting of family responsibilities in preference to work responsibilities.

> I know I could engage a maid to help but that just does not feel right – and my aunties will help but I don't feel I can ask them all the time – so I feel really conflicted.
>
> (SA 5)

The ability to engage domestic help did not dissipate the guilt these women felt. High levels of internal conflicts were reported as women tried to balance the competing demands of family responsibilities, family and tribal expectations and business success. This is particularly so if the woman was engaged in a more non-traditional field. There are strong perceptions as to what is an appropriate career for Saudi women. Often this is not as an entrepreneur. This is in contrast to the study of Danish and Lawton-Smith (2012) which found that entrepreneurship was an attractive career option for women.

Networking and relationship opportunities, especially informal gatherings are more difficult for women in Arab countries. Palestinian women spoke of the ease with which men can meet in coffee houses or network in cafes. 'It is more socially acceptable for men to meet in this way to discuss business issues' (PA4). Similar, concerns were expressed by the Saudi participants. Yet there was an acknowledgement that in Saudi, public spaces designed for women are becoming more common (Le-Renard, 2014).

These social-cultural constraints included male waiting staff not being comfortable taking orders from female employers, or being in close proximity to women as was reported in Palestine by PA8. This issue may not arise in Saudi Arabia as restaurants are staffed in the main by expatriate workers who may not have the same social mores in their home country. In this study a Saudi woman active in the hospitality industry reported no difficulty in having male staff taking instruction from her:

> I think that is because they are expatriate staff – and they are used to working with women.
>
> (SA 4)

There is a lack of Saudi nationals with the requisite skills for many of the new ventures that are being developed. In spite of the Saudization process many entrepreneurial ventures are still dependent on expat labour. For example, SA 5 who had her own Abaya design studio, was unable to find skilled Saudi nationals and was reliant on expatiate labour. If her male expat tailor did not have his visa renewed, her business would not survive. Also, the social mores prohibiting non-related men and women working alone together meant the tailor had to be situated in a separate location, thereby incurring an additional cost. Similarly in Palestine, there is also a shortage of key skills. One interviewee stated:

> We do business in a donor controlled economy where NGO's pay higher salaries. It becomes difficult to recruit qualified employees as our business is PR and advertising – (we) need creative employees and this major is not taught in local universities.
>
> (PA3)

This confirms the findings of Palestine Country Report (2012) and Khoury and McNally (2016), which mentioned the lack of alignment between competencies possessed by graduates and those of the labour market. A challenge faced by both male and female entrepreneurs.

Access to venture capital/ financial institutions

Access to venture capital was stated as another challenge to women entrepreneurs. In Palestine, 'often this access is complex, requiring multiple layers of security and collateral to be provided' (PA3). As Sadeq et al. (2011) found, not only was it more difficult for women to gain guarantors for loans, when they did, it was often from multiple sources. This increased the risk of the entrepreneur being caught in a cash flow crisis or having the business endangered, should one of the providers choose to withdraw. In addition, the findings give support to the assertion of Jones and LeFort (2014) that there was a perception that women were not taken seriously and there was lack of trust in the woman's ability repay loans.

Discussion and implications

This research builds on that of Jamali (2009), who identified the challenges confronting women entrepreneurs in Lebanon. Examining the challenges in Palestine and Saudi Arabia adds to the limited empirical literature in this field. The exploratory findings indicate that each country or context within the MENA region is unique. It is important that a 'one-size fits all approach' is not adopted. Future research should be conducted based on this premise.

There is evidence of a change taking place in Arab societies (Le-Renard, 2014; Vision-2030, 2016). In particular, the changes mooted under the Saudi Arabian Vision-2030 strategies. Changes include a shift from where the male is the sole breadwinner to one where both husband and wife work and husbands supporting their wives in their business endeavours. The micro-level factors were found to enable female entrepreneurs to overcome macro-level challenges. Factors such as education, exposure to other cultures and previous work experience can help provide better opportunities and drive pull motivation factors. Moreover, family support was revealed as being very important to the success and performance or otherwise of an entrepreneurial venture. It was evident that there needs to be proactive attempts to provide female role models via developmental experiences such as exchange programmes or as guest speakers in universities and colleges.

The study also identified successful female entrepreneurs who were able to sustain their non-traditional businesses despite the adverse conditions in their environment and the existing macro-level challenges. As result the study was able to negate the myth of female underperformance in entrepreneurship.

There are responsibilities for governments to implement supportive procedures that facilitate registration and establishment of entrepreneurial ventures. While there are challenges for both men and women, there needs to be greater acknowledgement of the needs of women in patriarchal societies. Moreover, there is a necessity for specialist solutions to be developed to support new ventures in Palestine. For example, female networking spaces. The geographical separation of the Gaza Region and the West Bank, and the resultant difficulty of access create challenges not evident in other contexts.

A change in perceptions with respect to female entrepreneurship is required. This includes adapting laws and regulations to take account of the constraints placed on female entrepreneurial performance. Media and educational institutions have a role in changing perceptions about the value of entrepreneurship as a career choice for women. This would facilitate a move away from the current perceptions that a worthwhile career is not one situated solely in an office.

As identified by Mazzarol (2005), human capital was identified as fundamental to the growth of entrepreneurial ventures, specifically, capacity building via the education and training of young people. Hence, the personal aspirations and characteristics of an entrepreneur are vital components in the success of ventures. As with Mazzarol (2005), this study also found that the ability of entrepreneurial firms to grow social capital arising from strategic networking and alliances related to women was an important contributor to success.

Conclusion

It is evident that it is not possible to have one formula for female entrepreneurs in the MENA region. There is a difference between the two countries. In Saudi Arabia, the challenges are normative and regulatory, whereas in Palestine political and regulatory factors create the more significant challenges. However, there are similarities that arose from the patriarchal nature of the context and the institutional systems and processes existing in each country. As this is an exploratory study it is important that further empirical work is undertaken to explore more fully the challenges identified in this paper.

References

Ahl, H. (2006). Why research on women entrepreneurs needs new directions. *Entrepreneurship Theory and Practice, 30*(5), 595–621.

Ahmad, S. Z. (2011). Evidence of the characteristics of women entrepreneurs in the Kingdom of Saudi Arabia: An empirical investigation. *International journal of Gender and Entrepreneurship, 3*(2), 124–143.

Al-Botmeh, S. (2013). *Barriers to female labour market participation and entrepreneurship in the occupied Palestinian territory.* Ramalleh. Palestine: The Centre for Development Studies, Birzeit University and the YWCA. Retrieved from www.ywca-palestine.org/UploadCenter/Files/1386108714.pdf.

Al-Munajjed, M. (2010). *Women's employment in Saudi Arabia: A major challenge.* Riyadh, Saudi Arabia: Booz and Company. Retrieved from https://ncys.ksu.edu.sa/sites/ncys.ksu.edu.sa/files/Women002_5.pdf.

Al-Rasheed, M. (2015). Caught between religion and the state: Women in Saudi Arabia. In B. Haykel, T. Hegghammer & S. Lacroix (Eds), *Saudi Arabia in transition: Thoughts on political, economic and religious changes* (pp. 292–313). New York: Cambridge University Press.

Arenius, P., & Minniti, M. (2005). Perceptual variables and nascent entrepreneurship. *Small Business Economics, 24*(3), 233–247.

Basaffar, A. A. (2012). *Understanding the entrepreneurial potential of female Saudi Arabian family and consumer sciences students and businesswomen.* (PhD dissertation). Iowa State University, Ames, Iowa (Paper 12604.)

Bhattacherjee, A. (2012). *Social science research: Principles, methods, and practices*: Global Text Project. [PDF document] Retrieved from https://www.pwc.de/de/internationale-maerkte/assets/doing-business-in-oman-2017.pdf.

Blanchard, A., & Warnecke, T. (2010). Shaping economic practices in China's post-command economy period: The interaction of politics, economics, and institutional constraints. *International Journal of Pluralism and Economic Education, 1*(4), 290–302.

Breen, J. (2010). Gender differences in home-based business ownership. *Small Enterprise Research, 17*(2), 124–136.

Danish, A. Y., & Lawton-Smith, H. (2012). Female entrepreneurship in Saudi Arabia: Opportunities and challenges. *International journal of Gender and Entrepreneurship, 4*(3), 216–235.

Elmuti, D., Khoury, G., & Omran, O. (2012). Does entrepreneurship education have a role in developing entrepreneurial skills and ventures' effectiveness? *Journal of Entrepreneurship Education, 15*, 83–104.

GEM (2012). *The Global Entrepreneurship Monitor: Palestine country report.* Babson Park, MA: Babson College and London Business School. Retrieved from www.gemconsortium.org/report.

GEM (2017). *Global Entrepreneurship Monitor: Saudi Arabia country report.* Babson Park, MA: Babson College and London Business School. Retrieved from www.gemconsortium.org/report.

Harvard-Kennedy-School (2015). *Back to work in a new economy: Background paper on the Saudi Labor Market: Evidence for policy design.* Boston, MA: Retrieved from http://epod.cid.harvard.edu/files/epod/files/hks-mol_background_paper_-_full_-_april_2015.pdf.

Jamali, D. (2009). Constraints and opportunities facing women entrepreneurs in developing countries: A relational perspective. *Gender in Management: An International Journal, 24*(4), 232–251.

Jones, G., & LeFort, A. (2014). *Female entrepreneurship in developing countries* (Vol. 9–807–018). Boston, MA: Harvard Business School.

Khoury, G., & McNally, B. (2016). Importance of fostering alignment to ensure sustainable nation building: The role of HRD in large Palestinian organizations. *Journal of Management Development, 35*(6), 718–734.

Le-Renard, A. (2014). *A society of young women: Opportunities of place, power and reform in Saudi Arabia.* Stanford, CA: Stanford University Press.

Marlow, S., & McAdam, M. (2013). Gender and entrepreneurship: Advancing debate and challenging myths: Exploring the mystery of the underperforming female entrepreneur. *International Journal of Entrepreneurial Behavior and Research, 19*(1), 114–124.

Mazzarol, T. (2005). A proposed framework for the strategic management of small entrepreneurial firms. *Small Enterprise Research, 13*(1), 37–53.

McGregor, J., & Tweed, D. (2002). Profiling a new generation of female small business owners in New Zealand: Networking, mentoring and growth. *Gender Work and Organization, 9*(4), 420–438.

Muna, F., & Khoury, G. (2012). *The Palestinian executive: Leadership under challenging conditions.* Farnham: Gower.

Naguib, R., & Jamali, D. (2015). Female entrepreneurship in the UAE: A multi-level integrative lens. *Gender in Management: An International Journal, 30*(2), 135–161.

Palestinian-Central-Bureau-of-Statistics (2016). *Results of the labour force survey.* Palestine: Palestine Central Bureau of Statistics.

Paprock, K. E. (2006). National human resource development in transitioning societies in the developing world: Introductory overview. *Advances in Developing Human Resources, 8*(1), 12–27.

PASSIA (2015). *Palestinian women.* Jerusalem: Palestinian Academic Society for the Study of International Affairs. Friedrich Ebert Foundation. Retrieved from www.passia.org/images/meetings/2015/dec/Women2015.pdf.

Pathak, S., Goltz, S., & Buche, M. W. (2013). Influences of gendered institutions on women's' entry into entrepreneurship. *International Journal of Entrepreneurial Behavior and Research, 19*(5), 478–502.

Sadeq, T., Mamed, M., & Glover, S. (2011). *Policies to promote female entrepreneurship in the Palestinian territory.* Jerusalem and Ramallah: Palestine Economic Policy Research Institute. Retrieved from www.palestineeconomy.ps/files/server/20152201112434–1.pdf.

Scott, W. (1995). *Institutions and organizations.* Thousand Oaks, CA: Sage.

Sheriff, M., & Muffatto, M. (2015). The present state of entrepreneurship ecosystems in selected countries in Africa. *African Journal of Economic and Management Studies, 6*(1), 17–54.

Solesvik, M., Westhead, P., & Matlay, H. (2014). Cultural factors and entrepreneurial intention. *Education and Training, 56*(8/9), 680–696.

Sparkman, T. E. (2015). The factors and conditions for national human resource development in Brazil. *European Journal for Training and Development, 39*(8), 666–680.

Strauss, A. L., & Corbin, J. M. (1990). *Basics of qualitative research: Grounded theory procedures and techniques.* Newbury Park, CA: Sage Publications.

Verheul, I., Stel, A., & Thurik, R. (2006). Explaining female and male entrepreneurship at the country level. *Entrepreneurship and Regional Development, 18*(2), 151–183.

Vision-2030. (2016). *National transformation program 2020.* Riyadh: Saudi Arabian Government.

Warnecke, T. (2013). Entrepreneurship and gender: An institutional perspective. *Journal of Economic Issues, 47*(2), 455–463.

Welter, F. (2004). The environment for female entrepreneurship in Germany. *Journal of Small Business and Enterprise Development, 11*(2), 212–221.

Welter, F., & Smallbone, D. (2008). Women's entrepreneurship from an institutional perspective: The case of Uzbekistan. *International Entrepreneurship and Management Journal, 4*(4), 505–520.

World Bank (2016). *Doing business report.* Washington, DC: The World Bank. Retrieved from www.doingbusiness.org/reports/global-reports/~/media/GIAWB/Doing%20Business/Documents/Annual-Reports/English/DB16-Chapters/DB16-Country-Tables.pdf.

Yamani, M. (1996). *Some observations on women in Saudi Arabia.* In M. Yamani (Ed.), *Feminism and Islam: Legal and literary perspectives.* New York: New York University Press.

Yousafzai, S.Y., Saeed, S., & Muffatto, M. (2015). Institutional theory and contextual embeddedness of women's entrepreneurial leadership: Evidence from 92 countries. *Journal of Small Business Management, 2015*(53), 3.

6 Women's entrepreneurship in Turkey

Promising initiatives and evidence for success in the face of culturally embedded barriers

Ceyda M. Eyiusta

Over the past decades, women have demonstrated significant progress in different fields, including health and education, as well as economics and politics (Global Entrepreneurship Monitor [GEM], 2015). They have not only become more visible in these fields but also achieved successful results in terms of performance outcomes as paid workers, managers and entrepreneurs. These developments have occurred simultaneously with the rise of women-owned businesses worldwide. In 2012 an estimated 126 million women initiated or ran new businesses in 67 economies around the world and 98 million ran established businesses (GEM, 2012). Although female entrepreneurs are growing in importance and making substantial contributions to world economies, their potential is still underutilized, with negative implications for job creation, innovation and wealth generation (Greene, Han, & Marlow, 2013). Moreover, a brief review of the research on women's entrepreneurship reveals that, even though the number of studies on the topic is increasing, there is a lack of reliable data and inferences on women's entrepreneurial activity in developing countries and emerging economies (Jamali, 2009).

Various categorizations of feminist theories have been offered so far to explain the context of female entrepreneurship. Ahl (2006) portrayed three diverse types of feminist theories: (1) theories that view women and men as essentially similar, such as liberal feminist theory and feminist empiricism; (2) theories that deem women and men to be essentially different, such as social, radical, and psychoanalytical feminist theories; and (3) theories that distinguish between sex and gender, describing gender as 'something that is "done," rather than something that "is"' (Ahl, 2006, p. 597), such as social constructionist and poststructuralist feminist theories.

Long before the criticisms of gendered assumptions in entrepreneurial research, Gunnerud (1997) challenged the implicit masculinity of entrepreneurship studies. The author suggested that scholars should keep in mind that when studying entrepreneurs, they are studying gendered beings in gendered places. He emphasized the difference that places make to gender relations and stated that we should conceive of place and gender as integral parts of entrepreneurship. As such, studies on female entrepreneurship should describe entrepreneurs within their material context, for example the labour market, and/or the socio-cultural context, such as the local attitudes toward entrepreneurship and social networks.

This study adopts the view that the entrepreneurial discourse can best be understood as embedded in the gendering of work; that is, entrepreneurship itself is a gendered process (Ahl, 2006). It proposes that the gendering of entrepreneurship influences the key drivers of women's entrepreneurship and the problems women entrepreneurs face.

Additionally, responding to Ahl's (2006) call for a more sophisticated view of female entrepreneurs and Gunnerud's (1997) request to study entrepreneurs and their ventures in their context, this study portrays the female entrepreneurship in Turkey, which is among the understudied geographies in entrepreneurship research. Specifically, it sheds light on the institutional context of entrepreneurship in Turkey, portrays the current situation of Turkish female entrepreneurs and examines the case of female subordination from different aspects.

In the light of the above discussion, the purpose of this chapter is to develop a clear picture of the entrepreneurship of women in Turkey by focusing on the following research questions. (1) What are the basic features of the institutional context that shapes female entrepreneurship in Turkey? What are the major support mechanisms to encourage female entrepreneurship? (2) What is the current position of women in the overall entrepreneurial landscape in Turkey? (3) What types of problems and challenges do Turkish female entrepreneurs face when initiating and running their business? (4) What are the key drivers and success factors for women's entrepreneurship in Turkey?

The first two questions are addressed through a literature review reflecting the findings of previous studies and statistical reports and the latter two questions are addressed through both a literature review and case studies.

The chapter consists of five sections including this introduction. In the next section, theoretical perspectives on female entrepreneurship are delineated and the theoretical perspective of this study is presented. Then, the extant literature on women's entrepreneurship in Turkey is reviewed followed by the research methodology and case studies of two successful female entrepreneurs. The chapter concludes with a discussion of the interview findings and policy recommendations to foster women's entrepreneurship in Turkey.

The institutional context of women entrepreneurship in Turkey

The Turkish Republic, established after the collapse of the 600-year old Ottoman Empire, is a democratic country founded in 1923. The population of Turkey is about 70 million and is predominantly Muslim, although the country is a secular state with no official religion (Cetindamar, Gupta, Karadeniz, & Egrican, 2012). Mustafa Kemal Ataturk, the founder of the modern Turkish Republic, introduced a number of social, political, linguistic and economic reforms to this predominantly Muslim country (e.g., Turkish women had the right to vote before women in many Western democracies had this right) (Aycan & Eskin 2005) to align Turkey with the modern world.

Historically speaking, ownership of private enterprises has not been a very popular activity among Turkish people. In the Ottoman Empire period, business enterprises were primarily run by non-Muslim minorities (Kasaba, 1988) and in the early days of modernization, state owned enterprises were the major source of production and investment (Kozan, Oksoy, & Ozsoy 2005). In the last two decades, however, Turkey witnessed significant changes in business environment due to (1) a dramatic shift from a predominantly agriculture-based economy to an increasingly industrialized and service-based economy (Cetindamar et al., 2012), (2) its entrance into a customs union with the EU in 1996, and inclusion among the candidate countries for EU membership in 1999 (Cetindamar et al., 2012) and (3) the expanded liberalization policies that have been ongoing since the mid-1980s (Arat-Koc, 2007). Liberalizing reforms have particularly increased under the Islamist

76 *Ceyda M. Eyiusta*

political party, Justice and Development Party (AKP), which has dominated Turkish politics since its remarkable electoral victory in 2002 (Ozkazanç-Pan, 2015).

Within this context, entrepreneurship has been considered an important mechanism to boost national prosperity and employment. As noted by Ozkazanç-Pan (2015), in the public sphere, this is evidenced through the Turkish government's support for high-profile entrepreneurship summits such as the Second Global Entrepreneurship Summit in Istanbul in 2011, following the inaugural 2010 summit in the USA. Similarly, the government has continuously supported entrepreneurs and start-ups through the state-run Small and Medium Enterprise Development Organization (KOSGEB) as well as through other financial incentives (Cin, 2012).

Turkish Statistical Institute statistics showed that there was a considerable increase (116%) in self-employment between 1988 and 2015 for women (Turkish Statistical Institute, TUIK Statistics, 1988–1999, 2015) while the percentage of Turkish women who are self-employed with employees (1.2%) is one of the lowest among the OECD countries (OECD, 2016). Besides, the ratio of male to female entrepreneurs in Turkey is the one of the highest, or most inequitable, among the efficiency-driven economies (GEM, 2012). Among the twenty-nine developing and developed countries in Europe, Turkey is ranked at number 4 for the ratio between male and female total early stage entrepreneurial activity (TEA) and number 1 for the ratio between male and female established business ownership. The GEM 2015 Report revealed that in Turkey women are less than half as likely as men to express entrepreneurial intentions, even though the intentions and TEA levels are above the regional average (i.e., the average of efficiency-driven economies in Europe) for women in Turkey.

Various governmental, non-governmental and national/international organizations have demonstrated a sustained effort to address the gender gap in entrepreneurship over the past two decades. These efforts primarily aimed at supporting and promoting women's entrepreneurial activities (Ecevit, 2007) which contribute to empowerment, gender equality and poverty alleviation (Ozkazanç-pan, 2015). Particularly with Turkey's ratification of Convention on the Elimination of All Forms of Discrimination Against Women (CEDAW) in 1985 (Kardam, 2005), women's entrepreneurship has become instrumental in achieving women's equal and full participation in society (Ozkazanç-Pan, 2015). Efforts to promote women's entrepreneurial activities in Turkey will be discussed in more detail in the following section.

Support mechanisms

Starting with 1990s, Turkish governments and non-governmental organizations began to support female entrepreneurs by offering business set-up financing at reasonable rates, organizing training activities and providing business support services to those women who want to start up businesses.

The Prime Ministry General Directorate on the Status of Women (KSGM) is one of the governmental units that was established following to Turkey's ratification of CEDAW in 1985 to ensure its implementation on the social level. Its major goals are to protect and to promote women's rights; to advance women's social, economic, cultural and political status; and to ensure that women have equal rights and opportunities in all aspects of life. To these ends, the directorate conducts and funds research projects with a policy orientation; cooperates with other public institutions, local administrations and women's associations; and increases awareness and consciousness about women's problems through the mass media.

The Small and Medium Enterprise Development Organization (KOSGEB), which operates under the Ministry of Trade and Industry, is another organization that encourages female entrepreneurship in Turkey by providing technical, managerial and marketing support to small and medium enterprises (SMEs). This organization arranges applied entrepreneurship training for general and specific target groups including women without charging any fees.

Organizations such as the Turkish Industry and Business Association (TUSIAD) and the Union of Chambers and Commodity Exchanges of Turkey (TOBB) also emphasize the important role of female entrepreneurs for Turkish economy through different platforms as well (Karatas-Ozkan, Inal, & Ozbilgin, 2010). TOBB has a specific unit for women entrepreneurs, named Women Entrepreneurs' Council, which develops general policies about the women's entrepreneurship and provides advisory opinions.

One important non-governmental organization that supports women's entrepreneurship is the Women Entrepreneurs' Association of Turkey (KAGIDER). KAGIDER carries out a number of projects, provides incubation and mentorship support and initiates training programmes for the (potential) female entrepreneurs. It has also close relationships with the regional and international women organizations and established sustainable project partnerships with different international institutions like the World Bank (WB) and the International Finance Corporation (IFC).

In addition to these continuous efforts, recently a number of local institutions and organizations in Turkey have begun microcredit and finance programme in collaboration with the Grameen Bank. However, initial assessment of these programmes reveals that most users are male, and the few women that start a business with the aid of such programmes are clustered in home-based craft businesses (Soyak, 2010).

Problems of Turkish female entrepreneurs

Female entrepreneurs face many obstacles to starting up and maintaining their business, including but not limited to the difficulty of finding capital (e.g., Minniti, 2009), the work-family interface (e.g., Williams, 2004), a lack of societal support (e.g., Jamali, 2009), and gender-based biases against women's entrepreneurship (Gupta, Turban, Wasti, & Sikdar, 2009). In the following parts, these problems and challenges are explained in more detail for Turkey.

Societal stereotypical perceptions of entrepreneurship

Although mainstream economic thought tends to consider itself as gender neutral (i.e., an entrepreneur is a rational, self-interested individual with no sex, gender, age, social class, religion or ethnicity) (Vossenberg, 2013), a significant amount of research has revealed that entrepreneurship tends to be considered as a stereotypically masculine endeavour (Jennings & Brush, 2013).

In Turkey society tends to attach a lower value to women's employment and entrepreneurship due to patriarchal values and associated gender roles, making it difficult for women to compete and survive within the league of male business owners. In a critical review of the extant research on women's entrepreneurship, Karatas-Ozkan et al. (2010)

stated that the recent developments in the country, particularly the rise of religious conservatism and patriarchal norms, have contributed to the segregation of women's roles to motherhood and homemaking which may deter women from engaging in entrepreneurial activities. The domination of male entrepreneurs in certain sectors, such as technology and construction, makes it even harder for female business owners to establish trust-based, long-lasting relationships with different stakeholders, particularly with those with gendered stereotypical representations of entrepreneurs (Maden, 2015).

Access to financial resources

Research on entrepreneurship has long highlighted that female entrepreneurs tend to have less access to external sources of capital than men when securing financing (Vossenberg, 2013).

Studies conducted in Turkey have also indicated that problems of obtaining financial capital are one of the most important constraints for women when starting their own business (Hisrich & Ozturk, 1999; Ufuk & Ozgen, 2001). Specifically, bank requirements of collateral to secure the loan, high credit interest levels, and the costs involved in applying for a loan create obstacles for female entrepreneurs in the establishment phase (Garanti Bank, 2014). Thus, female entrepreneurs are less likely to use formal loans and liquidation of assets as a source of initial capital and tend to use their own savings and other resources (e.g., financial support from their spouse, relatives and friends) as start-up capital (Maden, 2015; Ozdemir, 2010; Ufuk & Ozgen, 2001). These findings are supported by recent OECD figures showing that in 2013 the share of Turkish women declaring that access to money was an obstacle to starting a business (12%) was half the equivalent share for men (21%) and far below the OECD average for women (27%) (OECD, 2016).

Lack of societal support and work-family balance

Scholars have argued that the normative constraints and societal attitudes shaped by cultural and regional beliefs in some countries are not supportive of women's employment and entrepreneurship (Baughn, Chua, & Neupert, 2006; Jamali, 2009). In various parts of the world, the general perception is that entrepreneurship is a suitable career choice only for men and not for women (Vossenberg, 2013).

For female entrepreneurs in Turkey, the lack of societal support and the conflict between their family life and their work life are perceived as two distinct but related problems, both having links to the gender-stereotypic beliefs within the society. According to the traditional thought system, which is still prevalent particularly in eastern parts of the country, housework and care of children and the elderly are the primary responsibilities of women (Beduk & Eryesil, 2013). Women who are able to share these responsibilities with their husbands and/or other family members are more likely to consider creating a career path for themselves, either as regular employees or as business owners. Without a sufficient level of support, female entrepreneurs, just like female employees and managers, tend to experience work–family conflict (e.g., Maden, 2015) as well as role overloading and role conflicts in fulfilling their roles as wife, mother, housewife and business owner (Karatas-Ozkan et al., 2010 Ozgen & Ufuk, 1998).

In support of the previous arguments, previous research has revealed that female entrepreneurs in Turkey exert extra effort to be accepted in the patriarchal labour market while taking care of children and performing other household responsibilities (Garanti Bank, 2014). Recent rise of religious conservatism and patriarchal norms has made it even more difficult for Turkish women to fulfil the competing expectations of business and private life (Karatas-Ozkan et al., 2010).

Key drivers and success factors for women's entrepreneurship in Turkey

Previous studies have suggested that entrepreneurs are motivated by two different factors when starting their business. Some entrepreneurs establish independent enterprises to take advantage of external opportunities (i.e., opportunity entrepreneurship), while others resort to entrepreneurship as they lack other real sources of income (i.e., necessity entrepreneurship) (van Stel, Storey, & Thurik, 2007). This classification relies on the assumption that entrepreneurs can be pushed and pulled by some external drivers and internal motivations (Karatas-Ozkan et al., 2010). The empirical evidence indicates that female entrepreneurs in transitional and less developed economies tend to be motivated by necessity-based 'push' motivations rather than by opportunity motivations (e.g., Kelley, Brush, Greene, & Litovsky, 2011).

In contrast to these arguments, the GEM 2012 revealed that, in Turkey, only 33% of female entrepreneurs act with necessity motives in starting their business while 64% of female entrepreneurs have opportunity motives. These percentages are 30% and 68% for male entrepreneurs, respectively. The GEM 2012 data also showed that men and women have different attitudes toward entrepreneurship. A higher percentage of men (44%) than women (35%) perceive favourable business opportunities in the external environment for becoming involved in entrepreneurial activity.

Previous research on female entrepreneurs in Turkey has consistently shown that both push and pull factors are influential in motivating women to engage in entrepreneurial activity. As push factors, gender discrimination, bullying, continuous supervision, working with incompetent managers, boredom with being a housewife, relocation and frustration with previous jobs or occupations (Hisrich & Ozturk, 1999) have been reported as being influential in shaping women's self-employment decisions. Female entrepreneurs in Turkey are also influenced by various pull factors, including working independently and flexibly (e.g., Ozdemir, 2010; Maden, 2015), being productive and creating employment opportunities (e.g., Cetindamar, 2005), gaining a social status (e.g., Yilmaz, Ozdemir, & Oraman, 2012), meeting the family needs, and having better financial gains (e.g., Nayir, 2008). Among these factors, being independent, aiming for self-actualization and having one's own business have been reported as the most important motivators that pull women into entrepreneurship.

Key success factors

An analysis of the factors that contribute to the success of female entrepreneurs demonstrates that access to financial capital and social support from family and friends are two major factors that foster high-potential women's entrepreneurship in Turkey.

The Female Entrepreneurship Index (FEI) (2015), which analysed the conditions that foster high-potential female entrepreneurship in 77 countries, showed that Turkey is among the countries with the biggest gender inequalities in terms of female entrepreneurship.

80 *Ceyda M. Eyiusta*

Although the country has the highest score for technology absorption (i.e., the firm-level technology absorption capability in a country), it is at the lowest level for first-tier financing for female entrepreneurs (i.e., debt capital and financial literacy) (Terjesen & Lloyd, 2015, p. 38), inhibiting women's entrepreneurship in Turkey.

According to research findings, social support is another key driver that may influence the success of enterprises established by women in Turkey. For instance, Cetindamar et al.'s (2012) study indicated that, even though family capital (measured as family size) provides men with no advantage over women, at very high levels of family capital women are marginally more likely to engage in entrepreneurship than men. This may be associated with the necessity for women to make some financial contributions to the family or their chance of obtaining more social support from the family. The importance of family support and social networks for women's business establishment and development has also been emphasized in different academic studies (Ufuk & Ozgen, 2001; Maden, 2015; Ozdemir, 2010) as well as statistical reports. The Garanti Bank Report (2014) showed that the support given to female entrepreneurs by their families after the founding of a company, including assisting in the workplace, providing technical support, giving moral support and helping with household chores and childcare, is critical to the survival of their business.

As emphasized in the previous sections, female entrepreneurs are still provided with limited institutional support in Turkey. In establishing and maintaining their business, many female entrepreneurs apply to banks for loans and seek institutional support from KOSGEB, which encourages women's entrepreneurship by providing SMEs with technical, managerial and marketing support (Garanti Bank, 2014). On the other hand, to date there has never been extensive and multidimensional support in Turkey to promote a considerable increase in women's entrepreneurship, and very few female entrepreneurs are aware of the support provided by non-governmental organizations (Garanti Bank, 2014).

Research methodology

Before deciding on the research design of the study, the literature on women's entrepreneurship in Turkey was reviewed comprehensively. The literature was quite fragmented containing studies and research reports drawing attention to different aspects of female entrepreneurship. Consistent with the exploratory nature of the research, a qualitative case based approach was adopted (Yin, 2009) to complement the findings from the literature. The case data examined in this chapter were gathered from two Turkish female entrepreneurs who excel in their fields of business. The exploratory nature of the study required an approach that would allow narrative textual data to be gathered from available documents (i.e., previous interviews) on selected cases and semi-structured interviews.

In the next section, case studies that demonstrate the success stories of two Turkish female entrepreneurs are presented. The entrepreneurs introduced in the cases are the winners of the 'Turkey's Woman Entrepreneur Competition' in 2015.[1] They are different from many other female entrepreneurs in Turkey in the sense that they have managed to survive in difficult conditions but are still facing some barriers in their business. To draw a clear picture of their entrepreneurial process, with the integration of the drivers, challenges and key success factors, semi-structured interviews were conducted with these entrepreneurs.

The interviews focused on the three key areas that relate to the research questions of the study: the motivators of female entrepreneurs to establish their own business, the problems and challenges that they face, and the key factors contributing to their success. Each interview was transcribed, read carefully several times, and examined together with the text-based data from the participants' previous interviews.

Case 1: Mevlude Uygun (2015 Turkey's Woman Entrepreneur), Idilbebe[2]

Mevlude Uygun pursued her passion for fashion by designing and sewing clothes for her friends and herself until she opened a small, 50-square-metre shop in 1984 with the support of her family. Uygun worked as a sewing contractor until 1998 and experienced quite rough periods due to instabilities in the market. In 1998 a crisis hit the textile industry, which even led her to consider shutting down the workshop. However, she managed to turn the crisis into an opportunity by creating her own brand, Idilbebe. Mevlude Uygun describes the reasons behind her decision to establish her own brand and the reactions to her decision as follows:

> At the end of the 1990s, there was a serious crisis in the textile industry . . . I was at such a point that I would either shut down the workshop or find another solution . . . On the other hand, I had no experience of any other job than textiles . . . So, my decision to create my own brand was a kind of necessity.
> This decision was made at such a time that no one who heard it could believe it. Everyone I talked to believed that creating a brand would cost big money . . . When I looked at the products in the baby apparel market, there were mostly poor-quality products manufactured with poor workmanship. That's why my belief in myself was strong.

Regarding the obstacles that she faced in establishing her own brand, Uygun draws attention to a general obstacle faced by many female entrepreneurs in Turkey:

> When a woman decides to start up her business, first, the people around her warn her about the possibility of failure . . . If you are a woman and want to be a part of business life, you first conflict with your beloved ones . . . If you are successful, people try to find some other reasons (e.g., a supportive top manager) behind your success. I mean, in our society women's success is not easily recognized, and that's why you feel that you have to work more. May be the success originates from these challenges.

After creating her own brand, Uygun faced different obstacles. One was related to the suppliers and again turned out to be an opportunity for her. One of her competitors in the market told Idilbebe's fabric supplier that, if they worked with Idilbebe, they would stop buying fabric from them. After encountering this challenging situation, Mevlude Uygun decided to manufacture her own fabric, as she could not find high-quality goods in the market. In 2005 Mevlude Uygun decided to sell products to retailers, which helped her to achieve a growth rate of 40% or more every year.

Currently, Uygun operates twenty stores in seven different cities in Turkey and employs 230 people in her company. She is planning to increase the total number of stores to sixty by 2020. Moreover, Idilbebe exports to fifteen countries in Europe and the Turkic republics.

82 Ceyda M. Eyiusta

When asked about the key success factors in her case, Mevlude Uygun replies:

> As Idilbebe, we learnt to turn crises into opportunities . . . Our customers (mothers and babies) were always the focal point. We really manufacture as we manufacture for our own babies . . . We differentiated our apparel from our competitors' products . . . We even kept certain product lines (e.g., apparel for premature babies) with low sales potential since our customers asked for them.

Zehra Sema Demir (Turkey's Social Woman Entrepreneur), Living Museum[3]

Sema Demir's interest in museums started during her university life, while she was taking cultural studies courses at Hacettepe University's Turkish Folklore Department. After graduating from the university, she familiarized herself with the museology projects in Europe in which the architectural variety and pre-industry daily life of the relevant country were exhibited, together with the different exhibition techniques. She thought that this kind of museum would be very influential in attracting Turkish visitors and planned to create a similar museum in Turkey. She describes the key motivators for her entrepreneurship decision as follows:

> I can say that a key motivator for me was to realize my dream, which had been shaped in my mind since the university years. When I was a student at Hacettepe University, I had a special interest in museums, and as I became acquainted with museology projects in Europe, I wanted to initiate similar projects in Turkey . . . My interest became my passion.

While working as an instructor at Bilkent University, Sema Demir was looking for an organization that would be interested in her Living Museum project. In 2006 she received the good news from Mansur Yavas, the Mayor of Beypazari, that her project had been approved. Subsequently, Demir left her job at Bilkent University and became the founder, manager, curator, museum critic and even janitor of the Living Museum. With regard to the obstacles that she faced, Demir states:

> While making preparations for the Living Museum project, I was also working at Bilkent University Department of Music and Performing Arts as an instructor. As soon as I finished teaching the class, I used to go to Beypazari from Ankara. I was a woman who was a mother, teacher, doctorate student, and entrepreneur trying to establish a museum. It was a very tiring and gruelling, as well as a pleasant and exciting period.
>
> I can say that there is a huge gap between being an entrepreneur and being a female entrepreneur in our country. While it is already tough to be a "woman" in this patriarchal society, being a "woman entrepreneur" is much more difficult. In my case, I experienced some economic and bureaucratic problems in my business. But when people understand your real intention and rely on your capabilities, you can overcome these problems.

The Living Museum welcomed its first visitors on 23 April 2007, and two years after its establishment, the museum became one of the most visited museums in Anatolia. This dedicated effort was deemed worthy of an award by two prominent institutions, including Junior Chamber International (JCI). With the ideal of establishing a large museum in which Turkey's rich cultural heritage can be demonstrated and reviving tourism in Beypazari, Sema Demir initiated a new project named 'Anatolia Outdoor Museum.' With this project she aims to turn the Anatolian Values Association, of which she is the creator, into a foundation that supports research, review and documentation projects about Turkish cultural values. She links her success in various cultural projects with the following factors:

> When I look back to identify the factors that brought me to success, I think, the first one is living in a culturally rich geography like Beypazari and the presence of visionary local administrators such as Mansur Yavas in this region . . . For sure, the support of my family, particularly my husband, cannot be denied. While I was working on the Living Museum project, they supported me a lot . . . Finally, I think my undergraduate and graduate studies helped me a lot in establishing my museology projects and succeeding in each one of them.

Discussion

This chapter aims to explore (a) the basic features of the institutional context and the major support mechanisms that influence the women's entrepreneurship in Turkey, (b) the current position of women in the overall entrepreneurial landscape in Turkey, (c) the problems/challenges Turkish female entrepreneurs face when initiating and running their business, and finally (d) the key drivers and success factors for women's entrepreneurship in Turkey.

Literature review results and the findings from two case studies and interviews revealed that although the regulatory institutional context in Turkey supports women's entrepreneurship through various support mechanisms, Turkey is still behind the other efficiency-driven economies in the world with respect to female entrepreneurship rates. Recent reports have revealed that the percentage of Turkish women who run their own business is one of the lowest among all the OECD countries (OECD, 2016), and the ratio of male to female entrepreneurs is the one of the highest, or most inequitable, among the efficiency-driven economies (GEM, 2012). The extant gender gap in female entrepreneurship is mainly due to the normative and/or cultural context of the country, which is shaped by patriarchal norms and gender-stereotypical beliefs rather than to the regulatory context. Traditional roles that are prevalent in the society and the conservative executive power that has been dominant since early 2000s reinforce the segregation of gender roles (i.e., role of women as mothers and men as breadwinners) and make it difficult for women to build business networks and to access knowledge and financial capital particularly in male-dominated business fields.

In close relation to the previous remarks, the results of the previous studies together with the interview findings in this study demonstrate that female entrepreneurs in Turkey experience many problems, such as access to financial resources (e.g., Hisrich & Ozturk, 1999; Maden, 2015; Ufuk & Ozgen, 2001), maintaining a work–life balance (e.g., Garanti Bank, 2014; Maden, 2015) and a lack of societal support for women's entrepreneurship (e.g., Maden, 2015), in starting up and running their enterprises. The interview results specifically reveal that, for female entrepreneurs in Turkey, the lack of societal support and conflict

84   *Ceyda M. Eyiusta*

between their family life and their work life are two different but related problems, linked to the gender-stereotypical beliefs within the society. Patriarchal values and the associated gender roles stimulate the tendency to attach a lower value to women's entrepreneurship in Turkey, and this decreases women's ability to compete with male business owners in male-dominated sectors, such as technology and construction. These findings support the general perception in various parts of the world that entrepreneurship is a suitable career choice only for men and not for women (Vossenberg, 2013).

Although the accumulated empirical evidence has revealed that necessity-based, 'push' motivations are more prevalent amongst female than male entrepreneurs worldwide (Kelley et al., 2011; Minniti, 2010), a key finding of this study is that both push and pull factors motivate women to engage in entrepreneurial activity in Turkey. Among the push factors, gender discrimination, bullying and frustration with previous jobs or occupations are reported as influential elements. As emphasized in one of the interviews, changes in external circumstances (e.g., recessions in the economy and sectoral crises) may also lead women to consider self-employment as an option. Female entrepreneurs in Turkey are influenced by various pull factors as well, including working independently and flexibly, being productive and creating employment opportunities, gaining a social status and achieving better financial gains. Being independent, feeling self-actualization and creating a social benefit emerge as the most important motivators that pull women into entrepreneurship.

Finally, the key success factors for female entrepreneurs in Turkey are mostly associated with women's belief in their capabilities together with the support that they received from their family and friends. The support given to female entrepreneurs by their families after they start companies, including assisting in the workplace, providing technical support, giving moral support and helping with household chores and childcare is critical to the survival of women-owned businesses. This specific finding is consistent with the recent research results revealing that female entrepreneurs are more likely than their male counterparts to report that they benefit from various forms of family to-business enrichment (Powell & Eddleston, 2013). One of the female entrepreneurs interviewed emphasized that the support of her family, particularly her husband, in conjunction with her educational background enhancing her business-related capabilities, helped her considerably in succeeding in different business ventures. Considering the cultural and religious beliefs that are not supportive of women in entrepreneurship in some countries including Turkey, the support of male family members seems be particularly important for the success of Turkish female entrepreneurs.

Implications for policy

In the light of the discussions above, it is plausible to suggest that the promotion of women's entrepreneurship in Turkey is a multidimensional process. Policies should be established not only to create an appropriate regulatory environment for female entrepreneurship, but also to overcome the social biases or barriers against women who are running their own business. Specifically, these policies should focus on:

- Fostering an inclusive entrepreneurial eco-system for women by creating conditions in which they can smoothly establish and run their business. To this end, an important initiative is to make it easier for women to access financial capital with certain regulations that decrease bureaucratic procedures and provide financial privileges (e.g., low-interest and long-term credit) for women (Maden, 2015).

- Increasing institutional support to inform prospective and existing female entrepreneurs about market conditions (e.g., opportunities and threats) and encourage and guide them through different phases of business development (Garanti Bank, 2014).
- Enhancing women's self-confidence through training programmes that increase their capabilities in the fields of management, finance, marketing and communication. Although KOSGEB already organizes training activities for female entrepreneurs, these mostly focus on manufacturing sectors and their scope needs to be extended to other sectors such as the service sector, in which more and more female entrepreneurs operate (Maden, 2015).
- Initiating social reforms to transform the stereotypical gender role perceptions at the societal level. Both governmental and non-governmental organizations need to pursue awareness-raising activities directed to their members and to the general public to prevent discrimination against women in social and business life. Positive demonstrations of entrepreneurship within the popular press, educational materials, and academic studies as an attractive career option for women may help to transformation of the stereotypical gender roles in society (Maden, 2015).

Notes

1 Turkey's Woman Entrepreneur Competition has been organized by the Garanti Bank in cooperation with the *Ekonomist* magazine and the Women Entrepreneurs Association of Turkey (KAGİDER) since 2007 to support female entrepreneurs. The major aim of the competition is to uncover the business and social entrepreneurial spirit of women and to publicize their success stories as an example for women in Turkey and all over the world.
2 The story of Mevlude Uygun was compiled from the Garanti Bank's 'Turkey's Woman Entrepreneur Competition' web site, https://www.kadingirisimciyarismasi.com/mevlude-uygun.aspx?lang=EN and www.ekonomist.com.tr/her-yil-15-magaza-acmak-istiyoruz-haberler/8502.aspx?2.Page. The statements in the quotations are derived from the above website with the permission of the entrepreneur and combined with the interview responses. The researcher had the written consent of the entrepreneur to reveal her identity in this study.
3 The story of Zehra Sema Demir was compiled from the Garanti Bank's 'Turkey's Woman Entrepreneur Competition' web site, https://www.kadingirisimciyarismasi.com/zehra-sema-demir.aspx?lang=EN and www.isfikirleri-girisimcilik.com/muzeleri-yasatan-kadin-girisimci. The statements in the quotations are derived from the above website with the permission of the entrepreneur and combined with the interview responses. The researcher had the written consent of the entrepreneur to reveal her identity in this study.

References

Ahl, H. (2006). Why research on women entrepreneurs needs new directions. *Entrepreneurship Theory and Practice, 30*(5), 595–621.

Arat-Koc, S. (2007). (Some) Turkish transnationalism(s) in the age of capitalist globalization and empire: 'White Turk' discourse, the new geopolitics, and implications for feminist transnationalism. *Journal of Middle East Women's Studies, 3*(1), 35–57.

Aycan, Z., & Eskin, M. (2005). Relative contributions of childcare, spousal support and organizational support in reducing work-family conflict for men and women: The case of Turkey. *Sex Roles, 53*(7/8), 453–471.

Baughn, C., Chua, B., & Neupert, K. (2006). The normative context for women's participation in entrepreneurship: A multicountry study. *Entrepreneurship Theory and Practice, 30*(5), 687–708.

86 Ceyda M. Eyiusta

Beduk, A., & Eryesil, K. (2013). Women entrepreneurship & problems in Turkey. *Women Entrepreneurship & Problems in Turkey, 7*(5), 10–14.

Cetindamar, D. (2005). Policy issues for Turkish entrepreneurs. *International Journal of Entrepreneurship and Innovation Management, 5*(3/4), 187–205.

Cetindamar, D., Gupta, V. K., Karadeniz, E. E., & Egrican, N. (2012). What the numbers tell: The impact of human, family and financial capital on women and men's entry into entrepreneurship in Turkey. *Entrepreneurship & Regional Development: An International Journal, 24*(1/2), 29–51.

Cin, I. (2012). *Is dunyasinin bekledigi tesvik paketi aciklandi!* Retrieved from: www.girisimhaber.com/post/2012/04/05/Is-Dunyasinin-Bekledigi-Yeni-Tesvik-Paketi-Aciklandi.aspx/.

Ecevit, Y. (2007). *Turkiye'de Kadin Girisimciligine Elestirel Bir Yaklasim.* Ankara: Uluslararasi Calisma Ofisi.

Garanti Bank (2014). Research on women entrepreneurship [PDF document]. Retrieved from: http://assets.garanti.com.tr/assets/pdf/tr/diger/K.G. A_eng_dijital_v_1.pdf/.

Global Entrepreneurship Monitor (GEM) (2012). *Women's report* [PDF document]. Retrieved from: www.babson.edu/Academics/centers/blank-center/global research/gem/Documents/GEM%202012%20Womens%20Report.pdf/.

Global Entrepreneurship Monitor (GEM) (2015). *Women's report* [PDF document]. Retrieved from: http://gemorg.bg/wp-content/uploads/2015/11/gem-2014-womens-report-1447757361.pdf/.

Greene, F. J., Han, L., & Marlow, S. (2013). Like mother, like daughter? Analyzing maternal influences upon women's entrepreneurial propensity. *Entrepreneurship Theory and Practice, 37*(4), 687–711.

Gunnerud, B. N. (1997). Gender, place and entrepreneurship. *Entrepreneurship & Regional Development, 9*(3), 259–268.

Gupta, V. K., Turban, D. B., Wasti, S. A., & Sikdar, A. (2009). The role of gender stereotypes in perceptions of entrepreneurs and intentions to become an entrepreneur. *Entrepreneurship Theory and Practice, 33*(2), 397–417.

Hisrich, R. D., & Ozturk, S. A. (1999). Women entrepreneurs in a developing economy. *Journal of Management Development, 18*(2), 114–125.

Jamali, D. (2009). Constraints and opportunities facing women entrepreneurs in developing countries: A relational perspective. *Gender in Management: An International Journal, 24*(4), 232–251.

Jennings, J. E., & Brush, C. G. (2013). Research on women entrepreneurship: Challenges to (and from) the broader entrepreneurship literature, *The Academy of Management Annals, 7*(1), 661–713.

Karatas-Ozkan, M., Inal, G., & Ozbilgin, M. (2010). Turkey. In V. Fielden & M. Davidson (Eds), *International handbook of successful women entrepreneurs* (pp. 175–188). Cheltenham and New York: Edward Elgar Press.

Kardam, N. (2005). *Turkey's engagement with global women's human rights.* Burlington, VT: Ashgate.

Kasaba, R. (1988). *The Ottoman Empire and the world economy: The nineteenth century.* Albany, NY: State University of New York Press.

Kelley, D., Brush, C., Greene, P., & Litovsky, Y. (2011). *The global entrepreneurship monitor: 2010 women's report.* Wellesley, MA: Babson College & GERA.

Kozan, M. K., Oksoy, D., & Ozsoy, O. (2005). Growth plans of small businesses in Turkey: Individual and environmental influences. *Journal of Small Business Management, 44*(1), 114–129.

Maden, C. 2015. A gendered lens on entrepreneurship: Women entrepreneurship in Turkey. *Gender in Management: An International Journal, 30*(4), 312–331.

Minniti, M. (2009). Gender issues in entrepreneurship. *Foundations and Trends in Entrepreneurship, 5*(7–8), 497–621.

Minniti, M. (2010). Female entrepreneurship and economic activity. *European Journal of Development Research, 22,* 294–312.

Nayir, Z. D. (2008). Is ve ailesi arasındaki kadin: Tekstil ve bilgi islem girisimcilerinin rol catismasina getirdikleri cozum stratejileri, *Ege Akademik Bakis Dergisi, 8*(2), 631–650.

Organisation for Economic Co-operation and Development (OECD) (2016). *Women entrepreneurship – Key findings: Turkey* [PDF document]. Retrieved from https://www.oecd.org/std/business-stats/EaG-Turkey-Eng.pdf/.

Ozdemir, A. A. (2010). Motivation factors of potential entrepreneurs and a research study in Eskisehir. *Ege Akademik Bakis, 10*(1), 117–139.

Ozgen, O., & Ufuk, H. (1998). Kadinlarin evde gerceklestirdikleri girisimcilik faaliyetlerinin aile yasamina etkisi. In O. Citci (Ed.), *20. yuzyilin sonunda kadinlar ve gelecek* (pp. 285–302). Ankara: TODAIE Yay.

Ozkazanç-Pan, B. (2015). Secular and Islamic feminist entrepreneurship in Turkey. *International Journal of Gender and Entrepreneurship, 7*(1), 45–65.

Powell, G. N., & Eddleston, K. A. (2013). Linking family to-business enrichment and support to entrepreneurial success: Do female and male entrepreneurs experience different outcomes? *Journal of Business Venturing, 28,* 261–280.

Soyak, M. (2010). Kadin girisimciliği ve mikrofinans: Türkiye deneyimi. *Sosyal Bilimler Ensitüsü Dergisi, 24,* 129–144.

Terjesen, S. A., & Lloyd, A. (2015) *The 2015 Female Entrepreneurship Index (June 18, 2015).* Kelley School of Business Research Paper No. 15–51. Retrieved from https://papers.ssrn.com/sol3/papers.cfm?abstract_id=2625254.

Turkish Statistical Institute (TUIK) *1988–1999. Labor force statistics dynamic search – 1988–1999.* Retrieved from: https://biruni.tuik.gov.tr/isgucuapp/isgucu.zul?dil=2/.

Turkish Statistical Institute (TUIK) 2015. *Labor force statistics dynamic search.* Retrieved from: https://biruni.tuik.gov.tr/medas/?kn=72&locale=en/.

Ufuk, H., & Ozgen, O. (2001), The profile of women entrepreneurs: A sample from Turkey. *International Journal of Consumer Studies, 25*(4), 299–308.

van Stel, A., Store, D, & Thurik, R. (2007). The effect of business regulations on nascent and young business entrepreneurship. *Small Business Economics, 28*(2/3), 171–186.

Vossenberg, S. (2013). Women entrepreneurship promotion in developing countries: What explains the gender gap in entrepreneurship and how to close it? *Maastricht School of Management Working Paper,* No. 2013/08, March 2013.

Williams, D. R. (2004). Effects of child-care activities on the duration of self-employment in Europe. *Entrepreneurship Theory and Practice, 28*(5), 467–485.

Yilmaz, E., Ozdemir, E., & Oraman, Y. (2012). Women entrepreneurs: Their problems and entrepreneurial ideas. *African Journal of Business Management, 6*(26), 7896–7904.

Yin, R. (2009). *Case study research: Design and methods* (4th ed.). London: Sage.

Section 2

Gendered embeddedness of women's entrepreneurial activity in the entrepreneurship ecosystem

7 Developing gender-responsive trade ecosystems in the Asia-Pacific

Patrice Braun

Introduction

As part of an integrated, innovative and interconnected agenda, the Asia Pacific Economic Cooperation (APEC) forum –comprising twenty-one Pacific Rim member economies that promote free trade throughout the Asia-Pacific region – has for some time recognized the pivotal role of women-led enterprises in the development and prosperity of the region (APEC, 2011). Narrowing the gender gap is not just a matter of equity. It has the potential to contribute up to $28 trillion, or 26 per cent, to annual global GDP (McKinsey Global Institute, 2015). Acknowledging the importance of trade support for women, one of the foci of APEC is to strengthen economies' trade ecosystems to enhance the ability of small and medium size enterprises (SME) to internationalize.

Export by SME ranks among the highest priorities in both developed and developing economies. Export policies can, however, be subject to narrow criteria, leading to the exclusion of a large proportion of SME, especially in developing economies where weak ecosystems and multiple market failures prevail (Belloc & Di Maio, 2011). In the case of assistance to potential women exporters, the World Bank (2014) advocates government interventions that strengthen the trade enabling environment to eliminate the barriers typically faced by women entrepreneurs.

Trade support services are often dispersed across government agencies whose role may vary from trade to regional development, small business assistance and the empowerment of women. As a result, trade services operate within a complex ecosystem involving multiple actors across multiple domains. Typically, trade support services are gender neutral, or rather gender-blind. That is to say, they provide trade support to enterprises regardless of gender, which neither accelerates gender parity nor adequately stimulates gendered economic growth.

There are some notable exceptions in the field of women-focused trade services. Malaysia's Women Exporters Development Program (WEDP), for instance, has assisted women entrepreneurs to build their business and become ready for export. Australia, through its Women in Global Business (WIGB) programme, has provided dedicated support to female entrepreneurs wishing to engage in international business, the most common mode of which is exporting goods and services. Both these programmes have assisted hundreds if not thousands of women entrepreneurs to export. Such programmes remain uncommon, resulting in scant research on gender-responsive trade support.

Drawing on the experiences of the (recently folded) WIGB programme – which offered one-stop-shop access to information and resources, trade support and training, advocacy on behalf of women entrepreneurs, communication channels and networks – an intervention was designed to make developing APEC economies aware of gender-responsive trade support practices to enhance the internationalization of women-led enterprises.[1] The intervention ensued from the premise that most trade support services in APEC economies do not meet the needs of women, serving as a call to action for economies to understand the value of embedding gender-responsive practices in their trade ecosystems.

This chapter examines the intervention as a tool for the development of gender-responsive support services and strengthening of the overall trade ecosystem. It is exploratory in nature and process rather than data driven. The structure of the chapter is as follows. The next section positions the intervention within the literature, reviewing ecosystems in general and aspects that impact on women entrepreneurs in particular. This is followed by the research design and outcomes of the intervention. The chapter concludes with future directions pertaining to building inclusive trade ecosystems.

Positioning the research

The aim of the intervention was to put a gender lens on trade support and make developing APEC economies aware of the potential benefits of implementing gender-responsive trade practices. Interventions to improve organizational ability towards achieve gender parity are not new. Examples of human capital development and gender mainstreaming are well documented in the literature (Morgan, Baser, & Morin, 2010; Daly, 2005). However, interventions pertaining to trade support are generally only reported in technical texts, making it difficult to ascertain the impact of trade support and whether such services stimulate the propensity of women to internationalize[2] (Orser et al., 2004).

Liberal feminism theory holds that men and women are fundamentally equal and that gender differences in export propensity are due to systemic barriers and/or discrimination (Fischer, Reuber, & Dyke, 1993). Thus it could be argued that gender-neutral trade support inadvertently contributes to systemic discrimination. Scholars like Ahl (2006) advocate moving beyond liberal feminism theory, suggesting that the internationalization of SME is far from gender neutral. Women face additional barriers because of their gender and status, with firm size in part due to unequal access to resources required for enterprise growth.

Social feminism focuses on the need to understand and acknowledge women's experiences, skills, competencies and values (Orser et al., 2004). Envisioning a double bottom line 'feminist entrepreneurship theory' the latter authors propose to not just explain gender differences in export performance but to 'do something about' (p. 951). Researchers further suggest that trade support is most effective when focused on solving the specific needs of enterprises (Gundlach & Sammartino, 2013). To that end, the study tables a gender-responsive trade practices framework designed to improve access to resources and supports for women entrepreneurs in trade ecosystems.

Ecosystems

There is a rapidly growing body of literature that examines the interactions between entrepreneurial firms and the context within which such enterprises operate, commonly referred to as the entrepreneurship ecosystem. The definition of an ecosystem ranges from interactions and interdependences in the value chain (Adner & Kapoor, 2010) to an emphasis on actors, governance and the general enabling environment for entrepreneurial action (Stam, 2014). Mazzarol (2014) describes entrepreneurship ecosystems as a conceptual framework designed to foster economic development via entrepreneurship, innovation and small business growth.

Isenberg (2011) identifies six domains within the entrepreneurship ecosystem: a conducive culture, enabling policies and leadership, availability of appropriate finance, quality human capital, markets, and a range of institutional supports (Figure 7.1).

Comprising a multitude of interdependent components, aforementioned ecosystem domains echo every trade barrier faced by women entrepreneurs (Asia Foundation, 2013). Without paying heed to gender, entrepreneurship ecosystems may well perpetuate systemic discrimination, leading to male-led enterprises being more likely to export than female-led enterprises (Ahl, 2006). Stam (2014) suggests a supportive environment is the shared responsibility of the public and private sector, whereby policy inputs are interwoven with socially embedded factors to nurture entrepreneurship and growth. The latter tends to translate into institutional support for high-growth industries and firms, posing challenges for entrepreneurship ecosystems with a paucity of high-growth firms (Mason & Brown, 2014) as well as for women entrepreneurs who are generally under-represented in high-growth industries (Krause, 2015).

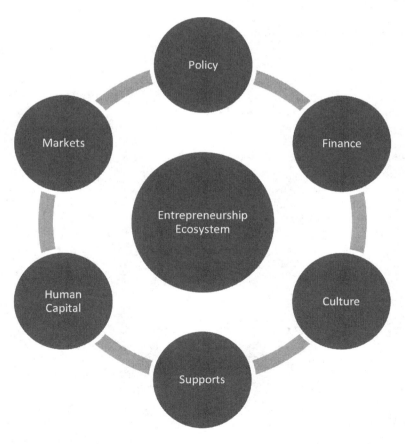

Figure 7.1 Entrepreneurship ecosystem domains (adapted from Isenberg, 2011)

94 *Patrice Braun*

Few studies have considered the entrepreneurship ecosystem from a trade support perspective, ignoring potential institutional shortcomings in this area. This research applies a gender lens to the entrepreneurship ecosystem and in particular to the merits of institutional supports for women entrepreneurs wishing to access the global trade ecosystem. For the purposes of the study, a trade ecosystem is defined as 'trade flows in and out of entrepreneurship ecosystems, including both regional and international trade development and flows'. The study builds on Ahl & Nelson's (2014) call to develop uniform policy for entrepreneurship supports that acknowledges the business landscape is gendered. It also follows Mason & Brown (2014) who believe ecosystem interventions must be holistic and consider the entire entrepreneurship environment to achieve inclusive growth.

Trade and gender

The relationship between trade and gender is an increasingly important theme in the economics and development literatures, yet the role of gender in international trade remains relatively unexplored (Orser, Spence, Riding, & Carrington, 2010). It has long been established that women play an important role in the economic development process (Boserup, 1970). It is similarly well established that women-led enterprises face a set of institutional constraints that limit their ability to thrive and grow (e.g., Brush, 1992; Brush 1997, Marlow, 2002). While women-led enterprises are not inherently less productive, the so-called second glass ceiling – a gender bias that obstructs women-led enterprises from equal access to trade ecosystem aspects such as finance and markets – prevents women-led SME from reaching their full potential, with the cost of this second glass ceiling being borne by the entire economy (Bosse & Porcher, 2012).

While not all women exporters may experience gender-related access barriers to finance and international trade, perceptions influence decision-making. Early gender research into trade points to women's disadvantaged position vis-à-vis international trade as predominantly based in education and experience with women lacking the knowledge and skills required to internationalize (Nelson, 1987). Orser et al. (1999) identified gender-specific challenges and traits that influenced internationalization, such as women not being taken as seriously as male-owned firms in export markets. Gender also influenced travel decisions related to internationalization, both in terms of personal safety as a woman traveller and the logistics of balancing family commitments (McClelland, 2004). Alternative views on why women did not export, e.g., research into the expansion of firms, suggests women-led enterprises remained small by choice (Carter and Allen, 1997).

Research conducted in the new millennium (ACOA, 2003) again points to women's confidence levels and perceived lack of credibility in foreign markets as barriers to export. Overcoming cultural conditioning is typically cited as one of the greatest export barriers for female entrepreneurs (McKay, 2001) with socio-cultural conditions appearing to maintain women entrepreneurs' economic vulnerability (Green et al., 2003). A decade on, research upholds long-standing financial, cultural and educational barriers, while also highlighting the roles of government and weak entrepreneurship ecosystems in deterring women in business (Asia Foundation, 2013). Internationalization also remains a challenge for women-led SME in developed economies (Gundlach & Sammartino, 2013), whereby ecosystem aspects such as finance, human capital and supports as identified by Isenberg (2011), continue to negatively impact the trade status of women (GEM, 2015).

Impediments notwithstanding, there is strong appetite among women-led SME for expansion into new markets.

Internationalization of women-led SME

International trade is the foundation of today's global knowledge economy in which SME are considered the critical engines of growth and innovation for economies. Globalization is changing the nature of trade facilitation and the support required by business. Enabled by information and communication technologies (ICT), SME now have many more options available to go global with new business models and platforms continuing to emerge (Braun, 2014; Weeks, 2001).

Globally, the number of formally registered women-led SME (excluding micro enterprises) already makes up close to one-third of all SME (International Finance Corporation, 2014) and it is estimated that by 2020, some 870 million women will enter the economic mainstream for the first time (World Bank 2012). This increases demand for trade support from women-led SME and would logically provide sound rationale for trade facilitation providers to embrace strategies that augment the export propensity of women-led SME (Orser et al., 2010). However, given women's entrepreneurial activity – typically clustered in service industries as compared to male-dominated high-growth industries (Gupta et al., 2009) – women are not considered a growth sector, despite the fact the Asia-Pacific region could generate an estimated US$89 billion annually if women-led SME were supported to develop to their full potential (McKinsey Global Institute, 2015).

Methodology

An intervention was designed to assist ten developing economies in APEC understand the value of embedding gender-responsive trade support in their domestic trade ecosystems. The study adopted Rodrik's (2010) evidence-based view that the best intervention approach entails a process through which participants gain a better understanding of their local trade ecosystem. As such, this chapter posits that, at best, institutions engaged in trade support see the value of embedding gender-responsive trade practices, and, at least, makes them aware that business practices are gendered (Ahl & Nelson, 2014).

A multi-prong methodology was adopted for the intervention. Components included (i) a background review of trade services, (ii) a questionnaire to establish a baseline on existing trade services in participating economies; and (iii) a workshop to collectively identify a gender-responsive trade practices framework. Each component is described in more detail below.

Trade services review

To get a solid understanding of trade services, a cross-section of technical literature was reviewed. Trade promotion programmes in a number of economies were studied; promotion materials, technical reports and trade agency websites were examined. WIGB programme services were analysed for potential good practice examples. A discussion on technical reports, trade and export programmes across economies falls outside the scope of this chapter.

Questionnaire

To establish a baseline of existing trade support practices, a brief questionnaire was distributed via email to participants nominated by their economy to attend the workshop. Invited delegates comprised twenty-one male and female trade officials and fourteen women entrepreneurs and business network representatives from ten developing APEC economies – Chile, China, Indonesia, Malaysia, Mexico, Papua New Guinea (PNG), Philippines, Peru, Thailand and Vietnam.

Separate but overlapping survey instruments were formulated for government officials and business representatives (see Appendix A, B). The instruments were designed to determine (1) availability of trade support services, (2) perceived differences on trade facilitation from a government vs. business perspective, and (3) common barriers/enablers to establish gender-responsive trade practices. Selected background reading[3] was circulated to delegates as part of their preparation for the workshop.

A total of thirty-five questionnaires were distributed, twenty-six of which were returned via email. Questionnaire responses ranged from very descriptive to minimalist with some economies simply returning the questionnaire as 'not applicable', reducing the total useable responses to fifteen public sector and seven private sector responses. Questionnaires were read, organized question-by-question, and analysed for commonalities and patterns using

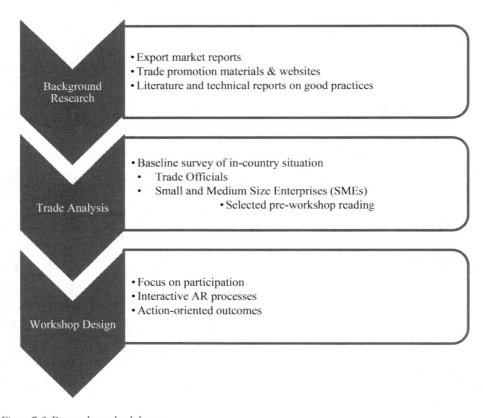

Figure 7.2 Research methodology

a word processing programme, and subsequently grouped by key themes as identified by government officials and private sector representatives.

Workshop

The workshop design was underpinned by an Action Research (AR) methodology. AR develops practical situations and competencies, is participatory, experiential and action oriented in nature (Reason and Bradbury, 2001). Considering the objective was to create awareness of and collectively determine gender-responsive trade practices, a clinical inquiry approach was adopted for the workshop (McDonagh & Coghlan, 2001). A participatory form of AR, clinical inquiry enables integration of the organizational, human and cultural aspects of an intervention. Using facilitated forms of dialogue, this type of AR intervention stimulates communication between participants, provides insights into organizational structures, and builds pathways to collective thinking and mutual learning (Braun, 2005).

Bringing together a heterogeneous group of delegates can be challenging from a facilitation perspective. This challenge was to a large degree overcome by ample interaction, both in terms of speaker and floor interaction and various participatory exercises. The seating arrangements also encouraged collaboration and bonding between delegates, while interactive plenary and panel structures gave all participants equal opportunity to share their thoughts and experiences. Through a series of break-out group exercises, delegates discussed gender-sensitive trade practices and related support needs. Outcomes of group discussions were presented in a final plenary session and organized by consensus into a cohesive gender-responsive trade practices framework.

Survey findings

With the exception of one developing economy (Malaysia), participating government officials all reported that no specific policies or dedicated trade support programmes were in place for women entrepreneurs, highlighting the lack of gender-responsive trade practices in most all participating economies.

Table 7.1 Trade support services

Economy	Gender neutral policies/ trade support programmes	Dedicated policies/trade support programmes for women entrepreneurs	Policies/trade support programmes spread across more than one agency
Chile	√	–	√
China	√	–	√
Indonesia	√	–	√
Malaysia	√	√	√
Mexico	√	–	√
PNG	√	–	√
Peru	√	–	√
Philippines	√	–	√
Thailand	√	–	√
Vietnam	√	–	√

98 *Patrice Braun*

Several officials emphasized that services for female exporters were provided as part of a full suite of trade support activities on the national, regional and local level. While some delegates stressed their trade support services were gender neutral, they did not appear to be aware that business practices are in fact gendered and, as such, do not consider business-women's trade support needs. As one official illustrated: 'All programs are important for SME, in this case women SME.' Another official responded that 'gender discrimination is not practiced among SME conducting international business' and establishing women-focused trade promotion services was neither necessary nor a priority for their economy. Most all officials (bar China which did not nominate a government official to attend the workshop) indicated the responsibility for trade support was dispersed across government departments, recognizing the spread across (often several) agencies as a key barrier to cohesive service delivery.

Several delegates resorted to listing the names of agencies involved in trade; only two economies identified coordination across agencies as a key enabler under collaboration. One economy listed the banking industry as a key player, illustrating the industry to be 'somewhat biased to men in terms of securing loans'. Most officials recognized human capital (training) and knowledge flows as key enablers.

Responses from private sector delegates reaffirmed trade assistance was generally dispersed across numerous agencies with little collaboration or transparency between agencies. Women-led SME reported they were bounced between departments, did not know who to talk to or where to get clear directives on regulatory and logistical issues. Said one female exporter: 'From our efforts of interaction, it has seem to shown [*sic*] that the existence of those 'agencies' have had a background of thick bureaucracy, making it difficult to get direct and significant assistance towards SME. However, from the government's recognition themselves [*sic*], reports have shown that SME development are [*sic*] going well, whereas in reality, the situation is otherwise'.

Other barriers cited by private sector delegates included a lack of recognition from government to acknowledge women entrepreneurs as economic actors. Voicing government inefficiency, SME delegates cited the lack of vision by government to treat women-led SME as a growth sector. One economy (Peru) pointed to programmes often being urban focused, overlooking women entrepreneurs in regional and rural areas where support is most needed. Two economies (Malaysia and Indonesia) cited traditional culture combined with household and family duties as key barriers for women entrepreneurs.

Table 7.2 Government official responses

Government Official Responses (n = 15)	Key Barriers: spread across agencies	Key Enablers: collaboration coordination between agencies	Skills & knowlegde key enablers for women exporters
Chile (1)	√	–	√
China (0)	–	–	–
Indonesia (2)	√	√	√
Malaysia (2)	√	√	√
Mexico (1)	√	–	√
PNG (1)	√	–	√
Peru (1)	√	–	√
Philippines (4)	√	–	√
Thailand (1)	√	–	√
Vietnam (2)	√	–	√

Table 7.3 Private sector responses

Private Sector Responses (n = 7)	Key Barriers: finance, bureaucracy, firm size, lack of skills	Key Barriers: programme concentration/eligibility; cultural	Key Enablers: finance, skills & export knowlegde, networks, partners & mentors
Chile (0)	–	–	–
China (1)	√	–	√
Indonesia (1)	√	√	√
Malaysia (1)	√	√	√
Mexico (0)	–	–	–
PNG (0)	–	–	–
Peru (2)	√	√	√
Philippines (1)	√	–	√
Thailand (1)	√	–	√
Vietnam (0)	–	–	–

Programme eligibility criteria were also seen as too restrictive. One SME delegate cited government's general focus on large enterprises as a barrier, suggesting 'there is a need for institutional strengthening of the public sector which should approach the private sector more openly and treat SME as an economic group that has the same characteristics as large enterprises'. This particular delegate also listed SME as enablers, mentioning the need for more public-private partnership approaches that foster collaboration between SME for internationalization purposes. 'They may be competitors in the domestic market but may be partners in the export industry'. All private sector delegates listed access to finance, training, export knowledge, networks, partners and mentors as key enablers.

Gender-responsive trade practices framework

A gender-responsive trade practices framework was developed by public and private sector delegates from ten developing economies during the workshop component of the intervention. The workshop commenced with a presentation of survey findings, followed by a series of moderated panels during which delegates had an opportunity to share their experiences related to barriers and opportunities for inclusive trade. It quickly became apparent to all present that there was a significant gap between sectors in terms of demand vs. supply of trade support services. At the end of the panel sessions delegates were in general agreement that there was a need to close this gap, evolve the relationship between the two sectors and work closer together to remove the barriers that limit the participation of women-led SME in global markets.

Having discussed the opportunities and barriers impeding businesswomen to internationalize, it was agreed women need transparent, cost-effective channels to access markets. The WIGB programme was tabled as a good practice example of gender-responsive trade support. Building on the five WIGB programme themes – (1) access to information and resources, (2) trade support and training, (3) capacity development supports; (4) communication channels and networks) and (5) advocacy on behalf of women entrepreneurs – break-out groups were formed to discuss each theme. The workshop concluded with

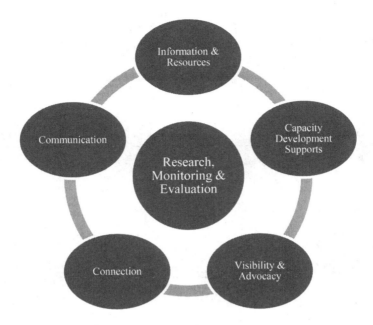

Figure 7.3 Gender-responsive trade services framework

groups reporting back on their chosen theme and delegates achieving consensus on adopting the themes into a gender-responsive trade practices framework. Delegates agreed that research, monitoring and evaluation had to be central to the successful implementation of such a framework (Figure 7.3).

Delegates further agreed there was a strong rationale for the adoption of a 'one-stop-shop' approach (both physical and virtual) to reduce fragmentation and streamline service delivery via a single entry point. Anecdotal evidence suggests that entry points would vary per economy, with developing economies typically building product quality and skill levels prior to exposing women to internationalization, whereas developed economies are more likely to step in when a woman-led SME has an established business and is close to export ready.

Discussion

While public and private sector delegates recognized the value of gender-responsive trade support, the trade landscape is both convoluted and evolving fast. Trade officials are under pressure to expand their services to meet the increased demand from both male and female entrepreneurs, yet face budgetary constraints to improve operations and reach new markets. This, according to officials, makes it difficult to provide dedicated services for women-led SME to support their participation in international trade. SME, on the other hand, are frustrated with the bureaucratic, inefficient nature of dispersed trade support.

Despite good intentions to evolve public-private and inter-agency collaboration, the gap between demand and supply of gendered trade support appears ever harder to bridge, especially in light of the recently folded Australian WIGB programme attributed to budget cuts and the assertion that gender-neutral trade support can adequately serve all would-be exporters. Such gender-blindness not only perpetuates systemic discrimination, it disregards the fact that the business landscape is gendered (Ahl & Nelson, 2014) and that women-led SME are a growth sector (McKinsey, 2015).

As this study has shown, women still face export barriers due to their gender and status, firm size and lack of access to resources. Since the internationalization of SME continues to be far from gender neutral (Ahl, 2006), the argument in favour of establishing (or maintaining) gender-responsive trade support services is strong. There is not only a need to understand and acknowledge women's experiences, skills, competencies and values (Orser et al., 2004), it is in the economic interest of trade ecosystems to provide entitlements and supports that are focused on solving the specific needs of women-led enterprises (Gundlach & Sammartino, 2013).

Adopting a gender-responsive framework for trade ecosystems has the potential to improve access to resources and supports for women entrepreneurs. Providing a holistic suite of services (Mason & Brown, 2014), the framework is designed to support the *entire* export process, addressing both entitlements (access to resources to enter markets and increase productivity) and capabilities (improving human capital and managerial capacity to deploy resources and increase market access) (Belloc & Di Maio, 2011). Neither government nor the private sector can reasonably be expected to accomplish such a task alone. Public-private partnerships (PPP) are a growing form of support for economic prosperity (Braun, 2007) with all parties in the ecosystem sharing responsibility for nurturing female entrepreneurship and agency (Stam, 2014). Indeed, partnership attention to equality in business is a key process for the transformation of economies and enterprises (Prügl & True, 2014).

Coordinated service provision notwithstanding, cultural norms remain a sticking point. The success of any trade ecosystem involved in building the export capacity of female entrepreneurs will depend on how it responds to existing cultural values (Isenberg, 2011), whether there is recognition that the business landscape is gendered (Ahl & Nelson, 2014) and needs to be supported accordingly.

Occupying a central position in the gender-responsive trade practices framework, research, monitoring and evaluation are crucial to understanding and tracking conditions within trade ecosystems. There currently is large heterogeneity in the evaluation of trade support (Belloc & Di Maio, 2011). Often measures do not go beyond input data and most economies do not collect sex-disaggregated data pertaining to the impact of trade support services on the internationalization of SME (APEC, 2011). Understanding the economic benefits and efficacy of gender-responsive trade practices creates an evidence-base to inform overall trade ecosystem policy.

Future directions

This chapter has reported on the outcomes of an intervention aimed at increasing institutional awareness of the value of gender-responsive trade support. Building on established social feminism theory (e.g., Orser et al. 2010, Ahl, 2006), the research makes a contribution to the entrepreneurship ecosystem discourse from a gendered trade perspective.

Exploratory in nature, the study proposes a gender-responsive trade practices framework to support the internationalization of women-led enterprises.

The proposed framework is based on the premise that current supports are far from gender neutral and hence do not accelerate inclusive growth. With male-led enterprises more likely to export than female-led enterprises (Ahl, 2006), the *raison d'etre* of the proposed framework is that improved trade ecosystem conditions for women-led enterprises will reduce systemic gender discrimination and encourage inclusive growth.

While the framework is practical in nature in terms of 'doing something' to stimulate the propensity of women to internationalize (Orser et al., 2004), to determine the actual value of implementing gender-responsive trade services requires the development of appropriate gender measurement instruments and attributes (Ahl, 2006). Adopting and sharing framework metrics across APEC economies will be a significant step forward towards recognizing women as a growth sector and evidence-based policy making. At the time of writing PPP roundtables were being conducted in participating economies to encourage inter-agency and public-private collaboration and identify gender-responsive measures to strengthen trade ecosystems, outcomes of which will be reported in future papers.

Even in economies with favourable export enabling environments, entrepreneurship ecosystems are made up of a complex set of actors and interdependencies with local or regional environment always influencing entrepreneurial activity (Stam, 2014). Building on the knowledge that access to resources and cultural constraints continue to be the biggest challenges for women-led enterprises (GEM, 2015), the proposed framework endorses a holistic and 'one-size does not fit all' intervention approach (Mason & Brown, 2014). To create inclusive growth, trade ecosystem actors are encouraged to undertake both institutional and firm-level capacity building and collectively design trade support services that remove systemic barriers.

Useful future research directions that would contribute to inclusive trade ecosystem development include mapping multi-stakeholder roles and services within local ecosystems, identifying good practices in access to finance, human capital development and other supports, tracking how women-led enterprises enter global value chains; and conducting cross-cultural studies on the value and potential impact of gender-responsive trade practices as a whole.

Notes

1 The author was the lead consultant for the intervention.
2 While internationalization involves much more than export propensity, in this chapter the two terms are used interchangeably.
3 Access to Trade and Growth of Women's SME in APEC Developing Economies: Evaluating Business Environments in Malaysia – Philippines – Thailand, APEC/Asia Foundation, February 2013. SME 11–2013 – APEC Train-the-Trainer Training Course for Women SME Service Exporters – Summary Report Ho Chi Minh City, Viet Nam 17–18 June, Small and Medium Enterprises Working Group, July 2014.

References

ACOA (2003). *A portrait of women business owners in Atlantic Canada in 2003.* New Brunswick: The Atlantic Canada Opportunities Agency.

Adner, R., & Kapoor, R. (2010). Value creation in innovation ecosystems: How the structure of technological interdependence affects firm performance in new technology generations. *Strategic Management Journal, 31*, 306–333.

Ahl, H. (2006). Why research on women entrepreneurs needs new direction. *Entrepreneurship Theory and Practice, 30*(5), 595–621.

Ahl, H., & Nelson, T. (2014). How policy positions women entrepreneurs: A comparative analysis of state discourse in Sweden and the United States. *Journal of Business Venturing, 30*, 273–291.

APEC (2011). *Declaration. High level policy dialogue on women and the economy.* Asia Pacific Economic Cooperation, San Francisco, 16 September 2011.

Asia Foundation (2013). Access to trade and growth of women's SME in APEC developing economies: Evaluating business environments in Malaysia – Philippines – Thailand. Retrieved 10/10/2014 from https://wlsme.org/sites/default/files/resource/files/2013_ PPWE_Access-Trade-Growth-Women-SMEs.pdf.

Australian Government Office for Women/Sensis (2009). Women in exports. An export profile of Australia's female operated small and medium exporters. Canberra. https://www.dss.gov.au/sites/default/files/documents/05_2012/women_and_exports.pdf.

Belloc, M., & Di Maio, M. (2011). *Survey of the literature on successful strategies and practices for export promotion by developing countries.* International Growth Centre, London School of Economics. Working Paper 11/0248. Retrieved 10/10/2014 from http://ssm.com/abstract=2001000.

Boserup, E. (1970). *Women's role in economic development.* New York: St. Martin's Press.

Bosse, D., & Porcher, L. (2012). The second glass ceiling impedes women entrepreneurs. *The Journal of Applied Management and Entrepreneurship, 17*(1), 152–68.

Braun, P. (2005) Action research methods: Case study. In S. Marshall, W. Taylor, & X. Yu (Eds), *Encyclopedia of regional communities with information and communication technology* (pp. 1–5), Hershey, PA: Idea Group Reference.

Braun, P. (2007). SME policy development in a global economy: An Australian perspective. In D. Hong (Ed.), *The policy environment for the development of SME.* Taipei: Pacific Economic Cooperation Council. http://trove.nla.gov.au/work/36990864?q&versionId=210668475.

Braun, P. (2014). Cooperative entrepreneurship and ICT: A path for social change. In E. Surjadi (Ed.), *Gender empowerment: For social life and harmonious living* (pp. 553–571). Jakarta: Sriya Harapan Jagra.

Brush, C. (1992). Research on women business owners: Past trends, a new perspective and future directions. *Entrepreneurship Theory and Practice, 16*(4), 5–30.

Brush, C. (1997). Women owned businesses: Obstacles and opportunities. *Journal of Developmental Entrepreneurship, 2*(1), 1–25.

Carter, N., & Allen, K. R. (1997). Size determinants of women-owned businesses: Choice or barriers to resources? *Entrepreneurship and Regional Development, 9*(3), 211–20.

Daly, M. (2005). Gender mainstreaming in theory and practice. *Social Politics: International Studies in Gender, State and Society, 12*(3), 433–450.

Fischer, E., Reuber, R., & Dyke, L. (1993). A theoretical overview and extension of research on sex, gender, and entrepreneurship. *Journal of Business Venturing, 8*(2), 151–168.

GEM (2015). Global Entrepreneurship Monitor Special Report: Women's entrepreneurship 2015. Accessed 08/12/2016 from http://gemconsortium.org/report/49281.

Green, P., Hart, M., Gatewood, E., Brush, C., & Carter, N. (2003). Women entrepreneurs: Moving front and center: An overview of research and theory. Retrieved 10/10/2014 from www.usasbe.org/knowledge/whitepapers/greene2003.pdf.

Gundlach, S., & Sammartino, A. (2013). *Australia's underestimated resource: Women doing business globally.* Women in Global Business and University of Melbourne. Retrieved 09/08/14 from https://www.austrade.gov.au/ArticleDocuments/1414/Australias-underestimated-resource-women-doing-business-globally-exec-summary.pdf.aspx.

Gupta, V., Turban, D., Wasti, S., & Sikdar, A. (2009). The role of gender stereotypes in perceptions of entrepreneurs and intentions to become an entrepreneur. *Entrepreneurship Theory and Practice, 33*(2), 397–417.

International Finance Corporation (2014). Women-owned SME: A business opportunity for financial institutions. International Finance Corporation. https://yali.state.gov/wp-content/uploads/sites/4/2016/03/WomenOwnedSMes+Report-Final.pdf.

Isenberg, D. (2011). The entrepreneurship ecosystem strategy as a new paradigm for economic policy: Principles for cultivating entrepreneurship. The Babson Entrepreneurship Ecosystem Project, Babson College, MA. Retrieved 03/10/15 from http://entrepreneurial-revolution.com/2011/05/11/the-entrepreneurship-ecosystem-strategy-as-a-new-paradigm-for-economic-policy-principles-for-cultivating-entrepreneurship/.

Krause, A. (2015). How can healthier entrepreneurial ecosystems help women succeed? Kaufman Foundation. Retrieved 08/12/2016 from http://www.kauffman.org/blogs/growthology/2015/06/women-entrepreneurs-in-ecosystems.

McClelland, E. (2004). Irish female entrepreneurs: Mapping the route to internationalisation. *Irish Journal of Management, 25*(2), 92–108.

McDonagh, J., & Coghlan, D. (2001). The art of clinical inquiry in information technology-related change. In P. Reason & H. Bradbury (Eds), *Handbook of action research*. London: Sage.

McKay, R. (2001). Women entrepreneurs: Moving beyond family and flexibility. *International Journal of Entrepreneurial Behaviour & Research, 7*(4), 148–65.

McKinsey Global Institute (2015). The power of parity: How advancing women's equality can add $12 trillion to global growth. Retrieved 04/10/15 from http://www.mckinsey.com/insights/growth/how_advancing_womens_equality_can_add_ 12_trillion_to_global_growth?cid=mckwomen-eml-alt-mgi-mck-oth-1509.

Marlow, S. (2002). Women and self-employment: A part of or apart from theoretical construct? *The International Journal of Entrepreneurship and Innovation, 3*(2) 2, 83–91.

Mason, C., & Brown, R. (2014). Entrepreneurial ecosystems and growth-oriented entrepreneurship. Final report to OECD. Paris. Retrieved 10/10/15 from http://www.oecd. org/cfe/leed/Entrepreneurial-ecosystems.pdf.

Mazzarol, T. (2014) *Growing and sustaining entrepreneurial ecosystems: The role of regulation, infrastructure and financing*. White Paper WP02–2014, Small Enterprise Association of Australia and New Zealand (SEAANZ). Retrieved 09/08/14 from www.seaanz.org.

Morgan, P., Baser, H., & Morin, D. (2010). Developing capacity for managing public service reform: The Tanzania experience 200–2008. *Public Administration and Development, 30*, 27–37.

Nelson, G. W (1987). Information needs of female entrepreneurs. *Journal of Small Business Management,* 2(53), 38–54.

Orser, B., Fischer, E., Reuber, R., Hooper, S., & Riding, A. (1999). *Beyond borders: Canadian businesswomen in international trade*. Ottawa: Royal Bank of Canada.

Orser, B., Riding, A., & Townsend, J. (2004). Exporting as a means of growth for women-owned Canadian SME. *Journal of Small Business and Entrepreneurship, 17*(3), 153–174.

Orser, B., Spence, M., Riding, A., & Carrington, C. (2010). Gender and export propensity. *Entrepreneurship Theory and Practice, 34*(5), 933–957.

Prügl, E., & True, J. (2014). Equality means business? Governing gender through transnational public-private partnerships. *Review of International Political Economy, 21*(6), 1137–1169.

Reason, P., & Bradbury, H. (2001). *Handbook of action research*. London: Sage.

Rodrik, D. (2010). Diagnostics before prescription. *Journal of Economic Perspectives, 24*(3), 33–44.

Stam, E. (2014). The Dutch entrepreneurial ecosystem. Retrieved 22/07/15 from http://ssrn.com/abstract=2473475.

Weeks, J. (2001). The face of women entrepreneurs: What we know today. OECD Proceedings, Second OECD Conference on Women Entrepreneurs. In *SME's: Realising the benefits of globalisation and the knowledge based economy* (pp. 127–144). www.oecd.org/industry/smes/1848305.pdf.

World Bank Group (2014). *Supporting growth-oriented women: Entrepreneurs: A review of the evidence and key challenges*. Innovation, Technology & Entrepreneurship Policy Note No. 5. Retrieved 22/07/2015 from www.worldbank.org.

World Bank (2012). *Toward gender equality in East Asia and the Pacific: A companion to the World Development Report*. Washington DC. Retrieved 22/07/2015 from www.worldbank.org.

Appendix A: Questionnaire for Government Officials

Table 7.4 Trade Analysis

Your assistance is requested in completing the below questionnaire. All responses will be treated confidentially and used for research/training purposes only.

Personal Information (please √ all that apply)

Government Official	☐
Entrepreneur	☐
Representative of a business network or group	☐

Policies, Programs and Export Initiatives – please provide details & web links where available

---

What government policies, trade promotion programs/ initiatives are in place in your economy to assist women-led SME to export?

Which have been most successful? Why?

Which have been least successful? Why?

What are the key barriers in your economy preventing women-led SME from exporting?

Generating Best Practices & Real Change – Deliberations prior to attending the workshop

---

How can your economy overcome the barriers that stand in the way of women-led SME exporters?

What are the enablers your economy can leverage to benefit women-led SME exporters?

Appendix B: Questionnaire for Business Representatives

Table 7.5 Trade Analysis

Your assistance is requested in completing the below questionnaire. All responses will be treated confidentially and used for research/training purposes only.

Personal Information (please √ all that apply)

Government Official	☐
Entrepreneur	☐
Representative of a business network or group	☐

Policies, Programs and Export Initiatives – please provide details & web links where available

---

In your opinion, what are the most successful practices in your economy to assist you/women-led SME to export?

Which government departments/trade promotion agencies have you accessed to help you export and what has been your experience with these interactions?

What are the key barriers in your economy preventing you from exporting?

Creating Best Practices & Real Change — Deliberations prior to attending the workshop

---

How can your economy overcome the export barriers that stand in your way?

What are the enablers you can leverage to benefit women-led SME like you?

8 Gender embeddedness in patriarchal contexts undergoing institutional change
Evidence from Nepal[1]

Mirela Xheneti and Shova Thapa Karki

Women have been considered as an important 'untapped source' of economic growth and development (Minniti & Naudé, 2010), making up 40% of the global workforce (Kelley et al., 2015). Yet, their participation is lower than that of men and often in vulnerable forms of employment in the informal economy as a result of the persisting gender gaps in many countries around the globe (ILO, 2015). The informal economy, defined as 'the diversified set of economic activities, enterprises, jobs, and workers that are not regulated or protected by the state' (Chen, 2012), is a feature of both developed and developing countries. The informal economy is, however, very extensive in developing countries, accounting for around 40–60% of their GDPs (Williams et al., 2016). South Asian countries, in particular, have very high percentages of women participating in the informal economy – 62% of labour active women are absorbed by the informal economy compared to 42% of men (ILO, 2015). Generally, women-owned enterprises in developing countries are of smaller scale, with slower growth trajectories than male-run enterprises, less efficient in terms of productivity, less profitable and with women having less control over profits (Kantor, 2005; Bardasi et al., 2011). Self-employed women in South Asia make up 25% of female employment, compared to 56% in the case of men (ILO, 2008).

The high emphasis of entrepreneurship scholarship on individual characteristics of women-owned businesses, however, has failed to acknowledge how these characteristics interact with contextual factors. This interaction would explain the different rates of entrepreneurship across and within countries, and between women and men (Kabeer, 2012; Pathak et al., 2013). Accordingly, scholars have called for gender analysis as more relevant in researching the 'entrepreneurial spaces' inhabited by women (Rouse et al., 2013), and the particular gender-based constraints that continue to impede women's participation in the formal sector, or entrepreneurship more broadly. These gender-based constraints include social norms that emphasize women's household roles, their lower access to education (Ramani et al., 2013; ILO, 2015), or the lack of access to support mechanisms, such as credit or official help (De Bruin et al., 2007; Bardasi et al., 2011).

In this chapter, we take the view that differences in the entrepreneurial behaviour of women can be explained by an exploration of the gendered nature of institutions. We focus on social institutions, such as family, caste, marriage and their interaction with regulatory institutions, in understanding entrepreneurial behaviour amongst women in a developing country context. Consistent with previous research, we define gendered institutions as those that re-enforce different expectations about men and women, through patterns of relations that systematically treat them unequally (Mabsout & Van Staveren, 2010; Pathak et al., 2013). Most research on women entrepreneurs to date comes from Western contexts despite various calls for entrepreneurship research to take into account experiences in diverse contexts (Zahra, 2007; Brush & Cooper, 2012). Thus, this chapter by focusing on how gendered institutions explain entrepreneurial choices in the informal economy in developing contexts contributes towards discussions on the contextual embeddedness of women's entrepreneurship. Empirically, we focus on the case of Nepal that is a patriarchal and highly stratified society whereby, power relations are not equal and the roles, behaviours and expectations for men and women are socially prescribed (ILO, 2015). Yet, Nepal, contrary to other South Asian countries has also the highest percentage of labour force participation for women (ILO, 2015), and has undergone a long process of instability, conflict, as well as institutional change. These features suggest interesting contextual dynamics worth exploring. Further, studies on women enterprise in Nepal are limited; the only exception is the study by Bushell (2008) that explored the various barriers faced by Nepalese women in engaging in entrepreneurial activities.

We draw on two sources of data: (i) policy documents of the Nepalese government; and (ii) empirical data from a qualitative project that was primarily concerned with women's enterprise transitions to the formal economy. The project involved interviews with ninety women in three different regions in Nepal. We use these data sources to illustrate our explorations of the interaction of institutions and women entrepreneurship. We show that the processes of institutional change and the conflicts the country has undergone have affected to a large extent the scope and nature of entrepreneurship for all individuals in the Nepalese society. We also draw particular attention to how several gendered institutions such as caste, marriage, family and the lack of rights over property and education have disproportionally affected women.

In achieving our objectives for this chapter, we start with a general discussion of the institutional environment for entrepreneurship and the nature of gendered institutions in a developing context. We then continue with an overview of the Nepalese economic and political environment that allows us to place into context the discussion of formal and informal institutions affecting the nature and scope for women entrepreneurship in Nepal. We conclude with some theoretical and policy implications.

(Women) Entrepreneurship and the institutional environment

Discussions of entrepreneurship and entrepreneurial behaviour have often centred on institutions (Baumol, 1990), recognizing that the nature and extent of entrepreneurship development and contribution is context dependent, reflecting the institutional development of a country (Boettke and Coyne, 2003; Welter, 2011) and the social structures in which entrepreneurship is embedded (Davidsson, 2003; Baker et al., 2005). Institutions have been defined as a system of rules that provide a framework for human interaction (North, 1990), simultaneously enabling and constraining human behaviour. They consist of formal rules, such as regulations, laws and constitutions, whose aim is to facilitate political or economic exchange, and social rules such as norms of behaviour, conventions and self-imposed codes of conduct (North, 1990). The latter emerge spontaneously through a process of problem-solving. They are embedded in a web of social norms, networks and trust in a society and are mainly enforced informally, as a by-product of ongoing social relationships (Granovetter, 1985; Nee, 1998; Thornton et al., 2011).

A stable political environment and simple and efficient regulatory frameworks are considered as enabling entrepreneurship (Klapper et al., 2006). On the other hand, normative and cognitive institutions – as in the values and norms of a society – influence the desirability and legitimacy attached to entrepreneurship. When regulatory (or formal) institutions are considered as unfair or inefficient, or they clash with the prescriptions of the social institutions, it is the latter, which guide individual behaviour, often legitimising participation in the informal economy (Webb et al., 2014; Welter & Xheneti, 2015). When taking gender into account, both formal and informal institutions may limit women's behaviour more than men's and privilege men as a group to the expense of women (Mabsout & Van Staveren, 2010). Gender-specific formal institutions include the overall constitution ensuring equal opportunities for women and men, as well as more specific formal institutions such as labour market polices, family law or property rights allowing for female ownership of land (Welter & Smallbone, 2008; Pathak et al., 2013). For example, women's lack of rights to property in many developing countries affects their interaction with financial institutions and hence, their inability to get a loan compared to men (Bushell, 2008; Khavul et al., 2009).

Caste and traditions, the value of family and the distribution of roles within it shape the standing of women in the society and the type of economic activities they can participate in. In this respect, it is not surprising that women engage predominantly in informal entrepreneurial activities or home-based activities as a means to sustain their livelihoods and generate income by combining the productive and reproductive roles for wider social benefits (Gough et al., 2003). The family can provide a safe and supportive network through which to launch an entrepreneurial career (de Bruin et al., 2007). However, expectations of women's domestic commitments limit time devoted to business development (Minniti & Naudé, 2010), restricting venture growth and pushing women to remain in the informal sector (Babbitt et al., 2015). Even when women's confidence and ability to manage a business grows, they face significant challenges and exposure to social injustice when attempting to formalise or grow their business (Ntseane, 2004). Thus, taking into account the gendered nature of institutions and most importantly the long-standing and deeply rooted nature of social institutions allows for a better understanding of women's entrepreneurial activities.

The social context in Nepal

Nepal is also a highly patriarchal and caste-based society influenced by Hindu religion, whereby women have a subordinate status. Traditionally, girls in Nepal were excluded from education whereas boys were entitled to good education and other familial privileges (Luitel, 2001; Mahat, 2003). This continues to be the case in many rural and undeveloped areas of Nepal where women are mainly confined to the household and simple agricultural works (Paudel, 2011). The Nepalese government has committed to practising no discrimination on the basis of caste, race, gender and ideology in its constitution of 1990 and the interim constitution of 2007. However, there is still discrimination on legal rights related to family issues (Bushell, 2008). The Gender Inequality Index is 0.489, ranking Nepal 108th out of 155 countries. In Nepal, 29.5% of parliamentary seats are held by women, and 17.7% of adult women have reached at least a secondary level of education compared to 38.2% of their male counterparts.

The caste system, a long-standing feature of the Nepalese society, ranks individuals into four different strata, manifested also in the different occupations of each of these groups. The Brahmin and Chettri upper-castes, for example, take up privileged positions requiring higher educational levels and qualifications (Karki et al., 2012). Although each caste inherits a position in the division of labour in the society, the lower caste people are shifting away from their inherited roles (Aoki & Pradhan, 2013; Subedi, 2014). Only 10 to 20 % of the population follows their caste-based occupations (Aoki & Pradhan, 2013). The country's economic, political and social development has affected people's attitudes about the caste system. Traditional cultural norms of the caste system are slowly disappearing both, in the urban and rural areas (Subedi, 2011) particularly so, during and after the Maoist conflict in Nepal. The latter advocated against any kind of discrimination on the basis of caste and gender (Nightingale, 2011). However, the differences in the level of resources such as knowledge, skills and capital are still visible amongst the different caste groups, negatively affecting individuals' socio-economic situation and their participation in governance (Villanger, 2012). It is this particular environment that has contributed to the features of entrepreneurship and gender relations we discuss in this chapter.

The formal institutional environment for (women) entrepreneurship development in Nepal

The contribution of entrepreneurship to employment generation, poverty alleviation and overall development has been recognized by the Nepalese government in several long term strategies and policies. Starting with the Ninth Development Plan (1997–2002) the Micro-Enterprise Development Program (MEDEP) was launched in 1998 supported by the UNDP, with the aim to alleviate poverty through the support of micro-enterprises (UDDP/GoN, 2013). The fourth phase of the MEDEP programme continues as part of the current Thirteen Development Plan of Nepal (2013–2018) with a focus on increasing the level of knowledge and skills of entrepreneurs, in line with the demands of national and international labour markets.[2] It also targets people living below the poverty line, disadvantaged women (divorced, women-headed households), disadvantaged caste groups, and disabled persons. The Industrial Policy of 2010 also prioritized the creation of an enabling environment for small-sized enterprises, especially by waiving various taxes (MoI, 2010). The Industrial Policy has also made special provisions to promote women's entrepreneurship, offering priority to venture capital funding, 35% reduction in the registration fee, 20% deduction in the registration of patents, designs and trademarks, and inclusion of women entrepreneurs in trade fairs and trainings.

The neo-liberal agenda and the promotion of micro-enterprises were also accompanied by the introduction of microcredit development banks, saving and credit cooperatives and financial NGOs. A total of thirty-four microcredit development banks, sixteen saving and credit cooperatives and thirty financial NGOs operate in Nepal, licensed and regulated by the central bank – Nepal Rastra Bank (MFDBs). Despite the exponential growth of the financial institutions (FIs), the credit market has not expanded and most financial services are limited to the urban areas (Ferrari, 2007). More than half of the country's households rely on informal financial access (Collinson et al., 2013). Larger financial institutions in Nepal have complex and time consuming loan procedures, which require collateral such as land and buildings. However, in almost 80% of the Nepalese households, women do not own any property (i.e. house or land) and when they do so the likelihood is that they reside in an urban area (CBS, 2012). This continues to be the case despite provisions made to reduce gender discrimination by furthering the rights of women to parental property and land. The National Code of 1963, which stated that the son is the only heir to the property, unless a daughter is unmarried and is over 35 years old, seems to prevail (Collinson et al., 2013).

Several governmental and non-governmental actors support women entrepreneurship in Nepal but they lack coordination and clear cut policies, inadequate financial and human resources, and poor implementation (Bhadra & Shah, 2007). Often those who participate in these programmes are privileged women from wealthier and more educated backgrounds rather than those who are actually the policy target – the resource-poor lower castes such as Dalit women (Bhadra & Shah, 2007). We turn now to discuss the social institutional environment and how it interacts with the formal institutional provisions and women's entrepreneurial behaviour.

Gendered institutions and women's entrepreneurship – Empirical evidence

In this section through our empirical evidence, we set out why the policy measures discussed above are not effective in promoting entrepreneurship amongst women. As institutional approaches suggest, countries' efforts to establish formal institutional infrastructures supportive of entrepreneurship can only be successful, if the values, attitudes, perceptions and behaviours of individuals change to accommodate these institutions. In other words, social institutions related to gender and entrepreneurship, including family, marriage, caste – should be also changing to accommodate the formal institutional changes. Economic circumstances such as migration mediate some of the effects of informal institutions.

The profile of women engaged in entrepreneurial activities

Unsurprisingly, most women interviewed for our study were engaged in services (41%) followed by trade (33%), handicrafts (13%), food processing (7%) and agri-business (6%), with half of the sample having been in operation for over five years. Services comprised activities such as tailoring, hairdressing or catering. Women engaged in trade were mainly involved in retail trade in activities such as grocery, cosmetics or clothing shops, which were often home-based or in nearby home locations. A good proportion of the sample was also involved in handicrafts using traditional skills women could utilize. Half of the sample was between 31 and 40 years old, of higher secondary education (up to ten years of schooling), married and with school-age children. As marriage is highly customary it was not surprising that our sample had only five single women. Additionally, three women were divorced and three widowed. Most women belonged to the higher castes of Brahmin and Chettri. Interestingly, and reflecting the high internal migration rates in the country, most women (and their households) were migrants to the regions where fieldwork was conducted.

Family

The family is one of the most influential social institutions as it can be a vital enabling source of general support, free labour, access to networks and financial support. The support from the family is essential also because women in developing countries lack formal education, which acts as a key barrier to their economic participation (Kantor, 2005). Families, however, also institutionalize social, religious and cultural norms especially in relation to expectations about women's behaviour (ILO, 2009). Our data allowed us to explore how family influences played an important role in women's choices of business activities directly through business inheritance or indirectly, by providing exposure to, or familiarity with, a particular line of business. This exposure and familiarity indirectly equipped women with unpaid skills and training, facilitating a comparatively low-cost start-up process. Unsurprisingly, the family's influence on business choices was also related to women's limited access to formal education, training or any other skills. Women, thus, were not only inclined to engage in activities they had been exposed to in their parental family or family in-law, but very often their decisions with respect to their business were directly influenced by family members (see Box 1).

Box 1   Business start–up and expansion decisions

Biratnagar 3.3.1 owns a hotel for just over a year. She opened it after discussing with her husband, who is currently working abroad. Her main reason for the choice of this business was the familiarity and exposure to this line of business. She had helped her sister, who owned a hotel business. She receives help from her father with looking after the kids. Being happy with her business, she would like to extend it but she is constrained by being on her own. As she states: *it is difficult to run the business alone as my husband is not here.*

Her choice of extending the business is also constrained by her husband's preferences for using one's internal sources of funding rather than loans. Her husband also dictates whether she can get involved in women support organisations.

These family dynamics, not unique to Biratnagar 3.3.1's case, have clear implications for business development and sustainability, as well as women's confidence and autonomy. (Biratnagar 3.3.1, 30 years old, with secondary education and married with young children)

As most women followed in their families' footsteps, they benefited from the access to networks of business partners, suppliers and customers, which the family had accumulated over time. Family networks acted as gateways and links to other broader social networks, enabling business development, as well as posing barriers. In subsistence markets, in which most women working informally engage, consumers and entrepreneurs play multifaceted and often overlapping roles (Viswanathan et al., 2010). Family networks are an essential part of these markets' structure. Families' own business history, or a current business venture within the extended family, were often the key to activating networks with suppliers. For example, family members running a similar business acted as the supplier of the business. Family-enabled networks, whilst provided access to end consumers, very often acted as consumers themselves (Box 2). This was particularly the case with food products that lacked the certification to be legally sold without incurring penalties in formal markets. These indirect relationships with markets, customers and suppliers also subverted the potential to develop personal networks that would enable women to be more responsive to market demands and changes (see also Kantor, 2005).

Box 2 Family-enabled networks

For Biratnagar 3.2.1, family links provide part of the market for her pickled products, which she has been trading for over five years. She points out that difficulties in the institutional infrastructure hinder her business development making the reliance on family networks even more important:

My husband had a job in an insurance company but the income was low. So, we decided to make pickles as we had our own lemon farm. One brother [neighbour/ family friend], who had studied a Bachelor in Food Technology helped us a lot while establishing the business. Now we are trying to acquire more funds for the expansion of the business . . . I supply pickles in my father's, niece's, cousins' and other distant relatives' houses, shops and offices (Sanima bank staff, school staff) . . . We can increase the production if there are no problems with electricity and transportation. (Biratnagar 3.2.1, 35 years old, university educated, married with two children)

Despite limiting the ability of women to develop their own networks and access to markets, families also influenced women's businesses through expectations about household roles. Thus, women's struggles to ensure their livelihoods related also to balancing household responsibilities with their business activities. For many women, the default option was to operate businesses from home, prioritizing household duties to their business activities. They dedicated less time to their business activities, often at the expense of losing customers to their competitors, or to expanding their business activities. Where the household environment was more supportive with childcare, women made better choices in relation to their business activities, such as locating outside the home location or increasing their goods/services' range (Box 3).

Box 3 Benefits of outside home location

Biratnagar 3.1.1 runs a tailoring business for six years. Having not faced family constraints in terms of business location, she reported the benefits of outside-home business location for providing visibility and therefore, increased customer base, increased confidence and business growth prospects. She clearly illustrates a combination of relevant skills and family assistance in the success and growth of her business.

At home, I had a limited number of customers, mainly neighbours, relatives and friends. As this shop is located in the main street, people from this and the surrounding areas know my tailoring shop. I have now more customers than before. Due to the central location, the business can be easily fostered here, with good prospects for growth. (Biratnagar, 3.1.1, 28 years old, with secondary level education, married with young children)

Thus, there appears to be a link between family history and entrepreneurial choices (Giannetti and Simonov, 2004), with families helping women to overcome limitations concerning formal education and skills by enabling access to networks. Families also limited market access and constrained opportunities for business expansion, through reproducing expectations of female roles as carers and mothers (Bardasi et al., 2011).

Marriage, property rights and access to finance

The central role the family played also highlighted women's subordinate status in the Nepalese society. Despite provisions made by law, women's lack of property rights made marriage the only way through which they could access economic resources. Women, as a result, were heavily dependent on their husbands and families-in-law more generally, for their livelihoods. Even when they owned land as collateral, they needed to ask their husbands for a guarantee and the bank would only disburse the loan following the husband's approval (see also Bushell, 2008). Whilst married women could negotiate the constraints of these social institutions, those not conforming to this norm, such as being single or divorced women, not fitting the norm, faced problems in gaining access to funding from financial institutions (Box 4).

Box 4   Access to finance

Kathmandu 1.2.5 is a divorced woman. After leaving her husband she moved to Kathmandu with one of her sons and opened the parlour in order to earn a living for her and her son. She moved to Kathmandu because her relatives already residing there could help her start a new life. They found a business space for her and helped with the furniture. Her father and brother helped with start-up funding. Having run this business for six years, she has dealt with many societal constraints related to her single woman status. As she states:

I am a single woman. Many people say I have laboured a lot for my living. But there are some people that disparage me and don't trust me as I am alone. They didn't trust me when I wanted to get involved in a group or asked for loans from the cooperatives. They asked me about my husband all the time. When they asked: 'Where is your husband?' I always questioned them: 'Why can't a single woman get a loan?' After I raised many issues, they accepted me in the group and also gave me a loan.

She believes her experience underlines a much wider societal attitude towards single women, coupled with the government's lack of provision for single women or divorcees, and the lack of low interest-rate loans for women entrepreneurs. (Kathmandu 1.2.5, 32 years old, university educated, divorced)

The high emphasis on women's easier access to credit in the developing countries often ignores how the provisions made by law or policy to support them are hindered by social expectations about women in the society, which jeopardize the impact of these policies.

Caste and social acceptance

Another long-standing social institution with implications for the nature of entrepreneurial activities run by women is caste. Women's entrepreneurial choices did not reflect caste-related labour division indicating the changes in the Nepalese society in the last twenty to thirty years. However, caste-related attitudes did affect the way respondents perceived the significance of their activities in the society, and their interaction with partners, family or business customers. For example, tailoring (or Damai) has been usually associated with work done by lower caste people. Involvement in this type of activity still positions individuals, independently of their caste, in the lower caste group. In turn, this influences their family and social standing. Getting involved in activities associated with different castes to their own was not an issue for a number of respondents, reflecting a change in attitudes in the society. Pokhara 2.1.5, for example, stated that: '. . . time is different now. This work doesn't belong to any caste. There is no shame in working and earning one's living. People of every caste can do tailoring'. For others, it took time to get accustomed to being associated with a different, often lower caste than their own (Box 5).

Box 5   Caste influences

Pokhara 2.2.3 is a tailor. Having lived in an extended family for many years and having not completed secondary education, she lacked the confidence to justify to her family in-law work outside the house. When her sister-in-law received formal education, she felt it was time for her to get some training. Her lack of formal qualifications constrained her choice of training to tailoring, for which she was hesitant at first because of the low caste association. She opened her own tailoring business and she recalls that it takes time for people to overcome the constraints related to caste and take ownership of one's chosen business activity:

But at first I felt ashamed of tailoring. I used to stay inside [the shop] for a whole year. When I went out, I felt like everyone noticed me . . . nowadays, I don't. My [current business] partner used to tell me: 'Why do you feel like that? I am also Brahmin. Is this work only for Damai?' Now my relatives enter my shop. I don't feel shame now; it is my profession . . . I learned that a woman could do business even when times are not favourable. The main thing is courage. (Pokhara 2.2.3, 50 years old, married with grown-up children)

The range of social institutions such as caste and marriage continue to ascribe certain roles and positions to women that hinder their access to good business opportunities. Yet again, formal institutional provisions for eliminating caste discrimination are in conflict with how people make caste-based associations. In our study, the categories of caste and marriage, together with women's low access to resources and education position this group of women in the informal sector. These place a double burden on them and indicate how the effects of the conflicts between formal and informal institutional provisions are disproportionally experienced by women.

Economic circumstances – Migration

Family, marriage or caste categories and the roles they prescribed to women were also mediated by the economic circumstances of women and the need to ensure an urgent livelihood for their families in the informal sector. The Maoist conflict (1996–2006) by displacing males from the rural areas (Menon & Rodgers, 2011), pushed women to work for ensuring their livelihoods not only in agricultural activities left behind by male migration but also in other types of (informal) work in urban areas. Narratives of migration revealed a number of enabling / constraining factors for households that migrated internally or for women 'loosing' a household member to international migration. International migration of a family member provided the needed capital for women to start up a business activity and often an increased decision-making power in relation to income spending and children's education (Box 6).

Box 6   Rural–urban migration

Following the decision of her household to migrate to the capital in order to ensure the education of her children, Kathmandu 1.3.2, who runs a grocery shop for four years stated:

I brought my children to Kathmandu to provide them with better education. The boarding schools in the village were all demolished by the Maoists. My husband had returned from abroad. We knew the money would finish soon. We had to do something for our livelihood and to run the family. We had no contacts or networks to help us with finding a job. We couldn't work in a hotel. So, we decided to start this grocery shop . . . We managed the start-up fund as we had some savings. The remaining amount was provided by my in-laws. So, we didn't have to ask for a loan . . . We had no prior experience in the field, neither received any training. (Kathmandu 1.3.2, 32 years old, secondary education, married with young children)

This woman's experience captured various dynamics affecting her choice of entrepreneurial activity, common to many households in that position. On the one hand, international migration provided the seed funding for many to start up business activities. On the other hand, this simple passage also shows the extent of family and business overlap in the collective effort of many families to sustain their living and also to ensure their children's education. These dynamics have implications for how households affected by migration become more dependent on women, who as a result, take a more active role in household decision-making. As illustrated elsewhere (Maharjan et al., 2012), this increases women's social status as a result of their strengthened household position. The strengthened household position goes hand in hand with the increased ability of women to integrate into their communities and markets given their limited access to extended family and other forms of social capital.

Conclusions

The potential of women's entrepreneurship for economic and social development is well recognized in the literature (i.e., Minniti & Naudé, 2010). Women, however, also 'fail' to fulfil this potential due to a number of gender-based constraints. Country-based studies frequently report the gendered nature of institutions that continue to affect how women engage in economic activities (Pathak et al., 2013). Yet, scholars also recognize the need for nuanced understandings of how gendered institutions are experienced and negotiated in these diverse contexts. Our aim in this chapter was to analyse the institutional environment for women's entrepreneurship in Nepal, a country that has received little attention in entrepreneurship studies. Years of conflict, migration and continuous regulatory changes have affected the scope for entrepreneurship within all groups of the population. By placing particular attention on a range of gendered institutions such as rights to education, property, caste, marriage and family, we showed how they are 'implicated' in women's experiences of entrepreneurship. As other studies also indicate, women's lack of education or skills as a result of their subordinate status in the society or their conformance with gender norms expecting women to attend to household duties affected to a large extent the type of activities they get involved in; often small, operated from home and in the case of Nepal, in sectors where there is family history. Interestingly, family despite its constraining influence on women's education, ownership of property or mobility also enabled them through access to finance and networks.

As importantly, we showed how despite the provisions made in the formal institutional environment for no caste or gender discrimination, these social institutions have long lasting effects in prescribing the behaviour and attitudes of individuals in the society. Although our chapter is structural in its approach by focusing primarily on the effects of institutions, we also showed how under some circumstances women were able to mitigate the negative influences of gendered institutions. These, for example, included internal migration as a clear case where women were less dependent on their families, or less concerned with social legitimacy, for making decisions with respect to their entrepreneurial activities and household decision-making.

This supports views that the nature of entrepreneurial activities is closely linked to the changing interplay of formal and informal institutions and the economic development of various contexts (Welter & Xheneti, 2015). Thus, it is important for (women) entrepreneurship to be studied in its formal and social institutional context, recognizing their dynamic nature over time. As such, our chapter contributes towards the increasing need for accounts of women entrepreneurship that emphasize the embeddedness of gender (Brush et al., 2009) instead of simplistic male-female binaries (Jennings & Brush, 2013). By highlighting the gendered nature of institutions and their effects on the nature of activities women are involved in, our chapter has implications about women's decisions to operate informally and stay small, suggesting the centrality of social expectation rationales rather than economic (functional) ones. The contextual and gendered nature of institutions, as well as the appeal and constraints of the informal sector for women cannot, thus, be overlooked in academic and policy discussions.

Notes

1 The empirical data collection was supported by the Centre for Economic Policy Research and the Department for International Development, UK within their Private Sector Development Scheme, Exploratory Research Grant No 2533. We thank the three Research Assistants, who supported the data collection process in Nepal.
2 https://dfat.gov.au/about-us/publications/Documents/nepal-medep-phase-iv-project-document.pdf (Accessed on 15.08.2015).

References

Aoki, C., & Pradhan, P. K. (2013). Impact of microfinance services on socio-economic empowerment of the women's group in Nepal. In P. K. Pradhan, J. Buček, & E. Razin (Eds), *Geography of governance: Dynamics for local development* (pp. 1–10). Bratislava: International Geographical Union Commission on Geography of Governance.

Babbitt, L. G., Brown, D., & Mazaheri, N. (2015). Gender, entrepreneurship, & the formal-informal dilemma: Evidence from Indonesia. *World Development, 72*, 163–174.

Baker, T., Gedajlovic, E., & Lubatkin, M. (2005). A framework for comparing entrepreneurship across nations. *Journal of International Business Studies, 36*(5), 492–504.

Bardasi, E., Sabarwal, S., & Terrell, K. (2011). How do female entrepreneurs perform? Evidence from three developing regions. *Small Business Economics, 37*(4), 417–441.

Baumol, W. J. (1990). Entrepreneurship: productive, unproductive & destructive. *Journal of Political Economy, 98*(5), 893–921.

Bhadra, C., & Shah, M. T. (2007). *Nepal: Country gender profile.* Kathmandu, Nepal: Japan International Cooperation Agency.

Boettke, P. J., & Coyne, C. J. (2003). Entrepreneurship & development: Cause or consequence? *Advances in Austrian Economics, 6*, 67–87.

Brush, C. G., & Cooper, S. Y. (2012). Female entrepreneurship & economic development: An international perspective. *Entrepreneurship & Regional Development, 24*(1–2), 1–6.

Brush, C. G., De Bruin, A., & Welter, F. (2009). A gender-aware framework for women's entrepreneurship. *International Journal of Gender & Entrepreneurship, 1*(1), 8–24.

Bushell, B. (2008). Women entrepreneurs in Nepal: What prevents them from leading the sector? *Gender & Development, 16*(3), 549–564.

CBS (2012). *National population & housing census 2011.* Kathmandu, Nepal: Central Bureau of Statistics, National Planning Commission Secretariat, Government of Nepal.

Chen, M. A. (2012). *The informal economy: Definitions, theories and policies.* Women in informal economy globalizing and organizing. WIEGO Working Paper 1. WEIGO.

Collinson, E., et al. (2013). *Growing potential: An analysis of legal & policy barriers faced by women in horticulture in Guatemala, Nepal, Tanzania, & Zambia.* Humphrey School of Public Affairs. Retrieved from the University of Minnesota Digital Conservancy, http://hdl.handle.net/11299/149584.

Davidsson, P. (2003). The domain of entrepreneurship research: Some suggestions. In J. Katz & D. Shepherd (Eds), *Advances in entrepreneurship, firm emergence & growth* (pp. 315–372). Oxford: Elsevier.

De Bruin, A., Brush, C. G., & Welter, F. (2007). Advancing a framework for coherent research on women's entrepreneurship. *Entrepreneurship Theory & Practice, 31*(3), 323–39.

Department of Cooperatives (DoC) (2016). *Statistics of cooperative enterprises, 2015.* Nepal: Department of Cooperatives (DoC), Ministry of Cooperatives & Poverty Alleviation, Government of Nepal.

Ferrari, A. (2007). *Access to financial services in Nepal.* Washington DC: World Bank Publications.

Giannetti, M., & Simonov, A. (2004). On the determinants of entrepreneurial activity: Social norms, economic environment & individual characteristics. *Swedish Economic Policy Review, 11*(2), 269–313.

Gough, K. V., Tipple, A. G., & Napier, M. (2003). Making a living in African cities: The role of home-based enterprises in Accra & Pretoria. *International Planning Studies, 8*(4), 253–78.

Granovetter, M. (1985). Economic action and social structure: The problem of embeddedness. *The American Journal of Sociology, 91*(3), 481–510.

IFC (2011). *Strengthening access to finance for women-owned SMEs in developing countries.* Washington, DC: International Financial Cooperation.

ILO (2008). *Global employment trends.* Geneva: International Labour Organisation.

ILO (2009). *The informal economy in Africa: Promoting transition to formality: Challenges & Strategies.* Geneva: International Labour Organisation.

ILO (2015). *World employment & social outlook: Trends 2015.* Geneva: International Labour Organisation.

Jennings, J. E., & Brush, C. G. (2013). Research on women entrepreneurs: Challenges to (& from) the broader entrepreneurship literature? *The Academy of Management Annals, 7*(1), 663–715.

Kabeer, N. (2012). *Women's economic empowerment & inclusive growth: Labour markets & enterprise development.* SIG working paper 2012/1. London: International Development Research Centre.

Kantor, P. (2005). Determinants of women's microenterprise success in Ahmedabad, India: Empowerment & economics. *Feminist Economics, 11*(3), 63–83.

Karki, L., Schleenbecker, R., & Hamm, U. (2012). Factors influencing a conversion to organic farming in Nepalese tea farms. *Journal of Agriculture & Rural Development in the Tropics & Subtropics (JARTS), 112*(2), 113–123.

Kelley, D., et al. (2015). *GEM special report women's entrepreneurship.* Boston, MA: The Centre for Women's Leadership, Babson College.

Khavul, S., Bruton, G. D., & Wood, E. (2009). Informal family business in Africa. *Entrepreneurship Theory & Practice, 33*(6), 1219–38.

Klapper, L., Laeven, L., & Rajan, R. (2006). Entry regulation as a barrier to entrepreneurship. *Journal of Financial Economics, 82*(3), 591–629.

Luitel, S. (2001). The social world of Nepalese women. *Occasional Papers in Sociology & Anthropology, 7*, 101–114.

Mabsout, R., & Van Staveren, I. (2010). Disentangling bargaining power from individual & household level to institutions: Evidence on women's position in Ethiopia. *World Development, 38*(5), 783–96.

Maharjan, A., Bauer, S., & Knerr, B. (2012). Do rural women who stay behind benefit from male out-migration? A case study in the hills of Nepal. *Gender, Technology & Development, 16*(1), 95–123.

Mahat, I. (2003). Women's development in Nepal: The myth of empowerment'. *PRAXIS The Fletcher Journal of International Development, 18*, 67–72.

Menon, N., & Van der Meulen Rodgers, Y. (2015). War & women's work: Evidence from the conflict in Nepal. *Journal of Conflict Resolution, 59*(1), 51–73.

Minniti, M., & Naudé, W. (2010). Introduction: What do we know about the patterns & determinants of female entrepreneurship across countries? *European Journal of Development Research, 22*(3), 277–93.

Ministry of Industry (MoI) (2010). *Government of Nepal: Industrial policy 2010*. Kathmandu, Nepal: Ministry of Industry.

Nee, V. (1998). Norms and networks in economic & organizational performance. *American Economic Review, 88*(2), 85–89.

Nightingale, A. J. (2011). Bounding difference: Intersectionality & the material production of gender, caste, class & environment in Nepal. *Geoforum, 42*(2), 153–62.

North, D.C. (1990). *Institutions, Institutional Change & Economic Performance*. Cambridge: Cambridge University Press.

Ntseane, P. (2004). Being a female entrepreneur in Botswana: Cultures, values, strategies for success. *Gender & Development, 12*(2), 37–43.

Pathak, S., Goltz, S., & W. Buche, M. (2013). Influences of gendered institutions on women's entry into entrepreneurship. *International Journal of Entrepreneurial Behaviour & Research, 19*(5), 478–502.

Paudel, S. (2011). Women's concerns within Nepal's patriarchal justice system. *Ethics in Action, 5*(6), 30–36.

Ramani, S. V., et al. (2013). *Women in the informal economy: Experiments in governance from emerging countries*. Maastricht, Netherlands: United Nations University – Maastricht Economic & Social Research Institute on Innovation & Technology (UNU-MERIT).

Rouse, J., et al. (2013). The gendering of entrepreneurship: Theoretical & empirical insights. *International Journal of Entrepreneurial Behaviour & Research, 19*(5), 452–459.

Subedi, M. (2011). Caste system: Theories & practices in Nepal. *Himalayan Journal of Sociology & Anthropology, 4*, 134–159.

Subedi, M. (2014). Some theoretical considerations on caste. *Dhaulagiri Journal of Sociology & Anthropology, 7*, 51–86.

Thornton, P. H., Ribeiro-Soriano, D., & Urbano, D. (2011). Socio-cultural factors & entrepreneurial activity: An overview. *International Small Business Journal, 29*(2), 105–118.

UNDP/GoN (2013). Micro Enterprise Development Programme (MEDEP IV) Project Document. Kathmandu, Nepal: United Nations Development Program (UNDP) & Government of Nepal (GoN).

Villanger, E. (2012). *Caste discrimination & barriers to microenterprise growth in Nepal*. CMI Working Paper 9. Bergen, Norway: Chr. Michelsen Institute.

Viswanathan, M., Echambadi, R., Venugopal, S., & Sridharan, S. (2014). Subsistence entrepreneurship, value creation & community exchange systems: A social capital explanation. *Journal of Macromarketing, 34*(2), 213–226.

Webb, J. W., Ireland, R. D., & Ketchen, D. J. (2014). Toward a greater understanding of entrepreneurship & strategy in the informal economy. *Strategic Entrepreneurship Journal, 8*(1), 1–15.

Welter, F. (2011). Contextualizing entrepreneurship: Conceptual challenges & ways forward. *Entrepreneurship Theory & Practice, 35*(1), 165–4.

Welter, F. & Smallbone, D. (2008). Women's entrepreneurship from an institutional perspective: The case of Uzbekistan. *International Entrepreneurship & Management Journal, 4*(4), 505–520.

Welter, F., & Xheneti, M. (2015). Value for whom? Exploring the value of informal entrepreneurial activities in post-socialist contexts. In G. McElwee & R. Smith (Eds), *Exploring criminal & illegal enterprise: New perspectives on research* (pp. 253–275). Bingley, UK: Emerald Publishing Group.

Williams, C. C., Martinez-Perez, A., & Kedir, A.M. (2017). Informal entrepreneurship in developing economies: The impacts of starting up unregistered on firm performance. *Entrepreneurship Theory and Practice, 41*(5), 773–799.

Zahra, S. A. (2007). Contextualizing theory building in entrepreneurship research. *Journal of Business Venturing, 22*(3), 443–452.

9 Opportunity creation for female entrepreneurs in the Welsh and Turkish entrepreneurial ecosystem

A social capital perspective

Shandana Sheikh, Aybeniz Akdeniz, Federica Sist, Shumaila Yousafzai and Saadat Saeed

While women entrepreneurship (WE) is identified as the 'way forward' (World Economic Forum, 2012), the discourse on the *'underperformance'* of women enterprises compared to their male counterparts still holds (Ahl, 2006; Marlow et al., 2008; Eddleston & Powell, 2008). Much of this debate results from the adopting a narrow approach to studying WE, one that focuses only on individual factors and disregards the impact of macro-level factors on WE, thus ignoring the factors that affect women performance. Such tendency is even more common in case of small-scale women entrepreneurs, those who may start a business from home or remain small due to resource constraints or personal preferences. Due to their size and visibility, small-scale women entrepreneurs are tainted with hues of underperformance, although these women may be creating several opportunities in their business. Considering the dangers of an individual level approach to study WE and the lack of contextual orientation within it, scholars have highlighted the need to move towards a contextually embedded approach to study WE, its antecedents, processes and outcomes (Zahra et al., 2014; Welter, 2011; Autio et al. 2014). It is crucial to recognize the embeddedness of WE activity in their entrepreneurial ecosystem (EE) (Isenberg, 2011); a set of interrelated factors (human capital, finance, markets, social support, policy and culture) that individually or interactively impact the performance and success of women-owned businesses. Past research documents that women entrepreneurs face several constraints within their entrepreneurial environment including gender based discrimination, financial, socio-cultural and institutional constraints that hinder their ability to perform well in business. Thus, analysing WE from a broader, multi-level approach, may help to understand that women entrepreneurs do not 'underperform' but are instead 'constrained' in their performance (Marlow et al. 2013; Van de Ven, 1993; Spilling, 1996).

Acknowledging the constrained performance of women in entrepreneurship and in line with the contextual embedded approach, we contend that although women face considerable challenges from their entrepreneurial environment or EE, their social networks (formal and informal) may enable them to be successful in their business and create opportunities within it. Our objective in this study is to identify the perceived weaknesses among the Welsh and the Turkish entrepreneurial ecosystem, thus highlighting the different elements that impact WE in each ecosystem. Additionally, we study how social capital (SC), primarily formal and informal social networks enable Welsh and Turkish women entrepreneurs to create opportunities in their business, despite of the weaknesses of their respective ecosystem. Based on the creation theory of entrepreneurial action, we focus on opportunity creation which seeks to explain the actions that entrepreneurs take to create and exploit opportunities (Venkataraman, 2003; Shane & Venkataraman, 2000, p. 211; Alvarez & Barney, 2007). In exploring the role of SC in opportunity creation, we focus on the relational, structural and cognitive embeddedness of SC and explain how these impact opportunity creation of women.

We incorporate six cases of women-owned enterprises, three each from Wales and Turkey and explore the extent to which SC enables women entrepreneurs to create opportunities in their business. Our findings suggest that while both Welsh and Turkish women entrepreneurs have different perceptions about their entrepreneurial ecosystem and its individual components, they create opportunities in their business utilizing their SC. Specifically, we find that women utilize both formal and informal SC to create opportunities in multiple contexts including *business, financial, human capital and social context*. Our findings also suggest that while all dimensions of SC (structural, relational and cognitive) affect the extent of opportunity creation in women businesses, cognitive SC restricts opportunity creation among women and thus impacts their business performance.

Women entrepreneurship in Wales and Turkey

Small business activity is a vital source of economic and social contribution in an economy. For the Welsh economy, small businesses are a backbone to the economy, accounting for 99% of all businesses in Wales (Kelsey 2015). However, despite of the importance of small businesses, the number of businesses, specifically those owned by women are low (Thomas, 2015). Recent Global Entrepreneurship Monitor (GEM) figures suggest that only 4.2% of working age women are engaged in setting up a business while 3.1% expect to do so in future years (GEM, 2013). Moreover, women businesses have a higher exit and failure rate as compared to men wherein most women tend to exit from entrepreneurship due to personal reasons or business failure itself. Major factors leading to lower WE rates in Wales include less positive attitudes of women towards starting a business compared to men (30% vs 38%) (Federation of Small Businesses, 2016), lack of support in case of failure (Meechan, 2013) lack of role models (Thomas, 2015), constrained access to funding and finance (Verhuel & Thurik, 2001), primarily due to the small-scale nature of women businesses (Carter & Rosa, 1998) and gender discrimination against them. Beyond financial constraints, women are under-represented on the government board of the Welsh enterprise zones and thus are less often viewed in the capacity of leadership positions, resulting in limited success stories and role models for prospective women who aspire to start a business.

In Turkey, gender gap in entrepreneurship is high with only 7.4% of all businesses being owned by women (Okten, 2013). Women-led enterprises in Turkey are concentrated in sectors that are low-profit generating including financial services, education and social services (Okten, 2013; Singh et al., 2001). Prominent factors that account for the lower WE rate in Turkey include fear of failure (41% for women versus 33% for men), access to finance (Ince, 2012; Okten, 2013), higher tax rates, malpractices of informal competitors, corruption and tax administration (37% for men and 38% for women), political instability (17% for women) perceived capability of starting a business (35% for women versus 53% for men). Moreover, the underlying social and cultural norms, gender-biased policies and regulations including lack of child-care provision and other support services for women (Cebeci & Essmat, 2015:30) deter women from achieving their entrepreneurial goals in Turkish EE.

Considering the challenges of their respective entrepreneurial ecosystems, Welsh and Turkish, efforts at the government level have been initiated to encourage and increase women entrepreneurial intentions, create employment and generate economic and social value through WE in Welsh and Turkish economies (Ecevit, 2007 Meechan, 2013).

Social capital and women entrepreneurship

SC is a significant contributor to knowledge production, research exchange, research and development processes and education (Westlund, 2006) and thus is considered a key driver of entrepreneurship (Doh & Zolnik, 2011). Although various definitions of SC are present in literature, our research builds upon Coleman's (1990) definition which refers to SC as 'an attribute of the social structure in which a person is embedded' and it is not 'the private property of any of the persons who benefit from it'. Thus, we consider the individual SC which arises because of an entrepreneur's personal and professional network relationships.

Female entrepreneurs face considerable constraints with regards to participation in formal SC for example business associations, societies and chambers of business leaders and thus may not have the opportunity to benefit from the essential skills and expertise that members of professional networks (Klyver & Terjesen 2007; Kumra & Vinnicombe 2010). Consequently, they tend to rely on informal SC including industry networks such as current or past customers, suppliers and employees of financial institutions and family and friends. Such informal networks may provide them with access to information and enable them to identify and exploit opportunities (Johannisson, 2000) and thus are a significant source of SC for female entrepreneurs (McGowan et al., 2015; Neergaard et al., 2005).

Social capital and opportunity creation

Entrepreneurship is the process of 'by whom', 'how', and 'what' affects opportunities to create future good and services are discovered, evaluated and exploited (Shane & Venkataraman, 2000). Entrepreneurs interact with various elements of their entrepreneurial environment and socially construct the opportunities for their businesses (Alvarez & Barney, 2007). This reflects the exogenous nature of opportunities suggesting that opportunities do not pre-exist in the market or industry but instead are created by entrepreneurs by utilizing the available resources in their entrepreneurial environment (Gartner, 1985; Sarasvathy, 2001; Berger & Luckmann, 1967). It also suggests that different entrepreneurs create different opportunities which differ in context, number as well as their impact on business. Previous scholars have discussed several factors that significantly affect opportunity recognition including knowledge stocks or behaviours of entrepreneurs (Shepherd and DeTienne (2005), entrepreneurial alertness (Gaglio & Kataz, 2001) and Human and SC (Ramos-Rodríguez et al. 2010; Alvarez & Busenitz, 2001), entrepreneurial environment (Tang, 2010; Casson & Wadeson, 2007).

Considering the dynamic entrepreneurial environment of entrepreneurs, opportunity creation is facilitated by social networks of entrepreneurs that help them to access scarce resources from their environment and create opportunities (Fuentes et al. 2010). For example, entrepreneurs may utilize their social networks to build human capital, thus creating more opportunities for their business (Alvarez & Barney, 2007). Additionally, social networks also increase the cognitive skills of entrepreneurs thus enabling them to create and exploit more opportunities (Baron, 2006). Of course, the extent of opportunity creation and exploitation depends upon the strength of ties in an entrepreneur's network, wherein weak ties tend to bring more informational benefits than strong ties (Alvarez & Busenitz, 2001; Ardichvili et al., 2003; Arenius & Clercq, 2005). Alternatively, strong ties bring strategic benefits for entrepreneurs, giving them greater access to resources and hence more opportunities (Granovetter, 1973; Hite & Hestery 2001.

Dimensions of social capital

Although SC has been viewed as a uni-dimensional construct, recent discussions incorporating SC have adopted a multi-dimensional approach to studying SC and its role in entrepreneurial activity. Based on Nahapiet and Ghoshal's (1998) categorization, we discuss three dimensions of SC including *cognitive, structural and relational SC with regards to their role in opportunity creation in WE.*

Cognitive SC refers to the shared understanding that individuals develop amongst each other because of the common language, norms and culture (Nahapiet & Ghoshal, 1998). Shared culture and goals facilitate the flow of knowledge between entrepreneurs, thus enabling them to benefit from each other's perceptual processes and sharing common ways of making sense of new information (De Carolis & Saparito, 2006; Nonaka, 1994). Thus, women possessing SC with a high cognitive dimension may enable them to create more opportunities as network members aid the flow of knowledge and information in an effort to achieve common goals.

> P1: Female entrepreneurs may create more opportunities when they have high cognitive SC.

Structural SC incorporates structural embeddedness or the overall pattern of the entrepreneur's network (Nahapiet & Ghoshal, 1998). It entails two components, notably '*Closure*' which refers to the extent of connectedness within a network group and '*Brokerage*' which represents the number of indirect ties between a network actor and other network members (Burt, 1992; 2000). Closure is based on the idea of information symmetry and becomes a source of SC due to the connectedness of social actors within a network group.

Brokerage or structural holes within networks relates to the asymmetry of information which results in advantages for individuals who may perform a bridging *role* in their networks (Burt, 2000, p. 356). Unlike closure where members within a group have access to the same information, structural holes enable to separate redundant information which may arise from cohesive or equivalent contacts in a group who share similar information. Based on the above, entrepreneurs with high closure networks have greater access to information since all information is equally accessible and known to each member within the network group. Additionally, women entrepreneur networks that consist of structural holes may benefit from early access information than other network members. Early access to a range of skills, resources and perspectives helps in creating opportunities with respect to customers, suppliers, employees, financing and other business aspects (Burt, 2000, p. 370).

> P2: Female entrepreneurs may create more opportunities when they have less closure in their structural SC.
>
> P3: Female entrepreneurs may create more opportunities when they have more brokerage in their structural SC.

Relational SC refers to the 'personal relationships people have developed with each other through a history of interactions' (Nahapiet & Ghoshal, 1998, p. 244). It is characterized by two main components including '*Closeness*' and '*Trust*', which determine the quality of relational exchange between network members. A high level of personal familiarity (relational closeness) (Uzzi, 1996) and a sense of reliability and faith (trust) (Coleman, 1990; McAllister, 1995; Nahapiet & Ghoshal, 1998) in a network contact determines the quality of relationships between network members and the strength of ties within it (Moran, 2005; Granovetter, 1985; Nahapiet & Ghoshal, 1998). Strong ties typically reflect a greater investment of time, emotions, intimacy, intensity and reciprocity among network members (Granovetter, 1985) and thus may enable entrepreneurs to create more opportunities than weak ties. Female entrepreneurial networks lacking relational trust (trust, norms and sanctions) in their networks face challenges in understanding the expected behaviour of other network contacts (O'Connor & Rice, 2001), accrue less benefits from their networks and create fewer opportunities. Based on this, we suggest that

> P4: Female entrepreneurs may create greater opportunities if their networks consist of strong ties than weak ties.
> P5: Female entrepreneurs may create greater opportunities when their networks are characterized with high quality, high level of trust, shared beliefs and cognition.

Method

We study the lived experiences of six women entrepreneurs (three Turkish and three Welsh) and seek to understand the role of SC in opportunity creation within their businesses as embedded in the EES. Face to Face and Skype interviews, lasting between 60 and 90 minutes were conducted with all participants. All respondents were briefed about the purpose and objectives of the research and in line with this, they were asked to share their perceptions about their entrepreneurial ecosystem (Strong/Weak). Next, the respondents were asked to narrate their experiences of how their SC helped them to create opportunities in business. Table 9.1 presents an overview of the six cases included in the study.

Table 9.1

Case	Industry (Business) – Clientele	Overview
WY	Social entrepreneurship (Substance misuse training design and development) – UK & Africa	WY is a social enterprise not-just-for-profit organization providing substance misuse awareness, education and training. Having considerable experience in the social care and health industry, the founder of WY set up the business with the aim of designing and and delivering bespoke training using the skills, knowledge and experience of volunteers, who are initially trained by the founder of WY. The business serves clients including statutory, voluntary and private sectors. The income generated from sales is used to build the capacity and skills base of the volunteers, meet our operational costs and to grow the business throughout Wales and internationally, through community partnerships projects in Africa.

(Continued)

Table 9.1 (Continued)

Case	Industry (Business) – Clientele	Overview
WT	Design and Architecture (Interior Design Consultancy) – UK	WT is a professional interior designing consultancy providing interior solutions to all its clients including individual, large companies as well as government agencies. It services include Interior design consultation, Space planning, 3D visualization, Mood boards, and Technical/working drawings. The founder of WL has considerable experience in design and architecture and aims to provide her customers with versatile interior designs within the constraints of their budget. She is also an active participant in the contribution to the design and property industries in Wales.
WL	Marketing and Communications (Content Writing, Social Media and Communications) – Wales & USA	WL provides content writing, proofreading and and copywriting services through social media. Its clients are a number of private and public sector organizations, offering them communication services that help them to set them apart from other competitors.
TA	Internet (Electronic Commerce, Online Retailing) – Turkey	TA is an online retailing company which was previously started in Silicon Valley, USA and has now and has 90,000 members is 'Turkey's greatest location platform'. It draws attention of customers to its e- commerce website by providing them with great offers from restaurants, accommodation facilities and occasional activities, make reservations, order goods or services and get information and reviews about potential places. TA which received a 1.5-million-dollar credit from Aslanoba Capital for investment and got into a partnership with Foursquare Turkey has gained an important place in the Turkish market. It has collaboration with famous brands including Shangri La Bosphorus, Lacivert, Hayal Kahvesi, Divan, Bath and Body Works.
TT	Marketing and Promotion (Word of Mouth Marketing) – Turkey	TT is a Word of Mouth agency, incorporating three business models, all of which support the power of Word of Mouth marketing. One of the models within the TA business constitutes a community of more than 80,000 women from 81 cities of Turkey. TA serves companies including L'Oreal, Philips, Procter and Gamble, Unilever, Tefal and Rowenta.
TP	Agriculture (Worm Fertilizer Production) – Turkey	TP was founded from a gap identified in the Turkish market for worm fertilizer production. Having extensive exposure through travelling opportunities, founder of TP saw worm manure abroad for the first time and upon her return to Turkey, she pre-tested the idea of her business by producing worm manure in the bathroom of her house, moving onto the garage and then garden of her house. Finally, in 2014, after considerable testing of her business idea and achieving efficiency, founder of TP started her business. Currently, TP covers an area of 380 meter squares, has more than 250 million worms and an annual manure production of 250 tons. In future, TP aims to expand its facility and is increasing the closed area to over 1000 meter squares.

Findings

Analysis of the interviews revealed important themes underlying the role of SC in opportunity creation in businesses of women.

Perception of Entrepreneurial Ecosystem among women entrepreneurs

Analysis of the accounts of women entrepreneurs revealed that women in Wales and Turkey had different perceptions regarding their respective EES. Having different experiences of setting up a business and operating in an environment characterized by unique financial, cultural, governmental, support systems, human capital pool and market factors, women in Turkey generally perceived the EES as weak to sustain and support entrepreneurial activity while women in Wales considered it to be strong and hence supportive towards entrepreneurial ventures. For example, one of the Turkish women entrepreneurs (TA), who had prior experience of working in US, expressed her perceptions of the Turkish EES as:

> I would definitely define the ecosystem in Turkey as weak. There are times when we think that it would have been better if we had started a business in the US.
>
> (TA, internet business, 29)

Welsh women overall had a positive perception about their EES mainly due to their experiences of starting up a business in a relatively supportive environment as compared to Turkey. Overall Welsh respondents felt that the EES in Wales had improved over the years and hence was supportive of entrepreneurial activity.

> I think more people are starting their own business in Wales, with all the different awards recognizing people and helping them achieve, mentality is changing. Support is there otherwise people won't be trying it. Recession pushed a lot of people initially but people have the confidence and have started a business and others, then follow them.
>
> (WT, Interior designer, 33)

Perceived strengths of Welsh and Turkish EES

Pertaining to the individual elements of the EES, Welsh women perceived the availability of support systems, human capital resource and access to markets to be a strong element in their EES. For Turkish women, support services including social support from professional networks and from friends and family was revealed as an important factor contributing towards the success. With regards to human capital, Welsh and Turkish women perceived it to be a significant resource in running a business and creating opportunities within it. In this regard, personal education and experience as well as the staff/ employees hired in the business were highlighted as important sources of start-up and current business management among Turkish and Welsh women entrepreneurs. The highest qualification that all but two women (TP, fertilizer production business, 32; WY, substance misuse training and design development, 59) had was Bachelor's degree while one woman had a Master degree (WL, content writing and media, 26). Despite of their educational qualifications, women perceived that their prior experience in business or paid employment was more beneficial in starting a business and creating opportunities within it. For example, a Turkish entrepreneur (TP, fertilizer production business, 32) narrated about her experience from international exposure while travelling to other countries for business purposes. Her observations of people, businesses and markets abroad helped her identified a gap in Turkey, and start her business. Beyond human capital, access to markets was perceived as crucial for identifying a clear gap for their products/services in the Welsh and Turkish market.

Perceived weaknesses of Welsh and Turkish EES

Pertaining to the weaknesses of EES, both Welsh and Turkish women perceived policy and finance to be weak elements in their ecosystem. Additionally, Turkish women also perceived culture as a weak element in the Turkish EES.

While Welsh women perceived culture to be a driving force behind the increase in the number of women entrepreneurs in Wales, Turkish women perceived culture to be a negative factor impacting their business activity. For example, one respondent (TP) expressed negative sentiments about cultural support, suggesting that the culture in Turkey discriminated against women entrepreneurs and hence was not supportive towards their entrepreneurial efforts. She narrated her feelings as:

> Turkey is not a good place for entrepreneurial spirit and it is even more difficult if you are a woman. It is just like two frogs who fall into a well, one comes out and the other dies. Then they say something to one who survives but it can't listen since he is deaf. This is what we need to do to ignore what people say to avoid failure.
>
> (TP, fertilizer production business, 32)

With regards to cultural support, Turkish women expressed a zero or very low tolerance for failure in Turkish culture. While women thought of failure as a pathway to success, the society did not have such perceptions and thus Turkish women felt a lot of pressure on themselves to be successful and not fail in their business. Failure was an individual's failure rather than a business or venture failure, suggesting the one-sided approach to analyse the performance of women entrepreneurial activity, wherein external factors are discounted. Contrary to this, Welsh women perceived that their culture had a high tolerance for risk and encouraged more people to start a business and learn from the mistakes within it.

Beyond cultural constraints, Policy was perceived as a negative/weak element in both Turkish and Welsh EES. Women entrepreneurs in both ecosystems perceived government policies to be discriminatory and stringent thus making it difficult for them to create opportunities and be successful in business. Specifically, Turkish women expressed their dissatisfaction with government policies regarding women business support. Women entrepreneurs (TA, Internet business, 29; TT, Internet business, 42) perceived government policies as highly bureaucratic and discriminatory and felt that the Turkish government only supported in the initial stages of business start-up and not in the later stage. Government laden constraints such as taxes and employee regulations were highlighted to be barriers for business development and for creating opportunities for business success.

> We strive in this environment to do a business and it is as if the state is a founding partner in it. I pay 40% of my revenue to the state at year end and hence I feel it definitely needs to support me.
>
> (TT, internet business, 42)

Furthermore, Financial constraints were highlighted as a common weakness of both Turkish and Welsh EES. Welsh and Turkish women perceived lack of funding to be a major constraint in achieving their business goals. All women except for two Turkish entrepreneurs (TA, Internet business, 29 who had an angel investor; TP, fertilizer production business, 32 received funding from a small and medium development organization in Turkey: KOSGEB), started their business with personal savings, funding from family or spouse. Major reasons for women to rely on personal savings include small-scale nature of their business which did not require massive investments, preference of avoiding dependency on financial institutions, and high cost of borrowing in the form of interest payments. Even in cases where some funding was received from external sources, women entrepreneurs perceived it to be inadequate or not readily available when required for business performance and growth. Thus, most women preferred family and personal sources of financing as these were perceived more reliable and readily available (TT, Internet business, 42). In expressing their dissatisfaction regarding availability of financial resources, some women entrepreneurs, particularly Turkish entrepreneurs highlighted the limited support of government in helping them to overcome financial constraints in business. Narratives of accounts revealed that while some Welsh women entrepreneurs received support such as grants and training programmes for business, Turkish women did not receive any government support. As one respondent narrated:

> The state definitely helps women entrepreneurs. First they provide trainings for women who wish to become entrepreneurs and then if you have innovative ideas, you will be given 35000TL as a grant which is without interest and repayable after one year. However, I did not benefit from any such support.
>
> (TA, internet business, 29)

Structural, relational and cognitive embeddedness of SC in opportunity creation

Structural SC

Overall, our findings suggest that women entrepreneurs benefit from knowledge exchange in their networks when they participate in large networking groups characterized with less closure. The average *size* of women networks ranged between 30 and 600 members. Although network density of some networks was high, the networks were characterized as moderately closed, especially large networks. Thus, women entrepreneurs part of large networks were able to benefit from new information and knowledge exchange thus enabling them to create new opportunities in financial, human capital, social and business context. However, more frequent interactions with new members led to familiarity among members, which suggested that over a period and with frequent interactions, networks became of high closure. This affected the extent to which women could create opportunities for their business through the networking events. Some women often considered this to be a positive element especially in mixed networks (males and females), or male dominated networks, where the presence of a previously known contact would become a source of comfort amid other members who would not be familiar and may appear as daunting (Participant WT, Interior Design and Consultancy business, 33, Wales).

For women who were part of smaller networks (fewer than thirty members), information and knowledge exchange was limited and much of the information was redundant, thus reducing the benefits of networks for opportunity creation. This was due to high closure since network members were closely connected to each other and that most events were attended by the same network members.

With regards to network positions of women entrepreneurs in all the networks were of both *bonding* and *bridging* nature. All women entrepreneurs expressed their role in networks as bonding with other members, actively seeking information from contacts and identifying and exploiting opportunities in business. Additionally, women also performed the broker-age role in networks by bridging the flow of information to other contacts who previously would not have access to information. This was particularly in case of Welsh respondents wherein women entrepreneurs benefited from various networking events because of an increased flow of information between contacts.

The extent to which women entrepreneurs performed a bridging role in networks was dependent on the *trust* and familiarity of relationship with a contact. For example, a contact would be recommended to another network member only if a woman trusts him, has knowledge about him and his work, and believes that other people think positively about him (Participant WT, Interior design and consultancy business, 33, Wales). Beyond trust and familiarity, motivation for being in a bridge in networks arises from reciproc-ity of relationships, the belief that bridging connections between people would lead to the same favour for one's own self in future (Participant WL, Content writing ad media business, 26, Wales).

The analysis also revealed that Welsh and Turkish women's perception of information sharing within their networks was somewhat neutral. All women entrepreneurs but one (Participant TT, Word of Mouth marketing business, 42, Turkey) believed that information was moderately shared between networking contacts, meaning that some contacts would share information openly while others would not. This was more common in Turkish than Welsh women entrepreneurial networks. Particularly, information constraints were industry specific and organizations specific.

> Contacts do share information openly but there are people over others you click with and they refer you first.
> (Participant WL, Content writing and media business, 26, Wales)

> There are some tricky organizations who won't share information because they want to get all the funding for themselves. It's easier for us, because the model that we have is different to anyone.
> (WY, substance misuse development and training business, 59, Wales)

> I feel that women in construction sometimes can feel intimidated in male networking. They feel like knowing someone in the networks then so that when they go to these events they already know someone, because the construction industry is mainly male

dominated and there are mostly men in these networks. When they know that you are the only female there, they are quite sexist and can pass comments.

(Participant WT, Interior design and consultancy business, 33, Wales)

Further, information constraints also arose due to networking dynamics, specifically for Welsh women participating in mixed networks or networks that were highly male dominated.

The relational embeddedness of SC which determined the extent of closeness between contacts in networks of women entrepreneurs was suggested to be neutral and thus opportunities created based on relational embeddedness of SC often too a long time to initiate. While Turkish women felt very close to their work contacts (those actively involved in the business), they kept a distance with others in their wider professional networks until a decent level of trust was developed in a contact. Welsh women overall felt close to their contacts in their professional networks, especially those whom they met frequently in networking events. Also, while Welsh women entrepreneurial networks were characterized with a lot of trust and honesty, Turkish women did not perceive their networks to be very trustworthy. There were some contacts in networks who were not trusted at all (Participant TP, fertilizer production business, 32, Turkey) while others were perceived as very honest and trustworthy (Participant TA, E-commerce business, 29, Turkey; Participant TT, Word of mouth marketing business, 42, Turkey)

However, once trust was established, women entrepreneurs performed a bonding and bridging role in their networks and thus created opportunities to grow their business. As a Welsh respondent explained:

Even if I do know people myself, the value of knowing that person is not as much as them introducing me to another key person, because my friend knows me and trusts me so has no problem referring and recommending me to someone else.

(Participant WY, substance misuse development and training business, 59, Wales)

Role of SC in opportunity creation of women entrepreneurs

In the presence of the unique challenges faced by women entrepreneurs in their respective entrepreneurial ecosystem, all women highlighted the critical role of their SC in helping them to create opportunities for their business. Despite being constrained in various aspects of business, women entrepreneurs aimed to do well in their business and create opportunities that will promote business growth, primarily by utilizing their formal and informal sources of SC.

Analysis of the accounts revealed that women entrepreneurs tap into their personal networks to create opportunities in four main contexts including *human capital context, business context, financial context and social context* (Figure 9.1). By utilizing formal or informal networks, women created opportunities that helped them to grow in business. However, incorporating the dimensions of SC, our findings suggest that while SC provides an advantage to women to overcome the challenges of their ecosystem and create opportunities, it also constrains the extent of opportunity creation among women entrepreneurs.

Role of SC in opportunity creation in human capital context

Our findings indicate that women entrepreneurs utilize their social networks to create opportunities for knowledge exchange, which in turn enabled them to build their customer base and grow their business. Primarily, formal networks of women in both ecosystems

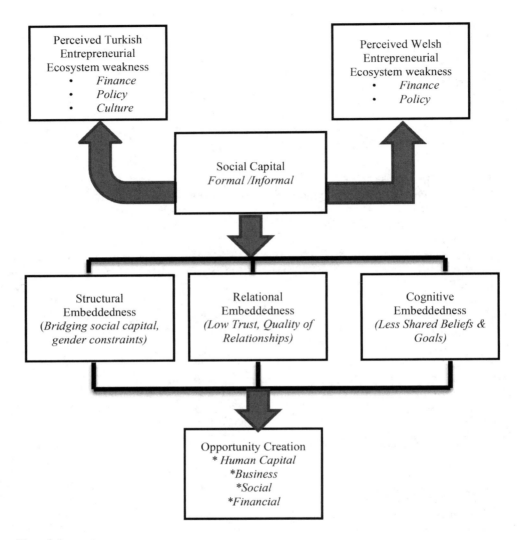

Figure 9.1

helped them to form linkages with academic institutions which facilitated the flow of information between universities and the business, while also enabling women to establish a presence and gaining recognition in the academic institutions. Women entrepreneurs shared knowledge of their business experiences with students, motivating them to develop positive entrepreneurial attitudes and mind-set and simultaneously benefited from the research conducted by universities. Presence in academic institutions also helped women entrepreneurs to indirectly market their business to others, thus building their reputation in the market. As one respondent narrated below:

> After becoming a member of "Turkish Win" (professional network), the entrepreneurship clubs of some universities accessed me and I visited universities and spoke to

students about how I started my business and brands associated with it. The universities had no contribution to us (business) in terms of creating links and contacts, and actually I find universities very underdeveloped in this regard.

(Participant TA, e-commerce business, 29, Turkey)

Beyond knowledge exchange, professional social networks also enabled a few women, particularly Welsh women to build their human capital. For example, WY, a social enterprise, managed to attract human capital (volunteers) through its links with the universities.

I deliver lectures and workshops twice a year at Cardiff university and Cardiff Metropolitan University and these help me to get volunteers from universities who assist me in the workshops designed on substance misuse.

(WY, substance misuse training, 59, Wales)

Social networks and opportunity creation in business context

Operating in challenging environments of their respective EES, our findings suggest that SC of Welsh and Turkish women entrepreneurs plays a significant role in providing business-related support. Women perceived that their social networks enabled them to overcome challenges in their broader entrepreneurial environment, both in the start-up stage and current stage of business. For example, because of the stringent and unsupportive regulatory policies regarding business set-up, women entrepreneurs' social networks enabled them to understand the business start-up procedures in the initial stages of their business. As one Turkish respondent narrated:

If you are doing a different business in Turkey, public authorities cannot help you. I wasted four months of my time at the time when I was starting my business and dealing with them. It was hard as I did not have any support to help me with complicated business procedures. Later, I found a consultant through a networking event I attended and he helped me with the significant parts of setting up my business.

(Participant TP, worm fertilizer production business, 32, Turkey)

Additionally, women entrepreneurs expressed their dissatisfaction regarding the strict government policies including stringent tax systems and employee regulations that impose a burden on small businesses. These created hurdles for women entrepreneurs to achieve their business goals and grow their business. However, despite of such regulatory burdens, our findings suggest that women entrepreneurs make use of the available resources, primarily their network base to manage various aspects of their business. For example, one Welsh respondent explained how she used her formal networks to manage business responsibilities since government's employee regulations and policies made it difficult for her to hire new employees.

Taxes, taxes, taxes! Oh my God! this is one of the reason I don't hire anyone and haven't expanded because I pay a lot of tax being a small business. If you look at companies like Starbucks, they pay less tax than me and that's really frustrating. It cripples the small businesses. If I take on a fixed employee, I will be responsible for paying their wage, their sick pay, their maternity pays and that would really affect my business. So, I just hire free lancers through people I know from my networks, or by connecting with people on social media, like Linked in.

(Participant WT, Interior Design and Consultancy, 33, Wales)

Narratives of women entrepreneurs also revealed lack of business-related support including information of setting up, business regulations and standard procedures, and availability of mentors and key personnel to guide through the initial stages of business set-up. The majority of Welsh and Turkish entrepreneurs felt that the government did not provide any business-related support to help them understand the basic procedures involved in setting up a business and that women had to search for information and look for existing entrepreneurs or consultants who could guide them on how to set-up a business. In this regard, women tapped their network base for mentoring purpose wherein women sought help from mentors in various aspects of business including registration process, tax systems and accounting procedures. For example, a Welsh respondent explained how her informal networks (her father's network base) enabled her in initial setting up stage of her business.

When I was thinking about starting my business, my father (informal networks) put me in touch with a professional who helped me with the practicalities of setting up, page structure, company registration process and all.

(WL, content writing and media business, 26, Wales)

Similarly, a Turkish respondent narrated her experience of how her formal networks helped her to solve problems that she encounters in business.

There is someone I met through a networking event 3 years ago, and she is now in my group of friends but I still consider her as a mentor so if I am working on a new idea or project and I have got any questions, I will send an email to her and ask her about her opinion and she will get back to me.

(WL, content writing and media business, 26, Wales)

Social networks and opportunity creation in financial context

Due to the weak financial ecosystem, both Welsh and Turkish women entrepreneurs faced significant constraints in their business. Majority of the women entrepreneurs relied on personal savings and other informal sources of finance to start their business with only one Turkish women who could benefit from a government grant and a loan from a formal financial institution. A major reason for women not tapping into formal finance sources was perceived inability to avail finances from formal sources. This was particularly true for Turkish women who felt that the cultural norms discriminated against women businesses and thus made it difficult for women to secure financial resources. Additionally, some women entrepreneurs, by virtue of their small-scale businesses and limited finances preferred to avoid large interest premiums associated with repayment of loans and thus did not apply for funding from external sources. However, despite of starting small-scale with minimum investment, all women entrepreneurs realized and expressed the need to acquire more finances to expand their business and create new opportunities in it. To achieve this, women entrepreneurs tapped on their social networks which enabled them to identify financial sources for their business needs. As expressed by a Welsh respondent:

> I started off myself, I was lucky I didn't have to buy any equipment, I just had the website and the business cards and some marketing, I had money myself and to be honest I didn't have to spend a lot of money. In the long run, if I am looking for an investor for my business, I would have to pitch in my personal network.
>
> (Participant WL, Content writing and media business, 26, Wales)

Formal networks including professional clients also helped women to build a recognition for themselves and their business. This in turn led to good will for the business and enhanced funding opportunities. In some cases, relationships that started professionally turned into informal friendships for women entrepreneurs and hence increased the probability of exploring financial opportunities for the business.

> Our first partner, Mr. A from U.S. A. loved business idea and showed his interested in partnering with us. Thanks to this, we had our first investment for our business. Later on, a very successful businessman Mr. B who appreciates our ideas and business and has heard us speak at events emailed and asked us to contact Mr. C, a person from one of the richest families in Turkey. Upon conversing with Mr. C, I gained a lot of confidence and self-esteem and secured an investment of 1 million dollars against some shares. Further, while reading the newspaper, I came to know that Mr. X was looking to invest in technology companies and hence I reached out to Mr. X through LinkedIn. We met over a cup of coffee and later on had the investment from him.
>
> (TA, E-commerce business, 29, Turkey)

Our findings also suggest that in the presence of lack of funding sources from formal networks such as venture capitalists and angel investment, women use their informal networks to overcome financial difficulties and grow their business. In this regard, family SC plays a significant role since women entrepreneurs acquire access to key financial resources either directly from family (parents and spouse) or from secondary contacts of family members.

> We started our business by taking support from KOSGEB, however we could not obtain that financial support immediately so we were in a very difficult situation at which point the support of the family was used and we handled our financial needs.
>
> (Participant TT, Word of Mouth marketing business, 42, Turkey)

Social networks and opportunity exploration in social context

Formal and informal networks do not only provide business and financial support to women entrepreneurs but also act as a source of social support. In the presence of weak regulatory policies and lack of government support for business, women entrepreneurs relied on the support from their family and friends. Additionally, by participating in formal networks, women get moral support which enables them to sustain their business activity and solve day to day business problems. For example, other entrepreneurs having similar industry experience (formal networks) act as a significant source of social support for women, giving them advice and assisting them through their own experiences in business. Moreover, through formal networks, women get the necessary push into the networks, which once obtained can trigger new connections and opportunities, for example access to new markets and customers.

> Formal networks like Turkish WIN provide an opportunity to get yourselves known to others, to promote your work. Personally, I had a friend who was working in Procter and Gamble and I received a briefing from this friend related to my current business and these advices helped me start my business. These networks have utmost benefit in terms of personal introduction to new contacts and hence new opportunities.
>
> (Participant TT, Word of Mouth marketing business, 42, Turkey)

Additionally, women get emotional support and confidence from their networks, which helps them to be consistent in their efforts of recognizing new business opportunities and overcome the weaknesses of their respective entrepreneurial ecosystem. For example, our findings suggest how women gain confidence of doing business through their formal and informal networks (Respondent WT, Wales) and cope with challenges presented by a weak cultural ecosystem, thus restoring their belief in their ability to do business (Respondent TP, Turkey).

> Friends have recommended me on projects or just made that introduction to potential clients. Also support from other entrepreneurs is a big one, this has helped me big time and I think without that, I wouldn't have the confidence to carry on.
>
> (Participant WT, Interior Design and Consultancy, 33, Wales)

> I hear demotivating expressions from people like, "Come on now, give it up, sit at home and take care of your children, you are doing that for nothing, you have incurred all those expenses and what if you fail and go bankrupt, you are wasting your time" Since I have a significant amount of motivation for success, due to the full support of my husband and people around me I can ignore what people say.
>
> (Participant TP, Worm Fertilizer production business, 32, Turkey)

With regards to informal networks, family and friends networks were identified as a critical factor of social support during various stages of business. Women entrepreneurs in Wales and Turkey relied on their family as this was perceived to be a reliable, trustworthy and readily available source of support, especially when other sources of network support were absent.

> My brother is a very smart person who knows the industry very well. He also has information to help me on this subject. When I have issues regarding business, I immediately call him and receive his support. Without him, there is nobody else from whom I can receive help, unless I spend some money.
>
> (Participant TT, Word of Mouth marketing business, 42, Turkey)

Barriers to opportunity creation

Our findings suggest that women entrepreneurs benefited from their formal and informal networks which enabled them to create opportunities in four main contexts including human capital, financial, social and business. However, narratives of women entrepreneurs also revealed the negative impact of their SC which impacted their ability to create opportunities for their enterprises and also created challenges for them to succeed in their business.

Threat to business reputation

Women entrepreneurs, specifically Welsh women, experienced threat from contacts in the form of replicating the product/service they offered, backstabbing and negative impact on reputation. Contacts which were unknown and not familiar would use the name of the business and portray that they are working with the founder, thus associating with her. This was considered as a threat to the reputation of the business and the founder since the nature and work ethics of the contact were not known. Thus, although new contacts could potentially be a source of opportunity recognition for women, they were also a threat to business reputation.

Backstabbing was another negative spill-over effect of networking identified in the interpretation of women entrepreneurs' narratives, wherein previously familiar contacts who were also good friends, tried to tarnish the reputation of a business to attract clients/ customers to their own business.

> I have had people whom I worked with before and I considered them friends. They tell people who I know through networking, that they don't know I know, that I only work on certain kinds of projects and they do this this kind of stuff. So, totally cutting me out. The person then called me and told me 'I have networked with so and so today and she told me that you just do specific projects'. I know that this particular person (friend) is going to all the NW groups that I go to, and I know they look at my LinkedIn profile and connect with the people I know.
>
> (Participant WT, Interior design and consultancy business, 33, Wales)

Due to such threats, women were more cautious and hence more active in maintaining relationships with clients and networking with other contacts. The presence in a network and hence in people's minds was essential to remain competitive in business, maintain existing clients and gain new opportunities.

Replication of product/service

Another threat from networks of women originated from replication of products and services, wherein other contacts would replicate the design, process, product or service of a business. This was experienced by founder of WY who observed someone else copying her design and training programmes and delivering a service. As a result of this, the founder stopped sharing any information about her training design and development with contacts, which consequently suggests a reduction in bonding role of the founder. Thus, even though close relationships with contacts were maintained, core information about the business was not shared with either formal or informal networks.

Cognitive SC of women entrepreneurs was found to be low among women entrepreneurs, specifically Turkish women entrepreneurs, and thus affected the extent to which women could create opportunities in any context. Turkish women had difficulties with professional networking contacts and work contacts since these did not share the same goals as the women did. Contrary to this, Welsh woman were satisfied and positively acknowledged the shared beliefs and goals of their contacts. Women believed that a shared belief among contacts was to help others and get help from others. However, there were exceptions to this, when some contacts or networks would not share the same goals as others. This was mainly observed in mixed or male dominated networks or industries which had a high level of competition wherein some contacts would consider others as threat to their business success.

Conclusion

Our research aims to highlight the important role of social capital of women entrepreneurs in opportunity creation of women entrepreneurs. Through our findings we suggest that despite the challenges of their respective entrepreneurial ecosystems, women entrepreneurs utilize their social capital and recognize and create opportunities in the social, business, financial and knowledge context. While women are tainted with the under-hypothesis image in entrepreneurship literature, our research reveals insights into the constrained performance of women entrepreneurs in two distinct entrepreneurial ecosystems, which present different set of challenges to women. Yet, women continue to over these challenges and succeed in business by utilizing their social capital, thus breaking the stereotypical image associated with them as entrepreneurs.

References

Ahl, H. (2006). Why research on women entrepreneurs needs new directions. *Entrepreneurship Theory & Practice, 30*(5), 595–621.

Alvarez, S. A., & Busenitz, L. W. (2001). The entrepreneurship of resource-based theory. *Journal of Management, 27*, 755–75.

Alvarez, Sharon A., & Barney, J. B. (2007). Discovery and creation: Alternative theories of entrepreneurial action. *Strategic Entrepreneurship Journal, 1*(2), 11–26.

Ardichvili, A., Cardozo, R., & Sourav, R. (2003). A theory of entrepreneurial opportunity identification and development. *Journal of Business Venturing, 18*, 105–123.

Arenius, Pia, & De Clercq, D. (2005). A network-based approach on opportunity recognition. *Small Business Economics, 24*(3), 249–265.

Autio, E., Kenney, M., Mustar, P., Siegel, D., & Wright, M. (2014). Entrepreneurial innovation: The importance of context. *Research Policy, 43*(7), 1097–1108.

Berger, P. L., & Luckmann, T. (1967). *The social construction of reality: A treatise in the sociology of knowledge.* Garden City, NY: Anchor Books Doubleday.

Burt, R. (1992). *Structural holes: The social structure of competition.* Cambridge, MA: Harvard University Press.

Burt, R. S. (2000). The network structure of social capital. *Research in Organizational Behavior, 22*, 345–423.

Carter, S., & Rosa, P. (1998). The financing of male and female owned business. *Entrepreneurship & Regional Development, 10*(3), 225–241.

Cebeci, T., & Essmat, S. (2015). *Women-led Enterprises in Turkey.* Online. Available at http://kadininstatusu.aile.gov.tr/data/54296a4b369dc32358ee2c3d/BEEPS-ENG_7.pdf.

Coleman, J. S. (1990). *Foundations of social theory.* Cambridge, MA: Harvard University Press.

De Carolis, D. M., & Saparito, P. (2006). Social capital, cognition, and entrepreneurial opportunities: A theoretical framework. *Entrepreneurship Theory and Practice, 30*(1), 41–56.

Doh, S., & Zolnik, E. J. (2011). Social capital and entrepreneurship: An exploratory analysis. *African Journal of Business Management, 5*(12), 4961–4975.

Ecevit, Y. (2007). *A Critical Approach to Women's Entrepreneurship in Turkey*. Online. Available at http://citeseerx.ist.psu.edu/viewdoc/download? doi:10.1.1.543.304&rep=rep1&type=pdf.

Eddleston, K. A., & Powell, G. N. (2008). The role of gender identity in explaining sex differences in business owners' career satisfier preferences. *Journal of Business Venturing, 23*(2), 244–256.

Federation of Small Business (2016). *Women in Enterprise: The Untapped Potential*. Online. Available at www.fsb.org.uk/docs/default-source/fsb-org-uk/fsb-women-in-enterprise-the-untapped-potential febc2bbb4fa86562a286ff0000dc48fe.pdf?sfvrsn=0.

Gaglio, C. M., & Katz, J. A. (2001) The psychological basis of opportunity identification: Entrepreneurial alertness. *Small Business Economics, 16*(2), 95–111.

Gartner, W. B. (1985). A conceptual framework for describing the phenomenon of new venture creation. *Academy of Management Review, 10*(4), 696–706.

Global Entrepreneurship Monitor (GEM) (2013) *UK: Wales Report*. Online. Available at http://gov.wales/docs/det/publications/140522gem13en.pdf.

Granovetter, M. S. (1973). The strength of weak ties. *American Journal of Sociology, 78*(6), 1360–1380.

Granovetter, M. S. (1985). Economic action, social structure, and embeddedness. *American Journal of Sociology, 91*, 481–510.

Ince, M. (2012). Obstacles and future prospects of women entrepreneurs: The Turkish context. *ECONOMIA MARCHE-Journal of Applied Economics, 31*(2), 61–73.

Isenberg, D. (2011). *The entrepreneurship ecosystem strategy as a new paradigm for economy policy: Principles for cultivating entrepreneurship*. Babson Park, MA: Babson Entrepreneurship Ecosystem Project, Babson College.

Johannisson, B. (2000). Networking and entrepreneurial growth. In D. L. Sexton and H. Landström (Eds), *The Blackwell handbook of entrepreneurship*. Oxford: Blackwell.

Kelsey, C. (2015). *Fast Growing Small Businesses are Responsible for a Third of Economic Growth in Wales, Report says*. Online. Available at www.walesonline.co.uk/business/business-news/fast-growing-small-businesses-responsible-10304409.

Klyver, K., & Terjesen, S. (2007). Entrepreneurial network composition. *Women in Management Review, 22*(8), 682–688.

Kumra, S., & Vinnicombe, S. (2010). Impress for success: A gendered analysis of a key social capital accumulation strategy. *Gender, Work and Organisation, 17*(5), 521–546.

McAllister, D. J. (1995). Affect-and cognition-based trust as foundations for interpersonal cooperation in organizations. *Academy of Management Journal, 38*(1), 24–59.

McGowan, P., Cooper, S., Durkin, M., & O'Kane, C. (2015). The influence of social and human capital in developing young women as entrepreneurial business leaders. *Journal of Small Business Management, 53*(3), 645–661.

Marlow, S., Shaw, E., & Carter, S. (2008). Constructing female entrepreneurship policy in the UK: Is the USA a relevant role model? *Environmental Planning C, 26*(1), 335–351.

Meechan, B. (2013). *New business start-ups in Wales lag behind UK, says ONS*. Online. Available at www.bbc.co.uk/news/uk-wales-25174973.

Moran, P. (2005). Structural vs. relational embeddedness: Social capital and managerial performance. *Strategic Management Journal, 26*, 1129–1151.

Nahapiet, J., & Ghoshal, S. (1998). Social capital, intellectual capital, and the organizational advantage. *The Academy of Management Review, 23*(2), 242–266.

Neergaard, H., Shaw, E., & Carter, S. (2005). The impact of gender, social capital and networks on business ownership: A research agenda. *International Journal of Entrepreneurial Behaviour & Research, 11*(5), 338–357.

Nonaka, 1. (1994). A dynamic theory of organizational knowledge creation. *Organization Science, 5*, 14–37.

O'Connor, G., & Rice, M. (2001), Opportunity recognition and breakthrough innovation in large established firms. *California Management Review, 43*(2), 95–117.

Okten, C. (2015). *Female entrepreneurship in Turkey.* Online. Available at https://openknowledge.world bank.org/bitstream/handle/10986/25410/102013-WP-P146215-PUBLIC-FEMALEENicindekiler.pdf?sequence=1.

Ramos-Rodríguez, A. R., Medina-Garrido, J. A., Lorenzo-Gómez, J. D., & Ruiz-Navarro, J. (2010). What you know or who you know? The role of intellectual and social capital in opportunity recognition. *International Small Business Journal, 28*(6), 566–582.

Sarasvathy, S. D. (2001). Causation and effectuation: Toward a theoretical shift from economic inevitability to entrepreneurial contingency. *Academy of Management Review, 26*(2), 243–263.

Shane, S., & Venkataraman, S. (2000). The promise of entrepreneurship as a field of research. *Academy of Management Review, 25*(1), 217–226.

Shepherd, D. A., & DeTienne, D. R. (2005). Prior knowledge, potential financial reward, and opportunity identification. *Entrepreneurship Theory and Practice, 29*(1), 9–112.

Singh, R. P. (2001). A comment on developing the field of entrepreneurship through the study of opportunity recognition and exploitation. *Academy of Management Review, 26*(1), 10–12.

Spilling, O. R. (1996). The entrepreneurial system: On entrepreneurship in the context of a mega-event. *Journal of Business Research, 36*(1), 91–103.

Thomas, G. (2015). *How can Wales Maximise the Contribution of Women to the Economy?* Online. Available at https://assemblyinbrief.wordpress.com/2015/06/09/how-can-wales-maximise-the-contribution-of-women-to-the-economy.

Uzzi, B. (1996). The sources and consequences of embeddedness for the economic performance of organizations: The network effect. *American Sociological Review, 61*(4), 674–698.

Van de Ven, H. (1993). The development of an infrastructure for entrepreneurship. *Journal of Business Venturing, 8*(3), 211–230.

Venkataraman, S. (2003). Foreword. In S. Shane (ed.), *A general theory of entrepreneurship: The individual-opportunity nexus* (xi–xii). Northampton, MA: Edward Elgar.

Verhuel, I. & Thurik, R. (2001). Start-up capital: Does gender matter? *Small Business Economics, 20*(4), 443–746.

Welter, F. (2011). Contextualizing entrepreneurship: Conceptual challenges and ways forward. *Entrepreneurship Theory and Practice, 35*(1), 165–178.

Westlund, H. (2006). *Social capital in the knowledge economy: Theory and empirics.* New York: Springer-Verlag.

World Economic Forum (2012). *Women as the Way Forward. Annual meeting.* Online. Available at www.weforum.org/videos/women-way-forward-annual-meeting-2012.

Zahra, S. A., Wright, M., & Abdelgawad, S. G. (2014). Contextualization and the advancement of entrepreneurship research. *International Small Business Journal, 32*(5), 479–500.

10 Effectuation thinking and the manifestation of socio-cultural complexities in Sri Lankan female entrepreneurs' business decisions

Nadeera Ranabahu and Mary Barrett

Female entrepreneurs in developing countries, including Sri Lanka, face many economic, cultural and social constraints in managing their businesses. Women in developing countries often lack steady employment and stable work histories, adequate collateral and verifiable credit histories (Ledgerwood & Earne, 2013). Many are illiterate and therefore unable to complete the paperwork needed to get conventional loans. To increase women's access to credit, microfinance institutions (MFIs) such as the Grameen Bank in Bangladesh, where microfinance originated, extend very small loans (microcredit) to impoverished borrowers – often women. As well as supporting entrepreneurship, microcredit has been used to help manage household risk and promote investment with an overall goal of poverty alleviation (Ledgerwood & Earne, 2013). Despite the lack of consensus about their impact, microcredit mechanisms are widely considered a sustainable way of financing women entrepreneurs and improving their well-being. For example, Pitt and Khandker (1998) and Khandker (2005) found that women increased their non-land assets and increased their consumption expenditure through microcredit. Similarly, Deininger and Liu (2013) found benefits associated with women's nutritional intake and general empowerment. Nevertheless, microfinance schemes are also criticized for maintaining gendered power structures and oppressive contextual practices (Ali, 2014; Karim, 2008; Wilson, 2015). For example, due to power relations within the household in a patriarchal society (Wilson, 2015), MFI loans are often controlled by men in the family (Garikipati, 2008) even though MFIs grant loans to women. Similarly, microfinance schemes are said to reinforce gendered roles and responsibilities requiring women to work close to home, balance income generation and household work, and take care of children and families (Karim, 2008; Wilson, 2015). Other social and cultural norms also influence women's borrowing and repayment practices. For example, the norm which regards women as custodians of family honour means wives, daughters or daughters-in-law have to make sacrifices to repay loans to avoid dishonouring the family (Ali, 2014; Karim, 2008; Wilson, 2015). Given these controversies, studies of women entrepreneurs who use microcredit (termed micro-entrepreneurs here) need to take careful account of context.

This chapter uses the theoretical framework of effectuation and causation thinking (see details later) to explore the entrepreneurial thinking and behaviour of Sri Lankan women business owners who use microcredit in their businesses, especially in terms of how their decisions are affected by the social and cultural context. Our research objective is to see whether and how women mobilize aspects of their social and cultural context in their businesses, even if it appears restrictive at some level. In other words, we want to know whether they apply a 'bird in the hand' approach, or whether they perceive restrictions purely as

Effectuation and causation perspectives on entrepreneurship

Effectuation and causation are process theories of entrepreneurship. They explain entrepreneurship in terms of 'what an entrepreneur does', that is, as an action-based phenomenon formed through an interrelated creative, strategic and organizing process (Moroz & Hindle, 2012) rather than, for example, in terms of the entrepreneur's personality ('who an entrepreneur is'). Effectuation theory, introduced by Sarasvathy (2001), distinguishes between means-driven thinking (effectuation) and predictive thinking (causation) in the process of starting a business. Effectual entrepreneurs focus on their available means such as their identity, resources, knowledge and network. They consider what they can afford to lose, form partnerships with others, and convert obstacles into opportunities using their own experience (Chandler, DeTienne, McKelvie, & Mumford, 2011; Fisher, 2012; Sarasvathy, 2001; 2008). In contrast, causal entrepreneurs start by setting business goals and select the means required to achieve those goals. Rather than converting obstacles into opportunities they seek to avoid obstacles by calculating risks and returns, and studying the market and their competitors. They establish control processes to achieve business goals by using predictions and forecasts (Chandler et al., 2011; Fisher, 2012; Sarasvathy, 2001; 2008). The early stages of successful enterprises tend to be characterized by effectual thinking while later development stages reflect causal decision-making (Read & Sarasvathy, 2005). Table 10.1 compares the two decision-making logics.

As Table 10.1 illustrates, at a theoretical level effectuation is the inverse of causation thinking. In practice, however, entrepreneurs use both logics (Read & Sarasvathy, 2005). Nevertheless, these authors argue that a clear preference for one or the other can be isolated in business start-ups and, as mentioned earlier, that the stage of business development affects the type of thinking entrepreneurs use.

Effectuation and causal perspectives have been used to study business start-ups in a variety of contexts, including manufacturing firms (Berends et al., 2013; Brettel et al., 2014), international businesses (Gabrielsson M. & Gabrielsson P., 2013; Mainela & Puhakka, 2009), technology or on-line businesses (Agogué, Lundqvist, & Williams, 2015; Kaufmann, 2013), not-for-profits (Yusuf & Sloan, 2015), multiple ventures (Morrish, 2009), and small and medium enterprises (SMEs) (Alford & Page, 2015; Crick D. & Crick J., 2015). However the vast majority of these studies were undertaken in developed countries and several focus on entrepreneurs in high-tech industries. In contrast, this study draws on female, low-tech micro-entrepreneurs such as door-to-door sellers, and owners of confectionery and dressmaking businesses, in a developing country, to explore whether and how they use effectuation and causation logic during business start-up.

The fact that micro-entrepreneurs operate in a credit-enabled environment is another contrast with previous studies of effectuation in entrepreneurship. Micro-loans made available by MFIs, though very small, still need to be repaid and many women use a range of financial and non-financial strategies to manage debt. Some rely on their networks and spread the liability for the loan among members of a group who guarantee each other's loans (Armendáriz & Morduch, 2010). However, the cost of not honouring one's repayment commitments within these groups may be akin to 'social suicide', leading to the loss of the social network, loss of family honour and social standing, and even greater financial pressures (Ali, 2014; Guerin, Morvant-Roux, & Servet, 2011; Karim, 2008). Hence, this

Women entrepreneurship in Sri Lanka   141

Table 10.1 Effectuation and causation views of entrepreneurship

	Effectuation	*Causation*
Problem space	Effectuation is used when markets are highly uncertain.	Causation is used when markets are reasonably certain and predictable.
Explanation	Entrepreneurs consider means as given and focus on creating possible effects.	Entrepreneurs consider particular effects as given and select between means to achieve those effects.
Underlying logic	To the extent that entrepreneurs can control the future, they do not need to predict it.	To the extent that entrepreneurs can predict the future, they can control it.
Fundamental principles	*Means-driven thinking:* The entrepreneur's identity, knowledge and network are the basis for making business decisions.	*Goals-driven thinking:* Goals are set for the business and appropriate means are sourced to achieve these pre-defined goals.
	Affordable loss: The entrepreneur puts at risk only what he or she is willing to lose.	*Expected returns:* The entrepreneur calculates likely risks and returns when making decisions.
	Alliances/pre-agreements: The entrepreneur forms partnerships to reduce uncertainty.	*Competitive market analysis:* The entrepreneur analyses market conditions and competition to reduce uncertainty.
	Acknowledging the unexpected: Unexpected events are considered as opportunities; hence, entrepreneurs are adaptive and flexible.	*Overcoming the unexpected:* Unexpected events are considered obstacles; hence, control practices are used to avoid them.
	Non-predictive control: Entrepreneurs use their own experience to make business decisions.	*Predictive control:* Entrepreneurs rely on forecasts and projections to make business decisions.

Source: Adapted from Brettel et al. (2012), Chandler et al. (2011), Dew, Sarasvathy et al. (2009), Fisher (2012), Sarasvathy (2001; 2008), Sarasvathy & Dew (2005), Wiltbank et al. (2009).

study also explores to what extent feelings of social pressure arising from using microcredit affect entrepreneurial thinking.

Country context: Sri Lanka

Sri Lanka, with a population of 20.7 million of whom 77% reside in rural areas, is a lower middle-income country with 10.5 million women (DCSSL, 2016a). Sri Lanka has a 54% labour force participation rate but men have more than double the participation rate of women (95% for males and 36% for females) (DCSSL, 2016b). This trend is visible in all age categories (DCSSL, 2016b). In addition, especially compared to men, women workers are concentrated in informal, low-income and low productivity sectors such as agriculture (i.e., paddy) and plantations (i.e., tea) and assembly line jobs such as in garment factories with upward mobility for women being limited, even when they have a job (ADB & GIZ, 2015). These gender inequalities have been argued to arise from a range of factors including cultural and status-related perceptions about married women working (Gunatilaka, 2013; The World

142 *Nadeera Ranabahu and Mary Barrett*

Bank, 2013), government legislation requiring employers to bear the entire cost of maternity leave benefits leading to discrimination in hiring females (Gunatilaka, 2013), lack of family friendly policies in the private sector (Gunatilaka, 2013), lack of access to information (Hancock & Edirisinghe, 2012), and the fact that women are overwhelmingly responsible for caring for children and the elderly (ADB & GIZ, 2015; The World Bank, 2013).

The management ranks of Sri Lankan micro and small enterprises also have an unequal women participation rate. Of the 935,736 micro-enterprises and 71,126 small enterprises recorded, only around 26% and 8% respectively are run by women (DCSSL, 2015). These women entrepreneurs face environmental, family and cultural challenges, and limited access to finance information and support structures (ADB & GIZ, 2015; De-Mel, McKenzie, & Woodruff, 2009; Kodithuwakku & Rosa, 2002; Women's Chamber of Commerce and Industry: Sri Lanka, 2015). Hence, government has developed programmes devoted to empowering women, widows and households headed by women, as well as specialized microfinance and SME financing schemes (Ministry of Finance: Sri Lanka, 2015).

Findings

To explore the research questions, we interviewed twenty-two female entrepreneurs who had borrowed from a large non-governmental MFI. The MFI has eighteen branches which operate across four of Sri Lanka's nine provinces. From each province one branch was selected as the data collection site. Five to seven women entrepreneurs were selected per branch, resulting in twenty-two interviewees. Twenty-one interviews were conducted in one of the local languages, Sinhalese, by one of the authors who is a native speaker; the remaining interview was done in the other local language, Tamil, with help from an interpreter. Table 10.2 presents some descriptive details about the interviewees and their businesses.

Table 10.2 Details of interviewees and their businesses

#	Business type	Management structure	MF loan/s used during business start-up (S) or development (D)?
1	Specialized services: vehicle upholstery	JMH	D
2	Food production: cake-making	SM	D
3	Food production: snacks and confectionery making	SM	D
4	Fisheries: owner of a multi-day fishing boat	Jointly managed with an outsider	D
5	Specialized services: garment sales	SM	D
6	Food production: confectionery making	JMH	D
7	Unspecialized retail sales: grocery shop and milk collection centre	JMH	D
8	Specialized services: dressmaking	SM	D
9	Specialized retail sales: a mobile tea seller	SM	S
10	Manufacturing: pillowcase and cement flower pot making business	SM	D

#	Business type	Management structure	MF loan/s used during business start-up (S) or development (D)?
11	Specialized services: dressmaking	SM	D
12	Specialized services: carpet making and packing snack foods and lamp wicks	SM	D
13	Unspecialized retail sales: a grocery shop	SM	D
14	Specialized services: dressmaking	SM	D
15	Specialized services: dressmaking under a forward sales agreement	SM	D
16	Specialized services: dressmaking and garment sales	SM	D
17	Agriculture related business: mushroom cultivation and sales	SM	D
18	Manufacturing: bra-making	SM	D
19	Specialized retail sales: a cut-flower and plant nursery business	JMH	D
20	Specialized retail sales: cut-flower business	SM	D
21	Food production: Kithul[1] treacle and jaggery[2] making	SM	S
22	Food production: confectionery making	SM	S

JMH = Jointly managed with husband; SM= Sole Managed.

The following sections explore the use of effectuation and causation thinking according to the five fundamental principles of each approach outlined in Table 10.1.

Means–driven vs goals–driven approaches

The means-driven sub-constructs of identity, knowledge and networks characteristic of effectuation thinking played a critical role in the business decision-making of micro-entrepreneurs. For example, interviewee 21's personal values of strong attachment to nature and tradition had led her to start a business producing Kithul honey and jaggery. In addition, social norms such as patriarchal practices related to livelihood activities, reinforced entrepreneurs' tendency to use means-driven approaches. For example, interviewee 2 had to substitute ingredients and use only the cake-making equipment she already owned because her husband did not allow her to travel to capital cities where she could have bought other ingredients and equipment.

Furthermore, the data suggested that micro-entrepreneurs relied on knowledge gained from previous experience in starting their businesses, including knowledge they had learnt by working as apprentices, from specific training, or from working in similar fields. For example, interviewee 14 said she had worked in a garment factory for five years before she started her dressmaking business, while interviewee 19 had completed a training programme on anthurium cultivation:

> I attended a training program for 3 days. I did not know anything before [about anthurium cultivation]. After the training, I started growing anthuriums as a small scale business with 200 plants.

> (Interviewee 19)

Similarly, interviewee 22 explained that her work as an insurance salesperson in a private company had helped her develop the marketing channels of her confectionery business.

The entrepreneur's family and social network also influenced their business start-up process. For example, interviewee 12's sister bought her the materials for her dressmaking business, interviewee 15's husband bought two sewing machines under a payment plan, and the husbands of interviewees 3 and 22 helped them with product deliveries. Interestingly, the husbands' contribution was necessitated by the restrictions on women travelling. In addition, family and relatives often played a role in providing informal training:

> Before I got married, when I was with my parents, my father owned a small shop. I helped my father to manage it. So, I knew how to manage this one [referring to her grocery shop].
>
> (Interviewee 13)

This kind of extensive support from the family members may reflect the importance of family and extended family in Sri Lankan society.

Some goals-driven approaches were also evident. For example, interviewee 8 had a general plan to expand her dressmaking business:

> In future, I want to expand this and have a showroom. In addition, I plan to hire at least two additional workers.
>
> (Interviewee 8)

Interviewees also used microfinance loans to achieve more specific goals. For example, interviewee 21 explained that she took out a loan to achieve a goal to expand her business:

> I did not have space to expand the production. At that time, I was doing this on a small scale, but had the idea of expanding. So, I took out a loan and made a separate space using the loan.
>
> (Interviewee 21)

However, most of the goals micro-entrepreneurs had were short-term, typically one or two years. The goals themselves often seemed to be inspired by chance observations or events which the entrepreneur then incorporated into the business. For example, from the cut-flower and plant nursery business owner:

> So, I one day thought that, after I saw a net house in one of their [other growers'] places, I would also build a net house before 2011 . . . So, every year like that [I have targets]. For example in 2014 I had the target for this net house [shows one to the researcher], and I constructed that. Like that, I have targets for the year. For this year [2015], we had vehicles earlier, but now we do not have any. So, this year, I am planning to buy a vehicle. In addition, I have a plan to build a net house for around 5,000 orchids this year.
>
> (Interviewee 19)

Due to the short-term orientation and means-driven nature of these goals it makes sense to consider these comments as evidence of effectuation rather than true causation thinking.

Women entrepreneurship in Sri Lanka   145

Affordable loss vs expected returns

Respondents used the effectuation principle of affordable financial loss. As Fisher (2012) explains, entrepreneurs identify a number of ways to start a business inexpensively, such as using borrowed equipment (e.g. interviewee 10), buying goods on credit (e.g. interviewee 6), and using second-hand equipment (e.g. interviewee 4):

> Initially, I did not purchase a cast to make flowerpots. I borrowed it from my sister.
>
> (Interviewee 10)

> There are retail and wholesale shops where you can borrow goods on credit. We [she and her husband] bought ingredients on credit, with the promise that we would repay the money in one or two days, or one week.
>
> (Interviewee 6)

> We [she and her husband] bought the engine for 115,000 [Sri Lankan Rupees-SLR]. Usually, a brand new one at that time would have cost around 300,000 [SLR]. So, we bought a used one.
>
> (Interviewee 4)

In addition, as Dew, Sarasvathy, Read, and Wiltbank (2009) explain, relying on loans or capital with a weak loan repayment structure such as non-interest loans obtained from friends and relatives (as with interviewee 1), is a common way to minimize losses:

> At that time we [she and her husband] did not have any cash in hand. So quickly we borrowed some money. But, that was not for interest. I just asked for some money from my sister and did the work and repaid her.
>
> (Interviewee 1)

Using personal resources or assets such as savings, cash in hand, pawning jewellery, personal labour instead of hired labour (e.g. interviewees 22, 3 and 19 respectively), and being cautious in initial money/resource investments were frequently mentioned. For example:

> . . . We had a small eggplant plantation. This eggplant harvest was sold to Dambulla [a town] wholesale market and, using that income, we bought goods for the grocery shop.
>
> (Interviewee 7)

Micro-entrepreneurs were clearly concerned about the likely loss of personal credibility, an unaffordable social loss, if they failed to repay their loans. For example, interviewee 9 explained the need to maintain regular payments so as not to lose the possibility of receiving more lenient treatment for her payments should an unexpected need arise:

> In our one [group], everyone does [repay on time]. When there is good attendance and repayment record, there can be leniency when I need it. Say there is funeral . . . If you are honest you can have that.
>
> (Interviewee 9)

In addition, interviewees 7 and 20 thought about whether they could repay the loan before borrowing to avoid potential future losses:

> I do not borrow much, thinking that if there is a sudden crisis, I would not be able to repay money. I request only the amount I can repay.
>
> (Interviewee 7)

At the same time, interviewees thought about the possibility of getting bigger loans in future:

> If you repay the microfinance loan continuously, you build trust. Then, you can even borrow a bigger loan.
>
> (Interviewee 18)

Occasionally some micro-entrepreneurs used causal thinking, calculating likely revenues. For example, interviewee 22 mentioned that she wrote down all her expenses and calculated the expected returns. However, micro-entrepreneurs did not appear to calculate likely returns as much as they considered affordable losses.

Pre-agreements/alliances vs competitive market analysis

Pre-agreements and alliances were used at business start-up. For example, interviewee 16 and 14 made dresses based on customer orders. Interviewee 7 had an ongoing agreement with milk collecting companies to supply raw milk. Interviewee 20 supplied cut flowers based on prior orders. However, establishing pre-agreements required some negotiations:

> this work [shows the interviewer some unfinished party huts],[3] I have to sew 10 huts. We charge 2,500 [SLR] per hut. The customers provided all the materials. However, the customer asked for a discount as there were 10 and we finally agreed on 1,750 per unit.
>
> (Interviewee 1)

While evidence about the use of competitive market analysis was limited, it was clear that at least two interviewees, 18 and 22, carefully explored what their competitors were doing:

> I removed one of their [a competitor's] packets and inspected the product [bras]. I saw that the competitor had used only one layer [of fabric] whereas we use two layers. So I showed the shop owner how my competitor had used only a single layer, and said that customers would not buy these bras and would return them. From the next month onwards, I had increased sales while the sales of other suppliers diminished.
>
> (Interviewee 18)

Acknowledging vs overcoming the unexpected

The use of adaptive practices in response to unforeseen difficulties (i.e., acknowledging the unexpected) was prominent. In fact, for interviewee 21, the failure of another local organization to properly manage a project that had been started by the United Nations was what prompted her to start her business:

> In 1998, this village was selected by the UNDP[4] for a project on products associated with Kithul. The UNDP time period for the project finished around year 2000 and they left here. Then, the process was handed to the local organization that UNDP worked with . . . The local organization could not manage the process properly . . . the money was not forthcoming [from the local organization]. A lot of honey and sap got wasted. Only then did I think to start the business.
>
> (Interviewee 21)

Interviewee 19 described unexpected sales and marketing problems that had made her change the direction of the business and explore different marketing options. She talked about how she reacted to a broken promise of an official in government:

> He [an officer from the agricultural department] was the one who sold us the plants. He said that he would buy cut flowers and seedlings from us. As a result, within [ABC] division [of the district] there were around 40 growers enrolled with this program. But after around eight months, just when the flowers were blooming, this person 'disappeared' . . . Meanwhile, my husband was a great help. He had contacts with government departments such as the Royal Botanical Garden in Peradeniya, and the Agriculture Department and we linked with all these places to provide flowers and seedlings and obtained orders to supply them.
>
> (Interviewee 19)

Gender-based social norms affected entrepreneurs' business options in important ways. For example, several interviewees were restricted in terms of how far they were allowed to travel. One (interviewee 11) said that the first time she travelled a major distance to buy garments to sell, she had to be accompanied by someone else. Some micro-entrepreneurs converted the barriers formed by these contextual norms into opportunities. For example, while interviewee 9's husband forbade her to travel around the country, he nevertheless bought tea in bulk from Colombo (the capital of Sri Lanka) and brought it back for her to sell locally.

In contrast, little direct evidence about control practices (i.e., overcoming the unexpected) appeared. Nevertheless some micro-entrepreneurs used control mechanisms to ensure the quantity and quality of their production. For example, interviewees 3 and 22 used fixed days and routinized production cycles:

> I produce on one day. I usually make around 8–10 kilograms of jujubes [a sweet] per night. The next day, with the help of the worker, I sugar coat them and then the next day packet them. Then, the next cycle starts.
>
> (Interviewee 22)

Non-predictive control vs predictive control

Non-predictive decision-making, that is, relying on your own experience, was prominent. For example, interviewees 7, 15 and 19 mentioned that they used their own experience in making business decisions. Interviewee 22 had transferred her experience in other areas to her current business, while interviewee 17 used her experience from failed attempts in mushroom cultivation in her current business. We did not find evidence that interviewees used predictive information. However it was not clear whether the interviewees had access to market forecasts which they could have used to make predictions, so this issue was difficult to judge.

Discussion

Overall, we found that female micro-entrepreneurs relied more on effectuation than causation in business start-up. They used all the effectual principles: means-driven approaches, affordable loss thinking, pre-agreements/alliances, acknowledging the unexpected, and non-predictive control. There were only isolated instances of causal approaches being used. This may, in part, be because the interviewees' businesses were not in complex sectors such as biotechnology, software development, solar or green energy, which typically feature unknown development paths requiring causal or 'hybrid' thinking (a combination of effectual and casual logics) (Kaufmann, 2013; Maine, Soh, & Dos Santos, 2015; Nummela, Saarenketo, Jokela, & Loane, 2014; Reymen et al., 2015). In addition, as most of these micro-entrepreneurs are in rural areas, the use of effectuation may be at least partly due to resource constraints (Read & Sarasvathy, 2005).

Certain social and cultural norms that operate differently for women and men in business had an impact. In particular, the study shows how patriarchal norms, such as the ideas that men are the breadwinners (Hewapathirana, 2011), that wives need to be obedient to their husbands (Fernando, 2012), and the restrictions and safety concerns associated with women travelling (Fernando, 2012), affect how women do business. Restrictions on travel made it necessary for women to use the means available to them (as with the cake-maker who substituted ingredients and used her existing equipment). But rather than seeing these as barriers preventing them from reaching 'two in the bush' – advantages that are unattainable because of cultural and contextual practices – some women made the barriers into opportunities. This was shown by the experience of interviewees 8 and 3, whose husbands sourced and delivered supplies for their wives' businesses. The solution is based in means-driven, effectuation thinking: a 'bird in the hand' approach.

Other findings reinforce the prominence of effectuation thinking. Women micro-entrepreneurs used their available knowledge, social networks and resources that could be found and leveraged at low cost, often from their immediate or extended family. They thought about the financial losses they could afford and used low-cost strategies to establish the business. In addition, they formed pre-agreements with customers, changed the business to meet contextual challenges, and grew the business slowly and steadily. Hence, at the time of interview, close to half the interviewees were managing their first business, and about half had been able to manage their businesses for more than ten years. These findings support previous research about the growth intentions of women micro-entrepreneurs. For example, Mukharlyamova et al. (2015) and Bulanova et al. (2016) found that women are more cautious in their businesses and more inclined to adopt a slow steady rate of expansion. Women's slow, steady growth intentions appear to be reflected in the effectual approach to business formation that was evident in this study, as effectuation allows entrepreneurs to explore their own capabilities using the means easily available and expand their businesses accordingly. However, the effect may also stem from the fact that most businesses in the study were the entrepreneur's first ever business, where entrepreneurs may tend to be cautious.

Another highlight of the findings is that disjoined institutional practices and lack of accountability from institutional providers may lead to entrepreneurial opportunities. Interviewees 21 and 19 both filled vacuums in the supply network created when limited-term institutionalized services finished or broke down. Given that micro-entrepreneurs in this study were from rural areas, lack of access to or breakdown in institutional services can create devastating social effects within communities. Hence, these micro-entrepreneurs performed a social service by acting as the link between rural producers or growers and outside markets, even though their businesses were small.

In addition, this study shows how microfinance loans influence business decisions. Lingelbach, Sriram, Mersha, and Saffu (2015) and Sarasvathy (2008) have explored the development of MFIs from an effectual perspective. For example, Sarasvathy (2008) explained the use of means-driven approaches, affordable loss and leveraging contingencies by examining the formation of the Grameen Bank. Lingelbach et al. (2015) used case studies from sub-Saharan African countries to show the use of effectuation thinking in financial sector innovations including microfinance. But these studies did not extend to the MFIs' borrowers. This study, by going beyond the institutional level, extends these findings to borrower level and thus contributes to the empirical evidence base of effectual research. In addition, this study shows that microcredit, as well as providing start-up or development capital, affects affordable loss thinking and becomes another means available to achieve entrepreneurial goals.

Microfinance lending mechanisms rely on timely loan repayment where defaulters may come to be seen as untrustworthy, making them unable to obtain future loans. Micro-entrepreneurs in the study were aware of this and it affected their social interactions. However, the interview evidence did not reveal any coercive loan collection practices of the kinds Ali (2014) and Karim (2008) found in Bangladesh. Still, micro-entrepreneurs clearly consider other losses, such as social loss and loss of future opportunities, as well as financial loss, and this can be seen as an extension of the affordable loss heuristic. Therefore, it seems that within the microfinance context, micro-entrepreneurs' business decision-making logic can only be comprehensively understood by considering whether other losses associated with the microfinance loan, not just financial losses, are affordable.

Findings in this study need to be viewed in the light of the fact that entrepreneurs in the study were operating in a credit-facilitated environment. As noted earlier, about 50% of the interviewees were managing their first business, so respondents are mostly 'non-experts'. Nevertheless, most of them had been able to manage their business for more than ten years. This suggests that even entrepreneurs with limited business exposure and experience use effectuation, not just the 'expert' entrepreneurs who were the subject of research by Dew, Read, Sarasvathy, and Wiltbank (2009) and Read, Dew, Sarasvathy, Song, and Wiltbank (2009). While they did not start out as expert entrepreneurs, they appear to have gained expertise by managing their businesses over the long term.

Implications for research and policy

Our findings indicate that effectuation thinking is prominent among micro-entrepreneurs who use microfinance loans. Effectuation logic allows us understand their decision process and to incorporate specific cultural and social influences on the decisions, including those related to managing the loan. However, some factors we identified are not limited to microfinance borrowers. For example, the way gendered roles and responsibilities influence business choice and activities, occasionally converting gender-related barriers into opportunities, is common to women entrepreneurs in other countries where gender differences vary from or are more marked than those in Western countries (Ahmad, 2011; Erogul, Rod, & Barragan, 2016; Tlaiss, 2014). These findings need to be further tested and, if validated, could be incorporated into effectual explanations when conceptualizing women entrepreneurship. In addition, future effectuation research among women microfinance borrowers should try to capture the multifaceted nature of the affordable loss heuristic and further explore how microfinance loans and other lending practices influence effectual and causal decision-making.

Our finding that micro-entrepreneurs' business reasoning has societal and cultural roots has implications for policy. Microfinance institutions should design their programmes carefully in order not to reinforce gender stereotyping and power structures within communities which adversely affect women, including as entrepreneurs. In addition, as women micro-entrepreneurs primarily use effectuation thinking at start-up, the institutional focus when assessing for loan eligibility should include on their current knowledge, network and capacities to manage a business rather than focusing only on their goals. Furthermore, as women rely more on non-predictive than predictive thinking during the start-up phase, institutions should provide forums for women to learn from each other and from experts in the field, and to obtain hands-on experience in business management. Capacity building and training programmes offered by MFIs should incorporate self-assessment tools that women (and indeed men) can use to evaluate the resources, capacities and networks they have, identify cheaper sources of finance within the means available, and overcome challenges by using flexible and adaptive strategies. Doing this would mean that MFI training could simplify management for micro-entrepreneurs rather than adding to it more burdensome, a criticism that has been levelled at MFIs (see Banerjee & Duflo, 2011).

Notes

1 Solitary fish-tail palm (scientific name: *Caryota urens*) [known as Kithul in Sinhalese].
2 A kind of a palm sugar: a by-product of sap taken from Kithul trees. It is made by traditional methods which, until recently, were passed down within families.
3 Cabana type structures made of fabric or leather.
4 The United Nations Development Programme.

References

Agogué, M., Lundqvist, M., & Williams, M. K. (2015). Mindful deviation through combining causation and effectuation: A design theory-based study of technology entrepreneurship. *Creativity and Innovation Management, 24*(4), 629–644.

Ahmad, S. Z. (2011). Evidence of the characteristics of women entrepreneurs in the Kingdom of Saudi Arabia: An empirical investigation. *International Journal of Gender and Entrepreneurship, 3*(2), 123–143.

Alford, P., & Page, S. J. (2015). Marketing technology for adoption by small business. *Service Industries Journal, 35*(11–12), 655–669.

Ali, H. M. A. (2014). Blaming the poor and legitimizing coercive loan recovery strategies: Unveiling the dark side of NGO practices in Bangladesh. *Anthropologica, 56*(1), 177–191.

Armendáriz, B., & Morduch, J. (2010). *Economics of microfinance* (2nd ed.). Cambridge, MA: MIT Press.

Asian Development Bank (ADB), & Deutsche Gesellschaft für Internationale Zusammenarbeit (GIZ). (2015). *Country gender assessment Sri Lanka: An update.* Retrieved from: www.adb.org/sites/default/files/institutional-document/172710/sri-lanka-country-gender-assessment-update.pdf.

Banerjee, A. V., & Duflo, E. (2011). *Poor economics.* New York: Public Affairs.

Berends, H., Jelinek, M., Reymen, I., & Stultiëns, R. (2013). Product innovation processes in small firms: Combining entrepreneurial effectuation and managerial causation. *Journal of Product Innovation Management, 31*(3), 616–635.

Brettel, M., Bendig, D., Keller, M., Friederichsen, N., & Rosenberg, M. (2014). Effectuation in manufacturing: How entrepreneurial decision-making techniques can be used to deal with uncertainty in manufacturing. *Proceedings of the 47th CIRP Conference on Manufacturing Systems Variety Management in Manufacturing, Procedia CIRP, 17,* 611–616.

Brettel, M., Mauer, R., Engelen, A., & Küpper, D. (2012). Corporate effectuation: Entrepreneurial action and its impact on R&D project performance. *Journal of Business Venturing, 27*(2), 167–184.

Bulanova, O., Isaksen, E. J., & Kolvereid, L. (2016). Growth aspirations among women entrepreneurs in high growth firms. *Baltic Journal of Management, 11*(2), 187–206.

Chandler, G. N., DeTienne, D. R., McKelvie, A., & Mumford, T. V. (2011). Causation and effectuation processes: A validation study. *Journal of Business Venturing, 26*(3), 375–390.

Crick, D., & Crick, J. (2015). Learning and decision making in marketing planning: A study of New Zealand vineyards. *Marketing Intelligence and Planning, 33*(5), 707–732.

DCSSL (2015). *Key indicators of industry trade and services sector-economic census 2013/2014* (press release). Retrieved from: www.statistics.gov.lk/PressReleases/Files/en/EC_20150714E.pdf.

DCSSL (2016a). *Mid-year Population Estimates by District & Sex, 2012–2016.* Retrieved from: www.statistics.gov.lk/PopHouSat/VitalStatistics/MidYearPopulation/Mid-year%20population%20by%20district.pdf.

DCSSL (2016b). *Quarterly Report of the Sri Lanka Labour Force Survey.* Retrieved from: www.statistics.gov.lk/samplesurvey/LFS_Q4_Bulletin_WEB_2016_final.pdf.

De-Mel, S., McKenzie, D., & Woodruff, C. (2009). Are women more credit constrained? Experimental evidence on gender and microenterprise returns. *American Economic Journal: Applied Economics, 1*(3), 1–32.

Deininger, K., & Liu, Y. (2013). Economic and social impacts of an innovative self-help group model in India. *World Development, 43,* 149–163.

Dew, N., Read, S., Sarasvathy, S. D., & Wiltbank, R. (2009). Effectual versus predictive logics in entrepreneurial decision-making: Differences between experts and novices. *Journal of Business Venturing, 24*(4), 287–309.

Dew, N., Sarasvathy, S. D., Read, S., & Wiltbank, R. (2009). Affordable loss: Behavioral economic aspects of the plunge decision. *Strategic Entrepreneurship Journal, 3*(2), 105–126.

Erogul, M. S., Rod, M., & Barragan, S. (2016). Contextualizing Arab female entrepreneurship in the United Arab Emirates. *Culture and Organization* [online]. doi:10.1080/14759551.2016.1244824.

Fernando, W. D. A. (2012). A social constructionist perspective of gender stereotyping at work: A case of highly skilled women in Sri Lanka. *Gender in Management, 27*(7), 463–481.

Fisher, G. (2012). Effectuation, causation, and bricolage: A behavioral comparison of emerging theories in entrepreneurship research. *Entrepreneurship Theory and Practice, 36*(5), 1019–1051.

Gabrielsson, M., & Gabrielsson, P. (2013). A dynamic model of growth phases and survival in international business-to-business new ventures: The moderating effect of decision-making logic. *Industrial Marketing Management, 42*(8), 1357–1373.

Garikipati, S. (2008). The impact of lending to women on household vulnerability and women's empowerment: Evidence from India. *World Development, 36,* 2620–2642.

Guerin, I., Morvant-Roux, S., & Servet, J. (2011). Understanding the diversity and complexity of demand for microfinance services: Lessons from informal finance. In B. Armendáriz and M. Labie (Eds), *The handbook of microfinance* (pp. 101–121). Singapore: World Scientific.

Gunatilaka, R. (2013). *To Work or not to Work? Factors Holding Women back from Market Work in Sri Lanka.* Retrieved from: www.ilo.org/wcmsp5/groups/public/—-asia/—-ro-bangkok/—-sro-new_delhi/documents/publication/wcms_250111.pdf.

Hancock, P., & Edirisinghe, I. (2012). Inclusion and empowerment of export processing zone women in Sri Lanka: Stakeholders perceptions and perspectives. *Labour and Management in Development, 13*, 1–20.

Hewapathirana, G. I. (2011). The role of social identity in internationalization of women owned small businesses in Sri Lanka. *Journal of Asia Business Studies, 5*(2), 172–193.

Karim, L. (2008). Demystifying microcredit: The Grameen Bank, NGOs, and neoliberalism in Bangladesh. *Cultural Dynamics, 20*(1), 5–29.

Kaufmann, D. (2013). The influence of causation and effectuation logics on targeted policies: The cases of Singapore and Israel. *Technology Analysis & Strategic Management, 25*(7), 853–870.

Khandker, S. H. (2005). Microfinance and poverty: Evidence using panel data from Bangladesh. *The World Bank Economic Review, 19*(2), 263–286.

Kodithuwakku, S. S., & Rosa, P. (2002). The entrepreneurial process and economic success in a constrained environment. *Journal of Business Venturing, 17*(5), 431–465.

Ledgerwood, J., & Earne, J. (2013). Credit. In J. Ledgerwood, J. Earne, & C. Nelson (Eds), *The new microfinance handbook: A financial market system perspective* (pp. 213–229). Washington, DC: The World Bank.

Lingelbach, D., Sriram, V., Mersha, T., & Saffu, K. (2015). The innovation process in emerging economies: An effectuation perspective. *International Journal of Entrepreneurship and Innovation, 16*(1), 5–17.

Maine, E., Soh, P-H., & Dos Santos, N. (2015). The role of entrepreneurial decision-making in opportunity creation and recognition. *Technovation, 39–40*, 53–72.

Mainela, T., & Puhakka, V. (2009). Organising new business in a turbulent context: Opportunity discovery and effectuation for IJV development in transition markets. *Journal of International Entrepreneurship, 7*(2), 111–134.

Ministry of Finance Sri Lanka (2015). *Annual Report 2015*. Retrieved from: www.treasury.gov.lk/docum ents/10181/12870/2015/68f51df3-5465-4805-ab6f-4a024ec672f6?version=1.1.

Moroz, P. W., & Hindle, K. (2012). Entrepreneurship as a process: Toward harmonizing multiple perspectives. *Entrepreneurship Theory and Practice, 36*(4), 781–818.

Morrish, S. (2009). Portfolio entrepreneurs: An effectuation approach to multiple venture development. *Journal of Research in Management and Entrepreneurship, 11*(1), 32–48.

Mukharlyamova, A. Y., Holuyeva, K. A., Mikhaelovna, L. G., & Irkinovna, I. N. (2015). Features of emotional sphere of entrepreneurs in trading business. *International Business Management, 9*(5), 877–884.

Nummela, N., Saarenketo, S., Jokela, P., & Loane, S. (2014). Strategic decision-making of a born global: A comparative study from three small open economies. *Management International Review (MIR), 54*(4), 527–550.

Pitt, M. M., & Khandker, S. H. (1998). The impact of group-based credit programs on poor households in Bangladesh: Does the gender of participants matter? *The Journal of Political Economy, 106*(2), 958–996.

Read, S., Dew, N., Sarasvathy, S. D., Song, M., & Wiltbank, R. (2009). Marketing under uncertainty: The logic of an effectual approach. *Journal of Marketing, 73*(3), 1–18.

Read, S., & Sarasvathy, S. D. (2005). Knowing what to do and doing what you know: Effectuation as a form of entrepreneurial expertise. *The Journal of Private Equity, 9*(1), 45–62.

Read, S., Sarasvathy, S. D., Dew, N., & Wiltbank, R. (2015). *Unreasonable assumptions in ASB*. Detail of discussion in Read, Sarasvathy, Dew, & Wiltbank (2016). Retrieved from: www.effectuation.org.

Read, S., Sarasvathy, S. D., Dew, N., & Wiltbank, R. (2016). Response to Arend et al.: Co-creating effectual entrepreneurship research. *Academy of Management Review, 41*(3), 528–536.

Reymen, I. M., Andries, P., Berends, H., Mauer, R., Stephan, U., & van Burg, E. (2015). Understanding dynamics of strategic decision making in venture creation: A process study of effectuation and causation. *Strategic Entrepreneurship Journal, 9*(4), 351–379.

Sarasvathy, S. (2001). Causation and effectuation: Toward a theoretical shift from economic inevitability to entrepreneurial contingencies. *Academy of Management Review, 26*(2), 243–263.

Sarasvathy, S. D. (2008). *Effectuation: Elements of entrepreneurial expertise*. Cheltenham: Edward Elgar Publishing.

Sarasvathy, S. D., & Dew, N. (2005). New market creation through transformation. *Journal of Evolutionary Economics, 15*(5), 533–565.

The World Bank (2013). *South Asia Human Development Sector Low Female Labor-Force Participation in Sri Lanka: Contributory Factors, Challenges and Policy Implications*. Retrieved from: https://openknowledge.worldbank.org/handle/10986/17871.

Tlaiss, H. A. (2014). Women's entrepreneurship, barriers and culture: Insights from the United Arab Emirates. *The Journal of Entrepreneurship, 23*(2), 289–320.

Wilson, K. (2015). Towards a radical re-appropriation: Gender, development and neoliberal feminism. *Development & Change, 46*(4), 803–832.

Wiltbank, R., Read, S., Dew, N., & Sarasvathy, S. D. (2009). Prediction and control under uncertainty: Outcomes in angel investing. *Journal of Business Venturing, 24*(2), 116–133.

Women's Chamber of Commerce and Industry (2015). *Fostering Women's Entrepreneurship in the SME Sector in Sri Lanka*. Retrieved from: www.wcicsl.lk/publications/WCIC%20Policy%20Advoacy%20Working%20Paper.pdf.

Yusuf, J. E., & Sloan, M. F. (2015). Effectual processes in nonprofit start-ups and social entrepreneurship: An illustrated discussion of a novel decision-making approach. *American Review of Public Administration, 45*(4), 417–435.

11 Cultural factors shaping women entrepreneurship in the Baltic Sea countries

Ewa Lisowska

The number of women entrepreneurs differs significantly in each of the Baltic Sea countries. The data show that the entrepreneurship rate for women, which expresses the percentage share of entrepreneurs in the women's total active labour force, is 14% in Poland, 7% in Lithuania, 8% in Latvia, 5% in Estonia, and 6% in Sweden (European Commission, 2014, p. 8). There are also differences in the share of women among all entrepreneurs: 34% in Poland, 40% in Lithuania and in Latvia, 28% in Estonia, and 26% in Sweden (European Commission, 2014, p. 24). While Lithuania and Latvia have the largest share of women among the total number of entrepreneurs, the highest female entrepreneurship rate is observed in Poland.

From these figures, the question that arises is why the entrepreneurship rate for women is twice as high in Poland as in Sweden. Is it caused by the fact that the conditions for the development of entrepreneurship are better in Poland than in Sweden? The ranking of the World Bank's *Doing Business* indicates that the best conditions for development of small and medium-sized businesses are in Sweden, whereas in Poland, they are the worst. Sweden is 8th in the ranking, Estonia is 16th, Lithuania is 20th, Latvia is 22nd, and Poland occupies the 25th position (Doing Business, 2016, p. 5). However, the relative conditions for business development in Sweden do not lead to a high share of women and men entrepreneurs. The situation in Poland is opposite: despite worse conditions for doing business than in Sweden, Estonia, Lithuania and Latvia, the phenomenon of entrepreneurship – both for female and male – is more evident in Poland and has a wider scope than what is observed in these countries, also compared to the European average. Therefore, a conclusion may be drawn that there are other factors besides those evident in the Doing Business ranking which explain differing levels of entrepreneurship in these countries.

In every Baltic Sea country, there is observed a visible entrepreneurial gender gap. It is also true that women's entrepreneurial activity is rather low in these countries compared with data from, for example, the United States. The explanation of the gap can be found in institutional theory and cultural factors, which are recognized as strongly influential on the social structure and the development of societies. Thus, the aim of the analysis in this chapter is to point out the role of cultural factors in shaping the phenomenon of women's entrepreneurship.

The analysis will be based on the literature, but the results of a questionnaire survey conducted in August–October 2015 in Estonia, Latvia, Lithuania, Poland and Sweden of 102 female entrepreneurs will be used to show that cultural factors are important for engaging women in entrepreneurial activity.

Cultural factors and female entrepreneurship

Cultural determinants have a significant meaning for perception of women's and men's roles in society and shaping the relationships between sexes (Bem, 1981; Krawiec, 2016; Mandal, 2004; Siemieńska, 2011). Over the last century, women exercised growing access to education, including tertiary schools, which sometimes led to a permanent place in the public sphere on the labour market, in economics and politics. The process of transition of women from the private sphere (home) to the public one was not easy because of persisting institutional patterns. Women taking up paid work did not translate automatically into the changes in family relationships, as husbands/partners did not want to assume more responsibility for housework and childcare (Titkow et al., 2004). In turn, work-related expectations and successful career patterns were defined by men to meet their needs and did not consider women's possibilities, needs and their desire to be treated equally (McKinnon, 1987; Ely et al., 2011; Bilińska & Rawłuszko, 2011). It became obvious that institutional aid in respect to care of dependent persons (children and elderly people) or help from individuals was necessary to realize professional ambitions of the contemporary women and to not waste their cultural potential (Siemieńska, 2011, p. 223). In the light of institutional theory, institutional environment (e.g., norms, rituals and conventions) strongly influenced the meaning what is appropriate (Meyer & Rowan, 1977; Amenta & Ramsey, 2010). From this point of view, the role of the state in development of anti-discrimination law and care institutions turned out to be the key one in supporting the economic activity of women.

According to the behavioural economists, stereotypes and prejudices against women and their competences (therefore cultural factors) currently present the main obstacles on the women's path to top managerial positions (Reuben et al., 2012; Wolfers, 2006). Prejudices against women also affect the position on the market of the companies managed by women, namely lower financial valuation of stock market companies and lower forecasts of their growth. They also cause the sale of shares of a company when a woman becomes its president (Wolfers, 2006, p. 3). However, the studies indicate that women, equally as well as men, cope with managing an enterprise and there are no statistically significant sex-related differences in the companies' financial performances (Wolfers, 2006; Lisowska, 2014). Then, the studies of Reuben et al.'s (2012) show that in the competition-minded environment, women are rarely chosen to a leadership position by a group, despite their high leadership competences. The reason lies in different perceptions and assessments of own skills and achievements and skills of the opposite sex: men show a tendency towards overrating their skills and underrating the skills of women, while women tend to underrate their own skills and overrate those of men. According to the Reuben conclusion, this mechanism leads to a lower representation of women among managers. Overrating men's skills and domination of the male experience in management results in making decisions that are not always optimal for the project team and its performance (Reuben et al., 2012, pp. 12–13).

Cultural barriers (the glass ceiling) in access to managerial positions are one reason for women to decide on self-employment. The glass ceiling mainly affects better-educated women aged 40 or over with experience in corporate work (Lisowska, 2010; Still, 2005). Since entrepreneurship is traditionally perceived as a male attribute, in almost all OECD countries fewer women than men are self-employed: on average 43.5% of men and 31.5% of women in OECD countries prefer self-employment to being an employee (Piacentini, 2013, p. 12). In the United States, both women and men often prefer self-employment. However, the gender gap is still visible: 43.8% of women and 58.3% of men prefer to be self-employed.

156   *Ewa Lisowska*

However, in the Scandinavian countries (e.g. Finland and Sweden), the least number of people opt for self-employment, whereas in countries such as Poland, the USA, Brazil, and Turkey their number is the highest (Piacentini, 2013, p. 13; Zbierowski et al., 2012).

Women, more often than men, conclude they lack the necessary knowledge and skills to establish their own company and believe that self-employment is not feasible. The exceptions to this perception are women from Finland and Sweden, who consider self-employment a feasible solution as often as men, albeit they usually declare that they prefer to work as employees (Piacentini, 2013, p. 14). In the case of Poland, the share of women reporting that it would be feasible for them to become self-employed within the next five years is at the level of Sweden. However, Polish women, more often than their Swedish counterparts, declare that it is better to be self-employed than to work as an employee, and in Poland more women are entrepreneurs (Piacentini, 2013; Lisowska, 2008).

Unemployment, gender equality and women entrepreneurship

A 2014 European Commission report pointed out a strong positive relationship between the level of unemployment and the female entrepreneurship rate. As shown in Table 11.1, while the female unemployment rate is lowest in Estonia and Sweden, the female entrepreneurship rate in these countries is also the lowest. In Poland one of the highest unemployment rates is observed and the female entrepreneurship rate is also the highest. Additionally, while Sweden has the highest and Poland has the lowest female employment rate, Poland is still at the top of the league when it comes to women entrepreneurship.

Table 11.1 Women and men on the labour market in the Baltic Sea countries

Country	Employment rate (2014)★ (age 20–64)		Unemployment rate (2014)★ (age 15–74)		Entrepreneurship rate (2012)★		Gender Equality Index★★	Sub-index in domain work★★★	Uncertainty Avoidance╪	
	Male	Female	Male	Female	Male	Female			Male	Female
Estonia	78.3	70.6	7.9	6.8	12	5	49.8	62.0	18.6	10.8
Lithuania	73.1	70.6	12.2	9.2	12	7	55.2	63.6	—	—
Latvia	73.1	68.5	11.8	9.8	13	8	46.9	63.3	—	—
Poland	73.6	59.4	8.5	9.6	23	14	43.7	55.5	36.7	17.8
Sweden	82.2	77.6	8.2	7.7	14	6	74.2	81.0	24.5	13.3
EU-28	78.3	63.5	10.1	10.3	19	10	52.2	61.9	—	—

★Eurostat 2014: http://ec.europa.eu/eurostat/web/lfs/data/main-tables (August 2016); European Commission 2014: Statistical Data on Women Entrepreneurs in Europe, September 2014, p. 8.

★★Gender Equality Index covers six core domains: work, money, knowledge, time, power and health. Its final value lies between 1 and 100, where the lowest value stands for inequality and the highest for equality.

★★★Domain of work covers: participation in employment (rate and duration of working time), segregation on the labour market (employment in education, human health and social work activities) and quality of work (flexibility of working time, safety, training at work, work-life balance).

Source: Gender Equality Index 2015 – Measuring gender equality in the European Union 2005–2012. European Institute for Gender Equality. Luxembourg: Publications Office of the European Union, p. 79.

╪ Women and men who very much agree or agree with the statement 'adventure and taking risks are important to have an exciting life' in chosen countries (%). Source: World Values Survey 2010–2014.

Looking at the Gender Equality Index, in the domain of work that covers participation in employment, segregation on the labour market and quality of work (flexibility of working time, work–life balance and training at work), Sweden received the highest index – 81.0 and Poland the lowest – only 55.5, while Estonia had 62.0, Latvia 63.3 and Lithuania 63.6 (EIGE, 2015, p. 79). In Poland, women work less often because of difficulties with finding a job. These difficulties concern young women and women re-entering the labour market after a longer break connected with childcare (Matysiak, 2007, p. 395). The employers focus mainly on employing men, because they perceive them as more available and free from childcare-related burdens. The results of qualitative research carried out in 2015 among women with basic vocational education indicated that women experience gender-related discrimination on the labour market. They are offered lower hourly pay rates than men with equal education levels and they less often have employment contracts (they are also employed more often for a limited duration than men). The employers are reluctant to conclude an employment contract with young women because they have concerns regarding maternity leave and breaks in work due to childcare (Lisowska, 2015a: 18; Lisowska, 2015b: 48–49).

Another problem is posed by the lower number of job offers for women, caused by stereotypes regarding jobs that can be performed by either women or men. The effect is segregation on the labour market, both horizontal and vertical (Sarata, 2011; Lisowska, 2010). The horizontal segregation concerns generally lower occupational possibilities for women than men, while the vertical segregation refers to women holding lower, often auxiliary, positions. The average women's and men's earnings are not equal; a gender pay gap is observed (Domański, 2011; Goraus & Tyrowicz, 2014; Grajek, 2003). It mainly concerns people with basic vocational education and university education (Lisowska, 2015a). This pay gap tends to discourage women from finding work or applying for managerial positions; thus, it consolidates traditional social roles (the woman as the homemaker, the man as the breadwinner). In a 2014 OECD Report concerning economic situation in Poland, the Polish labour market is described as 'heavily segmented', the female employment rate is low because of 'insufficient development of childcare', maternity leave is the longest among OECD countries and the pension system 'is generous for women' (OECD, 2014, pp. 10, 34, 75).

Despite European Union law regarding gender equality which has been obligatory in Poland for over a decade (respective provisions prohibiting discrimination were introduced into the Labour Code in 2004), there is no political willingness to supervise execution of this law. Research also indicates a lack of action promoting gender equality in the workplace and family (Lisowska, 2017; Zielińska, 2011). This differentiates Poland from Sweden where ensuring gender equality in practice has played a very important role in the state social policy. This gives Sweden the highest Gender Equality Index (GEI) among EU countries, whereas in Poland this indicator is below the EU average; it is also lower than the GEI for Latvia, Estonia, and Lithuania (see Table 11.1). Discrimination against women on the labour market in Poland results in higher indicators of female entrepreneurship than in other Baltic Sea countries.

The impact of social policy

It is also worth indicating another important element of social policy on behalf of families and combining work with childcare and its effects for the country's welfare. Social policy in Sweden is based on the social democratic regime of a welfare state, in accordance

158 *Ewa Lisowska*

with the Esping-Andersen typology (1990, pp. 26–29). The core idea of this is the state's responsibility for its citizens, including protecting people from negative effects of a market economy, and strengthening the family through services targeted at children, the elderly and disabled persons. In the social democratic regime, it is the state that guarantees a decent standard of living to the citizens. Thanks to the system of progressive and high taxes and individual taxation (there is no joint taxation for married couples) the state can finance allowances for all citizens in need. The social policy of Sweden focuses on occupational activation of all social groups, including women, and implementation of the model of the working family with the dual breadwinner (Anioł, 2013; Kondrat, 2015). It is possible due to a well-organized childcare infrastructure (crèches, kindergartens, dayrooms, etc.), as well as due to the inclusion of fathers into childcare and promotion of the positive aspects of fatherhood. As a result, Sweden is considered 'the first country to break patriarchal rules in the modern world' (Motiejūnaitė, 2008, p. 33).

A different situation is observed in Poland, a country with a liberal-conservative system where cultural and institutional determinant are 'highly unfavourable to combining work and family' (Matysiak & Mynarska, 2013, p. 5). The social policy of the government solidifies the traditional (patriarchal) division of roles in society. The solid evidence for this is the introduction on 1 April 2016 of the monthly financial allowance of PLN 500 for each second and successive child in all families (regardless of income) and for the first child if family income does not exceed PLN 800 (PLN 1,200 when bringing up a disabled child). The benefit is granted until a child reaches 18 years of age (Regulation, 2016). Such a form of the state aid to families (paying for having children) will probably result in 'pushing out' women from the labour market; the long-term effect can be lower female economic activity and the lack of financial security for the elderly. It seems that, women with lower levels of education and potentially lower earnings will be resigning from paid work. In no other country has such financial support for families been introduced; therefore, there is no research showing the extent to which this solution limits the economic activity of women.

The social policy offered by a state in the field of combining work with care responsibilities plays a significant role in the process of inclusion/exclusion women into/from the labour market. The lack of childcare infrastructure encourages women to favour self-employment as it is easier to combine family responsibilities with work duties than with full-time employment.

Uncertainty avoidance and women entrepreneurship

The European Commission analysis in 2014 indicated that the female entrepreneurship rate correlates negatively with the level of trust in people. The report offers a possible explanation in the following way: 'Less trust in people could stimulate entrepreneurship that can result in more autonomy and control' (European Commission 2014, p. 80). Such a relationship is also pointed out by Hofstede when describing the Uncertainty Avoidance dimension. In countries where the level of the Uncertainty Avoidance index (the degree to which members of a society feel uncomfortable with uncertainty and ambiguity) is high, more people, both women and men, are self-employed (Hofstede, 2005, p. 201). The results of the World Values Survey studies of 2010–2014, carried out via national representative samples, confirm evident differences in the level of trust among residents of Sweden, Poland, and Estonia (Latvia and Lithuania did not participate in this survey). The percentage of respondents who agreed with the statement 'most people can be trusted' comprised

22.2% in Poland, 39.0% in Estonia and 60.1% in Sweden, with 41.5% on average (www.worldvaluessurvey.org/wvsonline.jsp). It shows that Poland is among these countries with the relatively lowest level of trust in other people, while Sweden belongs to the group of countries with the highest level of trust.

Entrepreneurial attitudes, measured in the World Values Surveys with the respondents' attitude to the statement:'adventure and taking risks are important to have an exciting life', are most often observed in Poland (see Table 11.1). Both women and men from Poland most often identified with this statement (more often than the total number of those surveyed), while women and men from Estonia and Sweden chose this attitude decidedly less often. The data presented in Table 11.1 provide more evidence that in the Polish society, entrepreneurial attitudes are more frequent than in Swedish or Estonian society.

The factor 'trust in people' is one of the cultural determinants which greatly influence the entrepreneurship rate. It is interesting that another cultural factor – gender inequality– does not significantly influence the level of women entrepreneurs (European Commission 2014, p. 80). When analysing the data for the Baltic Sea countries, it may be observed that in Poland the scope of women's entrepreneurship phenomenon is larger than in Sweden, which is caused directly by discrimination against women on the labour market and their limited access to paid employment and managerial positions, while indirectly it is due to the lack of effective equality policy.

Therefore, cultural determinants may explain the varied level of women's entrepreneurship in the Baltic Sea countries. Beside the mentioned factors such as the unemployment rate and trust in people, there are other cultural factors influencing the level of women's entrepreneurship in a country, such as risk attitude and fear of failure, perceptions about entrepreneurs and entrepreneurship, as well as attitudes towards starting a business and ambition (Miller, 2012, p. 65). These factors were included into the questionnaire survey of women entrepreneurs in the Baltic Sea countries and are analysed below.

Method

As a part of the international project Gender, Innovation and Sustainable Development in the Baltic Sea Region (2014–2016), research among women entrepreneurs was conducted in the second half of 2015 with the use of an interview via questionnaire survey method, on a purposive sample. In each of the five countries (Estonia, Latvia, Lithuania, Poland, and Sweden), women were interviewed who for at least three years had been running their own business in the sector of tourism and the sector of creative industries or services. Female respondents were selected by local women's business organizations, with 50 chosen from each sector. The total number of interviews obtained was 102 (20 from each of the following countries: Sweden, Estonia and Lithuania, and 21 from Poland and Latvia).

For the research, businesses operating in catering, recreation and entertainment (tourist agencies; tourist services), accommodation (hotels and tourism farms) and tourist transport were classified as falling within the tourism sector. The sector of creative industries/services was defined according to the definitions of UNCTAD (2010, p. 7), Hesmondhalgh (2002, pp. 11–12), and Howkins (2001: 8) as IT, art and business, i.e. software and computer services; film, television and video production; computer games; music; visual arts; advertising; architecture; design and engineering.

The surveyed women most frequently had higher education, except for Sweden, where the number of women with secondary and post-secondary education was higher than the number of women with tertiary education. Their age was differentiated: the youngest ones

160   *Ewa Lisowska*

(aged up to 34 years) accounted for 23%; those aged 35–44 years, 27%; aged 45–54 years, 30%, and 55 years and older, 20%. Most of the respondents were owners of micro (with up to 10 employees) or small (10–49 employees) businesses, which were set up from scratch (only two in Sweden and two in Lithuania were created through inheritance or acquisition/ division of a private company) and mostly financed from own resources.

Findings

Opting for self-employment and development of the sector of small and medium-size companies are important for each economy, as they create new jobs, stimulate economic growth, reduce poverty and facilitate formalizing the informal sector (Ahmad & Hoffmann, 2012, p. 19). The phenomenon of entrepreneurship is determined by such factors as opportunities (caused by economic development), skilled people (obtained knowledge and skills) and resources (access to capital). All these factors are shaped by the culture and institutions of a given country, including entrepreneurship education, the law regulating economic relationships, involvement of the state in promotion of entrepreneurial attitudes and assistance in launching and maintaining companies. Culture influences the entrepreneurs' behaviour, attitudes and effectiveness; however, it is often unnoticed by the entrepreneurs because from a practical point of view the most visible influence for entrepreneurs is economic performance (Ahmad & Hoffmann, 2012, p. 22).

Risk attitude and fear of failure

Previous studies (Lisowska, 2010; Zbierowski et al., 2012) show that a positive perception of personal abilities and skills, as well as chances for success, is much higher for men, whereas a fear of failure is evidently higher among women. Therefore, it is more difficult for women to make decisions regarding initiation of self-employment (Lisowska, 2008). The situation is different when individuals have been already maintaining their own company; a lack of belief in achieving success is rare among women entrepreneurs. This is confirmed by the results of the studies in the Baltic Sea countries: only 12% of the total of respondents declared their lack of belief in achievement of success (Table 11.2).

About attitudes towards risk, women conducting their own businesses more often accept risk-taking than employed women. Nevertheless, among the female entrepreneurs in the

Table 11.2 Results of the questionnaire survey with 102 female entrepreneurs

	Estonia (n = 20)	Latvia (n = 21)	Lithuania (n = 20)	Poland (n = 21)	Sweden (n = 20)
Fear of failure, risk attitude and difficulties in combining work and family duties					
Lack of belief in success (12%)	1	3	4	1	3
Women who run own companies are afraid of taking a risk (49%)	11	10	12	10	7
Difficulties in combining work with caring for a child / elderly person (26%)	5	4	4	10	3

	Estonia (n = 20)	Latvia (n = 21)	Lithuania (n = 20)	Poland (n = 21)	Sweden (n = 20)
Opinions of female entrepreneurs about the situation of women in the country (number of 'yes' and 'probably yes' answers)					
Women have more difficulties and barriers in running own company as compared to men (43%)	10	5	9	7	13
Women have possibilities to receive support in starting own business (73%)	12	16	13	14	19
Socio-economic situation creates favourable environment for female entrepreneurship (56%)	15	15	7	12	8
Women are treated as equal partners in business (45%)	11	15	3	10	7
Opinions of female entrepreneurs about attitudes towards starting a business (number of 'yes' and 'probably yes' answers)					
Women have high entrepreneurial potential and are creative (96%)	17	21	19	21	20
Own business is the best way for women to reach a success in her professional life (55%)	15	9	12	10	10
Women are discriminated against on the labour market in my country (43%)	3	7	9	11	14

Baltic Sea countries, almost half declared that women who run their own companies are afraid of taking risk. Other studies confirm that conducting one's own business is in the opinion of many women burdened with high risk and one of significant reasons why they do not decide to take up self-employment (Lisowska, 2008).

Beside the above-mentioned difficulties which have their sources in cultural determinants, another factor to include is lack of work/life balance. The results of the surveys in the Baltic Sea countries show that one-fourth of female entrepreneurs' struggle with difficulties in combining work with caring for a child or elderly person. Among the surveyed countries, Poland is distinguished by a relatively high number of women indicating these difficulties, which are caused by limited access to institutional childcare.

Perceptions of entrepreneurs and entrepreneurship

In the opinion of a significant number of female entrepreneurs in the Baltic Sea countries, women face more barriers in running their own business compared to men. Such opinions are most often declared by women from Sweden, while they are voiced least often by women from Lithuania. The survey results also reveal that less than a half of women agree with the statement that women are treated as equal partners in business.

Making decisions about self-employment, as well as performing the role of the company owner, it is more difficult for women than for men because of cultural factors. About those difficulties some countries provide programmes supporting female entrepreneurship. These programmes most often comprise training aimed at strengthening the sense of one's own value and providing knowledge in the field of management of one's own company. There are also programmes that support women's export activities or offer credit guarantees. The majority of those surveyed in the Baltic Sea countries entrepreneurs report indicated that in their countries women may obtain support at the start of their own company. A distinctive country here is Sweden, where almost all women entrepreneurs (19 of 20 surveyed) agreed with this statement.

Slightly over half of women agreed that the country's socio-economic situation facilitates launching businesses by women. This was the most often stated by Estonian and Latvian women, while the least often by women from Lithuania and Sweden.

Attitudes towards starting a business

Contrary to the stereotypes, many women have entrepreneurial potential and they are creative persons. Almost all among the female entrepreneurs in the Baltic Sea countries agreed with the statement that women are entrepreneurial and creative. Slightly more than half of the surveyed women confirmed that own business is the best way for women to reach success in professional life. An interesting picture is provided by the respondents' reaction to the statement: 'Women in my country are discriminated against on the labour market.' Overall, 43% agreed with this statement. In Sweden, which holds the top position in the Gender Equality Index (EIGE, 2015) ranking, women entrepreneurs most often indicated the phenomenon of discrimination against women on the labour market (14 respondents of 20 surveyed women), while women from Estonia listed discrimination the least often (3 respondents per 20 surveyed women). These data indicate the awareness of the phenomenon of discrimination against women on the labour market, which is the highest in Sweden, rather than the actual scope of discrimination against women in a country.

Conclusions

The phenomenon of entrepreneurship of women is observed in many market economies; the intensity of it may be higher or lower, depending on the analysed country. The source of this phenomenon is based to a large extent discrimination against women on the labour market resulting in difficulties finding employment (high unemployment) and limited access to some occupations (gender-related occupational segregation), including access to managerial positions (the glass ceiling phenomenon). In the case of women slightly more often than in the case of men, a decision regarding self-employment is imposed rather than freely made. Difficulties with finding any paid work or a job offering decent earnings, the lack of chances for promotion and obtaining a managerial position, push women to self-employment. It is also worth pointing out that the studies on motivations for setting up own businesses indicate that regardless of the sex, the pulling to business factors are dominant over push factors (Hughes, 2003; Kariv, 2013; Lisowska & Rumińska-Zimny, 2016). Self-employment is undoubtedly one of the forms of economic empowerment of women threatened with unemployment or unemployed; it is also one of the ways of breaking the glass ceiling in women's access to decision-making positions.

Cultural factors (prejudices and stereotypes and the condition of law and institutions preventing prejudices and stereotypes and combating them) have a significant impact on the varied level of the entrepreneurship phenomenon countries, on entrepreneurial attitudes, and on the fact that women constitute a definite minority among entrepreneurs. Statistical data clearly show that the intensity of the women's entrepreneurship phenomenon in the Baltic Sea countries varies; the female entrepreneurs rate is the highest in Poland, while the lowest in other countries, where Estonia, Lithuania and Latvia are in this respect close to Sweden. In Sweden – the country with the most advanced equal treatment policy, the highest employment rate and the highest gender equality index – women less often choose self-employment than in other countries, which is probably caused by their high chances for paid employment. Female entrepreneurs from Sweden have great awareness of their opportunities on the labour market, including also the awareness of the fact that self-employment is an available choice for them, not a necessity. At the same time, more often than in the case of women from other countries, they realize their worse position on the labour market and in business, i.e. they are more sensitive to unequal treatment. In turn, female entrepreneurs from Poland slightly less often notice worse treatment in business and on the labour market than their Swedish counterparts, but, interestingly, they more often indicate difficulties in combining work and family responsibilities, although burdening only women with these responsibilities and the lack of institutional solutions including fathers' childcare is a manifestation of unequal treatment.

The results of the survey carried out in the Baltic Sea countries in 2015 confirm that female entrepreneurs are determined to achieve success and they believe in it. Half of the surveyed agreed with the opinion that one's own business is the best way for a woman to achieve success in her professional life. Almost all the surveyed declared that women are entrepreneurial and creative, albeit many of them indicated fears related to risk-taking. The surveys carried out in Germany proved that aversion to risk (higher in case of women than men) explained to the greatest extent the gender gap in entrepreneurship (Caliendo et al., 2014). Because of this (aversion to risk) women evidently less often than men make decisions regarding launching their own business activity. Thus, their participation among entrepreneurs is lower in each country.

One of the significant factors influencing entrepreneurial attitudes of women and men is education. Ahmad and Hoffmann (2012, p. 29) observe that:

> Entrepreneurship education has become an important component in many countries' attempts to affect the mindset of people, so they become more entrepreneurial. This type of education is not aimed at teaching specific skills that are relevant for entrepreneurship but more introducing the concept of entrepreneurship, its importance for society, and some of the key capabilities of entrepreneurs like pro-active.

The interest in becoming self-employed may be stirred through entrepreneurship education, which may also ease the fear of taking risk and failure, the factors which particularly hinder women's self-employment.

The findings presented here fit institutional theory which points out that cultural factors (tradition, history, norms, values) influence economic development and people's behaviour (Williamson, 1998, p. 26; Rosińska, 2008, pp. 15–16). In countries where there are more social guarantees for people and women have equal to men access to jobs in the public sector, entrepreneurial attitudes are rarer than in countries where social security is smaller

164 *Ewa Lisowska*

and limited to those who cannot handle their lives. In Sweden, where women's chances of finding work in the public sector are high, and institutional forms of care for children and elderly people are well-developed, women are less likely to own business than in Poland.

It should be underlined that the survey sample was small and the conclusions are not as strong as they could be if based on a larger sample of women entrepreneurs in the Baltic Sea countries. The results encourage further research on representative samples to strengthen the conclusions.

References

Ahmad, N., & Hoffmann, A. (2012). A framework for addressing and measuring entrepreneurship. In *Entrepreneurship determinants: Culture and capabilities*. Luxembourg: Eurostat Edition.

Amenta, E., & Ramsey, K. M. (2010). Institutional theory. In K. T. Leicht & J. C. Jenkins (Eds), *Handbook of politics: State and society in global perspective*. Handbooks of sociology and social research. © Springer Science+Business Media, LLC.

Anioł, A. (2013). *Szlak Norden. Modernizacja po skandynawsku*. Warsaw: Wydawnictwo IPS of the Warsaw University.

Bem, S. L. (1981). Gender schema theory: A cognitive account of sex typing. *Psychological Review, 88*, 354–364.

Bilińska, A., & Rawłuszko, M. (2011). Women managers for success 2011: Opportunities and obstacles to women's career path in Poland. *Women and Business, 1–4*, 42–59.

Caliendo, M., Fossen, F. M., Kritikos, A., & Wetter, M. (2014). The gender gap in entrepreneurship: Not just a matter of personality. *CESifo Economic Studies, 61*, 202–238.

Doing Business (2016). *Measuring Regulatory Quality and Efficiency*. Washington DC: The World Bank; www.doingbusiness.org/~/media/WBG/DoingBusiness/Documents/Annual-Reports/English/DB16-Full-Report.pdf.

Domański, H. (2011). Nierówności płci w latach 1982–2008. In K. Slany, J. Struzik, & K. Wojnicka (Eds), *Gender w społeczeństwie polskim* (pp. 251–266). Kraków: NOMOS.

EIGE (2015). *Gender Equality Index 2015: Measuring gender equality in the European Union 2005–2012*. European Institute for Gender Equality. Luxembourg: Publications Office of the European Union.

Ely, R., Ibarra, H., & Kolb, D. (2011). Taking gender into account. Theory and design for women's leadership development programmes. *Academy of Management Learning and Education, 10*(3), 474–493.

Esping-Andersen, C. (1990). *The three worlds of welfare capitalism*. Princeton, NJ: Princeton University Press.

European Commission (2014). Statistical data on women entrepreneurs in Europe. September.

Eurostat (2014). http://ec.europa.eu/eurostat/web/lfs/data/main-tables.

Goraus, K., & Tyrowicz, J. (2014). Gender wage gap in Poland: Can it be explained by differences in observable characteristics? *Working Paper, 11*. University of Warsaw.

Grajek, M. (2003). Gender pay gap in Poland. *Economic Change and Restructuring, 36*(1), 23–44.

Hesmondhalgh, D. (2002). *The cultural industries*. London: Sage.

Hofstede, G., & Hofstede, G. J. (2005). *Cultures and organizations: Software of the mind*. New York: McGraw-Hill.

Howkins, J. (2001). *The creative economy: How people make money from ideas*. London: Penguin.

Hughes, K. D. (2003). Pushed or pulled? Women's entry into self-employment and small business ownership. *Gender, Work and Organization, 10*(4), 433–454.

Kariv, D. (2013). *Female entrepreneurship and new venture creation: An international overview*. New York: Routledge.

Kondrat, M. (2015). Equal rights for women in Sweden. *Women and Business, 1–4*, 52–60.

Krawiec, A. E. (2016). Socio-economic implications of female inclusion in organizational structures and in leadership positions. *International Journal of Management and Economics, 49*, 106–134.

Lisowska, E. (2008). Analiza położenia kobiet na rynku pracy. In E. Lisowska & R. Kasprzak (Eds), *Zarządzanie mikroprzedsiębiorstwem. Podręcznik dla przedsiębiorczej kobiety* (pp. 159–193). Warsaw: Warsaw School of Economics.

Lisowska, E. (2010). *Równouprawnienie kobiet i mężczyzn w społeczeństwie.* Warsaw: Warsaw School of Economics.

Lisowska, E. (2014). Self-employment and motherhood: The case of Poland. In K. V. H. Lewis, C. Henry, E. J. Gatewood, & J. Watson (Eds), *Women's entrepreneurship in the 21st century: An international multi-level research analysis* (pp. 297–309). Cheltenham, UK; Northampton, MA: Edward Elgar Publishing.

Lisowska, E. (2015a). *Pay gap between women and men with basic vocational education: An Analysis of statistical data concerning the labour market, pay disparities and the opinions of the female respondents in 2015.* Warsaw: Karat Coalition; www.karat.org/wp-content/uploads/2015/09/Gender_pay_gap_vocational_education.pdf.

Lisowska, E. (2015b). Women with basic vocational education in the labour market: Situation in Poland. *Women and Business, 1–4,* 41–51.

Lisowska, E. (2017). Gender equality in the labour market and in the workplace. The case of Poland. In M. Warat, E. Krzaklewska, A. Ratecka, & K. Slany (Eds), *Gender equality and quality of life: Perspectives from Poland and Norway* (pp. 253–284). Frankfurt am Main: Peter Lang.

Lisowska, E., & Rumińska-Zimny, E. (2016). Innovativeness of women-owned businesses in the sectors of tourism and creative industries/services in the Baltic Sea countries. *Women and Business, 1–4,* 49–56.

McKinnon, C. (1987). *Feminism unmodified: Discourses on life and law.* Cambridge, MA: Harvard University Press.

Mandal, E. (2004). Stereotypical perception of female and male roles as determinant in professional careers and the functioning of the labour market. In *Gender and economic opportunities in Poland: Has transition left women behind?* (pp. 5–17). Warsaw: The World Bank.

Matysiak, A. (2007). Indywidualne przesłanki zwiększenia aktywności zawodowej. In I. E. Kotowska, U. Sztanderska, & I. Wóycicka (Eds), *Aktywność zawodowa i edukacyjna a obowiązki rodzinne w Polsce w świetle badań empirycznych* (pp. 383–403). Warsaw: Wydawnictwo Naukowe Scholar.

Matysiak, A., & Mynarska, M. (2013). Women's self-employment in Poland: A strategy for combining work and childcare? *Working Papers of Institute of Statistics and Demography Warsaw School of Economics, 28,* 1–30.

Meyer, J. W., & Rowan, B. (1977). Institutionalized organizations: Formal structure as myth and ceremony. *American Journal of Sociology, 83,* 340–363.

Miller, A. (2012). Training of entrepreneurs and future challenges for indicator construction. In M. Schmiemann (Ed.), *Entrepreneurship determinants: Culture and capabilities* (pp. 55–74). Luxembourg: Eurostat Edition.

Motiejūnaitė, A. (2008). Female employment, gender roles, and attitudes: The Baltic countries in a broader context. *Acta Universitais Stockolmiensis, Stockholm Studies in Sociology, 29.*

OECD (2014). *OECD Economic Surveys: Poland 2014.* OECD Publishing. http://dx.doi.org/10.1787/eco_surveys-pol-2014-en.

Piacentini, M. (2013). Women entrepreneurs in the OECD: Key evidence and policy challenges. *OECD Social, Employment and Migration Working Papers, 147.*

Regulation (2016). Rozporządzenie Ministra Rodziny, Pracy i Polityki Społecznej z dnia 18 lutego 2016 r. w sprawie sposobu i trybu postępowania w sprawach o świadczenie wychowawcze. Dziennik Ustaw z 19 lutego 2016, poz. 2014.

Reuben, E., Rey-Biel, P., Sapienza, P., & Zingales, L. (2012). The emergence of male leadership in competitive environments. *Journal of Economic Behavior and Organization, 83,* 111–117.

Rosińska, M. (2008). Analiza ekonomiczna przedsiębiorstwa w oparciu o teorie instytucjonalne: koncepcja 'instytucjonalizmu organizacyjnego przedsiębiorstw'. *Acta Universitatis Lodziensis Folia Oeconomica, 221,* 257–275.

Sarata, N. (2011). Rynek pracy w Polsce – płeć, obecność, uczestnictwo. In K. Slany, J. Struzik, & K. Wóycicka (Eds), *Gender w społeczeństwie polskim* (pp. 267–279). Kraków: NOMOS.

166   *Ewa Lisowska*

Siemieńska, R. (2011). Kontrakt płci. Między sferą prywatną i publiczną. In K. Slany, J. Struzik, & K. Wóycicka (Eds), *Gender w społeczeństwie polskim* (pp. 196–224). Kraków: NOMOS.

Still, L. V. (2005). The constrains facing women entering small business ownership. In S. L. Fielden, & M. J. Davidson (Eds), *International handbook of women and small business entrepreneurship* (pp. 55–65). Cheltenham: Edward Elgar Publishing.

Titkow, A., Duch-Krzystoszek, D., & Budrowska, B. (2004). *Nieodpłatna praca kobiet. Mity, realia, perspektywy*. Warsaw: Instytut Filozofii i Socjologii PAN.

UNCTACD (2010). *Strengthening the creative industries for development in Zambia*. New York and Geneva: United Nations.

Williamson, O. E. (1998). Transaction cost economics. How it works. Where it is headed. *The Economist, 1*, 26. doi:10.1023/A:1003263908567.

Wolfers, J. (2006). Diagnosing discrimination: Stock returns and CEO gender. *Journal of the European Economic Association, 4*, 531–541.

Zbierowski, P., Węcławska, D., Tarnawa, A., & Nieć, M. (2012). *Global Entrepreneurship Monitor: Poland*. Warsaw: Polish Agency of Entrepreneurship Development and University of Economics in Katowice.

Zielińska, E. (2011). Prawo wobec kobiet. In K. Slany, J. Struzik, & K. Wóycicka (Eds), *Gender w społeczeństwie polskim* (pp. 103–118). Kraków: NOMOS.

12 The business life-cycle and entrepreneurial ecosystem study of women entrepreneurs in the Polish tourism industry

Alina Zapalska and Erik Wingrove-Haugland

Entrepreneurship has been widely accepted as the most vital factor for economic growth and social development (Ramadani & Schneider, 2013; Dana, 2005). Governments are increasingly recognizing that entrepreneurial firms run by women have a strong positive impact on employment levels and on the creation of competitive advantages to a marketplace (Morrison et al., 2003; Ramadani et al., 2015). As an entrepreneurial gender gap between male- and female-owned businesses still exists (Mitra, 2002; Zapalska, 1997, Gupta et al., 2008), numerous organizations and institutions continue to address the needs of women entrepreneurs. Governments have become increasingly responsible for eliminating legal barriers and creating a regulatory environment in which women entrepreneurs can succeed (Davidsson et al., 2006; Hisrich et al., 2005). Understanding the environment of women entrepreneurs and how different it is from the environment of their male competitors is critical (Ramadani, 2013; Coleman, 2002).

Despite the fact that Poland is regarded as a leader in the process of entrepreneurial success in Eastern and Central Europe, Polish women entrepreneurial firms have been facing problems at various stages of their growth and development in Poland's transitional economy (Fogel, 2001). At each stage of business growth, it is important to identify and describe the environmental factors perceived to contribute to the problems faced by those businesses. This chapter analyses ten female entrepreneurs to understand how they have successfully grown their family businesses and what entrepreneurial barriers they faced over four stages of their growth.

Our findings are based on online surveys conducted with ten Polish female entrepreneurs who operate within the tourism industry. By analysing female entrepreneurship within the life-cycle model of the growth and development of an entrepreneurial firm, this study provides recommendations for policy makers to foster and encourage female entrepreneurship through targeted policy initiatives that reflect an understanding of the factors that constitute barriers to the success of female entrepreneurial activity. The experiences and strategies presented by ten female entrepreneurs generate recommendations for policy makers regarding business strategies and environmental conditions that foster successful entrepreneurial development and growth in the tourism industry.

This chapter is organized as follows. First, it provides a background on the Polish economy and the development of small businesses within the Polish tourism industry. Second, it presents a model of organizational life-cycle and entrepreneurial development that uses four stages of the business life-cycle to analyse the characteristics of Polish entrepreneurial firms within the tourism industry. The model also focuses on five factors affecting entrepreneurial success: *government policies and procedures; socioeconomic conditions; entrepreneurial and business skills; financial assistance*; and *non-financial assistance*. The last section of the chapter provides results of the research followed by conclusions and policy recommendations.

The context of women entrepreneurs in Poland

Poland is among the most diverse EU countries in respect to its culture and heritage, creating opportunities for entrepreneurial businesses to prosper within the tourism industry. Not only Polish history, culture and tradition but also Poland's natural beauty and wildlife influenced Polish females to start entrepreneurial activities in the tourism sector. During the Soviet regime, tourism in Poland was very limited (Sachs, 1994). The quality and amount of tourist services were inadequate due to lack of experience, insufficient infrastructure, and poor value in areas such as catering, advertising, transportation, and telecommunications brought by decades of ignorance and neglect (Zienkowski, 2000). However, several years before the collapse of the Soviet regime, Polish females took advantage of new market mechanisms introduced in the 1980s to create their first entrepreneurial businesses (Balcerowicz, 1995).

As soon as the Polish economy overcame the shock therapy at the end of 1990s, the private sector, and in particular the tourism sector, began to experience an economic and political environment that allowed entrepreneurial activities to develop, grow and create higher-value niche tourism products and services (Richards, 1996; Johnson & Loveman, 1995). Financial aid from Western institutions provided a source of support for infrastructure projects and encouraged further foreign investment in the small entrepreneurial sector of Polish tourism (Richards, 1996). Further assistance programmes provided the tourism sector with special EU funds and attention from the Minister of Sport and Tourism (Butler, 2001).

Female-run businesses within the tourism industry have developed in all parts of the Polish economy. They started simple and small while focusing on a relatively low-skilled segment of the market that offered accommodation and related services to domestic travellers. Poland's entry to the EU in May 2004 had a strong positive effect on the growth of the tourism sector (Kosmaczewska, 2007; GUS, 2012). Increasing prosperity in Poland has provided citizens with relatively more leisure time and discretionary income, which has allowed more Polish people to start enjoying the benefits and pleasure of domestic and international tourism, causing the growth of female entrepreneurial activities in the Polish tourism sector to skyrocket (Zapalska & Fogel, 1998). The growing trend towards involvement in travel and tourism has also come from the increasing number of Western European and North American tourists since the late 1990s (Jackson et al., 1999).

Today, the tourism industry supported by female entrepreneurs is one of Poland's fastest growing industries. Poland's current economic and political stability and the rising affluence of its population will continue to provide a solid base for sustained growth in the country's tourist services sector that is strongly supported by family based and female-run entrepreneurial firms (Kryk, 2008). Despite the fact that Poland has been regarded as a leader in the process of economic transformation, Polish small entrepreneurial ventures run by females have been facing many problems and obstacles. Therefore, it is important to identify the factors that contributed to success and failure of female-run entrepreneurial activities in Poland's tourism industry.

Empowering women is a challenge. Female entrepreneurship can help to meet this challenge. Female enterprises not only enhance local productivity and generate employment but also help develop economic independence, personal growth and social capabilities among women. Encouraged by these schemes, large number of women entrepreneurs from diverse socioeconomic backgrounds are coming forward to venture into business. Entrepreneurial growth in developing countries is often constrained by insufficient funds to set up ventures, and lack of ability to perceive opportunities, organize resources and establish and successfully operate the enterprise. Even when financial resources are made available, women entrepreneurs are not emerging because the potential entrepreneur who is dormant within them is not nurtured and cultivated.

The authors of this chapter hope to provide some directions on how to accelerate the formation of enterprises by women in other countries through imaginative development programmes and policies with sound institutional support. As this has been very well achieved in Poland in the last two decades, the case study presented in this chapter can provide some policy implications. The constraint of finance, which continues to prohibit the entry of many women entrepreneurs into business, has not been removed even in Western countries. Despite these problems, large number of women entrepreneurs from diverse socioeconomic backgrounds are coming forward and venturing into business. More open discussion of the financial constraints faced by women entrepreneurs and how to combat these barriers should help address this problem and eliminate the global gender gap.

Methodology and conceptual framework

The study of entrepreneurship is multi-dimensional (Baum et al., 2007; Kuratko et al., 2004). An increasingly popular approach explains entrepreneurs' success (or lack of success) by combining personal characteristics (psychological and physical predisposition), personal environment (role models, family factors and personal goals), business environment, and business ideas that promote or hamper the creation and development of successful entrepreneurship (Morrison et al., 2003). Several authors recommend examining entrepreneurs by analysing the characteristics of entrepreneurship as well as the internal or external factors that play key roles in stimulating or obstructing existing and prospective entrepreneurs seeking to grow or develop their businesses (Menguc et al., 2010; Henry et al., 2003). Storey (1994) defined the internal factors that influence growth and combined them into three components: *entrepreneur, firm* and *strategy*. According to the author, 'Entrepreneur' factors that affect growth of the SMEs include motivation, gender, unemployment, education, number of founders, management experience, family history, training, age and prior business failure, sector experience and firm size. Under *firm*, the author included the following factors: age, sector, legal form, location, size and ownership; and under *strategy*: working and management training, external equity, technology, market positioning and adjustments, planning, new products, management recruitment, state support, customer concentration, competition, exporting and information and advice.

Isenberg (2010 and 2011) proposed a holistic approach to analysing an 'entrepreneurial ecosystem', defined as a set of interrelated individual elements that include leadership, culture, financial and human capital that all together are critical for a sustainable entrepreneurial ecosystem. Isenberg's model represents a static model which does not represent challenges faced by firms over time across all stages of the firm's growth and development. Organizational life cycles and stages of development models analyse the entrepreneurial process based on the time factor (Lester et al., 2003). According to those models, firms pass through a sequence of stages where they face numerous problems and challenges; progressing to the next stage is highly dependent on how successful the firm was in addressing the issues in the previous stage.

This chapter contributes to entrepreneurship literature by advancing an analysis of female-run entrepreneurship activities over time. The model adopted in this chapter is based on Gnyawali and Fogel's framework (1994) that categorizes ecosystem factors into five general dimensions: government policies and procedures, socioeconomic conditions, entrepreneurial and business skills, financial assistance and non-financial assistance as illustrated in Figure 12.1. This chapter integrates Gnyawali and Fogel's framework into the four stages of growth and development proposed by Kazanjian (1988). As presented in Figure 12.1 those four stages are: Development, Commercialization, Growth and Stability.

Data was collected online based on responses provided by ten women who operate and manage family tourism businesses from different regions in Poland. A list of female entrepreneurs was obtained from the official tax office and a sample of ten female-run businesses was selected randomly. An invitation was sent out to each entrepreneur explaining the purpose of the research with a request to schedule a survey email interview. A follow-up email was sent out in order to increase the response rate. All ten entrepreneurs responded to the invitation and agreed to participate. Through an in-depth questionnaire and additional follow-up email conversations, the authors were able to obtain detailed and thorough information to complete this study. All participants gave permission to share their stories with the promise of confidentiality. The questionnaire elicited information on the size and nature of the entrepreneurial operation, business objectives, level of employment, financial assistance received and desired, non-financial support, business training needs, socioeconomic conditions, and opinions regarding policies on taxation, preferences and credit financing.

The questionnaire and responses were grouped into three distinctive categories to identify common factors that promote or inhibit the entrance of women into the entrepreneurial process, and to identify those factors that were critical, important or a matter of concern for growth and development across all four stages. This chapter summarizes research findings related to government policies and procedures, socioeconomic conditions, entrepreneurial

Figure 12.1 Model of organizational life-cycle and entrepreneurial development
Source: Developed by authors based on research results by Gnyawali and Fogel (1994) and Kazanjian (1988)

and business skills, financial assistance and non-financial assistance. Respondents were asked to evaluate the importance of five primary domains of entrepreneurship ecosystems across four stages of their firm's growth and development. Respondents' perceptions regarding which entrepreneurial ecosystem domains are 'critical', which are 'important' and which are 'satisfying' are presented and discussed to provide policy recommendations that support entrepreneurial development and growth.

Findings

The basic information of ten respondents and their characteristics is provided in Table 12.1. Nine of ten female entrepreneurs included in this study are not young; the average time of business operation is about twenty-seven years. Only one firm, medical tourism, has only been in operation for fifteen years. This indicates that the majority of the respondents had set up their ventures prior to 1990, which is when restrictions on private activity were lifted. The sizes of businesses are relatively small with staffing of between four and fifteen employees with 80 per cent of businesses extending their services to international customers. Six respondents have undergraduate college or technical education, while four respondents graduated from college with a diploma. Eight businesses were not developed by respondents but were inherited or taken over by children who had previously run them together with their parents. The median age of the respondent was 52, with a youngest of 31e and the oldest 65. All respondents were married and only six respondents had children.

Female entrepreneurs concentrate on sectors that are considered to be less profitable. The results of this study confirm this general claim. The female-run enterprises included in this study cover a wide spectrum of tourism services and products that include bed and breakfast, guesthouse and inn, agro-tourism, restaurant and café, art and culture-based activities, tourist wellness and health service, cultural, sport and recreation activities and training, and medical tourism (Table 12.1). Based on the responses, the most common tourist activities are visiting pilgrimage places, national parks and nature experiences, outdoor and recreational activities, arts festivals and cultural events, art and folklore related galleries and art or cooking seminars, visiting historical places, wellness and health related seminars and trainings, and recreational activities and sport-oriented training such as horseback-riding, wild-berry picking or pottery making.

Respondents' motivation for venturing into entrepreneurship referred to as their 'entrepreneurial spirit', goes beyond the desire to support their families and includes the desire to enjoy adventures, to push one's boundaries and to find out the limits of one's experience. Those results support other studies that argue that such characteristics are necessary for businesses to grow. Being inclined to 'take risks' or to make decisions based on longer-term visions of growth were all attributed to this 'entrepreneurial spirit'. The firms included in this study survived and experienced growth. In particular, the 2007 crisis did not affect tourism operations as female entrepreneurs focused on providing products and services that were of paramount importance to their customers. The females also concentrated on providing products and services with high-cost advantages by taking advantage of natural resources as well as cultural and historical elements of Polish society. The successful businesses focused on delivering products and services based on utilizing historical, artistic and natural resources present in Poland. They produced products and services of high quality that were unique to Polish heritage, culture and tradition. Respondents also expressed that prior to the 1990s, business skills were not as critical as they were after the collapse of the Soviet bloc.

172 *Alina Zapalska and Erik Wingrove-Haugland*

Table 12.1 Characteristics of ten female businesses within tourism industry in Poland

	Type of business	*Workers*	*Geographic.Location*	*Clients★*	*Selected examples of innovation strategies.*
1.	Art gallery and studio	10	City	D & I	new service, new marketing method, new organizational culture and climate
2.	Beauty salon and wellness spa	5	City	D & I	new product, new service, new supply, new administrative process
3.	Agro-tourism bed and breakfast	9	Country	D & I	new product, new service, new organizational culture and climate
4.	The farm and guesthouse	11	Suburb	D	new service, new strategy, new market, new organizational culture and climate
5.	The health and spa guesthouse	12	Suburb	D & I	new service, new strategy, new market, new organizational culture and climate
6.	Horseback–riding farm	5	Country	D	new strategy, new market
7.	The café shop	6	Small town	D & I	new product, new service, new strategy, new process of production, new organizational culture and climate
8.	Cosmetic, dental and plastic Surgery	15	Small town	D & I	new product, new market, new administrative process
9.	Horseback-Riding in the Wilderness	4	Suburb	D & I	new market, new organizational culture and climate
10.	The Pottery House	8	Small town	D & I	new product, new strategy, new supply, new organizational culture and climate

Note: ★ D = Domestic; I = International.

All respondents stated that finding a new and unique product or service that is based on Polish culture or tradition was a driving force for business success. They all were able to attract customers because of the type of products and services they provided. The country's unique natural resource base, socio-cultural, traditional and ecological characteristics form an environment in which female involvement in innovative entrepreneurial development and ownership is the norm rather than the exception. Finding an innovative product, a receptive market, effective strategies, and marketing practices made their businesses succeed particularly during financial crises. Examples of innovative locations and strategies exercised by respondents are summarized in Table 12.1.

Respondents agreed that the tourism sector in Poland managed to grow due to domestic tourists who wanted to get away from their professional responsibilities and take vacations. Polish tourists were not allowed to travel to Western Europe in the 1980s, and in the early 1990s they could not afford it. This growing trend towards domestic travel has become a vital element of the Polish economy. New entrepreneurs took advantage of the increasing opportunities to grow and expand their tourism businesses. They created successful businesses that provided at first an alternative income, but later after 1990 a primary source of income. While doing so, they also promoted the rise of cultural and environmental awareness in the local community, and contributed to the preservation of the rural region's culture, folklore and traditions.

Respondents business' growth was also tied to their commitment to enhance local prosperity and promote a product or service that meets the needs of consumers. Respondents (or their parents, in the case of inherited businesses) started their businesses from scratch. They were confident about their business direction, and their success was achieved after they recognized new market trends which led them to introduce an innovative strategy or develop a product or service that was new to their local economy. Finding an innovative product or service related to sustainable- or green-tourism made the businesses particularly successful. Female entrepreneurs were able to recognize and take advantage of the specific cultural and resource base in Poland.

The products and services offered by their businesses reveal an increasing trend towards sustainability tourism. Diversification and introduction of unique tourism products or services such as green-tourism, eco-tourism or sustainability tourism have also been greatly influenced by demographic and geographic changes in Poland and other countries of the EU. As a result of such changes, a generation of better informed and wealth-oriented consumers requires sustainable and environmentally friendly products and services. Demand for sustainable and culture-oriented tourism products and services have been growing in Poland since 1990. Today they are expected to continue to grow, given that the demand for Polish products and services is increasing among foreign customers who are attracted to lower prices, high quality, and unique services and products.

The respondents also expressed that their commitment to generate income and decent employment for their family and local community without affecting the environment and culture of the tourist destinations ensured the long-term viability and competitiveness of their enterprises. Their businesses have been a source of growth, wealth-creation and respectable employment for their local economy while at the same protecting the local environment. These female entrepreneurs expressed that their business success has been tied to their commitment to enhance local prosperity, increase happiness and provide health-oriented vacation services to their customers. They wanted their businesses to attract a large amount of spending that would be retained locally. The development and growth of their businesses provided a positive experience for local populations, other tourism industry sectors, workers and the tourists themselves.

Analysis of the entrepreneurial ecosystem characteristics

Business enterprises are presumed to face different crises, managerial problems and issues at different stages of growth. Our results demonstrate that respondents' perceptions regarding how entrepreneurial ecosystem domains were critical to the success of their firms across four stages of growth and development. The results based on the online interviews are summarized in Table 12.2.

Government policies and procedures

All ten respondents considered government policies and procedures to be a 'critical' domain that inhibited firms' growth and development, particularly during the first two stages (Table 12.2). All respondents stated that lack of proper policies supporting private sector growth in the 1980s and at the beginning of the 1990s prevented entrepreneurial businesses'

174 *Alina Zapalska and Erik Wingrove-Haugland*

Table 12.2 Entrepreneurial ecosystem factors results within life-cycle stage Model

Entrepreneurial ecosystem factors	Life-cycle stage			
	I	II	III	IV
Government policies and procedures.	10–0–10*.	10–0–10.	4–7–4.	3–7–3.
Socioeconomic Conditions.	10–10–4.	10–10–3.	10–10–0.	10–10–0.
Entrepreneurial and business skills.	10–4–2.	10–3–2.	10–3–5.	10–7–3.
Financial assistance.	10–0–10.	10–0–10.	7–6–5.	5–8–3.
Non-financial assistance	10–0–10.	9–0–10.	6–7–8.	5–70–9.

Source: Developed by the authors based on the interview results.

Note * is it critical for your success? – are you satisfied? – is it an important concern?

Stage I = Development; Stage II = Commercialization; Stage III = Growth; Stage IV = Stability.

growth. The perception on the concern of government policies and procedures decreased at the growth and stability stage (Table 12.2). The changes in government regulations and policies in the mid-1990s after the collapse of the Soviet regime allowed their businesses to expand. Entry barriers and rules and regulations that were prevailing during first two stages were considered the most critical. Seven out of ten respondents were satisfied with the extensive measures that EU policies established after Poland joined the EU in 2004. These policies stimulated the growth of the entrepreneurial activities, bringing economic growth and lower unemployment. Seven respondents were satisfied with government policies and procedures that applied to the tourism industry during their operations in last two stages. The respondents repeatedly expressed that the greatest hurdle to the growth of their businesses was a high level of taxation. Also, procedural requirements for registration and licensing were the most critical factors for successful development and growth.

Socioeconomic conditions

Socioeconomic conditions and entrepreneurial culture (what society offers and how individuals perceive entrepreneurship) were considered as critical entrepreneurial ecosystem domains for success during all four stages of growth and development (Table 12.2). The results are not surprising, since after the collapse of the Soviet regime, the importance of entrepreneurship, the population's willingness to take risks, and the desire to become an entrepreneur have increased with the acceptance of a market economy. The socioeconomic conditions in Poland continued to improve as society experienced the successful formation of entrepreneurial firms across all sectors of the economy. Table 12.2 reports that all ten respondents were 'satisfied' with socioeconomic conditions across all four stages. Respondents argued that there is no differentiation in the attitude towards doing business among men and women. The respondents stated that the greatest increase in the number of companies established by women was observed during the first years of transformation. Other studies confirm that during the whole period of transformation the number of self-employed women was relatively larger than that of men. The OECD (2010) indicating the percentage participation of women working on their own among all the employed, show that for many years Poland has been one of the leaders in this category. Moreover, in the whole of Europe the rate of women entrepreneurship in Poland, including the rate of the self-employed, has been one of the highest for years.

Entrepreneurial and business skills

Respondents mentioned that entrepreneurial and business skills were 'critical' and never at the 'satisfactory' levels across four stages. Despite that fact that new accounting standards, tax systems, more competitive economic conditions and government policies required female entrepreneurs to gain entrepreneurial and business skills, the majority of respondents argued that entrepreneurial and business skills were not 'an important concern'. According to respondents, business skills acquired before 1990 were not always useful in a new post-communist economic and political environment. However, the undergraduate or graduate degrees they acquired prior to establishment of entrepreneurial businesses allowed females to choose businesses that were the most efficient given their area of residence, their expertise and interest, and their business' competitive advantage. The results indicate 40 and 30 per cent satisfaction levels with entrepreneurial and business skills during first two stages, as their professional skills were suitable to establish and run an entrepreneurial tourism business. The level of satisfaction with entrepreneurial and business skills increased during the last two stages as female entrepreneurs were able to obtain some business training that increased their level of satisfaction (Table 12.2).

All respondents stated that they effectively communicated the projected plans of the firm to their employees and established interpersonal relationships with their workers. They all were able to meet the needs of their employees and the needs of their clients before their own personal needs, avoided the use of power for personal gain, demonstrated high moral standards and set challenging goals. Nine of the ten respondents motivated and inspired employees by displaying enthusiasm and optimism, involving the employees in decision making, communicating high expectations and demonstrating commitment to the shared goals. All respondents motivated their workers to be committed to their vision of their business organizations; it was not difficult to achieve those goals after the collapse of the Soviet bloc when spirit and drive were high.

The respondents also mentioned that they avoided the use of power or authority, but focused on personal characteristics such as charisma, interpersonal skills and personal contacts while running their family businesses. Charismatic personalities made the female leaders become role models who were respected and followed by their employees. Respondents recognized that the success of their business operations came also from caring leadership practices together with participative involvement of employees in decision making related to the direction and level of growth of the business. This participatory organizational culture had a positive effect on firms' performance and contributed to human resource development, employee satisfaction, more efficient communication and better cooperation. By working closely with their workers and clients, they were able to identify important problems and economic concerns faced by their small family entrepreneurial firms across four stages of growth and development.

Financial assistance

Financial assistance was considered to be a 'critical' domain for development and growth. Banks were not considered as a primary source of financing the growth of their businesses.

Lack of financial mechanisms available to entrepreneurs in the 1980s prevented them from achieving a desirable level of production to meet market demand. In all stages of development, the primary funding for women enterprises came from family and friends' savings. Those results are confirmed by other studies (OECD/European Commission, 2013; Piacentini, 2013). According to Table 12.2, nine respondents who started in the late 1980s had to rely on their own savings and financial support from their friends and families. Respondents also stated that higher levels of financial assistance were granted to males who operated in the construction or manufacturing sector over all stages.

The collapse of the Soviet bloc in the 1990s created some new opportunities for financing their firms' growth, which is reflected in an increase in their level of 'satisfaction' from zero to eight respondents expressing contentment. According to respondents, it was important to build a network of other professional women because women understand and support the businesses that women tend to run. However, women-dominated networks were also felt to be limiting because there were far fewer women working in venture capital firms. Respondents argued that this tended to minimize the success and potential of their business, compared to men. When applying to potential investors for financing, women were less able to generate confidence in their work and success compared to men. This was felt, by respondents, to be a result of ingrained gender behaviours which discourage women from highlighting their achievements, for fear that it would appear boastful. Access to venture capitalists or private investors was also a critical barrier as women-dominated networks are likely to be less influential in terms of facilitating access to funding. Based on the responses provided, it can be argued that women are likely to ask for less debt finance compared to male entrepreneurs and more likely ask for money to cover their immediate costs rather than money to enable them to grow. This was also felt to be a result of gender roles and different levels of 'entrepreneurial spirit' between genders.

Non-financial assistance

Overall, non-financial assistance was 'critical' and not 'sufficient' during the first two stages, and was considered a 'concern' during all four stages. The most critical element for the tourism industry was the availability of transport and communication facilities. Entrepreneurial networks increased in availability over the years, and hence respondents' level of satisfaction increased as presented in Table 12.2. Modern transport and communication facilities were always critical to our respondents across all stages. Their level of 'concern' was very high during first two stages before investment was fuelled by funds coming from the EU to improve infrastructure. The level of concern regarding a lack of modern transportation and communication facilities decreased over time, as the Polish economy has been growing fast and infrastructure kept changing in order to meet Western standards. Non-financial assistance to the entrepreneurs came from Western private investors who were seeing Poland as a coming success.

The respondents were concerned by a lack of consultancy for the active businesses, which would enable them to prepare the company's development plans, advise on the issue of new ideas and investments, introduce new ideas into the market, and provide information on available sources of financing and subsidies. Entrepreneurial networks were critical in the last two stages when markets became more competitive and complex after Poland joined the EU. Consultancy centres, according to the respondents, should be more available as well as more appropriately tailored for small female-enterprises. Another important 'concern' is the available networks that could support women entrepreneurs. For example, the network of public institutions providing care for small children is not sufficient. There is a lack of widely available access to nurseries and kindergartens, which would enable female entrepreneurs who are mothers to run a company.

Conclusions

For more than a decade, the Polish economy has been adjusting its laws and economic institutions to EU regulations. After the collapse of the Soviet bloc, it moved to establish basic market mechanisms and policies and opened its markets to international trade. These reforms were successful in generating entrepreneurship and economic growth. The transition from state-planning to a market-oriented economy in Poland has provided valuable lessons for developing countries and international assistance organizations seeking to accelerate private enterprise expansion. The private sector in the tourism industry operated by female entrepreneurs in Poland has stimulated economic growth and job creation. The Polish government and the EU tourism authorities recognized that Poland is rich in environmental and cultural assets and provided support and infrastructure to facilitate the development of sustainability and cultural tourism.

Polish female entrepreneurs preferred low-risk and return businesses. Most of the innovations within their operations were simple but ingenious and had their origins in an individual's ability to observe what was available and what was required by the market and to change their products or services to suit market needs. The success of these enterprises, as analysed across four stages of firms' growth and development, came from an optimal use of environmental resources and delivery of products and services that were unique to Polish heritage, culture, tradition and natural resources. These female-run businesses have become increasingly dynamic and subject to constant change and evolution towards sustainability, health and wellness. Entrepreneurship conducted by Polish women was accomplished primarily for the benefit of their local communities and the protection of natural resources. Their orientation towards eco-tourism and sustainable tourism services promoted a climate of respect for the socio-cultural authenticity of host communities. By providing positive experiences for both visitors and hosts, they also delivered direct benefits for conservation and financial benefits and empowerment for local people.

Female entrepreneurs included in this study experienced problems and concerns. Government policies and procedures, financial assistance and non-financial assistance were considered as obstacles to the firms' development and growth. The greatest hurdle to the economic growth of their businesses was related to a lack of access to financial assistance and as a result financial assistance continues to be based on their family or friends' savings. Government policies should be enacted to improve these conditions for women entrepreneurs in informal sectors such as tourism. Small enterprise development needs to be guided and managed strategically. The use of appropriate entrepreneurial ecosystem models of development that are sensitive to the cultures and entrepreneurial motivations of the local population would provide a foundation for an economic policy that will bring continuous growth and development in sustainability-oriented tourism. Developing business incubators, offering entrepreneurial and accounting consultancy, facilitating access to subsidies and other conveniences, offering free or partly paid trainings and workshops provide very practical knowledge in running a company, and simplifying the access to broadband Internet are the key tools policymakers can use to promote the development of small entrepreneurial firms.

Based on the results presented in this chapter, specific policy measures are needed to promote entrepreneurial growth. Innovation requires a clear vision of what an entrepreneurial firm wants to achieve. It is important that local authorities pursue economic and tax incentive policies to improve economic and financial conditions to support the growth of already operating firms and encourage the development of new entrepreneurial activities. However, there is a need for more research on the tourism industry in Poland and other countries of the region. Such focused efforts will help develop a more complete understanding of the causes, correlations, and consequences of successful, sustainable entrepreneurship.

References

Balcerowicz, L. (1995). *Wolność i rozwój. Ekonomia wolnego rynku*. Kraków: Znak.

Baum, J. R., Frese, M., & Baron, R. A. (2007). *The psychology of entrepreneurship*. Mahwah, NJ: Erlbaum.

Butler, R. (2001). Seasonality in tourism: issues and implications. In T. Baum & S. Lundtorp (Eds), *Seasonality in tourism* (pp. 5–22). Amsterdam: Pergamon.

Coleman, S. (2002). Constraints faced by women small business owners: Evidence from the data. *Journal of Development Entrepreneurship, 7*(2), 151–174.

Dana, L. P. (2005). *When economies change hands: A survey of entrepreneurship in the emerging markets of Europe from the Balkans to the Baltic States*. Binghamton, NY: International Business Press.

Davidsson, P., Delmar, F., & Wiklund, J. (2006). Entrepreneurship as growth: Growth as entrepreneurship. In P. Davidsson, F. Delmar, & J. Wiklund (Eds), *Entrepreneurship and the growth of firms* (pp. 21–38). Cheltenham: Edward Elgar Publishing.

Fogel, G. (2001). An analysis of entrepreneurial environment and enterprise development in Hungary. *Journal of Small Business Management, 39*(1), 103–109. doi:10.1111/0447-2778.00010.

Gnyawali, D. R., & Fogel, D. S. (1994). Environments for entrepreneurship development: Key dimensions and research implications. *Entrepreneurship: Theory and Practice, 18*(4), 43–62. doi:1042-2587-94-184$1.50.

Gupta, V. K., Turban, D. B., & Bhawe, N. M. (2008). The effect of gender stereotype activation on entrepreneurial intentions. *Journal of Applied Psychology, 93*, 1053–1061. doi:10.1037/0021-9010.93.5.1053.

GUS (Glowny Urzad Statystyczny) (2012). Turystyka w 2011. *Informacje i opracowania statystyczne*. Warsaw.

Henry, C., Hill, F., & Leitch, C. (2003). *Entrepreneurship education and training*. Aldershot: Ashgate.

Hisrich, R. D., Peters, M. P., & Shepherd, D. A. (2005). *Entrepreneurship*. New York: McGraw-Hill Irwin.

Isenberg, D. J. (2010). How to start an entrepreneurial revolution. *Harvard Business Review, 88*(6), 40–50.

Isenberg, D. J. (2011). *The entrepreneurship ecosystem strategy as a new paradigm for economic policy: Principles for cultivating entrepreneurship*. Boston, MA: The Babson Entrepreneurship Ecosystem Project. Babson Global.

Jackson, J., Klich, J., Poznanska, K., & Chmiel, J. (1999). The continued importance of business creation: The dynamics of the Polish economy 1990–1996. *Research Bulletin, 8*(1), pp. 5–40.

Johnson, S., & Loveman, G. (1995). *Starting over in Eastern Europe: Entrepreneurship and economic renewal*. Boston, MA: Harvard Business School Press.

Kazanjian, R. (1988). Relation of dominant problems to stages of growth in technology-based new ventures. *Academy of Management Journal, 31*(2), 257–279. doi:10.2307/256548.

Kosmaczewska, J. (2007). *Wpływ agroturystyki na rozwój ekonomiczno-społeczny gminy*. Poznan: Bogucki Wyd. Naukowe.

Kryk, B. (2002). Economic growth in Poland from 1990 to 2006. *International Journal of Economic Policy in Emerging Economies, 1*(2/3), 156–176. doi:10.1504/IJEPEE.2008.019261.

Kuratko, D. F., & Hodgetts, R. M. (2004). *Entrepreneurship: Theory process practice*. Mason, OH: Thomson South-Western.

Lester, D. L., Parnell, J. A., & Carraher, S. (2003). Organizational life cycle: A five-stage empirical scale. *The International Journal of Organizational Analysis, 11*(4), 339–354. doi:10.1108/eb028979.

Menguc, B., Auh, S., & Ozanne, L. (2010). The interactive effect of internal and external factors on a proactive environmental strategy and its influence on a firm's performance. Journal of Business Ethics, 94(2), 279–298. doi:10.1007/s10551-009-0264-0.

Mitra, R. (2002). The growth pattern of women-run enterprises: An empirical study in India. *Journal of Developmental Entrepreneurship*, 7(2), 217–237. Retrieved from http://uscga.idm.oclc.org/login?url=http://search.proquest.com/docview/208433866?accountid=10029.

Morrison, A., Breen, J., & and Ali, S. (2003). Small business growth: Intention, ability, and opportunity. *Journal of Small Business Management*, 41(4), 417–425. doi:10.1111/1540-627X.00092.

OECD (2010). *OECD Factbook 2010: Economic, environmental and social statistics*. Paris: OECD Publishing. doi:10.1787/factbook-2010-en.

OECD/The European Commission (2013). *The missing entrepreneurs: Policies for inclusive entrepreneurship in Europe*, Paris: OECD Publishing. doi:10.1787/9789264188167-en.

Piacentini, M. (2013). *Women entrepreneurs in the OECD: Key evidence and policy challenges*. Paris: OECD Publishing. doi:10.1787/5k43bvtkmb8v-en.

Ramadani, V., Gërguri-Rashiti, S., & Fayolle, A. (Eds) (2015). *Female entrepreneurship in transition economies: Trends and challenges*. London: Palgrave Macmillan.

Ramadani, V., & Schneider, R. C. (Eds) (2013). *Entrepreneurship in the Balkans*. Berlin and Heidelberg: Springer-Verlag. doi:10.1007/978-3-642-36577-5_1.

Richards, G. (1996). *Tourism in Central and Eastern Europe: Educating for quality*. Tilburg: Tilburg University Press.

Sachs, J. (1994). *Poland's jump to the market economy*. Cambridge, MA: MIT Press.

Storey, D. (1994). *Understanding the small business sector*. London: Routledge.

Zapalska, A. (1997). A profile of women entrepreneurs and enterprises in Poland. *Journal of Small Business Management*, 35(4), 76–83.

Zapalska, A., & Fogel, G. (1998). Characteristics of Polish and Hungarian entrepreneurship. *The Journal of Private Enterprise*, 8(2), 132–144.

Zienkowski, L. (2000). Regional pattern of economic growth in Poland 1995–1998. *Glowny Urzad Statystyczny, Research Bulletin*, 9, 3–4.

13 Women's entrepreneurial realities in the Czech Republic and the United States

Gender gaps, racial/ethnic disadvantages, and emancipatory potential[1]

Alena Křížková, Marie Pospíšilová, Nancy Jurik and Gray Cavender

Despite praise for women-owned businesses world-wide (White, 2015), evidence that women's businesses continue to underperform when compared to men's is worrisome (Vossenberg, 2013; World Economic Forum, 2015). Comparisons of female with male-owned enterprises ignore how success measures are rooted in men's experiences (Ahl, 2006; de Bruin, Brush, & Welter, 2007; Marlow & Swail, 2014). Research suggests that women's disproportionate responsibilities for unpaid care-work, historic concentrations in lower growth labour-intensive job and business sectors, and limited access to funding sources relative to men's contribute to women's lower performance on traditional success measures (Vossenberg, 2013). Such differences promote business precarity (Pearson & Sweetman, 2011). Feminist researchers suggest more research on how gender and entrepreneurship are intertwined (Bruni, Poggio, & Gherardi, 2005; Marlow, 2014).

Research (Vossenberg, 2013; World Economic Forum, 2015) finds that gender gaps and business practices differ across countries (Welter & Smallbone, 2011). They are shaped by historical market conditions, government policies, and normative frameworks that vary over time and across nations. More comparative research is needed to facilitate an understanding of the contextual embeddedness of women's entrepreneurship. Even within nations, there are variations in women's experiences by region as well as by ethnic, racial, age, sexual orientation, social class, migration, and marital/family stages (Essers & Benschop, 2009; Minniti & Naudé, 2010; Valdez, 2011). Women entrepreneurs are not a homogeneous group; intersectional approaches are essential to grasp how multiple dimensions of entrepreneurs' social identities converge to frame opportunities (Romero & Valdez, 2016; Welter, Baker, Audretsch, & Gartner, 2016).

Our study focuses on the experiences and ambitions of small, purposively selected samples of women business owners from two countries – the United States (US) and Czech Republic (CR) – by drawing on contextual embeddedness and intersectional perspectives. We were interested in understanding the barriers, opportunities and strategies identified in each country. Drawing on feminist intersectional perspectives (Collins, 2000; Crenshaw, 1988; Romero & Valdez, 2016), we expected that women's experiences would be differentially shaped by the convergence of multiple dimensions of social identities and women's institutional/geographical contexts. This convergence of multiple social identities and societal contexts has been termed *social location* (Zavella, 1991). A combined contextual embeddedness/intersectional approach to entrepreneurship suggests that interwoven dimensions of identities position entrepreneurs differentially in relation to the structural context in which they are located, including variations in historical patterns, national policies, market conditions and normative regimes (Valdez, 2011; Welter, 2011).

Our data are drawn from two parallel case studies of entrepreneurs and business support programmes in the US and CR; we concentrate here on interviews with nine CR and twelve US women entrepreneurs of varying race/ethnicities, family statuses and levels of economic security. Comparison of entrepreneurs from these two regions is important because the US and CR present an established market versus transitional market economy with differing norms, policies, market conditions, racial/ethnic composition and unique historical orientations toward business ownership. We analyse interview narratives to identify ways in which variations in social location may differentially position respondents in their decisions to start and their strategies for running their businesses.

Our intersectional framework recognizes the differing positioning of women even within the same country. This combined contextual embeddedness/intersectional approach complicates the notion of a singular entrepreneurial gender gap while illustrating how hierarchical structures shape life chances and business practices. Our analysis demonstrates that a gender-aware approach alone is insufficient for understanding women's entrepreneurship. Multiple dimensions of women's identities must be considered.

Theoretical Framing and study contexts

In traditional entrepreneurship research rooted in masculine-centred economic logic women have been viewed as 'underperforming' because structural factors such as different gender-role expectations and employment conditions for men and women were ignored (Marlow, 2014). Feminist approaches analyse businesses through another lens by investigating entrepreneurship as the interplay among gendered, racialized and heteronormative structural contexts and intersecting identities that situate women differently in terms of opportunities and barriers (Hozic & True, 2016; Romero & Valdez, 2016). We consider the similarities and the heterogeneity of women's experiences. Saskia Vossenberg (2013, p. 13) suggests that an intersectional approach facilitates the understanding of 'how characteristics of constructed identities impact on one's location in society and the economic, social and political rights and opportunities attached to it'. Mary Romero and Zulema Valdez (2016) elaborate an intersectional approach that provides insight into the ways that institutional arrangements structure entrepreneurial strategies. We consider the context of women's entrepreneurship as a structure of opportunities shaped by labour market structure, government policies, and services targeting women business owners. Informed by Welter (2011), we consider how national differences in norms and policies regarding gender roles, caregiving and paid employment influence gender and entrepreneurship.

The significant differences between US and CR make comparing entrepreneurship in the two countries a worthy research avenue. Business ownership is newer to the Czech Republic (CR) compared to the United States (US), because it was prohibited for decades and reinitiated when state socialism ended in 1989. Despite mandatory employment during CR state socialism, gendered job segregation (vertical and horizontal) and inferior women's wages endured. Post-1989, feminist demands for gender equality were discredited and followed by a re-traditionalization trend emphasizing women's domestic responsibilities (Hašková & Saxonberg, 2016). Data suggest significant US-CR variations in gender inequality (World Economic Forum, 2015; OECD, 2014) and that relative to US respondents, Czech respondents favour traditional gendered divisions of labour (Hašková, 2011; Parker, 2012).

US and CR family policies vary considerably. Czech family policy offers up to three years of paid parental leave, child allowances and state subsidized childcare for children age 3 and older. For CR children under 3 only costly, non-subsidized childcare is available. The US does not offer government-paid parental leave, but some employers provide limited paid parental/sick leave (rarely over six weeks) (World Economic Forum, 2015). Non-subsidized and expensive childcare is available for all ages in the US. The US offers limited economic support for children and childcare for families below poverty income levels.

US women sometimes take part-time jobs in order to care for children, but these offer lesser pay and benefits than full-time jobs. In the CR, part-time work is rare (OECD, 2014). Significant numbers of women in both countries report that they turned to entrepreneurship to create flexible opportunities for earnings while raising children (Carr, 2000; CZSO, 2014). However, benefits available to employees (e.g., family leave) are not readily available for women business owners in either country. Self-employment is increasing in the US and CR, especially for women with small children (CZSO, 2014; Valdez, 2011). Disadvantaged individuals are being pushed into self-employment by structural labour market changes and recurrent economic crises that have eroded the availability of secure jobs (Strier, 2010). Thus, research suggests that increases in female self-employment may not be simply an indicator of women's progress but also a result of gender inequalities (Budig, 2006). US women comprise only 38% and CR women 21% of all established business owners[2] (GEM Consortium, 2011). This figure indicates a significant gender gap within and between the countries. Therefore, exploration of perceived entrepreneurial motivations and barriers in these contexts is merited.

Creating entrepreneurship opportunities for women can improve women's economic and social position (Calás, Smircich, & Bourne, 2009). However, closing gender gaps requires attention to the differential positioning of women within structural contexts according to their multiple and interwoven identities. Focusing on the salience of gender alone overlooks variations in entrepreneurship for women across race/ethnicity and class groups (Hozic & True, 2016).

The US and CR exhibit interesting contrasts in the visibility and variety of racial and ethnic relations. Due to restrictive mobility under state socialism, the CR is largely homogeneous in terms of race/ethnicity. Data on race are not systematically collected in the CR and the terms nationality and ethnicity are used interchangeably. The largest CR ethnic minority (2%) is the Roma, most of whom have Czech or Slovak citizenship (CZSO, 2016). The US is more racially and ethnically diverse (Census.gov, 2010; CZSO, 2016). Historically, members of US racial/ethnic minorities have experienced discrimination in education, housing, employment, legal representation and restrictive immigration and naturalization policies. While each minority group has unique experiences (Omi & Winant, 2015), there are also commonalities. In both countries, stereotypes or 'controlling images' of racial/ ethnic minorities and immigrants are common and experienced at both institutional and interpersonal levels (Collins, 2000).

Hereafter, we use the concept of social location for our comparative contextual embeddedness/intersectional analysis to identify the ways multiple identities and geographical location converge to shape entrepreneurship experiences and approaches (Jurik, 1998; Zavella, 1991). Social location combines intersecting dimensions of identities with time and space-specific contexts associated with resources, market conditions, policies, values and stereotypes.

Regional institutional contexts influence businesses and family life (Jurik, Křížková, & Pospíšilová (Dlouhá), 2016) and gender norms, family policies, business climates and discourses about them vary across countries (Azmat, 2013). Women's perceptions of opportunities, barriers and strategies for business are influenced by their social location; perceptions might vary for women differentially located within the same country context. Our comparative analysis of women's entrepreneurship helps identify policy recommendations to challenge gender gaps within and across countries.

Methods

In 2014–2015, we conducted in-depth interviews with women entrepreneurs (twelve in the CR and nine in US).[3] The US sample came from entrepreneurial support provider referrals. These referrals generated primarily newer, smaller firms seeking business assistance. US owners came from the Phoenix area, and CR respondents came from several cities and small towns. Since the CR offered fewer business support services, we used matching methods (Neergaard, 2007) to draw a sample similar in composition to the US sample along the lines of varied ethnicity, class and family status. Because of contextual variations, sample composition was not a perfect match. For example, the relatively greater US racial/ethnic diversity is reflected in the US sample. Only a few respondents in either sample were under age 25; about half of each sample had children under 18 living with them.[4]

Findings I: Motivations for business

While some women were motivated to start a business for its own sake, most respondents in both countries described business as a solution to labour market problems. Women spoke about barriers as employees and the opportunities that entrepreneurship offered, at least temporarily. Despite cross-national commonalities, there were variations between CR and US respondent narratives and important within-country differences. These differences often implicated one or a combination of the following: gender, race/ethnicity, class resources and family status.

Entrepreneurship as opportunity to fulfil limited career mobility

In each country, some respondents emphasized the opportunities available through entrepreneurship. A common theme was 'blocked mobility' for employees. Consistent with prior research (Jurik et al., 2016), this sample referenced increased self-fulfilment, autonomy, freedom and challenge as reasons to start businesses (Jurik et al., 2016).

Geneva (US-3), described business as an opportunity for creative fulfilment. She was the daughter of immigrants and had worked in her parents' restaurant. Her parents and romantic partner provided financing to start her business. She stressed her lack of independence as an employee: 'I never stayed at a job more than eight months. I went from job to job because I didn't like people telling me what to do . . .' (US-3).

Geneva and another US respondent, Linda, identified the work ethic derived from their racial/ethnic and immigrant backgrounds as reinforcing their choices of entrepreneurship over corporate careers. Geneva came to the US with her parents from Cambodia when she was young; Linda is a second generation Latina.

184   *Křížková, Pospíšilová, Jurik and Cavender*

Linda thought she had limited mobility in her bank position. She attributed this disadvantage to both her gender and ethnicity: 'I had a lot of male mentors, and learned a lot through them . . . [but] I wasn't getting raises or getting promoted' (US-9).

A third, white respondent, Victoria (US-4), stressed gender disadvantage. After earning a university degree in economics she realized that there were no women in higher management: 'I call it 'the boys' network' . . . I didn't feel that the likelihood of my success was very high.' She started a consulting business.

Narratives constructing business as a response to limited career options also appear in two CR interviews. These women were frustrated with jobs that lacked space for creativity, independence or good salaries. Bára, who was employed in managerial positions in transnational companies, explains:

> The managerial environment allows for manifesting your individuality only in limited ways . . . There is limited space for your independent will . . . I am a person who needs her own rules, own system even going into the risk.
>
> (CR-4)

Bára stressed that meaning, creativity and development of potential were only available through entrepreneurship. Nad'a started her own business as a student because it was more 'financially rewarding' than employment: 'I can't imagine any CR company that would be appropriate for me' (CR-9).

These US and CR women were university-educated and childless at the time they formed businesses. Family concerns are not reflected in their motivation discussions. Interestingly, neither of the CR women constructed their employment barriers as gendered. These differences between CR-US respondent narratives may reflect the more traditional gender-role attitudes in CR men and women compared to the US (Hašková, 2011). In contrast, the US respondents directly referenced gendered disadvantage in their jobs. Linda and Geneva also identified their immigrant/ethnic background as an important factor in their socialization for entrepreneurship. All five women gained professional employment but believed that their mobility was limited.

Next, we discuss how race/ethnicity converged with gender and class position to shape perceived employment prospects. For this next group of respondents, entrepreneurship was often a forced choice.

Entrepreneurship as an alternative to blocked opportunity: Controlling images of gender, race/ethnicity and class

The US is a more racially heterogeneous society than the CR, and activism against racism is common (Omi & Winant, 2015). However, negative racialized images pervade both countries and limit employment options especially for poor individuals. Experiencing controlling images prompted some respondents' turns to entrepreneurship. Yet, negative images sometimes continued in business. The discrimination they described appeared more subtle in the US and more overt in the CR.

The CR's largest ethnic minority, the Roma, suffer from high rates of poverty, unemployment and low social status. Almost 75% of Roma experience discrimination seeking work (FRA, 2014; Hyde, 2006). Yvonna's Roma ethnicity led to discrimination when employers met her: 'If I called by phone, they told me that I had the job. But when I came in person . . . I could have been however clean, clean nails, brushed hair, but

I am still a Roma woman, and they didn't accept me' (CR-10). Her account illustrates the experience of employment discrimination but also reveals Yvonna's familiarity with controlling images of Roma as 'unclean'. Yvonna was from a poor family, while a more middle class, university-educated Roma respondent, Zuzana, said she had not experienced discrimination.

Another Roma woman, Šárka, who was from a poor background, described discrimination based upon her skin colour. Her bosses told her that she was 'inappropriate' for direct customer contact: 'After finishing school, I had problem finding a job, because I am dark. I had two good references for a job, two of my [lighter skinned] friends worked in the cosmetic salon I wanted to work in. And the manager didn't give me the job' (CR-12). Instead, Šárka was assigned to work in a position without customer contact. Dissatisfied, she started a cosmetic sales business. Her customers were friends so she did not have to fear discrimination.

Recall that Linda (US-9), a childless Latina, referenced gender and ethnicity as barriers in her employment career. These controlling images emerged in her business when several potential clients refused her services:

> Sometimes I do think that it could be that I am a woman . . . I just think because I am small, a lot of people don't think I can do all the stuff . . . Sometimes, you can tell when people are stuck on your CULTURE. And in those cases, I would always walk away . . . But then again: do I really know what I am talking about . . . I double question myself.

She tolerated negative images of gender but avoided doing business with people she suspected of ethnic bias. However, when racism is not directly stated, persons of colour may suspect but never know for certain.

Francesca (US-6) was a light-skinned black woman and mother of two with a middle class income. She discussed the negative connotations of being black in the US: 'I just happen to be lighter which might be less threatening to people, but I consider myself a black woman.' She explained that class position helped her counter racial disadvantages because her family could afford an affluent neighbourhood: 'It's a place where I definitely feel like I can do the kind of business I do, meet people, make more contacts.'

Our data highlight ways that social location shaped employment experiences and business motivations. Narratives suggest common barriers related to gender, race and class, but also differences in the ways those are experienced across social locations. The country contexts of differential gender and race consciousness also emerged in respondent narratives. CR respondents did not stress gender discrimination as an explanation of limited opportunities but reported more openly racist encounters. US respondents willingly described experiences of sexism and racism but their examples of racism were not as blatant as those in the CR. In the next section, we consider how having children combines with other features of social location to shape entrepreneurialism.

Searching for flexibility: Mothers of small children

Our data suggest that business ownership simultaneously produces opportunities and conflicts for mothers. Ownership offers flexibility for mothers who face limited flexible employment opportunities in the US – where pay and benefits for part-time work are limited – and in the CR – where part-time jobs are almost non-existent. Ironically, this finding held for women in both countries despite the more generous CR paid parental leave policies because long parental leaves often resulted in job loss for CR women despite some legal protections (Křížková, Maříková, Hašková, & Formánková, 2011). Yet, paid parental leave was costly for CR women business owners as was health insurance. These complications led CR respondents to define entrepreneurship more as a temporary or last resort solution when they could not find adequate jobs.

Several CR mothers turned to business as a temporary solution. Karolína describes the typical situation of mothers trying to find employment after parental leave. She preferred employment but chose entrepreneurship after failing to find a decent job:

> I was trying to find employment, but the fact that you have small children always comes up as a terrible problem in the labour market . . . most of those firms will prefer someone who does not have small children . . . So I tried, for about two, three jobs and it did not work out, so then I have not tried anymore.
>
> (CR-2)

Another mother's case illustrates the problems with family leave for self-employed women. Františka (CR-7) was employed for seven years. After an economic down-turn, she was forced to do the same work as a contractor to save her employer money. When pregnant with her first child, she realized that her self-employed status did not meet eligibility conditions for maternity allowance. 'Honestly I thought it was unfair because I was employed as a contractor in the same company.' Self-employed women must contribute to the leave system well before pregnancy. Before Františka had her first child, she had been able to contribute enough so as to collect some maternity allowance. However, before her second childbirth, she could not afford the contribution and lost entitlement. She received a parental allowance which is a lower amount. CR family leave terms actually disadvantage self-employed women, especially single mothers, because they must cease business operations during paid leave. This requirement reduces business viability.

Two CR Roma women were mothers. Yvonna turned to business due to the limited opportunities for lower-class Roma mothers to find jobs. Zuzana, who was middle class, used business to balance work and family obligations. By joining her partner's business, she was able to combine childcare with business work soon after childbirth:

> I took my daughter to work, I was returning step-by-step to work . . . We have time for the daughter at work. We made space there for her to play. We brought toys and blankets and everything she needs.
>
> (CR-11)

Zuzana described entrepreneurship as her only option for returning to work when her daughter was small.

Class-based resources helped balance earnings and childcare responsibilities. Zuzana was in business with her husband. Both Františka and Karolína had financial support from husbands to pay for childcare. A solo mother, Daniela (CR-5), preferred to remain employed after having her child. However, she could not find affordable private childcare and childcare hours conflicted with her work schedule. Entrepreneurship became the only viable solution.

US single mothers in low-paid, insecure jobs were also pushed into entrepreneurship for flexibility (Jurik, 2005). Rennie (US-2), a white woman, became a single mother after divorce when her second son was age 6. As breadwinner, she needed flexibility and was forced into precarious, part-time jobs. After struggling to make ends meet, she tried self-employment. 'The main reason . . . was that I was raising my son by myself . . . so I needed a flexible schedule.' Rennie's situation illustrates how self-employment is often chosen because flexible jobs are scarce in the US.

Having a spouse who can lend economic support made it possible for some US women to interrupt earnings activities to raise children. Victoria (US-4), interrupted her successful business, to have children and become a full-time mother. Francesca (US-6) quit a successful professional job to care for her children for seven years. Both women could take this time because of husbands' earnings. However, divorce changed Victoria's strategies.

After divorce, Victoria returned to her business. As a single mother, she required flexibility and shorter working hours: 'I don't have the availability like when I was 22. I have two kids to take care of . . . I don't have the luxury of spending 10 hours a day at work'. Thus, although flexibility was a common theme, variations in family status and class position produced important shifts in mother's responses to earnings/care conflicts in both countries.

Comments by US and CR mothers must be further located within their country context. Employment rates of women with school-age children and incidence of part-time employment are higher in US (72% and 12.4% respectively) compared to CR (63% and 5.4% respectively). These differences likely stem from the infrequency of US paid parental leave and the less traditional gender expectations compared to the CR's paid parental leave and more conservative gender-role attitudes. Women in both countries experienced inadequate flexible employment opportunities and expensive childcare for young children. Entrepreneurship was a strategy to address the earnings/care dilemma in both contexts. However, the costs to entrepreneurs entailed the loss of any leave and insurance benefits associated with employment.

Findings II: Business approaches to disadvantage

Entrepreneurship as a temporary solution

Our sample originated in referrals from business support organizations, so our respondents ran small and often precarious enterprises. Although not generalizable to the larger population of women owners in either country, our findings do speak to stereotypic male-centric images of entrepreneurship and undifferentiated views about small business as a solution for economic inequality. For most of our sample, entrepreneurship represented a survival strategy, particularly for women combining earning and childcare. Entrepreneurship also offered an alternative for women who faced barriers to career advancement (Thébaud, 2015) or the discrimination associated with social location. However, given our respondents' comments, one must ask if entrepreneurship is actually a solution for improving the position of women in society and economic development.

Since the 1990s, there have been many advocates who support women entrepreneurs, and women's businesses have been characterized as engines of development. Women's entrepreneurship has generally been presented as a solution for global poverty and underdevelopment (Jurik, 2005; Poster & Salime, 2002). With each new economic crisis, training, mentorship and loans are re-emphasized as strategies to boost women's business growth, resuscitate economies and reduce so-called gender gaps (Elias, 2016; Hozic & True, 2016).

Many business support programmes in the US include efforts to aid small start-ups that supplement or replace meagre wages, but also for incubating larger growth-oriented businesses (Feld, 2012). In contrast, CR entrepreneurship support focuses on training disadvantaged women in business skills, but long-term and financial support services are still missing (Dlouhá, 2015). Therefore, it is not surprising that CR women perceive fewer business opportunities than do US men and women and CR men. Women's business ownership in the CR is increasing but the percentages of women-owned businesses lag behind that of the US (GEM Consortium, 2011). Narratives portrayed entrepreneurship more as an escape strategy than a dream come true. It was often assessed against the quality and quantity of jobs. More so in the CR, the push toward entrepreneurship seemed a decision born of desperation; in the US, it was the more attractive option.

Dissatisfaction with employment and perceived business opportunities simultaneously pushed and pulled women into entrepreneurship. As Geneva stated,

> I was never satisfied even though I was doing great at my job. In the corporate world . . . you have to climb the ladder . . . Climbing that ladder takes time. I don't have a lot of patience.
>
> (US-3)

Business start-up was facilitated by contacts and support from spouses or other family members (Valdez, 2011). Without resources, start-up was more difficult. Start-up was complicated by racial or ethnic marginalization although such background helped in business for some.

Several CR respondents described entrepreneurship as a temporary solution to the shortage of flexible jobs for mothers. Respondents' view of entrepreneurship as temporary may reflect the more limited emphasis on entrepreneurship in the CR, and CR women's perceptions that there are fewer business opportunities. Self-employed CR women have difficulty claiming paid maternity leave and insurance benefits available to employees. Loss of these benefits is an expensive price to pay for business ownership. Health insurance was expensive in both countries when not provided through employment. Paid employee parental leave and health insurance were not as available in the US (Thébaud, 2015), so it is not surprising that US respondent narratives described entrepreneurship as a more acceptable fall-back plan.

The problem with viewing entrepreneurship as a solution to work-family conflicts is that it is often accompanied by low, insecure earnings, self-exploitation and vulnerable contractual conditions (Jurik, 1998). Daniela (CR-5) notes: 'The advantage of being a contractor is that I can be there for my daughter, more than being an employee . . . Disadvantages? It is extremely financially uncertain.' The insecurity of entrepreneurship makes it difficult for mothers to grow successful businesses and thereby reinforces gender business gaps and overall gender inequalities.

The situation of single mothers in both countries is more vulnerable than that of partnered mothers: single mothers do more childcare and need more flexibility. Fathers may not pay child support. There is no method to discipline non-paying CR fathers and methods in the US are often ineffective. In the cases of Rennie, Francesca and Victoria, husbands' earnings allowed women to temporarily assume the role of full-time mothers. Rennie said: 'I was married with my son until he was five and I did not work outside of home. He (husband) was self-employed and I helped him run his business' (US-2). However, divorces for Rennie and Victoria forced them to assume primary earnings and childcare responsibilities.

Class resources and marital/family status shape entrepreneurial motivations and experiences in different ways. The convergence of racism and sexism in the labour market of both countries may provide women of colour with incentives to get out of the job market and try entrepreneurship. However, it is always possible that entrepreneurship becomes just another version of economic insecurity and work-family conflict.

Emancipatory approaches to entrepreneurship

US and CR narratives revealed that some women used entrepreneurship to help disadvantaged groups. We refer to this theme as an emancipatory approach (Jurik & Bodine, 2014). Empowering others was grounded in respondent's experiences of disadvantage and connection to common problems confronting their targeted clientele. Key features of this emancipatory approach included 1) focus on the effects of gender in combination with other dimensions of social identities (e.g., race/ethnicity); 2) a recognition of structural sources of disadvantage; 3) the role of history; 4) the importance of personal experience.

First, gender was a focus of emancipatory strategies typically in combination with social disadvantages related to motherhood and/or race/ethnicity. Karolína (CR-2) said:

> I am employing mothers with children because I know that they are very good employees. Today, I am looking for mothers with children, even small children, because women appreciate the work more and they are more effective . . .

Karolína started her business because she faced discrimination as a mother and could not find employment after parental leave. She stressed the unequal position of women with children in the labour market and focused on strategies to remedy it.

Second, respondents recognized the role of structural context in disadvantaging their target groups. Two respondents addressed the damage caused by the forced segregation of CR Roma into dilapidated urban areas. Yvonna (CR-10), a social worker and leader of a Roma artistic group, orients her business activities around extending employment opportunities in the disadvantaged Roma community. She is opening a cleaning business that will hire disadvantaged groups, especially mothers: 'I will hire . . . mothers after parental leave. They don't have jobs because it is too far for them to travel to work . . . they (mothers) spend much money for transport to work so in the end they have nothing'. A US respondent targeted the harm produced by the treatment of American Indians who live on reservations. Mary (US-5), who identifies as an American Indian, is orienting her outdoor experience business toward troubled youth. She hopes her business services will alleviate the '. . . historical trauma that has been passed down – grandparents to the parents to the kids' in Native-American communities.

Third, Yvonna and Mary illustrate that emancipatory approaches connected their own history of disadvantage with efforts to empower others. Yvonna drew from her experiences as a Roma woman and mother of four. She had worked in low-paid, temporary jobs and faced discrimination due to ethnicity, gender and motherhood. Mary used her memories as a restless child from a mixed race/ethnic (native-American, black) family to inform her business operations. She wanted to address gender and social exclusion. After being introduced to dog training as a girl, she reported feeling safe and self-confident: Thereafter, 'It was always me and the dog.' Francesca (US-6), had a successful employment career before turning into a full-time mother, but felt overwhelmed by the pressure to be the perfect

190 *Křížková, Pospíšilová, Jurik and Cavender*

mother and family manager. She created a consulting business for mothers with similar experiences aiming to help them organize and eliminate self-doubt.

We use the term emancipatory to describe this approach as it refers to autonomy-seeking strategies. Rindova, Barry, and Ketchen (2009) define emancipatory as 'the act of setting free from the power of another,' and differentiate between individual freedom-seeking and freedom-seeking for social collectives. In the gender and entrepreneurship literature, empowerment is usually understood as a process of improving the entrepreneur's position and autonomy (Al-Dajani & Marlow, 2013). This is typically a more individual-centred project, while the entrepreneurial activities here target a group or community for empowerment (e.g. Mosedale, 2005; also see Young, 1994) on collective empowerment).

Despite the barriers in employment and entrepreneurship due to social location, some respondents used experiences of disadvantage in efforts to emancipate their communities. These goals provided them with meaning and hope as individuals and members of multiple social groups. Social location was a source of both barriers and opportunities, and to some degree, a strategy for challenging entrepreneurial or at least social and economic gender gaps.

Discussion and conclusion

Our findings provide some explanation of the gender gap or so-called underperformance of women-owned businesses. We analyse the opportunities and barriers confronting women in varying social locations including their intersecting memberships in varied social groups (gender, race/ethnicity, class) and their residence in two different countries – the CR and US. We use a combined contextual/intersectional approach to examine women's narrative accounts.

The US scores higher on gender equality and lower on gender-traditional attitudes than does the CR, although women's labour force participation is similar in the two countries. US women are more represented in management and entrepreneurship and they perceive greater opportunities for starting a business compared to CR women. Some women in both countries stressed entrepreneurship as a solution to blocked mobility, although US respondents more directly labelled the barriers as a gender issue than did CR women. Racial/ethnic discrimination and combined gender/race discrimination were noted by women of colour in both countries but class advantage sometimes mediated disadvantage related to skin colour. The higher level of reflexivity among US respondents is probably related to the relatively lower presence of gender-traditional attitudes and greater sense of gender equality. The degree of race consciousness is greater in the US than in the CR although overt racism still occurs in the US. Nevertheless, our findings reveal ways that gender interacts with race/ethnic, class, and family status in each country to form barriers and, on occasion, opportunities for entrepreneurship.

Mothers in both countries stressed entrepreneurship as a flexible alternative to employment that improved work/life balance. Entrepreneurship is more often described as a last resort or temporary solution for CR mothers; entrepreneurship was more positively viewed by US mothers. Single mothers, especially single mothers who were women of colour, described the most precarious entrepreneurial experiences. Even the more generous CR paid parental leave failed to fully ease pressures for either women employees or entrepreneurs. The length of the leave discouraged hiring women (Křížková et al., 2011) and the paid leave was less feasible for women entrepreneurs (Jurik et al., 2016).

The barriers that women faced help explain why women-owned business often have limited growth potential and provide limited income or 'underperform' according to male-centric measures. Our findings also demonstrate that a gender-aware analysis alone is insufficient. Other dimensions of social location must be considered whenever possible. Thus, our study contributes to research (Al-Dajani & Marlow, 2013; Jurik, 2005) suggesting that blanket recommendations for women's entrepreneurship as a solution to feminized poverty or economic crises should be viewed with caution.

Work/life balance options supporting employment of mothers of small children are lacking in both countries. When it becomes a last resort for work/life balance, entrepreneurship can reinforce disadvantage and precarity. Focus should be placed on dismantling stereotypes and policies that hinder the access of mothers and racial/ethnic minorities to employment advancement and viable business opportunities.

Despite insecurity, entrepreneurship can represent important sources of satisfaction, meaning and a sense of coping with barriers. Some women use their experience with disadvantage as a resource to create businesses focused on emancipation for socially marginalized groups. Encouraging entrepreneurship defined along these lines could contribute to increased community cultural and economic enhancement. However, state support will be needed to facilitate such ventures and challenge discrimination against women and minority race/ethnic communities (Al-Dajani, Carter, Shaw, & Marlow, 2015; Al-Dajani & Marlow, 2013).

This chapter demonstrates the utility of a combined comparative contextual/intersectional analysis. It adds to the still under-examined topic of gender and entrepreneurship in a post-socialist society compared to that of an established entrepreneurship-oriented country.

Notes

1 The authors wish to acknowledge funding in support of this research from the following sources: The Czech Science Foundation (grant no. GA15–13766S), Arizona State University's Institute for Social Science Research and School of Social Transformation and The Fulbright Foundation.
2 Percentage of the population aged 18–64 who are currently an owner-manager of an established business, i.e., owning and managing a running business that has paid salaries, wages or any other payments to the owners for more than 42 months.
3 We also interviewed men entrepreneurs and business support providers but we focus here on women entrepreneurs. Interviews were conducted in English (in US) and Czech (in CR) and translated into English for this paper by the researchers.
4 For more information regarding respondents please contact the authors.

References

Ahl, H. (2006). Why research on women entrepreneurs needs new directions. *Entrepreneurship Theory and Practice, 30*(5), 595–621.

Al-Dajani, H., Carter, S., Shaw, E., & Marlow, S. (2015). Entrepreneurship among the displaced and dispossessed: Exploring the limits of emancipatory entrepreneuring. *British Journal of Management, 26*(4), 713–730.

Al-Dajani, H., & Marlow, S. (2013). Empowerment and entrepreneurship: A theoretical framework. *International Journal of Entrepreneurial Behaviour & Research, 19*(5), 503–524.

Azmat, F. (2013). Opportunities or obstacles? Understanding the challenges faced by migrant women entrepreneurs. *International Journal of Gender and Entrepreneurship, 5*(2), 198–215.

Bruni, A., Poggio, B., & Gherardi, S. (2005). *Gender and entrepreneurship: An ethnographic approach.* New York: Routledge.

Budig, M. J. (2006). Intersections on the road to self-employment: Gender, family and occupational class. *Social Forces, 84*(4), 2223–2239.

Calás, M. B., Smircich, L., & Bourne, K. A. (2009). Extending the boundaries: Reframing 'entrepreneurship as social change' through feminist perspectives. *Academy of Management Review, 34*(3), 552–569.

Carr, D. (2000). The entrepreneurial alternative. In D. M. Smith (Ed.), *Women at work: Leadership for the next century* (pp. 208–229). Upper Saddle River, NJ: Prentice Hall.

Census.gov. (2010). *United States. Census 2010.* Retrieved 3 September 2016 from www.census.gov/2010census/.

Collins, P. H. (2000). *Black feminist thought: Knowledge, consciousness, and the politics of empowerment.* New York and London: Routledge.

Crenshaw, K. W. (1988). Race, reform, and retrenchment: Transformation and legitimation in antidiscrimination law. *Harvard Law Review, 101*(7), 1331–1387.

CZSO (2014). *Zaostřeno na ženy a muže* (Focused on women and men). Retrieved 17 December 2016 from https://www.czso.cz/csu/czso/4-prace-a-mzdy4259.

CZSO (2016). *Foreigners in the Czech Republic.* Retrieved 8 March 2017 from https://www.czso.cz/csu/czso/foreigners-in-the-czech-republic.

de Bruin, A., Brush, C. G., & Welter, F. (2007). Advancing a framework for coherent research on women's entrepreneurship. *Entrepreneurship Theory and Practice, 31*(3), 323–339.

Dlouhá, M. (2015). Czech Republic case study. In E. Schulze (Ed.), *Women's entrepreneurship: Closing the gender gap in access to financial and other services and in social entrepreneurship* (pp. 35–39). Brussels: European Parliament.

Elias, J. (2016). Whose crisis? Whose recovery? Lessons learned (and not) from the Asian crisis. In A. A. Hozic & J. True (Eds), *Scandalous economics: Gender and the politics of financial crises* (pp. 109–125). New York: Oxford University Press.

Essers, C., & Benschop, Y. (2009). Muslim businesswomen doing boundary work: The negotiation of Islam, gender and ethnicity within entrepreneurial contexts. *Human Relations, 62*(3), 403–423.

Feld, B. (2012). *Startup communities: Building an entrepreneurial ecosystem in your city.* New York: John Wiley & Sons.

FRA (2014). *Roma Survey – Data in Focus Poverty and Employment: The Situation of Roma in 11 EU Member States.* Luxembourg. Retrieved 20 January 2017, from http://fra.europa.eu/en/publication/2014/poverty-and-employment-situation-roma-11-eu-member-states.

GEM Consortium (2011). *Global Entrepreneurship Monitor.* Retrieved 14 January 2017, from www.gemconsortium.org/data/sets#baps.

Hašková, H. (2011). Proměny časování a způsobu návratu matek do zaměstnání (The changing timing and ways of mothers' returning to the workplace). *Gender, Rovné Příležitosti, výzkum/Gender, Equal Opportunities, Research, 12*(2), 40–52.

Hašková, H., & Saxonberg, S. (2016). The revenge of history: The institutional roots of post-communist family policy in the Czech Republic, Hungary and Poland. *Social Policy & Administration, 50*(5), 559–579.

Hozic, A. A., & True, J. (2016). Making feminist sense of the global financial crisis. In A. A. Hozic & J. True (Eds), *Scandalous economics: Gender and the politics of financial crises* (pp. 3–20). New York: Oxford University Press.

Hyde, A. (2006). *Systemic exclusion of Roma from employment.* Budapest: European Roma Rights Centre.

Jurik, N. C. (1998). Getting away and getting by: The experiences of self-employed homeworkers. *Work and Occupations, 25*(7), 7–35.

Jurik, N. C. (2005). *Bootstrap dreams: U.S. microenterprise development in an era of welfare reform.* Ithaca, NY: Cornell University Press.

Jurik, N. C., & Bodine, R. (2014). Social responsibility and altruism in small- and medium-sized innovative businesses. *Journal of Sociology & Social Welfare, 41*(4), 113–142.

Jurik, N. C., Křížková, A., & Pospíšilová (Dlouhá), M. (2016). Czech copreneur orientations to business and family responsibilities: A mixed embeddedness perspective. *International Journal of Gender and Entrepreneurship, 8*(3), 307–326.

Křížková, A., Maříková, H., Hašková, H., & Formánková, L. (2011). *Pracovní dráhy žen v České republice* (Working paths of women in the Czech Republic). Prague: SLON.

Marlow, S. (2014). Exploring future research agendas in the field of gender and entrepreneurship. *International Journal of Gender and Entrepreneurship, 6*(2), 102–120.

Marlow, S., & Swail, J. (2014). Gender, risk and finance: Why can't a woman be more like a man? *Entrepreneurship & Regional Development, 26*(1–2), 80–96.

Minniti, M., & Naudé, W. (2010). Introduction: What do we know about the patterns and determinants of female entrepreneurship across countries? *European Journal of Development Research, 22*(3), 277–293.

Mosedale, S. (2005). Assessing women's empowerment: Towards a conceptual framework. *Journal of International Development, 17*(2), 243–257.

Neergaard, H. (2007). Sampling in entrepreneurial settings. In H. Neergaard & J. P. Ulhøi (Eds), *Handbook of qualitative research methods in entrepreneurship* (pp. 253–278). Cheltenham: Edward Elgar Publishing.

OECD (2010). *Entrepreneurship and Migrants.* Retrieved 17 January 2017 from www.oecd.org/industry/smes/45068866.pdf.

OECD (2014). *OECD Family Database.* Retrieved 28 December 2016 from www.oecd.org/els/family/database.htm.

Omi, M., & Winant, H. (2015). *Racial formation in the United States from the 1960s to the 1990s.* New York: Routledge.

Parker, K. (2012). *Women, Work and Motherhood: A Sampler of Recent Pew Research Survey Findings.* Retrieved 13 January 2017 from www.pewsocialtrends.org/2012/04/13/women-work-and-motherhood/.

Pearson, R., & Sweetman, C. (2011). Introduction. In R. Pearson & C. Sweetman (Eds), *Gender and the economic crisis* (pp. 1–14). Oxford: Oxfam.

Poster, W., & Salime, Z. (2002). The limits of micro-credit: Transnational feminism and USAID activities in the United States and Morocco. In N. A. Naples & M. Desai (Eds), *Women's activism and globalization* (pp. 189–219). London: Routledge.

Rindova, V., Barry, D., & Ketchen, D. (2009). Entrepreneuring as emancipation. *Academy of Management Review, 34*(3), 477–491.

Romero, M., & Valdez, Z. (2016). Introduction to the special issue: Intersectionality and entrepreneurship. *Ethnic and Racial Studies, 39*(9), 1553–1565.

Strier, R. (2010). Women, poverty, and the microenterprise: Context and discourse. *Gender, Work and Organization, 17*(2), 195–218.

Thébaud, S. (2015). Business as plan B: Institutional foundations of gender inequality in entrepreneurship across 24 industrialized countries. *Administrative Science Quarterly, 60*(4), 671–711.

Valdez, Z. (2011). *The new entrepreneurs: How race, class, and gender shape American enterprise.* Stanford, CA: Stanford University Press.

Vossenberg, S. (2013). *Women entrepreneurship promotion in developing countries: What explains the gender gap in entrepreneurship and how to close it?* Maastricht: Maastricht School of Management.

Welter, F. (2011). Contextualizing entrepreneurship: Conceptual challenges and ways forward. *Entrepreneurship Theory and Practice, 35*(1), 165–184.

Welter, F., Baker, T., Audretsch, D. B., & Gartner, W. B. (2016). Everyday entrepreneurship: A call for entrepreneurship research to embrace entrepreneurial diversity. *Entrepreneurship Theory and Practice, 41*(3), 311–321.

Welter, F., & Smallbone, D. (2011). Institutional perspectives on entrepreneurial behavior in challenging environments. *Journal of Small Business Management, 49*(1), 107–125.

White, G. B. (2015). *Women are Owning More and More Small Businesses.* Retrieved 13 January 2017 from https://www.theatlantic.com/business/archive/2015/04/women-are-owning-more-and-more-small-businesses/390642/.

World Economic Forum (2015). *Global Gender Gap Report 2015.* Retrieved 15 January 2017 from http://reports.weforum.org/global-gender-gap-report-2015/rankings/.

Young, I. M. (1994). Punishment, treatment, empowerment: Three approaches to policy for pregnant addicts. *Feminist Studies, 20*(1), 32–57.

Zavella, P. (1991). Reflections on diversity among Chicanas. *Frontiers: A Journal of Women Studies, 12*(2), 73–85.

14 Women's entrepreneurship in Swedish forestry

A matter of adaptation or transformation?

Marie Appelstrand and Gun Lidestav

At global, national and local levels, women's entrepreneurship is increasingly recognized as an important driving force in sustainable and inclusive societal development (SOU, 20171: Warren-Smith & Jackson, 2004). This development is important especially for rural development, where entrepreneurship and diversification in the natural resource sectors have been encouraged as means of compensating for the decline of employment due to centralization and mechanization (Risku-Norja et al., 2010). Still, migration from rural areas, in the search for work opportunities in urban settings, has become an increasing challenge. Many rural regions, not least in Scandinavia, suffer not only from a declining and ageing population, but also from a lack of young women (Hjort, 2009). Paradoxically, despite the consequent overall reduction in the need for labour, the issue of labour shortage has been a recurring theme in the natural resource sectors or 'green industries' of Scandinavia and Canada (KSLA, 2015). Since the 1980s, the absence of women in forestry enterprises (or women's lack of interest in forestry), has been recognized as a particular problem for the forestry sector in the Nordic countries (Lidestav & Wästerlund, 1999; Ministry Series (Ds), 2004:39). More recently, the lack of a defined identity for women as forest owners and lack of personal involvement in the management of their forests has been observed (see e.g. Follo, 2008; Lidestav & Berg Lejon, 2013). Further, as pointed out in a 'Background report' prepared by one of the expert groups set up under the National Forest Programme (Swedish Government, 2016), strengthening the roles of women both as forest owners and as entrepreneurs is important for the achievement of gender equality in the forestry sector, which is considered a means of invigorating the sector's competiveness. The connection between entrepreneurship and rural development is also noted through references to the ongoing work of the Parliamentary Countryside Committee. However, research that brings forth and scrutinizes the actual preconditions for women's entrepreneurship in forestry is scarce, and studies that problematize the changing roles of women forest owners as innovators and entrepreneurs are even more rare.

Against this background, the purpose of this chapter is to contribute to the understanding of the preconditions for and movement towards enhanced gender equality in Swedish forestry. Based on the construction of the dominant gender order in the sector, we discuss how gender in forestry has been understood over time and in relation to our key concepts: 'modernization', 'identity' and 'entrepreneurship'. Thus, we aim to explore the potential for 'transforming' the dominant gender order through women's entrepreneurship in a changing forestry sector. In line with Bruni et al. (2004), we argue that the understanding of the identity and motivation of women as (potential) entrepreneurs in forestry must be interpreted in the context of the prevailing norms and traditions, i.e. the male 'culture', of the sector, namely the framing of gender equality through a greater focus on timber production and technical skills and knowledge: its industrial male normative.

For this purpose, literature on the topics of the gendering of forestry and gender reproduction in forestry, including family owned forestry businesses and entrepreneurship, gender equality policies, entrepreneurial identity and soft governance, has been reviewed. Regarding policy documents, we have identified three key contexts where gender equality issues in forestry have been raised and put forward as a problem that needs to be addressed through measures and actions of varying specificity. These are (i) gender equality in a rural development context, (ii) gender equality and competiveness in the forestry sector, (iii) gender equality and the renewal and multi-functionality of forests. After having identified and analysed the central policy documents, we then traced supporting documents and commentaries relating to these central policy documents. We apply a broad definition of the term '*entrepreneurship*', where we consider self-employment within family held forest businesses to be of particular interest. Further, in using this term, we consider the entrepreneurial activity to consist of traditional activities such as timber production, forestry contracting and the processing of wood and forest fuel, but we also use it when referring production and services revolving around the 'soft' value of forests deriving from non-wood forest products and services (NWFPS), such as tourism, game farming, and 'Green Care'/health services.

In our exploration of the 'gender gap' in a Swedish forestry context, we base our analysis on three interacting concepts: firstly, the process of 'modernization'; secondly, the construction of 'entrepreneurial identities'; and finally, the definition of 'entrepreneurship' as exposed to women in the forestry sector (holistic approach, etc.) (Figure 14.1). The 'gap' is made visible by, on the one hand, the apparent intertwining of modernization, identity and entrepreneurship and the formation of a specific masculinity, and on the other, a similar apparent absence of a connection with the formation of femininity.

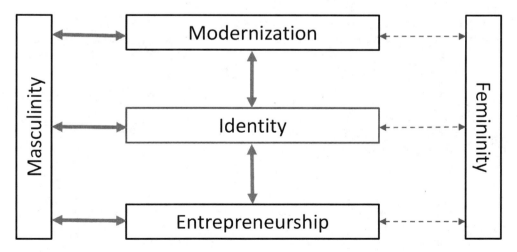

Figure 14.1 The gender gap in relation to the three interacting concepts: modernization, entrepreneurial identity and entrepreneurship

Gender equality policies in the Swedish forestry sector

Bridging the gender gap?

For more than a century, forestry has been one of the backbones of the Swedish economy, providing timber to sawmills and other industries, fuel in the form of wood and chips to households, district heating plants, and to the extractive chemical industry. Thus, there is an apparent interrelation between forestry as a rural and area-based business and the industrial processes and enterprises that depend on the raw material produced. During the early stages of the incorporation of industrial production logic into the sector, forestry was regarded as a modernizing force in Swedish society (Johansson, 1994; Kardell, 2004).

Given the fact that there are 28 million hectares of forestland in Sweden, over half of which is in the hands of 330,000 private individuals (Swedish Forest Agency, 2014), it can be argued that from an entrepreneurial perspective great potential exists for providing services and products based on the 'soft' value and rural environment of forests in combination with, or as an alternative to, traditional timber production (Appelstrand, 2012; Umaerus et al., 2011). However, this potential has yet to be fully developed by large-scale forest companies, whose business concepts focus on industrial timber and forest wood fuel, or by small-scale private owners developing their enterprises (Government Bill, 2007/2008:108; Swedish Forest Agency, 2014). At present, only a quarter of all small-scale forest owners engage in forest-related activity outside traditional forestry (Umaerus et al., 2013). This is also the case for entrepreneurship in small-scale forestry enterprises, which to a large extent are dominated by men (Häggström et al., 2013; Umaerus et al., 2013). With regard to the diversification of forest products and services, which has been proposed as a means of forest business development in rural areas, the omnipresent male dominance is considered a hindrance to women's involvement in forestry activities and thus hampers new enterprising businesses (Ministry Series (Ds), 2004:39; Official Reports of the Swedish Government (SOU), 2017:1). This phenomenon emphasizes one of the most important challenges facing the feasible development of women's entrepreneurship in green industries: the overall gender inequality in the forestry sector. Although the proportion of women forest owners has increased substantially in the last four decades, from an estimated 20% in 1976 (Lidestav, 1997) to 38% in 2014 (Swedish Forest Agency, 2014), the forest sector is still one of the most gender-segregated in Sweden and has not followed the trend seen in other business sectors towards greater gender equality (Ministry Series (Ds), 2004:39). As the Swedish government is taking the gender perspective into consideration at all levels and in all sectors, gender inequality indicates a policy failure, which has implications not only for democracy and legitimacy but for the economy as well. More precisely, the overall objectives of Swedish gender policy are an equal distribution of power and influence between women and men and the same rights and opportunities to shape society and their own lives (Government Communication, 2011/2013:3).

Thus, the key aspects of and criteria for a modern society, that is, the modernization project is at stake if one of the most important industries in Sweden is characterized by gender inequality. The discrepancy between the increasing proportion of women forest owners and entrepreneurs and the level of their active involvement in forest management has been noted by the Government (cf. Ministry Series (Ds), 2004:39; Government Bill, 2007/2008:108), which has found that increased gender equality is a precondition for the sector's continued development and competitiveness. To promote equal and sustainable rural development with more jobs and increased growth, the Ministry of Rural Affairs initiated a programme of action named 'The Forest Kingdom', which included a *National Gender Equality Strategy* (NGES). This strategy was promoted under the heading 'Competitiveness requires gender equality', and the objective was that women and men should have the same opportunities to own and manage forest and to work in or do business within forest management' (Ministry of Rural Affairs, 2011b, p. 3). However, what exactly does this imply for achieving gender equality? And, how can it contribute to bridging the gender gap in the forestry sector? To begin with, greater knowledge must be acquired about the background to the current inequality of opportunity for women as against men in terms of material conditions and cultural constraints, i.e. the gendering of the Swedish forestry sector. Thereafter, it is necessary to explore whether gender equality in forestry, as expressed in the strategy (NGES), is about fostering women's adaptation to the prevailing forestry culture and norms or if it specifically promotes creating opportunities for women to be included on their own conditions, i.e. in line with the overall Swedish gender policy (cf. Government Communication, 2011/2013:3). In the former case, little or no space for women as innovators and entrepreneurs can be expected, while in the latter case, the transformation of gender norms as well as forestry as a business ought to be facilitated.

Gender equality strategies: A matter of adaptation or transformation?

Prior to the development of the National Gender Equality Strategy, a governmental report on the lack of gender equality in agriculture and forestry was presented (Ministry Series (Ds), 2004:39). In that report, the unequal material conditions and gendered practices in family owned forestry businesses were revealed and discussed in the context of rural development, highlighting issues of justice and democracy and the arguments surrounding the profitability of gender equality. It was stated that although women have increasingly entered the forestry sector, both as professionals and as forest owners, the process has been slow and the nature of their participation differs from men's (Follo et al., 2016). On one hand, the inheritance of family estates may appear to be more gender-equal nowadays than the previous tradition of passing land on to one male child. On the other hand, it reflects a conception that women may own, but not manage, a forest estate as an enterprise. Thus, it can also be claimed that the lack of expectation on women and daughters, as compared to men and sons, in combination with little or no training and intergenerational socialization with others involved in forest management, hampers the development of entrepreneurship among female forest owners (Lidestav, 2010). The fact that the forestry sector at large is male-dominated, with only one in eight permanent positions held by a woman and only 4 % of those employed in contract firms being female (Swedish Forest Agency, 2014), provides little incentive and few role models for women and serves as an additional constraint.

Following the recommendations of the governmental report (Ministry Series (Ds), 2004:39), the National Gender Equality Strategy (NGES) for the forestry sector was launched in April 2011 (Ministry of Rural Affairs, 2011a). The NGES recognizes that gender inequality is a problem for the sector at large, partly because of the failure to attract and recruit competent co-workers throughout the population as a whole, and partly because gender inequality indicates a policy failure. The basis for gender equality has thus moved from matters of justice, democracy, inclusiveness and legitimacy to being regarded increasingly as a matter of business interest, which should be viewed as a form of voluntary 'contract' between the state and the sector at large. Thus, gender equality is in line with the soft governance approach of the new Swedish forest policy of 1993, which focuses on 'soft' policy instruments with few or no sanctions in the case of non-compliance (Appelstrand, 2007; Appelstrand and Lidestav, 2015).

The strategy can be seen as the outcome of two parallel and partially interwoven processes rooted in Swedish politics and the Swedish parley model. The first was a politically driven process based on a tradition of a general interest and involvement in gender equality issues, as reflected in the governmental investigation of gender equality in the agriculture and forestry sectors (Ministry Series (Ds), 2004:39). In that report, the appointed investigator summarized the situation by stating that 'it is going slowly', which led the government to include the issue of the gender inequality in the forestry sector and the need for action in the subsequent Governmental Bill 'A forest policy in line with the times' (Governmental Bill prop., 2007/08:108). The second process was born of an even longer tradition of negotiation, consensus-seeking and collaboration between the state, the forest industry and the private forest owners on several issues related to forestry in the broad sense (cf. Törnqvist, 1995; Appelstrand, 2007). Therefore, all major stakeholders in the Swedish forestry sector have been involved in the development and implementation of the strategy, striving towards a voluntary 'contract' between the state and the sector. In contrast to the overall objectives for gender equality policies in Sweden, the NGES does not raise issues of power and influence and does not consider current practices and culture as essential aspects of gender inequality (Holmgren and Arora-Jonsson, 2015). Rather, the strategy can be seen as a way of meeting the need for the forest industry to stay competitive.

Gender and the process of modernization

The construction of modernity in the Swedish forest sector

According to the ethnologist Ella Johansson (1994), it was through forestry work that the man of the north of Sweden became 'modern', i.e. an individual who explored and transformed nature in accordance with the idea that planning, calculation and rational decisions would lead to progress, a better life and a better society. Between 1860 and 1940, a large section of the male population in this region was involved in the winter season logging operations and this induced a material and mental change in the perception of men and of society. Thus, forestry became a force and industry, which in contrast to the traditional farming society, offered freedom from paternalistic relationships between the landed and the landless men, and gave the latter access to independent and equal social and economic status. The piece-rate system, i.e. payment by performance in terms of logs or 'pieces' processed per day's work, increased the predictability of recognition for merit. The lumberjacks that worked the hardest were the most skilful at inventing and applying more efficient work methods and tools and received the highest earnings and respect among their peers. This 'contract for harvesting' was the cornerstone of forestry work and economic organization and had a decisive influence on the social organization of the forest camp as well as on the identity formation of the individual man (Johansson, 1994; Ager, 2014). Significantly, the name for such a contractor in the Swedish language is 'entreprenör' and many of the step-by-step improvements and efficiencies have been, and still are, initiated and developed by these contractors (Ager, 2014). In this very male environment, where women rarely appeared or were recognized at all, a specific 'modern forestry masculinity' developed. This gendering of forestry as a distinct male arena has led to a prevailing set of norms and a culture (Hugosson, 1999; Hultåker, 2006) that has implications for today's female entrepreneurs as they enter the sector. In relation to the questions raised above, it must be considered how and in what form women may develop entrepreneurship and if identity formation is possible within the prevailing culture by adjusting to and replicating the male norms or by encoding forestry in 'feminine' terms, i.e. transforming the sector into an environment based on gender-equal norms involving a change of perspective or even paradigm.

During the manual logging epoch, the lack of visibility and recognition of women in forestry work may, according to Johansson (1994), be regarded as indicating that in that period it would have been too challenging even to imagine women as forestry workers and entrepreneurs. More recent research shows that both men and women in forestry have a common interest in gender non-visibility, stating that gender does not matter (Lidestav and Sjölander, 2007). If women are made visible but at the same time perceived as deviating from the norm solely by their physical presence in the room, they become invisible as knowledge subjects. In an industry sector characterized by gender stereotypes, i.e. masculine norms and standards, and where a certain type of physical (practical) and technical forestry knowledge and expertise lends credibility to its practitioners, women risk being perceived as not conforming to these norms and therefore as less competent (Johansson, 2015). However, to be made visible as a woman can also be problematic because of the (male) expectation that 'she' will represent women as a group, or that 'she' will be expected to contribute to the organization/industry with new and different values, ideas and visions (Lidestav et al., 2011).

Gender and identity

The emergence of a new paradigm?

In recent decades the emergence of the concept of '*ecosystem services*' has introduced a new perception of forestland, placing the ecosystem as a whole in focus and thereby placing value on all kinds of services that are produced by forestry ecosystems. This means that, for example, the production of a pine tree in a forest ecosystem both provides an industrial raw material but also an experience of beauty and scent which can be appreciated by those using forests for recreational experiences. Furthermore, the forest ecosystem supports a multitude of other ecosystem services: providing mushrooms, berries and game, which also have a value both as products and in association with recreational use of forests (Haines-Young and Potschin, 2013). However, the industrial paradigm of forestry (i.e. the male norm) still has the decisive influence on which products and services are most valued in the management of the forest ecosystem (Ambjörnsson et al., 2016). Consequently, the key stakeholders: forest owners and forest professionals who plant and harvest the forests and the associated management and operations, are usually trained and raised in the approach of this industrial paradigm. A similar problematic experience has been put forward by Piper Coutinho-Sledge (2015) in her study of forestry and forest professionals in the United States. She suggests that the gendering of forestry as 'a distinctly masculine profession has led to a wide range of negative outcomes', and argues for a shift in public values to a more 'feminine language'. This shift would focus on caring and holistic approaches to forestry, emphasizing a closer connection to nature, and could function as an agent of change recoding the forestry culture in order to capture the feminine forms of knowledge and interaction. If this were achieved, women's entrepreneurship might challenge the prevailing culture and norms in the sector.

In view of the momentum for this paradigm shift, we thus ask in this chapter: what is the potential for 'altering' gendered norms in a sector under change? Must forestry be 'encoded' in feminine terms, that is, are we moving towards a 'feminized forestry' as Coutinho-Sledge (2015) argues, or are women to adopt the male gender stereotypes: must they 'act like a man', thereby reinforcing male experience as a preferred normative value (Appelstrand & Lidestav, 2015)? Bruni et al. (2004, with ref. to Schwalbe et al., 2000) uses the expression, 'the othering of the non-male' to give visibility to the gender subtext of the discourse on entrepreneur mentality where women's organizations are portrayed as 'the other', thereby reinforcing the male normativity prevailing in the sector. The inherent dilemma is that for the forestry sector to consider 'normatively feminine values as agents of change' (Coutinho-Sledge, 2015), women must be recognized as competent, professional and legitimate knowledge subjects – not 'softer' or 'better' than men.

The role of entrepreneurial identity formation for a feminized forestry

In the light of this, it is of particular importance to understand what expressions women's entrepreneurial identities may take within the framework of the dominant gender order in the forest sector. Here, the focus must be on both the cognitive and normative understandings of women's views and actions on steps and measures taken at the societal, community and individual levels. Egan (1997) points out the importance of role models and mentors in order for women to develop an *entrepreneurial identity*, marking the shift that has occurred from the previous focus on rural women and issues regarding the division of labour, to this more recent interest in identities (cf. Trauger et al., 2008). Identity formation is thought to take place foremost at the individual level, but as the different levels are interdependent they must be considered equally important. In legal research on gender, the lack of positive results in sectors or areas with a high degree of gender inequality is discussed in terms of the disconnection and disparity between the institutional and the individual levels (Svensson, 2001). It has been highlighted that the measures introduced to bridge this gap have not been laws, policies or strategies that mandate that everyone should be treated equally, nor has the eradication of gender-related norms been achieved. One explanation offered for the lack of positive results is that soft governance policies and strategies that declare gender equality as a political goal at the institutional level, do not function automatically as a means of change at the individual level (Appelstrand, 2012; Appelstrand & Lidestav, 2015).

As mentioned above, the NGES is based on an implicit 'contract' between the state and the forestry sector, implying the adoption of voluntary measures by the stakeholders as a precondition for staying competitive by allowing women to enter the sector. Vedung and Danielsson (1997) stress that vague policy goals – as in the case of the NGES – are often justified as a necessary precondition for hindering a deep-rooted interest conflict – for example gender equality, in terms of allowing women the same power as men – to be fully visible at the central (institutional) level. In order for such a 'voluntary' measure to work, it has to be legitimate and fully accepted by all stakeholders, that is the forestry sector as a whole. As the NGES was implemented mainly by means of 'soft' steering methods such as education, knowledge transfer and information, not carrying any sanctions in the case of non-compliance, the incentive for the sector and its stakeholders to reach the goal of gender equality is derived from what is clearly expressed in the strategy as: *the ideological goal of growth*. The business rationale shaping the framework for the strategy is driven by arguments of efficiency and profitability, which state that the sector must stay competitive enough for business to continue as usual, that is, *within* the industrial paradigm. The potential for a normative change of the gendered culture in the forestry sector then becomes circumscribed.

Despite the lack of support at the institutional level: in our case policy programmes, strategies and support from the relevant authorities (cf. Warren-Smith & Jackson, 2004; Ahl, 2006), there is evidence that there are still incentives for women to develop and build an entrepreneurial identity at the individual level – at least within the space that they are afforded, that is, in their own business area – and thus to narrow the gender gap. At the individual level, several factors may function as motivators when women start or expand a business: social factors such as different kinds of *networks* may be a driver and women's personal cognitive abilities, values and motivation will also play an important role. Lidestav (2010) has shown that women in their identity forming process can move from their traditional, subordinated role as 'transitive elements' to adopting a position as '*transformative agents*', i.e. as forest owning women/entrepreneurs who position themselves as active managers, adapting their management style/business so that it reflects their own agenda. This suggests that, while the overall culture of forestry remains distinctly masculine, efforts at the individual level provide a point of entry for thinking through how feminist values and norms can be used to influence the creation of new institutional norms.

Gender and entrepreneurship

Women as 'transitive elements' or 'transformative agents'

Although several studies have shown that women forest owners generally are less engaged in the outdoor operational activities related to their forests than male owners, their active involvement in silviculture and the administration of their forestry businesses should not be overlooked (e.g. Lidestav & Nordfjell, 2005; Follo, 2008). According to Umaerus et al. (2013), the large majority of female owners are, similar to male owners, running traditional forestry businesses only (timber production for sale). Among those that run forest-related activities other than traditional forestry, about one-fifth are women. While men are more likely to engage in businesses such as forestry contracting or wood processing, i.e. forestry related activities much associated with rural masculine competence (cf. Brandth & Haugen, 2005), women are more likely to operate businesses in 'Green Care'/health services or tourism, i.e. activities related to typical female activities and professions. At the same time, these service-oriented businesses are introducing a certain novelty and diversification into Swedish forestry, in line with a more ecosystem-service-oriented paradigm. Thereby, it may be claimed that women as innovators and entrepreneurs can contribute to the transformation of the forestry sector. According to Lidestav (2010), some forest owning women have managed to do this by positioning themselves as '*transformative agents*' (Lidestav, 2010), i.e. transforming their ownership into active management and thus adapting the management to their own life goals. Others, who can be labelled as '*transformative elements*', do not engage actively in forestry management but have developed a relation to the forest as such, and may still be open to forest-related activities other than traditional forestry. As pointed out by Umaerus et al. (2013), the transformative agents have used their skills and complementary competence to go beyond traditional patterns by pursuing the opportunities connected to changing market demands. Regarding the transformative elements, we may assume that some external support or incentives are needed to activate their transforming potential.

With this new positioning of women forest owners we may also expect that '*a new type of entrepreneurial identity*' may occur.

Women's networks as a transformative strategy

In the governmental report from 2004 (Ministry Series (Ds), 2004:39), the low representation of women in public and corporate organizations and women's limited access to networks in the forestry sector was seen as an obstacle to the achievement of gender equality within the forestry sector. Hence, the formation of women's networks has been recognized as a means for women to gain access to the sector (Lidestav & Wästerlund, 1999; Brandth et al., 2004; Brandth & Haugen, 2005; Arora-Jonsson, 2005). In a study by Andersson and Lidestav (2016), two nationwide and four regional women's networks were identified and analysed. Five of these are networks of individual forest owners comprising up to 400 women each, while the sixth network comprises female elected representatives from the four main forest owners' associations (FOA). By establishing their own networks, female forest owners have created alternative platforms for articulating their interests and needs. In addition they can be regarded as a way of challenging gendered notions of what forestry and forest ownership is about. Further, the alternative and less hierarchical form of organization encourages and fosters higher degrees of participation based on individuals and resources and thereby also generates a group identity. Through their joint experiences and activities, a group identity for these women allows them to speak from their own position and identity, articulating alternative and even oppositional interpretations of key themes of the industrial forestry paradigm. As such, the networks empower women (Reineltl, 1994), and some of the network members report that they have been invited by forestry organizations at the local level to provide an 'expert opinion' as a female forest owner (Andersson & Lidestav, 2016). Three of the women's networks were also invited to participate in the process of developing the NGES. Thus, there are some signs of integration and participation of women in Swedish forestry through their networking activities. However, Andersson and Lidestav (2016, p. 42) argue that 'to be transformative, a strategy for empowerment by organizing space for non-hegemonic actors must, within the processes of gender mainstreaming in forestry, be combined with a strategy for displacement. Thus from the position of the counterpublics, the women's forest networks contribute to challenging and transforming the present rationales and organization of forestry and forest research'.

Concluding discussion

The forestry sector is no longer a modernizing force, but rather one that preserves the status quo through (i) fixing of the industrial paradigm for forestry, (ii) the male norm and (iii) the traditional understanding of entrepreneurship in the forestry sector. Women conforming to the contractor norm does not amount to modernization of the forestry sector. The dominant gender order is only cemented by development in that direction. The 'modern' identity is defined by men in relation to other men. In other words, the masculinity created – the modern man of Norrland – is created in relation to other men and does not work particularly well in a modern society which aims for gender equality in the context of rural development.

The gendering of the Swedish forest sector has led to a number of negative outcomes, not just for gender equality, but also for economic prosperity and ecosystem vitality.

Conventional forest management based on the industrial paradigm is no longer considered environmentally sustainable. At the same time, the profitability of the sector is declining. Thus, the hegemonic status of the industrial paradigm as 'the only game in town' is being challenged. A complete change in the notion of forestry as a business may not be possible or even desirable. Instead, a rethinking and 'encoding' of forestry with a transformed culture that allows different voices, competences and management practices is needed to revitalize and modernize the sector. In this chapter, we have discussed the preconditions for women to take their place and act as a transforming force, which in the terminology of Coutinho-Sledge (2015) would facilitate movement towards a 'feminized forestry'.

Based on our policy analysis, we argue that the gender aspect is not understood or taken into account by the regular actors in the policy-making process at the institutional level, which has resulted in the articulation of a gender equality process which takes place separately from other processes, for example at the individual level. Thus, the issue of power and legitimacy claims, e.g. in terms of competence, are then kept 'extraneous to the subject' and do not become problematic. However, in line with Coutinho-Sledge (2015) and Johansson (2015), we argue that to achieve gender equality it is vital that these aspects are thoroughly considered. Not least, the idea of 'forestry competence' should be scrutinized and stripped of gendered notions, so that women as forest owners or professionals can be recognized as competent, professional and legitimate knowledge subjects.

The path forward seems thus to require that changes occur across multiple facets of the sector, to provide more opportunities for the development of holistic knowledge, social engagement and caring approaches in forest use. As shown by our examples of women that position themselves as transformative agents and the emerging women's networks, transforming movements exist irrespective of how the forestry sector understands and frames strategies for gender equality. The effect of these initiatives is, however, limited because, as argued by Coutinho-Sledge (2015): 'Every time femininity enters into forestry it is through extremely limited means with a responsibility to alter the entire culture of the profession. It is important to realize that a professional culture has multiple components and a shift in one component does not automatically transfer to the others'.

References

Ager, B. (2014). *Skogsarbetets humanisering och rationalisering från 1900 och framåt* [The humanization and rationalization of forest work from 1900 and forward]. (Doctoral thesis). Luleå Technical University, Luleå.

Ahl, H. (2006). Why research on women entrepreneurs needs new directions. *Entrepreneurship Theory & Practice, 30*(5), 596–623.

Ambjörnsson, E. L., Keskitalo, E. C. H., & Karlsson, S. (2016). Forest discourses and the role of planning-related perspectives: The case of Sweden. *Scandinavian Journal of Forest Research, 31*(1), 111–118.

Andersson, E., & Lidestav, G. (2016). Creating alternative spaces and articulating needs: Challenging gendered notions of forestry and forest ownership through women's networks. *Forest Policy and Economics, 67*, 38–44.

Appelstrand, M. (2007). *Miljömålet i skogsbruket – styrning och frivillighet* [The environmental goal of Swedish forest policy: Regulation and voluntariness] (Doctoral dissertation). Studies in Sociology of Law, Lund University, Lund.

Appelstrand, M. (2012). Developments in Swedish forest policy and administration: From a 'policy of restriction' towards a 'policy of cooperation'. *Scandinavian Journal of Forest Research, 27*, 186–199.

204 *Marie Appelstrand and Gun Lidestav*

Appelstrand, M., & Lidestav, G. (2015). Women entrepreneurship: A shortcut to a more competitive and equal forestry sector? *Scandinavian Journal of Forest Research, 30*(3), 226–234.

Arora-Jonsson, S. (2005). *Unsettling the order: Gendered subjects and grassroots activism in two forest communities.* Uppsala: Dept. of Rural Development and Agroecology, Swedish University of Agricultural Sciences.

Brandth, B., & Haugen, M. S. (2005). Doing rural masculinity: From logging to outfield tourism. *Journal of Gender Studies, 14*, 13–22.

Brandth, B., Follo, G., & Haugen, M. S. (2004). Women in forestry: Dilemmas of a separate women's organization. *Scandinavian Journal of Forest Research, 19*, 466–472.

Bruni, A., Gherardi, S., & Poggio, B. (2004) Entrepreneur-mentality, gender and the study of women entrepreneurs. *Journal of Organizational Change Management, 17*(3), 256–268.

Coutinho-Sledge, P. (2015). Feminized forestry: The promises and pitfalls of change in a masculine organization. *Gender, Work & Organization, 22*(4), 375–389.

Egan, M. (1997). Getting down to business and off welfare: Rural women entrepreneurs. *Affilia, 12*, 215–228.

Follo, G. (2008). *Det norske familieskogbruket, dets kvinnelige og mannlige skogeiere, forvaltningsaktivitet og metaforiske forbindelser* [The Norwegian family-owned forestry businesses, its female and male forest owners, the management activities and metaphorical connections]. Trondheim: Norwegian University of Science and Technology (in Norwegian).

Follo, G., Lidestav, G., Ludvig, A., Vilkriste, L., Hujala, T., Karppinen, H., Didolot, F., & Mizaraite, D. (2016). Gender in European forest ownership and management: Reflections on women as 'New forest owners'. *Scandinavian Journal of Forest Research, 32*(2), 174–184.

Government Bill (prop.) (2007/2008:108). En skogspolitik i takt med tiden [A forest policy in line with times]. Stockholm: Sveriges Riksdag.

Government Communication (Regeringens skrivelse) (2011/2013:3). *Jämställdhetspolitikens inriktning 2011–2014.* [The focus of gender equality policy 2011–2014]. Stockholm: Ministry of Education.

Haines-Young, R., & Potschin, M. (2013). *Common international classification of ecosystem services (CICES): Consultation on version 4, August–December 2012.* EEA Framework Contract No EEA/IEA/09/003.

Hjort, S. (2009) *Socio-economic differentiation and selective migration in rural and urban Sweden.* GERUM 2009:1, Umeå University.

Holmgren, S., & Arora-Jonsson, S. (2015). The forest kingdom – with what values for the world? Climate change and gender equality in a contested forest policy context. *Scandinavian Journal of Forest Research, 30*(3), 235–245.

Hugosson, M. (1999). *Constructing cultural patterns from actors' views on industrial forestry in Sweden: An interpretive study based on assessments of conceptualizations and definitions in organizational culture theory.* (Silvestria 113). Uppsala: Swedish University of Agricultural Sciences.

Hultåker, O. (2006). *Entreprenörskap i skogsdrivningsbranschen — En kvalitativ studie om utvecklingen i små företag.* Uppsala: Sveriges lantbruksuniversitet.

Häggström, C., Kawasaki, A., & Lidestav, G. (2013). Profiles of forestry contractors and development of the forestry-contracting sector in Sweden. *Scandinavian Journal of Forest Research, 28*(4), 395–404.

Johansson, E. (1994). *Skogarnas fria söner. Maskulinitet och modernitet i norrländskt skogsarbete* [Free sons of the forest: A study of masculinity and modernity among loggers in northern Sweden 1860–1940] (Nordiska museets Handlingar 118). (Doctoral dissertation). Nordiska museet, Stockholm.

Johansson, M. (2015). *Att göra jämställdhet – motiv, motstånd och möjligheter i det svenska skogsbruket.* Luleå Technical University, Luleå.

Kardell, L. (2004). *Svenskarna och skogen. Del 2. Från baggböleri till naturvård.* Jönköping: Skogsstyrelsens förlag.

KSLA (Kungl. Skogs- och Lantbruksakademien) (The Royal Swedish Academy of Agriculture and Forestry) (2015). *Skogsnäringens framtida kompetensförsörjning.* En rapport från KSLA:s Kommitté för kunskaps- och kompetensförsörjning. Kungl. skogs- och lantbruksakademiens tidskrift. No. 2, 2015 Vol. 154.

Lidestav, G. (1997). *Female forest owners and female forest holdings: A structure analysis.* Research Notes. No. 298. Department of Operational Efficiency, Faculty of Forestry, Swedish University of Agricultural Sciences, Umeå.

Lidestav, G. (2010). In competition with a brother: Women's inheritance positions in contemporary Swedish family forestry. *Scandinavian Journal of Forest Research, 25*(Suppl. No. 9), 14–25.

Lidestav, G., & Wästerlund, D. (Eds) (1999). *Women and Forestry.* Proceedings of the Nordic–Baltic Workshop in Balsjö, Sweden, 7–9 December 1998; TemaNord 1999: 571. Copenhagen: Nordic Council of Ministers.

Lidestav, G., & Nordfjell, T. (2005). A conceptual model for understanding social practices in family forestry. *Small-scale Forest Economics, Management and Policy, 4,* 391–408.

Lidestav, G., & Sjölander, A. (2007). Gender and forestry: A critical discourse analysis of forestry professions in Sweden. *Scandinavian Journal of Forest Research, 22,* 351–362.

Lidestav, G., Andersson, S., Lejon, B., & Johansson, K. (2011) *Jämställt arbetsliv i skogssektorn – underlag för åtgärder Institutionen för skoglig resurshushållning,* Arbetsrapport 345. Sveriges lantbruksuniversitet.

Lidestav, G., & Berg Lejon, S. (2013) Harvesting and silvicultural activities in Swedish family forestry: Behavior changes from a gender perspective. *Scandinavian Journal of Forest Research, 28*(2), 136–142.

Ministry of Rural Affairs (2011a). Konkurrenskraft kräver jämställdhet – Jämställdhetsstrategi för skogsbrukssektorn [Competitiveness requires gender]. Stockholm: Ministry of Rural Affairs.

Ministry of Rural Affairs (2011b). *The Forest Kingdom – with values for the world. Action plan.* Stockholm: Ministry of Rural Affairs.

Ministry Series (Ds) (2004:39). *Det går långsamt fram . . . Jämställdheten inom jord- och skogsbrukssektorn.* [Slow to advance . . . gender equality in the agricultural and forestry sector]. Stockholm: Ministry of Agriculture.

Official Reports of the Swedish Government (SOU) (2017:1) *För Sveriges landsbygder – en sammanhållen politik för arbete, hållbar tillväxt och välfärd. Slutbetänkande av parlamentariska landsbygdskommittén.* Stockholm: Ministry of Enterprise and Innovation.

Reineltl, C. (1994). Fostering empowerment, building community: The challenge for state-funded feminist organizations. *Human Relations, 47,* 685–705.

Risku-Norja, H., Voutilainen, O., & Yli-Viikari, A. (2010). Rural development in Finland: Revival of a natural resource sectors' perspective. *Society and Natural Resources, 24,* 75–84.

Svensson, E.-M. (2001). *Genusforskning inom juridiken* [Gender research in the fields of law]. Kalmar: Högskoleverket.

Swedish Forest Agency (2014). *Statistical yearbook of forestry.* Jönköping: Skogsstyrelsen.

Swedish Government Report (2016). *Tillväxt, mångbruk, värdeskapande av skogen som resurs.* Underlagsrapport från arbetsgrupp 1 inom nationellt skogsprogram. Stockholm: The Swedish Government.

Trauger, A., Sachs, C., Berbercheck, M., Keirnan, N. E., Braiser, K., & Findeis, J. (2008). Agricultural education: Gender identity and knowledge exchange. *Journal for Rural Studies, 24,* 432–439.

Törnqvist, T. (1995). *Inheritors of the woodlands: A sociological study of private, non-industrial forest ownership.* Uppsala: Swedish University of Agricultural Sciences.

Umaerus, P., Lidestav, G., & Högvall Nordin, M. (2011). *Business activities in family farm forestry in a rural development context.* Working papers 330. Umeå, Sweden: Swedish University of Agricultural Sciences.

Umaerus, P., Lidestav, G., Eriksson, O., & Högvall Nordin, M. (2013). Gendered business activities in family farm forestry: From round wood delivery to health service. *Scandinavian Journal of Forest Research, 28*(6), 596–607.

Vedung, E., & Danielsson, M. (1997). *Riksdagens skogspolitiska intentioner. Om mål som uppdrag till en myndighet* [The Parliament's political intentions regarding forestry. On the objectives for public authorities]. Skogsstyrelsen meddelande 13:1997.

Warren-Smith, I., & Jackson, C. (2004). Women creating wealth through rural enterprise. *International Journal of Entrepreneurial Behaviour & Research, 10*(6), 369–383.

15 Women's business survival and the institutionalization of entrepreneurial support in the Malaysian handicraft industry

Salmah Topimin, Clare Brindley and Carley Foster

Based on a review of the literature on the concepts of gender, women's business survival and the institutionalization of entrepreneurial support, this chapter highlights the bias that surrounds our understanding of women entrepreneurs. To address this bias, we present a conceptual framework for women's business survival that includes the significant influence of contextual differences on women entrepreneurs by drawing on the Malaysian handicraft industry as the context (Figure 15.1).

This framework was developed based on the contention that entrepreneurship is a result of the dynamic interactions between individual and environmental factors (Shane, 2003; Welter, & Smallbone, 2011). However, understanding the process related to women's business survival is problematic, as the literature tends to separate women from their environments. For example, research on women's entrepreneurship has placed too much emphasis on explanations related to individuals while neglecting the complexity of their social arrangements (Ahl, 2006) that affect women's activities in the public sphere. This reality cannot be revealed without acknowledging the importance of using a gender lens in researching women's entrepreneurial activities (Brush, 2006; Loscocco & Bird, 2012). The lack of research that explains how social arrangements shape gender relations and society (Huq & Moyeen, 2008) also suggests the importance of recognizing other institutional elements in women's environments that affect their entrepreneurial success. As a result, the need for a multidimensional framework that takes into account the context in which the female entrepreneur is positioned is clear. This chapter contextualizes the discussion by describing the present state of the handicraft industry in Malaysia and women's involvement in it.

Women entrepreneurs in the handicraft industry in Malaysia

Since the Fourth Malaysia Plan[1] (1981–1985), the Malaysian handicraft industry has been recognized as a sector because of its growth through its export activities (Redzuan & Aref, 2011). The growth of the Malaysian handicraft industry is supported by the growth of related industries, such as the tourism industry (SME Corp., 2010). Recognizing the importance of the Malaysian handicraft industry, the government introduced a wide range of initiatives to help its development. A major government initiative to ensure the industry's sustainable development was the establishment of the Malaysian Handicraft Development Corporation (MHDC), which provides support programmes that focus on manufacturing and marketing efforts for handicraft producers and entrepreneurs (Mat Amin, 2006). However, despite the government initiatives, issues and challenges plague almost all levels of the

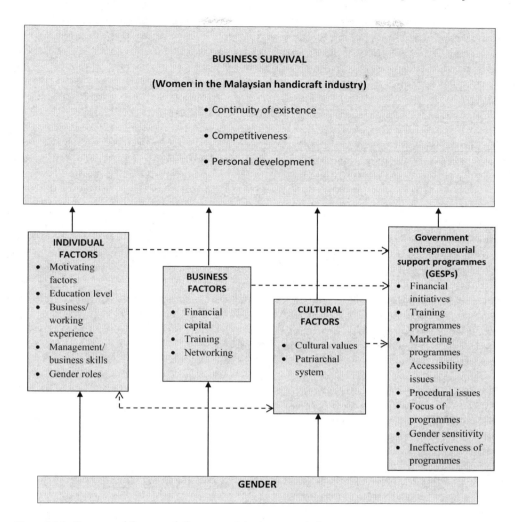

Figure 15.1 Conceptual framework for women's business survival

Malaysian handicraft industry, including production, research and development, marketing, human resources and regulations (Mat Amin, 2006). The constraints faced by the industry can be grouped into demand constraints and supply constraints, which include issues like lack of competitiveness, lack of creativity (e.g., outdated designs) and lack of quality control (Redzuan & Aref, 2011).

Most handicraft businesses in Malaysia are run by women. Based on data from the MHDC, women handicraft producers in Malaysia account for 61.8 per cent of the sector (Mat Amin, 2006), with Bumiputera women entrepreneurs (BWEs) dominating. 'Bumiputera', which means 'sons of the earth', refers to indigenous people (Ahmad, 1998), the largest population group in Malaysia. As Al-Dajani and Marlow (2013) noted, the skills required to produce craft products are held by women. Perhaps as a result, their businesses tend to be small (Habib Shah, 2004; Muda, Wan Mohd Amin, & Halim, 2011), home-based

Development of a conceptual framework for the survival of women's businesses

The framework developed in this chapter (Figure 15.1) draws on concepts that are evident in the entrepreneurial literature: that micro-level factors are determinants of entrepreneurial behaviour (Welter & Smallbone, 2011), that entrepreneurial behaviour is influenced by both individual and environmental factors (Shane, 2003), and that three institutional environments – economic, political and socio-cultural – influence people to engage in entrepreneurial activities (Shane, 2003). Although individual and environmental factors are not mutually exclusive, individual factors feature more heavily in the literature (Shane, 2003; Welter & Smallbone, 2011). Perhaps it is not surprising that women entrepreneurs are discussed in the early entrepreneurship literature as individually responsible for the success of their businesses (e.g., Hisrich & Brush, 1984), as the view that, even when women's socialization processes are considered, it is a woman's responsibility to choose a business strategy that fits with their individual competencies is prevalent (Carter, Williams, & Reynolds, 1997). However, studying individual experiences makes only a limited contribution to explaining the reality of women's entrepreneurship, so we consider factors that are beyond the individual in explaining the survival of women entrepreneurs' businesses.

The current literature on women's entrepreneurship has outlined that individual, business (Boden & Nucci, 2000; McGowan, Redekar, Cooper, & Greenan, 2012) and cultural factors (Mordi et al., 2010) are significant influencers of success. In addition, the review of the literature on the institutionalization of entrepreneurial support for women illustrates the relationship between public support and women's entrepreneurial activities (e.g., Jamali, 2009; Sadi & Al-Ghazali, 2010). The Malaysian government is influential in shaping the country's supportive environment for women entrepreneurs (Dechant & Lamky, 2005), but because of the dynamic interaction between gender and other external factors that women experience in the social environment (Bradley, 2007), the gender concept is as a pervasive theme in the framework. The inclusion of the gender concept enhances our insights into women's experiences (Ahl, 2006; Brush, 2006; Brush, de Bruin, & Welter, 2009) because it allows us to explore the complexity of gender relations within a social environment. Therefore, the conceptual framework (Figure 15.1) includes the interactions between the women's business survival process and the five constructs: the individual, the business, the culture, government entrepreneurial support programmes (GESPs) and gender.

Although there is significant institutional support for women entrepreneurs in Malaysia, its effectiveness is a matter for debate (Lee at al., 2011; Tambunan, 2007). For instance, programmes that support women entrepreneurs should meet women's expectations (e.g., Brush, Carter, Gatewood, Greene, & Hart, 2004; Welter, 2004), yet it is unclear whether such programmes actually address women's needs (Huq & Moyeen, 2006). Consequently, the extent to which GESPs facilitate women's business survival is closely linked to women's individual, business and cultural needs. Indirect links are also represented in the framework (Figure 15.1), and while they are less tangible, they are still significant. The direct and indirect links between the five constructs and the process of women's business survival indicate the complexity of women's entrepreneurial activities within the social and entrepreneurial environments in which they operate.

Business survival

In Figure 15.1 illustrates the five constructs that are significant in influencing the business survival of women's handicraft businesses in Malaysia. The *business survival* concept consists of three elements: *continuity of existence*, *competitiveness* and *personal development*. The first two issues reflect the notion that growing businesses are more likely to survive in the long term than are businesses that are not growing (Basu & Goswami, 1999). From a theoretical perspective, a business is a 'workable business entity' (Churchill & Lewis, 1983, p. 4) that is successful in overcoming crises at the inception stage (Scott & Bruce, 1987). In this sense, the business concept refers to a firm's ability to stay in business for a specific time period (e.g., Bekele & Worku, 2008). However, this view is likely to place women entrepreneurs at a disadvantage in at least two situations. First, the assumption that business survival is a natural business phenomenon does not recognize the intensity of the challenges women entrepreneurs face (Brush & Gatewood, 2008). Second, the view does not acknowledge the complexity of women's social environments. Women's business survival is more than an issue of existence; it is a dynamic process that requires women entrepreneurs to manage the environment in which they operate so their businesses continue to operate and remain competitive and financially healthy.

In addition, the practice of using hard indicators to evaluate the performance of women's businesses discriminates against women entrepreneurs (Ahl, 2002; 2006) because of for example, the lack of disaggregated data. The business concept (Figure 15.1) includes personal development as one dimension of business success and business performance for women entrepreneurs (Shaw, Marlow, Lam & Carter, 2009). In the Malaysian context, prevailing traditions and values determine the appropriateness of work for both men and women (Daud, 1988), and prejudice against women and the gendering practices to which women have been exposed at home and in other institutions (e.g., school) are accepted as the way things are (Hashim, Yusof, Ismail, & Raihanah, 2011). To overcome this prejudice, women incorporate strategies of empowerment, including becoming entrepreneurs. For example, in investigating the entrepreneurial aspirations of Malaysian women entrepreneurs, Osman et al. (2011) found that women entrepreneurs experience a high sense of empowerment. Their abilities in making business decisions and in accessing resources and information for business activities offer women entrepreneurs a sense of psychological empowerment that can boost their self-esteem and make inroads into the status quo such that women go from being traditionally passive in the community to being active players. Therefore, women entrepreneurs in general and in Malaysia in particular should consider how their businesses affect their personal development. Therefore, incorporating the three elements continuity of existence, competitiveness and personal development (Figure 15.1) helps to clarify the business concept for women entrepreneurs by reducing the domination of the time period as an indicator in explaining a firm's survival (e.g., Bekele and Worku, 2008; Boden & Nucci, 2000) and minimizing the discrimination effect of financial performance indicators on women entrepreneurs (Ahl, 2002, 2006; Brush, 1992). Furthermore, the framework acknowledges that women's business survival experiences cannot be separated from their environment.

Construct: business factors

Figure 15.1 shows that *business factors* like *financial capital*, *training* and **networking** are also central to women's business survival activities. Limited capital (Alsos, Isaksen, & Ljung-gren, 2006), skills, knowledge and experience in business (Roomi et al., 2009) and poor social networks (McGowan & Hampton, 2007) have been identified as factors in women's competitive disadvantage. In Malaysia, although a handicraft business can be started with a small investment, increasing the market competitiveness of the handicraft products requires a more substantial investment (Redzuan & Aref, 2011). Although women may seek external financing, the private capital market offers less favourable credit terms (Coleman, 2000) and charges higher interest rates to women (Muravyev, Talavera, & Schäfer, 2009). Alternatively, women entrepreneurs could use the subsidized loans and loan guarantees that governments provide (Verheul & Thurik, 2001), but the amount of money provided by government financial assistance is limited and less focused on business expansion (Devi, 2011). In this sense, women entrepreneurs who are past the start-up stage often find that government financial assistance is inadequate to support the survival of their businesses.

Roomi and Parrott (2008) argued that the lack of business management skills is women entrepreneurs' greatest challenge after access to finance. Women's lack of business-related skills is the result of their having usually been previously employed in low-paid, unskilled or semi-skilled positions in the service sector (Carter, 2000). One way to improve women's business skills is through their involvement in business-related training (Ayadurai & Ahmad, 2006), although the women's entrepreneurship literature has criticized training initiatives for women entrepreneurs for being based on the experiences of men and their lack of con-cern for women's needs (Huq & Moyeen, 2006, 2011). In Malaysia, although programmes like the Women Exporters Development Programme (WEDP) are specifically designed for women entrepreneurs, the fact that women's handicraft businesses in Malaysia are relatively small (Habib Shah, 2004; Muda, Wan Mohd Amin & Halim, 2011) makes the exporting programme less attractive and less appropriate for them.

Women's social networks also limit their access to information about training oppor-tunities (Teoh & Chong, 2008) because women have small social networks that include a high proportion of family and extended family members (Roomi et al., 2009). This pattern is also common in Malaysia (Ayadurai & Ahmad, 2006). This type of network is helpful only in the early stage of business development; to ensure business growth, women need networks of professional advisers (McGowan & Hampton, 2007). Therefore, women's usual networks can hinder their business survival.

Construct: The individual

Several *individual factors* influence women's business survival. Motivating factors, for exam-ple, are individual factors that influence women's involvement in entrepreneurial activities. Research has highlighted the importance of pull and push factors for women entrepreneurs (Van der Boon, 2005). Push factors are associated with a negative environment that forces women toward entrepreneurship, while pull factors are related to positive developments that encourage women to try entrepreneurship (Ahmad, 2011). However, the use of push and pull factors in explaining women's motivation for going into business does not reflect the complexity of the individual factors that are associated with each category (Humbert & Drew, 2010). For example, although men and women entrepreneurs are similarly motivated by push and pull factors, when their marital status is added to the context, the need to improve their work–life balance appears to be a significant motivational factor for women entrepreneurs. Women could also be motivated to become entrepreneurs by the socio-cultural context (Ahmad, 2011). In a context in which women struggle to improve their status, women's see involvement in business activities as one way to improve their status (Mboko & Hunter, 2010). In Malaysia, strong socio-cultural norms place women in a disadvantaged position in relation to men in the public sphere (Yusof, 2006). Any study of women entrepreneurs should not dissociate them from their social environment, as this environment brings a variety of challenges and experiences to women's entrepreneurship and to the likelihood of women's business survival.

Other individual factors that are significant in influencing women's business survival are *educational level, previous business or work experience* and *management or business skills*. These factors all relate to women's human capital and are key determinants of a firm's survival (Boden & Nucci, 2000). However, research has shown that individual barriers, such as a women's lack of qualifications and work experience, are important influencers of business growth (Roomi, Harrison, & Beaumont-Kerridge, 2009). Although no gender differences with respect to education have been found in developed countries (Shaw et al., 2009), education equality is uncommon in developing countries because of the structural barriers in women's social environments (Leach, 2000). This situation pertains to the handicraft entrepreneurs in Malaysia, where the majority of women business owners have a low level of education, knowledge and skills in producing their handicraft products (Redzuan & Aref, 2011). The women's lack of knowledge about business support is the result of their level of human capital, including their lack of managerial experience and access to networks (Roomi et al., 2009). While the significance of business support systems in influencing the success of women entrepreneurs has been discussed extensively, particularly in the context of developing countries (e.g., Lee et al., 2011; Sadi & Al-Ghazali, 2010), women's lack of human capital can prevent women entrepreneurs from accessing these support programmes.

Gender roles are one of the individual factors that influence women's business survival. Studies have suggested that women perform multiple gender roles throughout their lives, leading to gender-related obstacles in terms of running their businesses and restricting their mobility (Ahmad, 2011; Roomi & Parrott, 2008). Research on Malaysian women entrepreneurs have found that gender roles pose a major problem (e.g., Yusof, 2006; Selamat et al., 2011). In investigating the influence of socio-cultural traits on BWEs, Yusof (2006) found that managing the dual roles these women have has posed challenges to their ability to pursue their entrepreneurial activities. Yusof (2006) claimed that, although there BWEs have a degree of social and economic independence, their independence is still subject to a certain amount of control by the social order. For example, women must negotiate their cultural and business expectations in terms of dealing or travelling with male counterparts (Selamat, Razak, Gapor, & Sanusi, 2011).

Construct: The culture

The *cultural factors* that influence BWEs' business survival include *cultural values* and *patriarchal systems*. Cultural effects on entrepreneurial behaviours vary and are specific to the cultural context (Ahmad, 2007). In Malaysia, national values are associated with a collectivist culture, a strong emphasis on relationships (Abdullah & Lim, 2001) and mutual in-group support (Nordin, Williams, & Zimmer, 2002). In the Malaysian collectivist culture,

Bumiputera are likely to have collectivist inclination, where they give priority to 'we', rather than 'I', in order to maintain harmonious relationships in society (Zawawi, 2008). In this society, people consider the group's interests as the most important goal, so it may be expected that the Malaysian collectivist society offers informal support that can be beneficial to women's businesses. Figure 15.1 accounts for Malaysian collectivism and explores its impact on BWEs. In addition, the gender literature has argued that gender inequality subjugates women to males throughout society (e.g., Bradley, 2007), as society conforms to a patriarchal system. For women entrepreneurs in patriarchal systems, women's business potential is restricted, as they operate in a society that favours male norms (Ahmad, 2011; Roomi & Parrott, 2008). Therefore, women must negotiate with men and compromise their domestic responsibilities (Al-Dajani v Marlow, 2010). In the context of Malaysia, where patriarchal values are prevalent and the stereotypical role of women is consistent with the social–cultural norms (Ariffin, 1999), women are viewed as less independent and more emotional, gentle and weak (Hashim et al., 2011) than men are, and they must retain their traditional image even when they are involved in the modernization process (Daud, 1988).

Construct: GESPs

As Figure 15.1 shows, institutional support, which refers to the *GESPs*, contains eight elements: financial initiatives, training and marketing programmes, accessibility and procedural issues, focus of programmes, gender sensitivity and ineffectiveness of programmes. The importance of governmental influence in facilitating women's businesses is apparent throughout the literature (e.g., Lee et al., 2011). In the context of Malaysia, the government's support is a vital factor in women's ability to succeed in their entrepreneurial activities (Ariffin, 2009). Government funding is important for BWEs, and their entrepreneurial capacity and capability (e.g., entrepreneurial skills and product development) can be enhanced through strong and comprehensive government support (Shah, 2004). As such, GESPs have significant influence on women's business survival.

The most common support programmes cited in the literature involve financial initiatives and *training programmes* (e.g., Welter, 2004). These initiatives help to overcome women's low level of human and social capital and business resources (McGowan et al., 2012). Research has also shown that marketing can both contribute (Roomi et al., 2009) and constrain (Huq & Moyeen, 2006) the growth of women's businesses. These types of support programmes are available in Malaysia, offered by a government organization that is responsible for the development of the handicraft industry. However, the appropriateness of these programmes in supporting the survival of Malaysian women's handicraft businesses is questionable. While the training programmes focus on nurturing young handicraft producers, the programmes' marketing efforts are limited to one-off activities like handicraft carnivals, road shows and the yearly National Craft Day (Shahadan, 2001). In addition, credit facilities for Malaysian women entrepreneurs tend to be related to micro-financing (Teoh & Chong, 2008), which is appropriate for starting a business but may not be sufficient to support the growth that is necessary for its survival. Therefore, despite the availability of the government's financing, training and marketing support programmes, the extent to which these initiatives facilitate the business survival of BWEs in the handicraft industry in Malaysia requires further investigation.

The literature on institutional approaches has revealed that, for several reasons, women do not always participate in entrepreneurial support programmes (Schmidt & Parker, 2003).

First, women have *accessibility* and *procedural* issues that are related to poor marketing of the programmes (Mahajar & Yunus, 2006), bureaucratic issues (Ahmad, 2011), and extensive (Jamali, 2009) and complicated procedures (Hung, Effendi, Talip, & Rani, 2010). Research conducted on GESPs in Malaysia has supported this view, showing that inappropriate methods are used to disseminate information about the programmes offered (Ong, Ismail, & Yeap, 2010; Shah, 2004) and that complicated procedures to access support require that women present numerous supporting documents and negotiate significant amounts of bureaucratic red tape (Hung et al., 2010). These issues constrain women entrepreneurs from using the institutional support provided, particularly in Malaysia.

The entrepreneurial support programmes also suffer from their failure to identify women's needs and interests in relation to their business. The lack of focus of programmes on women entrepreneurs and the absence of gender sensitivity in implementing such programmes have led to a one-size-fits-all approach (Huq & Moyeen, 2006) that does not incorporate the unique needs of women entrepreneurs in the areas of, for example, growth aspirations (Brush et al., 2004; Roomi et al., 2009) and upgrading business capacity (Tambunan, 2007). For example, while the public support for SMEs in Malaysia helps women to create new enterprises, the initiatives seem to discourage them from going beyond their micro-businesses, as evidenced in the limitation to micro-financing and the limited scope of training (Teoh & Cong, 2008). The need to include women entrepreneurs as role models in training programmes and mentoring schemes in the Malaysian context has also been proposed (Teoh & Chong, 2008). In Malaysia, where women's social position is lower than men's (Ariffin, 1999), there is a need to challenge the male-oriented approaches and to increase sensitivity to gender issues in entrepreneurship development programmes.

The final issue concerns the *effectiveness of the programmes* for women entrepreneurs (Tambunan, 2007). The literature has pointed to a lack of initiatives that seek to understand the impact that entrepreneurial programmes have on their target groups (Lenihan, 2011). Even where evaluation processes are in place, they do not focus on women entrepreneurs. For example, evaluation processes concentrate more on resource input than on the programme's outcomes (Tambunan, 2007), and women are less involved in evaluation roles than men are (Landig, 2011). This issue applies to the context of GESPs in Malaysia, particularly since the evaluation process does not produce gender-specific data as an outcome (Shah, 2004). According to Ram and Smallbone (2003), sex-disaggregated data is essential for support agencies to target their services effectively to clients and to monitor their ability to penetrate various target groups. In this respect, the impact of GESPs on women entrepreneurs is difficult to evaluate.

Construct: gender

Scholars have argued that the gender concept is a useful category for researching women, as it helps to clarify the complexity of human relations in society (Bradley, 2007; Connell, 2009). However, the dynamic interactions between gender and other social factors in society does not make gender an easy solution for the long-standing debate about women's subordination or disadvantage in relation to men, particularly when the social dynamics of human interactions are closely linked with cultural systems (Bradley, 2007). In some contexts, such as that of Malaysia, the influence of the socio-cultural framework on women is apparent, as women's secondary status in relation to men in Malaysian society can be seen, for example, in terms of career choices. The prevailing traditions and values that determine the appropriateness of work for men and women (Daud, 1988) often force women to choose between upward career mobility and family stability in the home (Ismail, 2009). Although institutional support programmes encourage women to become involved in entrepreneurial activities, such programmes give little attention to strategies for capitalizing on women's entrepreneurial interests, skills and abilities (United Nations Development Programme, 2008). As a consequence, women's entrepreneurial activities tend to be associated with income-generating projects that are conducted simultaneously with their reproductive and caring roles in the private sphere, thus reinforcing women's homemaker roles. Hence, gender is included as one of the constructs in the framework (Figure 15.1) that would enable information to be collected about women's business survival process based on their real experiences.

Conclusion

This chapter develops a conceptual framework for women's business survival that is contextualized in the handicraft industry in Malaysia. The framework developed here is based on gaps and issues identified in the literature. The analysis of BWEs in the Malaysian handicraft supports the argument that women's human capital characteristics influence their entrepreneurial activities. However, in addition to the low level of human capital women have, Figure 15.1 highlights the influence of gender roles as one of the factors that limits the involvement of Bumiputera women in their handicraft businesses. Strong social customs and traditions in the Malaysian cultural landscape have caused women to struggle in managing their multiple roles, thus limiting their ability to commit to their businesses.

Our analysis also shows the significance of business-related factors in influencing the business survival of Bumiputera women in the handicraft industry. Adequate financial capital, appropriate business training and effective networking are important factors in the business survival process. While it is not uncommon for these factors to create competitive disadvantages for women, the situation can be improved by means of GESPs that are designed after considering women's needs, including adequate financing to support women's businesses beyond their start-up stage. Appropriate business training programmes that are consistent with women's business needs at the survival stage and effective networking with government officials who can act as professional business advisers are also key.

The framework makes clear that the Malaysian cultural setting has a system of social relationships that has a great effect on Bumiputera businesses. The analysis of the literature has shown that interactions between people in the Malaysian collectivist society are developed based on a mutual in-group support. As such, this society could provide informal support for BWEs to minimize their business challenges. The analysis highlights that BWEs in the handicraft industry have to confront cultural challenges that derive from the values practised in Malaysia. The Malaysian patriarchal system places BWEs in a difficult position in their efforts to maximize their business potential, particularly in ensuring that their efforts are consistent with the demand of the social order. In this respect, we provide unique insights into the dual effects of culture on women's entrepreneurial activities.

Finally, this chapter has identified the significance of GESPs in women's business survival process. However, there is an issue of gender bias that minimizes women's participation in the GESPs and creates a gap between what is offered and what women entrepreneurs need. Consequently, while women tend to view the current entrepreneurial support programmes as inadequate to meeting their business survival needs, providers like government organizations continue to view women as unresponsive to the programmes offered. This misunderstanding could work to make women entrepreneurs even less visible in the institutional environment for entrepreneurship development. By offering a framework (Figure 15.1) that recognizes the influence of various contextual differences in explaining the survival of women's businesses, this chapter provides a new research perspective that departs from using individual-related factors alone to explain women's entrepreneurial activities. The framework highlights the significance of interactions between contextual factors, thus adding a new dimension to the literature on women's entrepreneurship and supporting the idea of an institutional perspective that provides more meaningful research in the women's entrepreneurship discipline.

Note

1 The Malaysia Plan is a five-year blueprint that derives from the country's economic development.

References

Abdullah, A., & Lim, L. (2001). Cultural dimensions of Anglos, Australians and Malaysians. *Malaysian Management Review, 36*(2), 1–17.

Ahl, H. (2002). *The making of the female entrepreneur: A discourse analysis of research texts on women's entrepreneurship* (Doctoral thesis). Jönköping University, Sweden. Retrieved from www.researchgate.net/publication/265533157.

Ahl, H. (2006). Why research on women entrepreneurs needs new directions. *Entrepreneurship Theory and Practice, 30*(5), 595–621.

Ahmad, A. (1998). *Country Briefing Paper: Women in Malaysia*. Retrieved from www.onlinewomeninpolitics.org/malaysia/adb_my.pdf.

Ahmad, N. H. (2007). *A cross cultural study of entrepreneurial competencies and entrepreneurial success in SMEs in Australia and Malaysia* (Doctoral thesis). The University of Adelaide, Australia. Retrieved from https://digital.library.adelaide.edu.au/dspace/bitstream/2240/48199/9/01.

Ahmad, S. Z. (2011). Evidence of the characteristics of women entrepreneurs in the Kingdom of Saudi Arabia: An empirical investigation. *International Journal of Gender and Entrepreneurship, 3*(2), 123–143.

Al-Dajani, H., & Marlow, S. (2010). Impact of women's home-based enterprise on family dynamics: Evidence from Jordan. *International Small Business Journal, 28*(5), 470–486.

Al-Dajani, H., & Marlow, S. (2013). Empowerment and entrepreneurship: A theoretical framework. *International Journal of Entrepreneurial Behaviour and Research, 19*(5), 503–524.

Alsos, G. A., Isaksen, E. J., & Ljunggren, E. (2006). New venture financing and subsequent business growth in men and women led businesses. *Entrepreneurship Theory and Practice, 30*(5), 667–686.

Ariffin, J. (2009). *Readings on women and development: Tracing for decades of change*. Malaysia: MPH Group Publishing Sdn Bhd.

Ariffin, R. (1999). Feminism in Malaysia: A historical and present perspective of women's struggles in Malaysia. *Women's Studies International Forum, 22*(4), 417–423.

Ayadurai, S., & Ahmad, W. R. (2006). A study on the critical success factors of women entrepreneurs in small and medium enterprises (SMEs) in Malaysia. *Journal of Asia Entrepreneurship and Sustainability, 2*(3), 91–125.

Basu, A., & Goswami, A. (1999). South Asian entrepreneurship in Great Britain: Factors influencing growth. *International Journal of Entrepreneurial Behaviour and Research, 5*(5), 251–275.

Bekele, E., & Worku, Z. (2008). Women entrepreneurship in micro, small and medium enterprises: The case of Ethiopia. *Journal of International Women Studies, 10*(2), 3–19.

Boden, R. J., & Nucci, A. R. (2000). On the survival prospects of men's and women's new business ventures. *Journal of Business Venturing, 15*(4), 347–362.

Bradley, H. (2007). *Gender*. Cambridge: Polity Press.

Brush, C. G. (1992). Research on women business owners: Past trends, a new perspective and future directions. *Entrepreneurship Theory and Practice, 16*(4), 5–30.

Brush, C. G. (2006). Women entrepreneurs: A research overview. In M. Casson, B. Yeung, A. Basu, & N. Wadeson (Eds), *The Oxford handbook of entrepreneurship* (pp. 611–628). Oxford: Oxford University Press.

Brush, C. G., de Bruin, A., & Welter, F. (2009). A gender-aware framework for women's entrepreneurship. *International Journal of Gender and Entrepreneurship, 1*(1), 8–24.

Brush, C. G., Carter, N. M., Gatewood, E., Greene, P. G., & Hart, M. M. (2004). *Clearing the hurdles: Women building high growth businesses*. London: Financial Times/Prentice Hall.

Brush, C. G., & Gatewood, E. J. (2008). Women growing businesses: Clearing the hurdles. *Business Horizons, 51*(3), 175–179.

Carter, S. (2000). Improving the numbers and performance of women-owned businesses: Some implications for training and advisory services. *Education and Training, 42*(4/5), 326–333.

Carter, N. M., Williams, M., & Reynolds, P. D. (1997). Discontinuance among new firms in retail: The influence of initial resources, strategy and gender. *Journal of Business Venturing, 12*(2), 125–145.

Churchill, N. C., & Lewis, V. L. (1983). The five stages of small business growth. *Harvard Business Review, May–June*, 2–11.

Coleman, S. (2000). Access to capital and terms of credit: A comparison of men and women owned small businesses. *Journal of Small Business Management, 38*(3), 37–52.

Connell, R. (2009). *Short introductions: Gender* (2nd ed.). Cambridge: Polity Press.

Daud, F. (1988). Women's economic role in Malaysia. In: M. Nash (Ed.), *Economic performance in Malaysia: The insider's view* (pp. 111–128). New York: Professors World Peace Academy.

Dechant, K., & Lamky, A. (2005). Toward an understanding of Arab women entrepreneurs in Bahrain and Oman. *Journal of Developmental Entrepreneurship, 10*(2), 123–140.

Devi, S. C. (2011). A study on the role of government: The focus on growth of women entrepreneurs in small scale sectors. *International Journal of Exclusive Management Research, 1*(2), 1–11.

Full potential of handicrafts industry yet to be realised. (2012). *The Financial Express*, 11 October, pp. 1–4.

Habib Shah, F. (2004). *Mainstreaming potential women exporters in international markets through ICT: Malaysia*. APEC Committee on trade and investment.

Hashim, R., Yusof, N., Ismail, S., & Raihanah, M. M. (2011). Rethinking Malaysian perspectives of gender constructions through ethnographic-oriented approach. *Procedia Social and Behavioural Sciences, 18*, 420–426.

Hisrich, R. D., & Brush, C. (1984). The woman entrepreneur: Management skills and business problems. *Journal of Small Business Management, 22*(1), 30–37.

Humbert, A. L., & Drew, E. (2010). Gender entrepreneurship and motivational factors in an Irish context. *International Journal of Gender and Entrepreneurship, 2*(2), 173–196.

Hung, D., Effendi, A. A., Talip, A. L. S., & Rani, A. N. A. (2010). A preliminary study of top SMEs in Malaysia: Key success factor vs government support program. *Journal of Asia Entrepreneurship and Sustainability, 6*(1), 111–124.

Huq, A., & Moyeen, A. (2006). Gender responsiveness of business development services for micro and small enterprises in Bangladesh. *Journal of Business Administration, 32*(1), 21–42.

Huq, A., & Moyeen, A. (2008). Addressing gender in enterprise development programs: Current practices and a proposed approach. Paper presented at the 2008 International Council for Small Business World Conference, Nova Scotia, Canada. Retrieved from https://researchbank.rmit.edu.au/view/rmit:12336.

Huq, A., & Moyeen, A. (2011). Gender integration in enterprise development programmes. *Women's Studies International Forum, 34*(4), 320–328.

Ismail, M. (2009). The gendered nature of careers: Evidence from a Malaysian university. *The Journal of International Management Studies, 4*(2), 175–184.

Jamali, D. (2009). Constraints and opportunities facing women entrepreneurs in developing countries: A relational perspective. *Gender in Management: An International Journal, 34*(4), 232–251.

Landig, J. M. (2011). Bringing women to the table: European Union funding for women's empowerment projects in Turkey. *Women's Studies International Forum, 34*(3), 206–219.

Leach, F. (2000). Gender implications of development agency policies on education and training. *International Journal of Educational Development, 20*(4), 333–347.

Lee, J. H., Sohn, S. Y., & Ju, Y. H. (2011). How effective is government support for Korean women entrepreneurs in small and medium enterprises? *Journal of Small Business Management, 49*(4), 599–616.

Lenihan, H. (2011). Enterprise policy evaluation: Is there a 'new' way of doing it? *Evaluation and Program Planning, 34*(4), 323–332.

Loscocco, K., & Bird, S. R. (2012). Gendered path: Why women lag behind men in small business success. *Work and Occupations, 39*(2), 183–219.

McGowan, P., & Hampton, A. (2007). An exploration of networking practices of female entrepreneurs. In N. M. Carter, C. Henry, B. Ó. Cinnéide, & K. Johnston (Eds), *Female entrepreneurship: Implications for education, training and policy* (pp. 110–134). Abingdon: Routledge.

McGowan, P., Redekar, C. L., Cooper, S. Y., & Greenan, K. (2012). Female entrepreneurship and the management of business and domestic roles: Motivations, expectations and realities. *Entrepreneurship and Regional Development: An International Journal, 24*(1–2), 53–72.

Mahajar, A. J., & Mohd Yunus, J. (2006). The effectiveness of government export assistance programs on Malaysia's small and medium enterprises (SMEs). *Problems and Perspectives in Management, 1*, 58–71.

Mat Amin, I. (2006). *Manufacturing and marketing of traditional crafts: Malaysian perspective.* Paper presented at the APEC/SME seminar on support for local and cottage industries, Hanoi, Vietnam. Retrieved from www.asiaseed.org/apec2006sme/presentation_pdf/session3_2ismail.pdf.

Mboko, S., & Smith-Hunter, A. (2010). Zimbabwe women business owners: Survival strategies and implications for growth. *Journal of Applied Business and Economics, 11*(2), 82–103.

Mordi, C., Simpson, R., Singh, S., & Okafor, C. (2010). The role of cultural values in understanding the challenges faced by female entrepreneurs in Nigeria. *Gender in Management: An International Journal, 25*(1), 5–21.

Muda, M. S., Wan Mohd Amin, W. A. Z., & Halim, A. M. (2011). Craft entrepreneurs in Malaysia: Analysis of relationship between product innovation, business commitment and business expansion. *Prosiding PERKEM, Conference Proceedings, Malayisia 6*(2), 208–217.

Muravyev, A., Talavera, O., & Schäfer, D. (2009). Entrepreneurs' gender and financial constraints: Evidence from international data. *Journal of Comparative Economics, 37*(2), 270–286.

Nordin, F., Williams, T., & Zimmer, C. (2002). Career commitment in collectivist and individualist cultures: A comparative study. *The International Journal of Human Resource Management, 13*(1), 35–54.

Ong, J. W., Ismail, H., & Yeap, P. F. (2010). Malaysian small and medium enterprises: The fundamental problems and recommendations for improvement. *Journal of Asia Entrepreneurship and Sustainability, 6*(1), 39–51.

Osman, I., Ahmad, N. H., Husin, A., Tanwir, N. D., Abu Bakar, S., & Ahmad, Z. A. (2011). Entrepreneurial aspirations and empowerment of rural women in ecotourism SMEs: A preliminary analysis. Paper presented at the *Global Business and Social Science Research Conference*, China. Retrieved from http://wbiconpro/456-Istan.pdf.

Ram, M., & Smallbone, D. (2003). Policies to support ethnic minority enterprise: The English experience. *Entrepreneurship and Regional Development: An International Journal, 15*(2), 151–166.

Redzuan, M., & Aref, F. (2011). Constraints and potentials of handicraft industry in underdeveloped region of Malaysia. *African Journal of Business Management, 5*(2), 256–260.

Roomi, M. A., Harrison, P., & Beaumont-Kerridge, J. (2009). Women-owned small and medium enterprises in England: Analysis of factors influencing the growth process. *Journal of Small Business and Enterprise Development, 16*(2), 270–288.

Roomi, M. A., & Parrott, G. (2008). Barriers to development and progress of women entrepreneurs in Pakistan. *Journal of Entrepreneurship, 17*(1), 59–72.

Sadi, M. A., & Al-Ghazali, B. M. (2010). Doing business with impudence: A focus on women entrepreneurship in Saudi Arabia. *African Journal of Business Management, 4*(1), 1–11.

Schmidt, R. A., & Parker, C. (2003). Diversity in independent retailing: Barriers and benefits: The impact of gender. *International Journal of Retail and Distribution Management, 31*(8), 428–439.

Scott, M., & Bruce, R. (1987). Five stages of growth in small business. *Long Range Planning, 20*(3), 45–52.

Selamat, N. H., Razak, A. R., Gapor, A. S., & Sanusi, Z. A. (2011). Survival through entrepreneurship: Determinants of successful micro-enterprises in Balik Pulau, Penang Island, Malaysia. *British Journal of Arts and Social Sciences, 3*(1), 23–37.

Shahadan, F. (2001). Bumiputera commercial and industrial community in the food-processing industry: An analysis of institutional support. *Humanomics, 17*(1/2), 86–98.

Shane, S. (2003). *A general theory of entrepreneurship: The individual-opportunity nexus.* Cheltenham: Edward Elgar Publishing.

Shaw, E., Marlow, S., Lam, W., & Carter, S. (2009). Gender and entrepreneurial capital: Implications for firm performance. *International Journal of Gender and Entrepreneurship, 1*(1), 25–41.

SME Corp. (2010). *SME Annual Report 2009/10.* Retrieved from www.smecorp.gov.my/index.php/en/resources/2015–12–21–11–07–06/sme-annual-report.

Tambunan, T. (2007). Development of SME and women entrepreneurs in a developing country: The Indonesian story. *Small Enterprise Research, 15*(2), 31–51.

Teoh, W. M., & Chong, S. C. (2008). Improving women entrepreneurs in small and medium enterprises in Malaysia: Policy recommendations. *Communications of the IBIMA, 2*, 31–38.

United Nations Development Programme (2008). *Malaysia nurturing women entrepreneurs.* Retrieved from www.undp.org.my/uploads/UNDP_Malaysia_NurturingwomenErs publication.pdf.

Van der Boon, M. (2005). Women into enterprise: A European and international perspective in S.L. Fielden, & M. J. Davidson (Eds), *International handbook of women and small business entrepreneurship* (pp. 161–177). Cheltenham: Edward Elgar Publishing.

Verheul, I., & Thurik, R. (2001). Start-up capital: Does gender matter? *Small Business Economics, 16*, 329–345.

Welter, F. (2004). The environment for female entrepreneurship in Germany. *Journal of Small Business and Enterprise Development, 11*(2), 212–221.

Welter, F., & Smallbone, D. (2011). Institutional perspectives on entrepreneurial behaviour in challenging environments. *Journal of Small Business Management, 49*(1), 107–125.

Yusof, R. (2006). Socio-cultural traits and entrepreneurship among Malay rural businesswomen in Malaysia: An analysis through a feminist perspective (Doctoral thesis). Lancaster University, UK. Retrieved from http://ethos.bl.uk/OrderDetails.do?uin=uk.bl.ethos.442718.

Zawawi, D. (2008). Cultural dimensions among Malaysian employees. *International Journal of Economics and Management, 2*(2), 409–426.

16 Developing an understanding of entrepreneurship intertwined with motherhood

A career narrative of British Mumpreneurs

Shandana Sheikh, Federica Sist, Aybeniz Akdeniz and Shumaila Yousafzai

In the UK, there are around 1.2 million self-employed women of which approximately 300,000 are mumpreneurs ('an individual who discovers and exploits new opportunities within a social and geographical context that seeks to integrate the demands of motherhood and business ownership' (Ekinsmyth, 2011, p. 105), contributing £7.4bn to the UK economy each year (Start Up Donut, 2014). Recognizing the contribution of women in UK's economic growth, recent efforts to reduce the gender gap in entrepreneurship have been initiated by the UK government to encourage women, particularly mothers to engage in entrepreneurial activity (Harding, 2007; Women Enterprise Task Force, 2009). Yet, women entrepreneurship (WE) rates fail to keep up with the government's target.

Several *push* and *pull* factors (e.g., soaring childcare costs, glass ceiling, inflexible nature of employment, desire for independence and autonomy and a desire to achieve a better work-family balance) have led mumpreneurship to become a common pathway for a number of British mothers (Grady & McCarthy, 2008; Mallon & Cohen, 2001; Patterson & Mavin, 2009; Rouse & Kitching, 2006). Approximately 65% of British mothers, with children under the age of 10 years, consider starting a business from home in the next three years (Direct line Survey, 2014). However, the desire of attaining a balance between self-employment and family is a complex one (Shelton, 2006) and thus the extent to which mothers can take entrepreneurship as a career choice depends on the support they receive from their entrepreneurial eco system (Isenberg, 2011). The entrepreneurial eco system (EES) entails a variety of factors including policy, finance, culture, markets, human capital and social support, all of which individually or interactively affect entrepreneurial intentions and thus activity of mumpreneurs across different contexts. For this study, we focus on the policy element of the EES and explore how regulatory policies affect mumpreneurs' activity in the UK. Specifically, we study how mumpreneurs construct their experiences of moving into entrepreneurship and how regulatory family policies support or constrain them in simultaneously balancing their dual responsibility of business ownership and motherhood. In the UK, while there are current family policies such as childcare benefits, tax credits, maternity leaves and parental allowances, the impact of these policies on mumpreneurship has not been studied. Hence, by adopting a career narrative approach to examine the lived experiences of twenty-five British mumpreneurs, we study how the family policies of the British government may support or constrain mumpreneurs who juggle between their family and business responsibilities and aim to achieve a balance between the two.

Our study may potentially contribute to the existing literature on women/mumpreneurship, by highlighting the constraints that mumpreneurs face in achieving work-family balance. This may encourage policy makers to revise the strategies targeted towards mumpreneurs including better state provision of childcare facilities, parental leaves, tax policies and business policies for women. Our findings may also potentially encourage and motivate prospective mothers who juggle between the demands of paid employment and motherhood, to take up entrepreneurship as a career choice. It could thus encourage more women to become mumpreneurs, thus contributing towards the growth of British economy.

Exploring mumpreneurship amidst institutional domain

Although the number of working mothers in the UK has increased to 5.3 million since 1996 (*The Telegraph*, 2013), there is consistent evidence that women have paid the price of becoming mother by not only losing out on financial independence and career progression but also face considerable role-conflict and strain, termed as the 'motherhood penalty' (Gentleman, 2009; Daly, 2011). It is not a personal preference that women adapt their work and family roles but that such adaptation is made with little choice and is mostly a result of the structural realities of family life as well as the societal attitudes and pressures on a woman (Leahy & Doughney, 2006). Additionally, the expectations of managing the demands of work and family responsibilities simultaneously become cumbersome in the absence of institutional policies that facilitate women and help them to achieve a work-family balance.

The institutional support, in terms of family welfare policies, have the potential in various degrees to reconcile the tension between work and family obligations (Sjöberg, 2004). Measures for better work-life reconciliation and gender equality, for example, maternity leave and the provision of childcare have become a major policy issue on the European social agenda (Ciccia & Verloo, 2012; Fagnani, 2011), yet policy makers in the UK have largely ignored the link between family and work. For example, in the market-oriented model of UK, which puts most of the care responsibilities with families and provides little state support (Korpi et al., 2013), working mothers face greater work-family conflict. Compared to this, the pro-family model of Scandinavian countries facilitates women and encourages their participation in the workforce by giving them time to pursue their professional development (Gornick et al., 1997; Petit & Hook, 2005).

The Labour government reforms since the 1990s have aimed to assist families with children by focusing on employment and social policies such as greater incentives for women to work, longer maternity leaves and subsidized provision for childcare (Harkness & Evans, 2011). Despite such reforms, a gap remains within the UK's family welfare policies to reconcile family and work. For instance, with an increase of 10% each year, the childcare costs in the UK are the highest as compared to other OECD countries (Family and Childcare Trust, 2013). Per recent estimates British parents with two children could pay as much as £12,000 in a year (*The Telegraph*, 2014). Moreover, the state funded childcare provision for children less than 3 years of age is made for a few hours, implying that mothers resort to other private or informal arrangements or choose part-time working patterns (Ciccia & Bleijenbergh, 2014). Additionally, the deficit reduction plans of the Coalition government in 2010 has made matters worse by cutting down on welfare spending and public service provision, including cuts in public sector jobs, wages and pensions, state services and benefits thus resulting in a 'triple jeopardy' for women (Annesley & Scheele, 2011). This is reflected in the drop in working mothers (24%) who had to stop work due to the cuts in child tax credit by 10% (Resolution Foundation, 2011).

Lack of supportive family policies, make it difficult for women to manage employment responsibilities and thus push them to find other ways to continue their career path while simultaneously balancing their family responsibilities. Starting a business from home provides one such opportunity to women to manage both family/house and work responsibilities simultaneously while also giving them flexibility in working hours, as opposed to paid employment. Although an increasing number of women are becoming mumpreneurs, the challenge to juggle the demands of work and family, remains, mainly due to the institutional voids, which prevent these women from realizing their full potential in business.

To generate a holistic view of how mumpreneurship is constructed in the UK, it is important to study the experiences of mumpreneurship amidst these institutional voids, primarily regulatory family policies which directly impact work-family balance of mumpreneurs in UK. To achieve this and in line with feminist researchers' proposition for an epistemological shift towards a constructivist inquiry that utilizes more qualitative methods to study the various aspects of WE (Ahl, 2006; Bird & Brush, 2002; Henry et al., 2016, we adopt a constructionist approach to understand the lived experiences of mumpreneurs in the UK. Through in-depth interviews, lasting between sixty and ninety minutes with twenty-five mumpreneurs, we studied the experiences of mumpreneurs and the challenges they face in balancing the dual responsibility of motherhood and business. All mumpreneurs interviewed had home-based businesses, based in the UK, although some had global clientele.

Journey from mum to mumpreneur: Typology, motivations and aspirations

Based on Jayawarna et al.'s (2011) typology and analysis of the interviews, five mumpreneurs (Emily, Samy, Viks, Tash and Taz) could be termed as *convenience mumpreneurs* due to their simultaneous aspirations and goals in business and a desire to prioritize their children, thus reflecting a tension in identities i.e. being a good mother and a good entrepreneur. Four mumpreneurs (Chloe, Jenny, Pensy and Dee) could be classified as *learning and earning mumpreneurs* based on their desire of expanding their businesses, increasing product lines, becoming bigger and even opting for franchising. While children were still their main priority, these women were different from others as strived to move up on their learning curve and were passionate about growing their business to a level where they would be considered at par with the mainstream high performance entrepreneurs. Additionally, these women could also be associated as *social mumpreneurs* as they provided mentorship or expressed to help other mothers who were thinking of starting a business or just started one. As Sina expressed her future aspirations to be:

> I want to make a statement online so that I am able to help as many people as I can.
> (Sina, multiple businesses – cooking, interior designer, mentoring)

With respect to the future aspirations, all mumpreneurs except Emily (who wanted her business to remain small so that she could manage it around her daughters) aspired to expand their business, increase growth opportunities and sales and hire more people to be able to manage the increased growth of their enterprise.

In line with previous research, the interviewees' narrative identified a combination of push and pull factors that motivated mumpreneurs for starting an enterprise (Duberley & Carrigan, 2012; Jayawarna et al., 2011). These include flexibility (pull) (Zen, Samy, Taz and Lizy), to be available to look after their children and spend time with them (pull), due to the exorbitant costs of childcare (push), being one's own boss (pull) (Jenny and Pensy), passion (pull) for what they loved doing, redundancy from paid employment (push) (Viks) and recognition for a need for a product that did not exist in the market (push) (Emily).

> because if you go back to work, you would just be paying your childcare and that's sort of ridiculous . . . that is one of the reasons I started because I wanted to be home with my kids, I didn't want to put them in childcare.
>
> (Samy, organic baby products business)

> When my youngest daughter was 7 months, I was still breastfeeding her, I was diagnosed with breast cancer . . . led to the chain of treatments one of which was chemotherapy as a result of which I lost my hair. I felt I had to cover up all the time and all I really wanted was to have this need for a baby hat like my daughter was wearing.
>
> (Emily, hair products business)

Juggling mumpreneurs: Tensions in balancing work-family responsibilities

The task of striking a balance between business and family responsibilities for women was a difficult one. Women expressed their pride in being capable of managing their work around their children's routine but labelled it as a 'constant juggling act where if one ball drops the whole lot would drop' (Viks). As Emily described:

> I try and give as much time to both . . . the girls are in school from 9 to 5 so I am back at my desk at 9 o'clock and I work through until 3.15 after which I go to the post office to deliver the orders and then go pick the girls . . . and then depending on what we are doing, I can still answer a few emails on my phone, I can do a few bits . . . once they have gone to bed, I work at least an hour or two on jobs that I don't really need to think about the next day.
>
> (Emily, hair products business)

In their efforts to manage work-family responsibilities simultaneously, only a few women expressed social support from spouse or family (Chloe, Zen, Dee and Taz).

> My husband is very lucky because he works for a company that lets him do flexible hours. He works in the beginning of the week, so Mondays, Tuesdays and Wednesdays, I would do the school runs and everything and then Thursdays, Fridays and Saturdays, he would look after the children so that I can work longer hours.
>
> (Chloe, organic food business)'

> I actually don't think I could have gotten to the level I am at if mum hadn't been able to help, because he can occupy himself to an extent but he has special needs of autism. He is still in nappies so with that u have to constantly leave what you are doing to change a nappy and things like that . . . so I couldn't have done that with the business. I was happy that mum retired and took over.
>
> (Viks, children toys business)

Other times, they had to fight a balance between motherhood and career boundaries and in doing so, mumpreneurs experienced lack of time for themselves. In this context, the narratives reflected the perks of paid employment wherein at least they could work for fixed hours and have the remaining time to themselves. Thus, while self-employment gave them the flexibility to work around their children, it reduced the time that they could have for themselves as they did when they were in paid employment.

> The business gets time and the kids get time but the biggest thing for me is that I don't get time for myself. I don't watch films and even when I do it on my laptop or iPad while washing dishes and it takes two weeks to watch a film. It is things like that, I kind of miss, while before when kids were in bed at 7 or 8 o'clock that was me free to watch a film or play the computer. This is the hardest thing for me and some days it doesn't bother me but some days it does.
>
> (Viks, children products)

Institutional impediments in juggling work-family responsibilities

Insufficient childcare provision

Pertaining to the institutional voids in their entrepreneurial ecosystem, all women expressed a lack of government support for providing good quality and low cost childcare. Women expressed that the provision for free childcare was not sufficient, especially for children below school age. The resulting high cost of private childcare pushed women towards working for longer hours. Narrative also reflected preferences of women (except Sina, Jenny and Lizy), for private childcare even in the presence of the few hours offered by state nurseries, primarily due to the longer opening hours of private nurseries (Taz and Zen), better care provision, quality of staff, low staff to children ratio, better facilities and better learning and development (Dee and Zen).

> she is due for free entitlement to the government nursery but I am probably just continuing with the private one. The government one is 2.5 hours per day and by the time I drop her, get an hour of work done, it's time to go back . . . its absolutely impractical unless you are a stay at home mum, it doesn't work for you.
>
> (Zen, Café business)

Mumpreneurs also expressed a need for greater support for childcare during the school holidays since presence of children at home during holidays restricted the amount of work women could.

> I wish there was more provision for families during the holiday period. My children are going to be off for 10 weeks during the summer and I think we do have to take our foot off the pedal during that 10-week period. It's very difficult to keep the momentum off when you have three kids at home and it's very difficult for my staff who have children to continue to work during that time, particularly the mums who work for me.
>
> (Dee, children products business)

Amongst childcare constraints, the narratives also revealed a perceived lack of childcare support for children with special needs. There was no provision in the state school/nursery for one to one support for children with special needs. Moreover, the limited resources and funding from the government was perceived to be a major constraint to the quality of teaching and learning for special children in state funded primary schools.

> Unless the government gives resources to the teachers, you are stuck. Jay's teacher makes a lot of effort for Jay but she does not get any extra credit for doing that from the Education board.
>
> (Viks, children toys business)

Moreover, Viks, a single mother having two children with special needs, felt that the government did not provide relief but made it even more difficult for parents with children having special needs. She expressed her dissatisfaction with the lack of provision for a caretaker, even though both her children had special needs. Additionally, despite being in receipt of the Disability Living Allowance (DLA) for her children she felt that the application process was a pain. Hence, due to such constraints Viks juggled between her children, the business and her housework by working during the nights for her business and home-schooling her children and fulfilling home responsibilities during the day.

Soaring childcare costs and child tax credit

Mumpreneurs (Chloe, Zen, Tash and Viks) perceived themselves to be worse off as compared to non-working mothers, considering the surge in childcare costs. Despite working for longer hours in business women perceived that the non-working, stay-at-home mothers could avail a similar provision for childcare from the state. In this regard, women criticized the government's policy regarding free childcare to every mother regardless of their working status and believed that a separate policy with better provision should be devised for working mothers.

> while I was working and doing my job, there were all those mums who were taking their kids into free childcare but didn't work . . . and because there kids are in nursery, they can go off to the gym . . . that's a problem when you give free child care to everybody, people who don't necessarily need it occupy the spaces and those who do need it don't get any.
>
> (Chloe, organic food business)

While, women perceived the cost of childcare to be unaffordable, they appreciated the child tax credit (CTC: 70% of the childcare costs) and child benefit that was provided by the government for parents.

> had it not been for tax credits, I wouldn't have been in business . . . when I got divorced, the girls would have severely disadvantaged . . . i would have got at least part time job, probably a full time job really . . . the girls wouldn't be able to go to brownies, no swimming lessons, no piano . . . I am very grateful for that opportunity to have tax credit.
>
> (EY, hair products business)

However, only a few women were in receipt of CTC because of their ineligibility due to a higher income bracket, which was again expressed as an unfair policy of the government by women. Mumpreneurs criticized the criteria of the government for calculating the eligibility for CTC, i.e. by taking into account incomes of both partners and basing it on the previous year's income instead of real time income (Samy, Zen).

> Me and my partner have two children from our previous marriage so our money isn't joint, when you have something like CTC, our money goes on it as joint but we don't essentially share our money and thus we don't get the child tax credit. I am earning and he is earning but we have two other children.
>
> (Samy, organic baby products business)

> it's a shame, we feel it because we have three children and that is 299 pounds per week . . . that was for my children, their extra curricular, swimming lessons and all used to be funded by that money.
>
> (Zen, café business)

Lack of business support

Beyond childcare, mumpreneurs expressed a lack of governmental support for women entrepreneurs in terms of training courses that could help them to develop and learn skills such as marketing, accounting, finance, PR and social media, which are critical for running an effective and efficient business. Narratives of women revealed a lack of knowledge and training for entrepreneurship and the difficulties it presented working mothers (Zen and Sina). Women who could afford specialized help for their business acknowledged the constraint faced by other mumpreneurs who were not able to do and expressed that, 'you are the jack of all trades, something goes wrong, you have to fix it, there is no IT department'. In the absence of adequate business support, some women resorted to self-help and teaching (Viks), thus enabling themselves to learn business skills while others relied on their informal social capital, taking help from family and friends (Samy, Zen, Jenny, Pensy)

> I had to teach myself proper photography, taking photos with shadows and stuff like that. I have resorted to using google. I had a camera that I used but had to figure out the buttons so again I turned to youtube! Yes, a lot of things, I had to learn and teach myself because if I were to go to professionals, there would be no profit left.
>
> (Viks, children toys business)

In addition to the perceived inadequate support in business, mumpreneurs also believed that the little support that was available from the government was not well marketed and communicated. Women expressed that there was lack of information available as to what support was available and how it could be accessed. The only source of information was social networks of women entrepreneurs or social media where women accessed relevant business information.

Lack of funding

Analysis of the narratives of women revealed a perceived lack of financial resources for women entrepreneurs, mainly due to mumpreneurship being perceived as a hobby instead of an actual 'serious business'. In this regard, women expressed that due to their small savings and high risk associated with business, they preferred to start small and thus could not compete with the high-street businesses which had adequate funds and support.

> You see because its safe area for mums to start a business doing what they love, so you know if someone is making cupcakes and cakes, it all starts as a hobby, of course you do want to test your water, you don't want to launch big and then end up failing. So, mums start small, they see the water and see if people are generally interested as they get the feedback and response. Once the seed takes off, they start doing it.
> (Sina, multiple businesses – cooking, interior designer, mentoring)

Additionally, women expressed gender and business type discrimination suggesting that even if the government had available funds to distribute, the banks were hesitant to lend it out to mumpreneurs (Lizy, Zen and Viks).

> because I don't have a great business idea and I don't have a massive factory, its classed as a hobby, nearly to where you are not taken seriously. You are taken as a stay at home mom where you decorate few things. The government doesn't understand that if someone sells a cushion or something, there are skills involved in that, you are spending time in that, there is work involved.
> (Viks, children toys business)

Allowance for sick leaves

All women expressed that they could not take time off in case of illness or other emergencies, since they couldn't afford to shut their business and lose out on customers as well as money. Moreover, it was impossible for these women to take holidays and even when they did, they would be constantly working from their laptops or phone, thus referring entrepreneurship as *a 24/7 job where one are working all the time*.

Juggling between motherhood and business, women felt that as compared to paid employment, there was no state support in terms of sick leave allowances for self-employed or business oriented mothers.

> I don't have sick leaves and that's a major issue being in and out of hospitals quite a lot. A couple of years ago, I had a major surgery, so what do you do? You still carry on and do every little that you can.
> (Emily, hair products business)

Further, Viks (*personalized children products business*) narrated her experience when she was sick and it took her a month to recover. Being the only person responsible for making orders and dispatching them, she fell behind orders due to her being unwell. Moreover, she did not want her customers to know that she was sick, as she did not want to gain sympathies nor wanted to lose customers.

> What would take me half an hour was taking me one day and I felt the pressure, I tried to go to the office in my pajamas trying to complete the orders for the simple fact that I couldn't afford 4 weeks off.
> (Viks, personalized children products business)

Entrepreneurship intertwined with motherhood: Reflections of Mumpreneurs

While women owned businesses are increasing in number, the discourse of underperformance of women enterprises compared to their male counterparts still hold (Ahl, 2006; Marlow et al., 2008; Eddleston & Powell, 2008). However, this myth of underperformance has been criticized by feminist researchers, suggesting that it is not under performance but rather *constrained performance* of women entrepreneurs which differentiates them from male entrepreneurs (Marlow & McAdam, 2013). Therefore, to explain reasons for underperforming, one must look beyond just gender differences but rather pay attention to structural factors that affect women's entrepreneurial activity in a country. The concept of mumpreneurship is often associated with the objective of simultaneously being a good mother and a good business owner. In researching this unique form of entrepreneurship, the boundaries between work, motherhood and home are made flexible and permeable, suggesting a need to focus more on work that originates within the household and community places (Oberhauser, 2002) and the factors that influence it. Through our study, we have highlighted the role of institutional family policies on mumpreneurship in the UK and identified factors that constrain the ability of mumpreneurs to balance their work-family responsibilities. We present these findings through a framework in Figure 16.1.

Reflecting upon their experiences of entrepreneurship in the UK's entrepreneurial ecosystem, all mumpreneurs expressed that more needed to be done for self-employed mothers. All women faced identity tensions wherein they struggled and juggled to balance

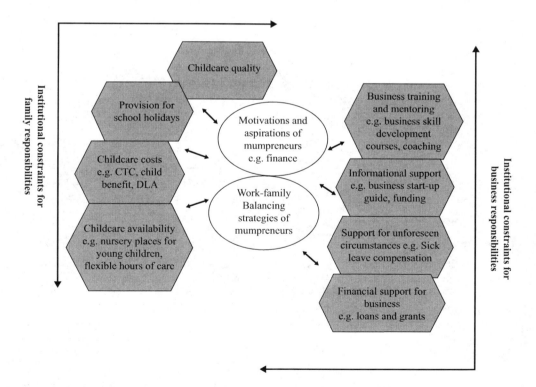

Figure 16.1 Mumpreneurs' perceived institutional constraints for work-family balance

their work and family responsibilities to become a good mother and an entrepreneur simultaneously. Mumpreneurs were challenged by their current institutional barriers which made it difficult for them to balance work and family responsibilities. Expressing about the constrained regulatory environment, women compared UK's family policies with those of other countries and suggested that UK had to increase efforts on several fronts to support women in business. For example, Lizy believed that European countries had a much better stance in supporting a mumpreneur's juggle between being a good mother and a good business woman. Additionally, with regards to sickness allowance, Sina compared her experience in Norway where one could get a financial compensation based on the income. With regards to maternity policy Emily explained how Germany's pro-family policies supported women in work and entrepreneurship. Referring to Germany's three-year maternity leave policy, she suggested that although the entire three-year period was not paid but social security and the right to one's job was guaranteed during this period.

> it's a diff mindset in Germany . . . that whole attitude of family is so important and it has worked really well for Germany . . . in UK if someone said I need 3 years off to have my child, the company would be quite annoyed about it. In Germany the whole mindset is that you need to be at home to look after your children when they are very young and there is no fear of losing your job whereas in this country there is a lot of pressure to go back to work as soon as possible.
>
> (Emily, hair products business)

Policy makers in the UK have largely ignored the link between family and work. UK's policy frameworks have worsened the work-family reconciliation instead of attempting to support it. The transition to motherhood in a woman's life is a change in her preferences of employment versus business ownership (Ekinsmyth, 2013). A woman's caring role and family responsibilities are deeply associated with her leading to a trade-off between the caring role as a mother and the desire to be independent and follow one's career. Women use home-based businesses as an optimum strategy to achieve work-life balance, which consequently limits their economic growth and success (Loscocco & Smith-Hunter, 2004). Analysis of mumpreneurs' narrative reveals that they are constrained in their daily lives by domestic responsibilities, which in turn determine the amount of time they can devote to their business. In balancing their work-family responsibilities, only three out of twelve women indicated that they got help from their husbands in managing children, reflecting the gendered division of labour between paid and unpaid work where most of the responsibility of housework and family is on women (Jennings & McDougald, 2007). The distribution of paid and unpaid work is also affected by the role of institutions, which have implications for access to resources and business development (Welter, 2011).

Our findings suggest that most mumpreneurs have started a business from home to work around their children. While this fulfils the good motherhood expectation, which is socially constructed by social norms of the society, it affects the performance and growth opportunities of the businesses run by these women, mainly due to their constrained institutional environment. All mumpreneurs expressed a deficiency in the provision of local childcare, a barrier that constrained them to work for their business. While CTC and child benefit schemes were acknowledged by mumpreneurs, it was insufficient to cover the costs of childcare. This is supported by recent evidence which suggests that two-thirds of parents who use formal care for their children pay for it while only 6% pay for informal care (Huskinson et al., 2013). Problems including access to free spaces in nurseries, timings of free provision which mismatched working hours and absence of childcare provision during school holidays, poor quality of childcare and learning and development in state provided childcare centres further impacted women's ability to balance work–family tensions. These inefficiencies in government's family policies had implications for mumpreneurs who juggled between their roles of a good mother and a successful business owner.

The importance of social networks for women entrepreneurs has been highlighted in previous research (Manolova et al., 2007). Lack of formal childcare highlighted in the narratives of mumpreneurs, reveals the importance of social networks and family in achieving work–family balance of mumpreneurs. Our findings suggest that most mumpreneurs rely on their informal social capital including family and friends for work–life balance as well as acquiring and learning key business skills. Such reliance on informal networks is an outcome of unavailability of support from the government for mumpreneurs, as a result of which social capital enables women to manage their dual identities of a good mother and a business woman.

Despite the significant contribution of home-based enterprises and specifically mumpreneurship to economic growth of UK, their importance has been undermined. There has been previous evidence suggesting that the invisibility and hobby like image of home-based businesses makes them get ignored by the government (Mason et al., 2011). Nearly all mumpreneurs in this study agreed with this perception and attributed this to the negligible support they received from the government. This points towards the general discourse of disintegration of motherhood and entrepreneurship where two are not associated. In comparison to the entrepreneur, the social and cultural construction of motherhood is more trivial, which results in mother owned businesses being perceived as less serious and limited in performance and scope. Such trivialization of motherhood poses an enduring challenge to mother entrepreneurs who struggle to balance their roles of a good mother while being a good business owner. We believe that to visualize the growth of mumpreneurship, attention must be given to the context within which these businesses are embedded. The narrative accounts of mumpreneurs signify that women have multi-tasking abilities, are naturally talented and can have all walks of life. With the necessary support and resources, these women can contribute significantly to a happy family and prospering economy.

Moving forward

This small-scale exploratory study attempted to trace the institutional embeddedness of mumpreneurship. While the trend of mumpreneurship has been on the rise, there are challenges in managing such businesses. We aimed to highlight some of the challenges that mumpreneurs face in balancing their dual identities of being a good mother and a successful business owner, in the light of government's family policies. While the UK government is making several efforts to support families, women and children, the outcomes of these efforts have not been evaluated. Our research suggests that the major reason for starting a business for mothers is to spend more time with their children and to manage work around their caring role. However, this does not suggest that mumpreneurs spend less time in work and have low ambitions for themselves or that they underperform. Our findings suggest that despite having dual responsibilities, mumpreneurs work hard to achieve their aspirations and career objectives, thus fighting between multiple identities of being a good mother and a good business woman. However, their ability to do so is severely constrained by the institutional support, more specifically in term of childcare provisions and training and financial support. As revealed through our findings, the small-scale nature of mumpreneur businesses makes them invisible and unimportant for government support.

Although we believe that this study offers rich insights to the phenomena under study, it is limited in its scale. Due to the nature of qualitative approach that we followed, the findings of the study are not representative of all mumpreneur businesses, particularly across different contexts and business sectors. Although, the use of phenomenological interviews helped to uncover the experiences of mumpreneurs and challenges they faced in current time-period, these experiences may change due to individual circumstances and given the dynamic nature of entrepreneurship. For example, when children start attending school, mumpreneurs may be able to put in longer hours in their business and could develop their business successfully, thus achieving a better balance between work and family life. Moreover, certain policies may become irrelevant to mumpreneur's work-family balance while some other may be more relevant in future, depending upon the nature of business activity and life stage (Jayawarna et al., 2011). We urge future researchers to conduct comparative studies with women with and without caring responsibilities to highlight the differences in performance outcomes as well as challenges between these groups of women. Finally, one could also compare family policies and their effect on mumpreneurs in UK and Scandinavian countries, which follow a pro-family model. This would help to build a model for the future of family policy for the UK.

References

Ahl, H. (2006). Why research on women entrepreneurs needs new directions. *Entrepreneurship Theory & Practice, 30*(5), 595–621.

Annesley, C., & Scheele, A. (2011). Gender, capitalism and economic crisis: Impact and responses. *Journal of Contemporary European Studies, 19*(3), 334–348.

Bird, B., & Brush, C. (2002). A gendered perspective on organizational creation. *Entrepreneurship Theory and Practice, 26*(3), 41–65.

Ciccia, R., & Verloo, M. (2012). Parental leave regulations and the persistence of the male breadwinner model: Using fuzzy set ideal type analysis to assess gender equality in an enlarged Europe. *Journal of European Social Policy, 22*(5), 507–528.

Ciccia, R., & Bleijenbergh, I. (2014). After the male breadwinner model? Childcare services and the division of labor in European Countries. *Social Politics, 21*(1), 50–79.

Daly, M. (2011). What adult worker model? A critical look at recent social policy reform in Europe from a gender and family perspective. *Social Politics, 18*(1), 1–23.

Direct Line Group (2014). *The Rise of the Mumpreneur: Two Thirds of Mums Consider Launching a Business from Home.* Online. www.directlinegroup.com/media/news/brand/2014/03–04–2014.aspx.

Duberley, J. & Carrigan, M. (2012). The career identities of 'mumpreneurs': Women's experiences of combining enterprise and motherhood. *International Small Business Journal, 0*(0), 1–23.

Eddleston, K. A. & Powell, G. N. (2008). The role of gender identity in explaining sex differences in business owners' career satisfier preferences. *Journal of Business Venturing, 23*(2), 244–256.

Ekinsmyth, C. (2011). Challenging the boundaries of entrepreneurship: The spatialities and practices of UK 'mumpreneurs'. *Geoforum, 42*(1), 104–114.

Ekinsmyth, C. (2013). Managing the business of everyday life: The roles of space and place in 'mumpreneurship'. *International Journal of Entrepreneurial Behavior & Research, 19*(5), 525–546.

Fagnani, J. (2011). *Work-Family Life Balance: Future Trends and Challenges.* Online. https://hal.archives-ouvertes.fr/halshs-00663849/document.

Family and Childcare Trust (2013). *Childcare Costs Survey.* Online. www.fct.bigmallet.co.uk/sites/default/files/files/Childcare_Costs_Survey_FCT_2013_FINAL.pdf.

Gentleman, A. (2009). Motherhood 'devastates' women's pay, research finds. *The Guardian*. Online. www.guardian.co.uk/lifeandstyle/2009/jul/10/mothers-wages-fawcett-society.

Global Entrepreneurship Monitor (2012). *Global Report*. Online. www.gemconsortium.org/docs/download/2645.

Gornick, J. C., Meyers, M. K., & Ross, K. E. (1997). Supporting the employment of mothers: Policy variation across fourteen welfare states. *Journal of European Social Policy, 7*(1), 45–70.

Grady, G., & McCarthy, A. (2008). Work–life integration: Experiences of mid-career working mothers. *Journal of Managerial Psychology, 23*(5), 599–622.

Harding, R. (2007). *State of women enterprise in the UK*. Norwich: Prowess.

Harkness, S., & Evans, M. (2011). The employment effects of recession on couples in the UK: Women's and household employment prospects and partners' job loss. *Journal of Social Policy, 40*(4), 675–693.

Henry, C., Foss, L., & Ahl, H. (2016). Gender and entrepreneurship research: A review of methodological approaches. *International Small Business Journal, 34*(3), 217–241.

Huskinson, T., Pye, J., Medien, K., Dobie, S., Ferguson, C., & Gardner, C., with Gilby, N., Littlewood, M., & D'Souza, J. (2013). *Childcare and early years survey of parents 2011*. SFR08/2013. London: Department for Education.

Isenberg, D. (2011). The entrepreneurship ecosystem strategy as a new paradigm for economic policy: Principles for cultivating entrepreneurship. *Presentation at the Institute of International and European Affairs.*

Jayawarna, D., Rouse, J., & Kitching, J. (2011). Entrepreneur motivations and life course. *International Small Business Journal, 29*(1), 1–23.

Jennings, J. E., & McDougald, M. S. (2007). Work-family interface experiences and coping strategies: Implications for entrepreneurship research and practice. *Academy of Management Review, 32*(3), 747–60.

Korpi, F., Ferrarini, T., & Englund, S. (2013). Women's opportunities under different family policy constellations: Gender, class, and inequality tradeoffs in Western countries re-examined. *Social Politics, 20*(1), 1–40.

Leahy, M., & Doughney, J. (2006). Women, work and preference formation: A critique of Catherine Hakim's preference theory. *Journal of Business Systems, Governance and Ethics, 1*(1), 37–48.

Loscocco, K., & Smith-Hunter, A. (2004). Women home-based business owners: Insights from comparative analyses. *Women in Management Review, 19*(3), 164–173.

Manolova, T., Carter, N., Manev, I., & Gyoshev, B. (2007). The differential effect of men and women entrepreneurs' human capital and networking on growth expectancies in Bulgaria. *Entrepreneurship Theory and Practice, 31*(3), 407–426.

Marlow, S., Shaw, E., & Carter, S. (2008). Constructing female entrepreneurship policy in the UK: Is the USA a relevant role model? *Environmental Planning C, 26*(1), 335–51.

Marlow, S. & McAdam, M. (2013). Gender and entrepreneurship. *International Journal of Entrepreneurial Behavior & Research, 19*(1), pp. 114–124.

Mason, C. M., Carter, S., & Tagg, S. (2011). Invisible businesses: The characteristics of home-based businesses in the United Kingdom. *Regional Studies, 45*(5), 625–639.

Oberhauser, A. (2002). Relocating gender and rural economic strategies. *Environment and Planning A, 34*(7), 1221–1237.

Patterson, N., & Mavin, S. (2009). Women entrepreneurs: Jumping the corporate ship and gaining new wings. *International Small Business Journal, 27*(2), 173–192.

Petit, B., & Hook, J. (2005). The structure of women's employment in comparative perspective. *Social Forces, 84*(2), 779–801.

Resolution Foundation and Netmums (2011). *Childcare Tax Credit Survey*. Online. www.resolutionfoundation.org/media/press-releases/childcare-tax-credit-survey/.

Rouse, J., & Kitching, J. (2006). Do enterprise programmes leave women holding the baby? *Environment and Planning C: Government and Policy, 24*(1), 15–19.

Shelton, L. (2006). Women entrepreneurs, work–family conflict and venture performance: New insights into the work family interface. *Journal of Small Business Management, 44*(2), 285–297.

Sjöberg, O. (2004). The role of family policy institutions in explaining gender-role attitudes: A comparative multilevel analysis of thirteen industrialized countries. *Journal of European Social Policy, 14*(2), 107–123.

Start Up Donut (2014). *Why Does the Number of Female Entrepreneurs Continue to Rise?* Online. www. startupdonut.co.uk/blog/2014/03/why-does-number-female-entrepreneurs-continue-rise-uk.

The Telegraph (2013). *Working Mothers Rise by a Fifth in a Generation.* Online. www.telegraph.co.uk/finance/economics/10333890/Working-mothers-rise-by-a-fifth-in-a-generation.html.

The Telegraph (2014). *Rise of the 'Mumpreneurs' as Childcare Costs Hit £12,000.* Online. www.telegraph.co.uk/finance/personalfinance/10772101/Rise-of-the-mumpreneurs-as-childcare-costs-hit-12000.html.

Welter, F. (2011). Contextualizing entrepreneurship: Conceptual challenges and ways forward. *Entrepreneurship Theory and Practice, 35*(1), 165–184.

Welter, F., & Smallbone, D. (2011). Institutional perspectives on entrepreneurial behavior in challenging environments. *Journal of Small Business Management, 49*(1), 107–125.

Women's Enterprise Task Force (2009). *Greater returns on women's enterprise: The UK Women's Enterprise Task Force's final report and recommendations.* London: Department of Business, Innovation & Skills.

17 An interdisciplinary framework to deconstruct second-generation gender bias

Ethné Swartz and Frances Amatucci

The gender-neutral paradox

Has sufficient progress been made in women's emancipation and labour force participation in the United States of America (USA) to move to the implementation of gender-neutral policies? Are we at a point where we can agree that gender discrimination has been 'solved', or that we have reached a 'grand convergence'?

> Of the many advances in society and the economy in the last century, the converging roles of men and women are among the grandest. A narrowing has occurred between men and women in labor force participation, paid hours of work, hours of work at home, life-time labor force experience, occupations, college majors, and education, where there has been an overtaking by females. And there has also been convergence in earnings . . .
>
> (Goldin, 2014, p. 1091)

We have not yet reached the stage where gender-neutral policies are appropriate in entrepreneurship. Evidence abounds that many barriers exist for women who receive a very small proportion of total external equity investment dollars compared to males (Brush, Greene, Balachandra & David, 2014; Robb & Coleman, 2009). Women approach the development of companies in a different way to men, developing different products or services and using half as much capital as male counterparts to start companies (Fetsch, Jackson & Wiens, 2015). Many researchers have called for a nuanced understanding of gender as a variable in policy making in entrepreneurship (deBruin, Brush & Welter, 2009). This call is now being echoed in economics (Wolfers, 2016). Consider the outcomes of research in the USA that looked at the effect of gender-neutral policies related to stopping tenure clocks for male and women academics (Wolfers, 2016; Antecol, Bedard, & Stearns, 2016); male academics were advantaged, making it even more difficult for women economists to obtain tenure at the best economics departments.

We share this example precisely because economists such as Claudia Goldin at Harvard University insist that it is difficult to show empirical evidence of discrimination based on gender. While this might be so, the empirical nature of labour economics can help to illustrate the unequal odds that women face in labour markets and, by extension, entrepreneurship. Similarly, evidence from law can augment the gender-focused research in management and entrepreneurship to build an analytical framework that explains current experiences of women entrepreneurs. Second-generation gender bias (Ibarra, Ely, & Kolb, 2013; Sturm, 2001) provides such an analytical framework and we attempt to develop an interdisciplinary review of the concept, drawing from gender and negotiation, labour economics and law. In the final section of the chapter we present a graphic representation of the elements that constitute second-generation gender bias.

This chapter arose from findings from our own research that gender still matters in successfully negotiating term sheets. In our recent research among women entrepreneurs in the USA most respondents reported no experience of discrimination when negotiating for external equity capital, defined by us to include angel and venture capital investment (Swartz, Amatucci, & Coleman, 2016a). One respondent opined that her gender had helped rather than hindered her during negotiations; yet, outcomes from our predictive statistics suggested something different. Negotiating teams which included a male as a member of the team emerged as more successful in securing external equity investments while simultaneously enabling the entrepreneur to retain more equity than those without a male on the team (Swartz, Amatucci & Coleman, 2016b). These findings appeared contradictory and caused us to seek answers in the literature on gender, labour economics and second-generation bias.

Second-generation gender bias (Sturm, 2001) has been applied in organizational leadership, resulting in Ibarra, Ely, and Kolb's *Harvard Business Review* article in 2013 that advocated for popularizing the concept. It has also found application in the field of entrepreneurship and risk capital investing (Swartz, Amatucci, & Coleman, 2016 b) as the best framework to explain research outcomes on gender and entrepreneurial negotiations. Using key findings from research about negotiating term sheets for growth capital, this chapter seeks to do justice to the concept of second-generation gender bias. We think that the application of the concept in the field of law (Sturm, 2001 and Krieger, 2004) must be explored further and combined with data from labour economics (Blau & Khan, 2017, Goldin, 2014; Goldin & Katz, 2016), social psychology (Greenwald and Banaji, 1995; Banaji and Greenwald, 2013), management (Ibarra, Ely, & Kolb, 2013) and entrepreneurship (Swartz, Amatucci, & Coleman, 2016b) to explore the processes that comprises second-generation gender bias.

Women entrepreneurs negotiating term sheets for equity funding

Women-owned businesses constitute 36.3% of the non-farm, privately held business population in 2012, translating into nearly 10 million companies that generate $1.4 trillion in revenues (https://www.nwbc.gov) in the USA. The United States (US) Census defines a company as woman-owned business when 51% or more of the equity is owned by a woman. The National Women's Business Council analysis of the 2012 Survey of Business Owners show a growth in women-owned business of 26.8% from 2007. Despite this growth, women receive a very small proportion of total external equity investment dollars compared to their male counterparts (Brush et al., 2014; Robb & Coleman, 2009), evidenced in Figure 17.1.

Data from the Kauffman Foundation reveals that the gender financing gap is persistent and women receive only 3% of equity financing through angel investments and venture capital (Krause, 2016). Women also appear to start their companies with half as much capital as male counterparts and they are less likely to access external networks in their search for funding. In an update of the Diana Project, Brush, et al. (2014) found firms with a woman

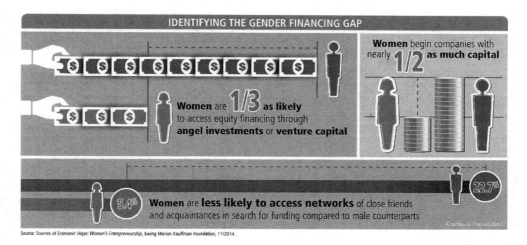

Figure 17.1 Identifying the gender financing gap
Source: Fetsch, Jackson, & Wiens, 2015.

on the executive team obtained 15% of all equity funding – up from 5% in the original 1999 study. Both female entrepreneur and investor respondents noted the presence of gender bias in the venture capital industry.

Our interest in growth companies, gender and negotiation led us to focus on term-sheet negotiation and the processes that women experience when negotiating with angel investors or venture capital investors. It is critical for entrepreneurs to finance growth companies with capital obtained under reasonable terms. Given the low rates of participation in obtaining equity funding, we were keen to better understand the experiences of those women entrepreneurs who do participate. Specifically, our concern was to understand what strategies these women found to be effective, what major challenges they experienced and whether they could identify problematic or advantageous negotiation styles and behaviours when negotiating term sheets.

Table 17.1 provides respondent demographics about our sample of women entrepreneurs who completed an online survey that contained quantitative and qualitative prompts. Data collection took place between 2010 and 2014, and respondents were recruited through conventional networks and online social media sites used by women entrepreneurs. A total of fifty-two responses were gathered, of which thirty-nine were usable. Our descriptive analyses show that women entrepreneurs were seeking to raise capital for start-up and growth, including acquisitions. One-quarter of the respondents was seeking less than $500,000, while another quarter was seeking over $10 million; the largest cohort of firms needed capital in the range of $1 to $5 million. Novice entrepreneurs constituted 33% of the sample; the remaining 67% had previously negotiated term sheets for private equity. At the time of completing the survey, more than 80% had raised equity, while the rest were either still in the process of negotiation or had walked away from a deal.

Our regression analyses used models for negotiation outcomes for funding, retention of equity and satisfaction and provided an objective measure against which to compare qualitative data. Two key findings are of importance: *First*, we find that human capital matters a great deal when raising equity funding. In examining the relationship between the

236 *Ethné Swartz and Frances Amatucci*

Table 17.1 Respondent demographics and purposes and uses of capital sought

Respondent demographics	Purposes and uses of capital and industries represented
Age:	**Purposes and uses of capital:**
27%: 20–40 years	Equity needs ranged from less than $500k (24%) to over $10m (22%), with 46% seeking $1m–$5m.
36%: 40–50 years	
33%: 51–60 years	More than 80% had raised equity.
3%: over 60 years	20% were still negotiating or had walked away from the deal.
Education:	
100% college educated;	Reported purposes for additional capital were for start-up (62%) and growth (56%), including acquisition of other companies.
68% had a graduate degree, including doctoral level training	
Career backgrounds:	**Industries represented:**
94%: Sales and marketing	Telecommunications, healthcare, retail, biotechnology, aerospace, Internet-related, education, transportation, financial services, consumer electronics, music and 'other', which included banking, fuel cell manufacturing, public digital screen advertising, commercial real estate, legal, optics and clean technologies.
29%: Research and development	
23%: Finance/accounting	

percentage funding raised, the characteristics of the entrepreneur, her firm and the investor, we found that older entrepreneurs and those launching either biotech or Internet-related firms had a greater likelihood of raising most or all the funding they were seeking. Our data also suggest that dealing with male investors did not appear to represent a disadvantage to women in our sample of whom 36% were over the age of 50 and 36% were in their forties. Most of our sample had experience in sales and marketing, including online marketing, and 29% had science or research and development backgrounds. Women with professional backgrounds in finance and accounting professions made up 23% of the sample. *Second,* strategies for successful negotiation emerged as conducting Internet research and including a male as a principal negotiator on the negotiating team. These two factors enabled entrepreneurs to raise at least 90% of the funding they were seeking.

The finding on human capital suggests that the position that women occupy in labour markets determines the type of company they build once they leave corporate life, as proposed by Goffee and Scase (1985) in their analysis of entrepreneurial women in the United Kingdom. Entrepreneurs' human capital determines the type of companies they start and, as our data suggest, those who have science and technology backgrounds are more likely to be successful negotiating for equity funding. The use of a male 'surrogate' on negotiation teams suggests that women entrepreneurs in our sample were expecting to encounter homophily, that they did not possess the requisite skills themselves or that they would not experience fair treatment without a man on the negotiation team. Homophily is the tendency for people to seek out others who are like them (McPherson, Smith-Lovin, & Cook, 2001).

Social psychology, gender bias and negotiation

Our original investigation of women entrepreneurs and term-sheet negotiations was informed by a well-established program of research on gender and negotiation in such fields as organisational behaviour, social psychology and conflict management (Stuhlmacher & Walter, 1999; Babcock & Laschever, 2003; Riley & McGinn, 2002; Brooks & Schweitzer, 2011). The seminal book, *Women Don't Ask*, by Babcock and Laschever in 2003 ushered gender and negotiation into the popular discourse. It suggested that women seemed to be more likely to settle for less optimal outcomes, and that negotiation was a man's game with women less likely to push for higher salaries. Even today this appears to be so – data from the Kauffman Foundation reveal only 16% of women attempt to negotiate their own salaries (Krause, 2016).

Current research findings on gender suggest a more nuanced picture influenced by contextual and psychological factors (Bowles & Kray, 2013; Brooks & Schweitzer, 2011; Chen & Chen, 2012; Eriksson & Sandberg, 2012; Bowles & Flynn, 2010; Kolb & McGinn, 2009; Kolb & Williams, 2003). Researchers are increasingly adopting a 'gender-in-context' perspective. In the legal field, Krieger (2004) provides excellent examples of how empirical results from the field of psychology can and are used in specific legal cases to consider whether gender might have been a consideration when decisions are made in litigation outcomes.

Field and laboratory studies in psychology have usefully been incorporated into research in management, revealing complex and unconscious factors that impact interactions. Bowles and Flynn (2010) cite the social psychological research to suggest that women are highly attuned to the need to be discriminating in how to respond during social interaction, using either lower-status or assertive behaviours as befit the circumstances. Women discern when to adopt appropriately assertive and less assertive behaviour to achieve desired outcomes. Bowles and Flynn (2010) cite Deaux and LaFrance (1998) on gender and social interaction to suggest that women tend to modify their behaviour in line with the gender of their 'opponent'. Women tend to be more aware of the need to reach out, bridge to opponents and be sensitive to situation cues. These behaviours are those typical of low-status actors in situations in which they lack control over outcomes.

Additionally, women finely modulate their speech patterns to the gender of their opponent during a disagreement, using more tentative (lower-status) speech patterns with male than with female opponents (Carli, 1990; Carli, LaFleur, & Loeber, 1995). The outcome is that women are more successful with men during such interactions. Finally, Bowles and Flynn (2010) show that research on social interaction among children suggest that girls, more than boys, change their behaviour to be more assertive when interacting with boys. Nonetheless, many obstacles remain. We know, from the field of linguistics, that a woman's voice is perceived more negatively than a man's (Sumner, 2015; Sumner, Kim, King, & McGowan, 2013), vindicating the decision to have men on a negotiating team when it matters, as was found in our research on term-sheet negotiation!

In the mid-1990s a team of social psychologists began their research on social interactions among individuals and groups, and how our biases are implicit or unconscious in nature (Greenwald and Banaji, 1995). Implicit bias may occur based on gender, as with second-generation gender bias, but also on race, ethnicity, age, religion, etc. These 'blindspots' can create flawed perceptual biases (Banaji and Greenwald, 2013). The negative consequences for women may include decreased representation in leadership positions and in STEM-related fields (Correll & MacKenzie, 2016). Likewise, implicit bias and negotiation are important in entrepreneurship because, although our research focused just on term-sheet negotiation, the entrepreneurial process involves myriad opportunities for effective negotiation strategies with suppliers, customers, employees and other stakeholders.

238　*Ethné Swartz and Frances Amatucci*

Implicit gender-related bias can lead to decreased self-efficacy, or confidence in one's ability to perform a specific task (Bandura, 1977; Gist, 1987). This stereotype type threat (Robertson & Kulik, 2007; Steele, 1997) which results in lower self-efficacy, in turn, may lead to gender-related underperformance as a 'self-fulfilling prophesy'. Research has explored the linkage between self-efficacy and entrepreneurship with regard to entrepreneurial intention (Wilson et al. 2007, financial management (Amatucci & Crawley, 2011) and negotiation (Amatucci & Swartz, 2011).

Labour market economics and gender bias

Our research shows the importance of human capital in negotiating term sheets and we believe the wage gap reveals a structural impediment on that journey. Labour market segregation means that women dominate professions that are paid less and associated with lower human capital than those historically occupied by men. Concomitantly they are at a disadvantage in regards to human capital, financial resource and social networks when they move into entrepreneurship and entrepreneurial negotiations. We are not arguing that women entrepreneurs cannot develop effective negotiation skills and that a senior, well-educated background in a growth industry is *de rigueur* for running a successful company.

The early studies on gender bias focused on negotiation in the personal domain, considering whether and how women negotiated salary or job conditions. Salary negotiation can result in profound and life-long inequities if conducted ineffectively. Women were and are still paid less for comparable work than men in most industries (Blau & Khan, 2017). US Department of Labor data illustrates women's median earnings in 1968 to be 58% of the earnings for men. NBER data shows that the educational achievements that women made during the 1970s and 1980s helped to erase some of this inequality (Blau & Khan, 2017) but that the oft-cited statistic of the median earnings for women being 77 cents compared to that for men is accurate, increasing to 79 cents by 2014 (Blau & Khan, 2017). Kazal-Thresher (1990), under the guidance of Myra Strober at Stanford, analysed the occupations and wages of thirteen cohorts of Stanford MBA students from 1973 to 1985. They show gender-related earnings differences even after allowing for hours worked, experience, unemployment and occupation. Being female was associated with slower wage growth and a negative impact on earnings. Data from the Women's Bureau at the US Department of Labor, illustrated in Figure 17.2, plots the growth in earnings for women as a percentage of earnings for white, non-Hispanic men.

Some of the earnings differential is due to actions by women themselves. Even when women possess the power to do otherwise, they continue to pay themselves less. A survey of participants in the Goldman Sachs 10,000 Small Business Program showed women entrepreneurs paid themselves 20% less than their male peers (Mandelbaum, 2014). As discussed earlier, implicit bias, stereotype threat and low self-efficacy may help explain this phenomenon. These constructs may also explain why Hispanic women today have a median earnings ratio lower than the median for all women in 1968 (Women's Bureau United States Department of Labor, 2016). US median earnings in 2014, when broken out into different ethnic groups, range from a high of 83.5% for Asian-Americans to 75.4% for White non-Hispanic women, to 60.5% for African-American women and a low of 54.6% for Hispanic women. These data for the period 1987–2014 show that median earnings for Hispanic women in 2014 ($39,428) represented a marginal decrease from 2013 ($39,798).

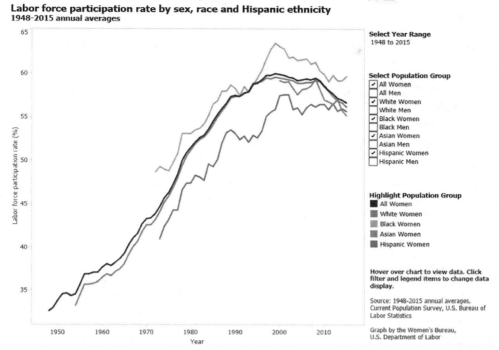

Figure 17.2 Median annual earnings by sex, race and Hispanic ethnicity

Goldin (2014) questions the use of median earnings as evidence related to occupations that require specific types of education and work experience – in sum, human capital make it necessary to compare 'apples to apples' (Goldin, 2014). One obstacle is the lack of such earnings data. Few sources track data on gender for specific industries and, in cases where they are tracked, other associated variables are needed to conduct analyses. To date compelling evidence exists for only one US industry where the male-female wage disparity appears to be changing – professionally educated pharmacists (Goldin & Katz, 2016).

Blau and Khan (20167 argue that for the 1980–2010 period gender compensation is determined by variables such as occupation and industry rather than gender and other human capital variables. They acknowledge that psychological and other non-cognitive skills as a 'newer' explanation, contribute a small or 'moderate' portion of the pay gap. Krieger (2004) explores these differences in her work on how situational factors influence behaviour on the part of women, managers and especially judges who sit in judgement during US labour discrimination litigation. Goldin and Katz (2016) have consistently argued that while it is true that in certain occupations women earn less than do men when considering median wages, the question we should be asking is whether this is an outcome of discrimination or is it tied to other factors? Their research has not unearthed evidence of outright discrimination and they conclude that the best that can be done is to research specific occupations to uncover how wage discrimination mechanisms have worked. It would appear that these psychological and non-cognitive factors would assist in that effort.

Jacobsen, Khamis, and Yuksel (2015) suggest that time allocation in labour markets, in addition to human capital, structural changes and social norms, combine to explain differential labour outcomes (Jacobsen, Khamis, & Yuksel, 2015). Using fifty years of data (1964–2013) these authors estimate that men worked an average of 200 hours per year more than women. Wage discrimination begins as women move 'up the ladder' following their entry-level jobs. Ascending the ladder coincides with having children and requiring greater 'temporal flexibility' about where and when work can be performed, with women more likely to seek such accommodations (Goldin & Katz, 2011). Temporal flexibility carries a care tax (Slaughter, 2015) which explains the split in professional career choices, including becoming a business owner. So, even professional women in well-compensated fields (finance, law or science) find their care responsibilities lead them to work fewer hours and unable to satisfy the disproportionate physical work presence demanded of senior professionals. 'Quite simply the gap exists because hours of work in many occupations are worth more when given at particular moments and when the hours are more continuous' (Goldin, 2014, p. 1116).

The biggest wage differentials occur in corporate roles, typically in finance, where the human capital associated with one individual is not easily substituted (Goldin & Katz, 2011). The smallest wage differentials occur in science, technology and healthcare fields. Goldin (2013) posits a 'pollution' theory of discrimination in which there is asymmetric information regarding the value of an individual woman in a new occupation. Asymmetry arises from 'incomplete information by those who confer prestige on workers and the group who confers prestige is society . . .' (Goldin, 2013, p. 2). Incomplete information does not refer to worker ability so much as the societal view of the fit of a woman in an occupation previously dominated by males. In Goldin's model a 'female' median predicts that all occupations requiring specific productivity characteristics higher than that median will be segregated by sex and below it will be integrated.

The wage gap persists because of multiple factors: time allocation in labour markets, subtle discrimination in some fields, assumptions regarding the role of women, the lack of bargaining by women themselves and, finally, differential standards for the promotion of women. Some elements of the wage gap remain because of assumptions about women's fit for certain roles.

Contributions from law to second-generation gender bias

Second-generation bias in the social sciences literature has its origins in the literature on discrimination and the impact of US civil rights legislation in curtailing explicit discrimination (Sturm, 2001). It has spilled over into the gender and organization development literature (Ibarra, Ely, & Kolb, 2013) and is beginning to reach the field of women and entrepreneurship (Swartz, Amatucci, & Coleman, 2016 b).

First-generation bias involved the overt exclusion of women and minorities, segregated job opportunities, conscious stereotyping, dominance in a workplace by an individual who excludes women and minorities, and the use of job requirements that helped solidify segregation of occupations (Sturm, 2001). Most of these practices were legal until the passing of the Equal Pay Act of 1963 and the 1964 Civil Rights Act which, under Title VII, prohibited employers from discriminating against employees based on sex, race, colour, national origin and religion (Krieger, 2004). Murphy (1970, p. 615) commented on the roots of sex discrimination being far more insidious and deeper than even discrimination based on race or ethnicity:

> When federal legislation to correct this imbalance was proposed, congressional opposition took many forms, but underlying all the disguising rhetoric, fashioned with euphemistic 'legal' and 'constitutional' terminology, there seemed to be a fairly representative attitude amongst males that 'women are more prone to homemaking and motherhood than men'.

The above quotation came from a member of the United States House Committee on Education and Labor. Today explicit expression of such an assumption about the role of women may be perturbing. However, such attitudes co-exist with explicitly stated egalitarian ones. Second-generation bias, whether with respect to race or gender, lacks the crassness and explicitness of the measures described earlier. Instead, biases are manifest in subtle ways, inhering in organizational cultures, beliefs and practices. Explicit and more tacit forms of bias co-exist. The nomenclature of 'a second-generation' does not imply a sequential evolution of bias but rather a careful avoidance of overt discrimination without questioning underlying decision processes that entrench bias, stereotyping and unequal access. Sturm (2001) advocates institutional remedies to counter such practices.

Krieger (2004), writing specifically about the 'maternal wall' and the intransigence to change of the legal field, expresses views that broadly support the case that Sturm (2001) makes for second-generation gender bias while not using the exact terminology. Civil rights legislation has not solved all issues of bias. Krieger argues that many legal outcomes are left to courts and judges, who function as 'intuitive psychologists' in their interpretation of discrimination, using inaccurate and outdated assumptions and perceptions about intergroup relations. 'Unlike actual research psychologists, the courts and the judges who staff them often use definitions of discrimination that are inadequate to address many modern forms of gender bias' (Krieger, 2004, p. 836).

Discriminatory acts can be sparked by circumstances. Krieger (2004) argues that social psychology shows that explicit, egalitarian attitudes influence people when they engage in deliberative thought. When behavioural responses are spontaneous, and when people lack the opportunity or motivation to deliberate over a decision, implicit attitudes tend to play a more dominant role. Dual attitudes co-exist and our unconscious biases are important factors that shape decisions. A summary of the research discussed in the previous sections is provided in Table 17.2.

Conclusion

This chapter began with a reference to research by Antecol, Bedard and Sterns (2016) showing how a gender-neutral policy, intended to ease employment conditions for women academics appeared to have had the opposite outcome. The lesson is salutary and supports Sturm's (2001) contention about the complexity involved in enacting anti-bias measures. We now conclude by framing the elements of second-generation gender bias. Linked with the literature in Table 17.2, we believe that the framework in Figure 17.3 helps to set a research agenda for second-generation gender bias. Moving from the explicit to the implicit, Figure 17.3 displays the elements as discussed in this chapter. Lines are porous

242　*Ethné Swartz and Frances Amatucci*

Table 17.2 An interdisciplinary deconstruction of second-generation gender bias

Discipline	Authors	Primary themes
Entrepreneurship/ management	Swartz, Amatucci, & Coleman (2016a; 2016b)	Presence of second-generation bias in term-sheet negotiation
	Ibarra, Ely, & Kolb (2013) Brush et al. (2014)	Second-generation bias as a barrier for women's leadership development
	Krause (2016)	Presence of gender bias in the venture capital industry
	Slaughter (2015)	Low levels of equity funding obtained by women 'Care tax'
Social psychology	Banaji & Greenwald (2013,) Greenwald & Banaji (1995)	'Blindspots' create unconscious flawed perceptions
	Sumner (2015)	Implicit or unconscious bias
		Female voice perceived more negatively than male voice
Labour market economics	Blau & Khan (2017) Goldin (2013, 2014)	Women paid less for comparable work in most US industries – median is 79 cents
	Goldin & Katz (2011, 2016) Mandelbaum (2014)	Pollution theory of discrimination; Grand convergence between males and females
	Murphy (1970) Jacobsen, Khamis, & Yuksel (2015)	Human capital requires comparison of wage gap within industries
		'Temporal flexibility' also factor in explaining wage gap;
		Gender gap in median wages
		Time allocation in labour markets, social assumptions contribute to wage gap
Law	Sturm (2001) Krieger (2004)	Anti-bias efforts post landmark civil rights legislation leads to structural and compliance approaches to managing discrimination in workplaces, perversely sometime leading to lack of addressing second-generation bias.
		The courts and judges use definitions of bias that lack understanding of modern forms of gender bias

to illustrate movement across boundaries, based on greater understanding of salient issues; alternatively, movement can also occur when setbacks occur, particularly during periods of political change.

Assumptions about the role of women are at the centre of the second-generation gender framework. These assumptions are taken-for-granted and surface at times of change or crisis, as evident in Murphy's quotation earlier in this chapter. In contrast, the most explicit aspect of the framework is the wage gap and what it tells us about human capital development. Claudia Goldin and other economists have already made huge contributions in noting the changes that have occurred in this arena and for specific industries. The wage

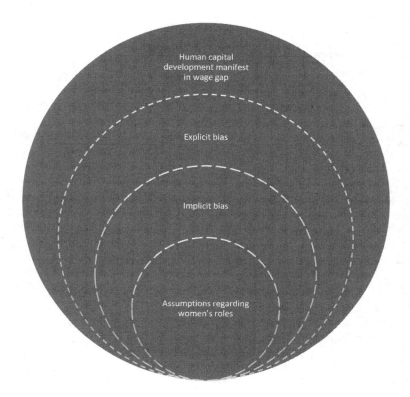

Figure 17.3 Second-generation gender bias model

gap is structural and its 'sorting' effects are far-reaching. For growth entrepreneurship, the sorting effect is evident in the companies that women start.

The entrepreneurship literature lacks a coherent consideration of the effects of the wage gap on human capital accumulation, despite the emergence of interesting approaches by scholars in strategic management (Ployhart et al., 2014). Explicit gender bias in the US has been curbed through civil rights legislation. Legal scholars, such as Krieger (2004) and Sturm (2001), have contributed to our understanding of second-generation gender bias issues while implicit gender bias permeates organizational (and personal) cultures, beliefs and practices. Furthermore, these phenomena co-exist and create complex stages on which entrepreneurs perform. We must deconstruct the effect of the wage gap on human capital accumulation and the implication for women's entrepreneurship. That understanding will come primarily from interdisciplinary research such as what we have attempted to provide in this chapter.

References

Amatucci, F., & Crawley, D. (2011). Financial self-efficacy among women entrepreneurs. *International Journal of Gender and Entrepreneurship*, 3(1), 23–37.
Amatucci, F., & Swartz, E. (2011). Through a fractured lens: Women entrepreneurs and the private equity negotiation process. *Journal of Developmental Entrepreneurship*, 16(3), 23–37.

Antecol, H., Bedard, K., & Stearns, J. (2016). *Equal but inequitable: Who benefits from gender-neutral tenure clock stopping policies?* IZA Discussion Paper # 9904 pp: 43. Downloaded from: http://ftp.iza.org/dp9904.pdf.

Babcock, L., & Laschever, S. (2003). *Women don't ask: Negotiation and the gender divide.* Princeton, NJ: Princeton University Press.

Banaji, M. R., & Greenwald, A. G. (2013). *Blindspot.* Random House: New York.

Bandura, A. (1977). Self-efficacy: Toward a unifying theory of behavioural change. *Psychological Review, 84,* 191–215.

Blau, F., & Khan, L. (2017). The gender wage gap: Extent, trends and explanations. *Journal of Economic Literature, 55*(3), 789–865.

Bowles, H. R., & Flynn, F. (2010). Gender and persistence in negotiation: A dyadic perspective. *Academy of Management Journal, 53*(4), 769–787.

Bowles, H. R., & Kray, L. (2013). Negotiation is a man's game: Ultimate truth or enduring myth? Paper presented at the gender and work research symposium, Harvard Business School. Downloaded from: www.hbs.edu/faculty/conferences/2013-w50-research-symposium/Documents/bowles_kray.pdf.

Brooks, A. W., & Schweitzer, M. E. (2011). Can nervous Nelly negotiate? How anxiety causes negotiators to make low first offers, exit early and earn less profit. *Organizational Behavior and Human Decision Processes, 115,* 43–54.

Brush, C., deBruin, A., & Welter, F. (2009). A gender-aware framework for women's entrepreneurship. *International Journal of Gender and Entrepreneurship, 1*(1), 8–24.

Brush, C., Greene, P., Balachandra, L., & David, A. (2014). *Diana report women entrepreneurs 2014: Bridging the gender gap in venture capital.* Arthur M. Blank Center for Entrepreneurship, Babson College. Downloaded from: www.babson.edu/Academics/centers/blank-center/global-research/diana/Documents/diana-project-executive-summary-2014.pdf.

Carli, L. L. (1990). Gender, language and influence. *Journal of Personality and Social Psychology, 59,* 941–995.

Carli, L. L., LaFleur, S. J., & Loeber, C. C. (1995). Nonverbal behavior, gender and influence. *Journal of Personality and Social Psychology, 68,* 1030–1041.

Chen, H., & Chen, Q. (2012). The mechanism of gender difference and representation role in negotiation. *Public Personnel Management, 41*(5), 91–103.

Correll, S., & MacKenzie, L. (2016). To succeed in tech, women need more visibility. *Harvard Business Review Digital Articles,* 13 September, 2–5. .https://libaccess.fdu.edu/login?url=http://search.ebscohost.com.libaccess.fdu.edu/login.aspx?direct=true&db=bsh&AN=118683851&site=ehost-live&scope=site.

Deaux, K., & LaFrance, M. (1998). Gender. In D. T. Gilbert, S. T. Fiske, & G. Lindsey (Eds), *The handbook of social psychology.* Boston, MA: McGraw-Hill.

Eriksson, K. H., & Sandberg, A. (2012). Gender differences in initiation of negotiation: Does the gender of the negotiation counterpart matter? *Negotiation Journal, 30*(4), 407–428.

Fetsch, E., Jackson, C., & Wiens, J. (2015). *Women Entrepreneurs are Key to Accelerating Growth.* Downloaded from: www.kauffman.org/what-we-do/resources/entrepreneurship-policy-digest/women-entrepreneurs-are-key-to-accelerating-growth.

Gist, M. (1987). Self-efficacy: Implications for organizational behaviour and human resource management. *Academy of Management Review, 12*(3), 472–485.

Goffee, R., & Scase, R. (1985). *Women in charge: The experience of female entrepreneurs.* London: Routledge.

Goldin, C. (2013). A pollution theory of discrimination: Male and female differences in occupations and earnings, revised. *NBER Working Paper No. 8985,* June 2002. www.nber.org/chapters/c12904.

Goldin, C. (2014). A grand gender convergence: Its last chapter. *American Economic Review, 104*(4), 1091–1119.

Goldin, C., & Katz, L. F. (2016). A most egalitarian profession and the evolution of a family-friendly occupation. *Journal of Labor Economics, 34*(3), 705–746. Downloaded from: http://scholar.harvard.edu/files/lkatz/files/jole_gk_pharm_published.pdf.

Goldin, C., & Katz, L. (2011). The cost of workplace flexibility for high-powered professionals. *The Annals of the American Academy of Political and Social Science, 638,* 1–24. Downloaded from: http://scholar.harvard.edu/files/goldin/files/the_cost_of_workplace_flexibility_for_high-powered_professionals.pdf.

Greenwald, A. G. and Banaji, M. R. (1995). Implicit social cognition: attitudes, self-esteem and stereotypes. *Psychogical Review, 102*(1), 4–27.

Ibarra, H., Ely, R., & Kolb, D. (2013). Women rising: The unseen barriers. *Harvard Business Review, 91*, 61–66.

Jacobsen, J., Khamis, M., & Yuksel, M. (2015). Convergences in men's and women's life patterns: Lifetime work, lifetime earnings and human capital investment. In S. W. Polachek, K. Tatsiramos, & K. F. Zimmermann (Eds), *Research in labor economics: Gender convergence in the labor market* (pp. 2–33). Bingley, GB: Emerald Group Publishing.

Kazal-Thresher, D. (1990). *Employment and earnings patterns of Stanford MBAs: Gender comparisons among thirteen graduating classes* (Order No. 9108849). Available from ABI/INFORM Collection. (303884576). Retrieved from: https://libaccess.fdu.edu/login?url=http://search.proquest.com/docview/303884576?accountid=10818.

Kolb, D., & McGinn, K. (2009). Beyond gender and negotiation to gendered negotiations. *Negotiation and Conflict Management Research, 2*(1), 1–16.

Kolb, D. M., & Williams, J. (2003). *Everyday negotiation: Navigating the hidden agendas in bargaining.* Hoboken, NJ: Jossey-Bass.

Krause, A. (2016). *Gender pay gap doesn't stop for women entrepreneurs.* 22 July 2016 [Blog post]. Retrieved from: www.kauffman.org/blogs/growthology/2016/07/gender-pay-gap-doesnt-stop-for-women-entrepreneurs.

Krieger, L. H. (2004). The intuitive psychologist behind the bench: Models of gender bias in social psychology and employment discrimination law. *Journal of Social Issues, 60*(4), 835–848.

MacKenzie, L. N. (2016). A model for inclusive workplaces: blocking bias in the employee lifecycle. *Presentation at the American Association for Collegiate Business Schools (AACSB) national conference*, Minneapolis, Minnesota, 2016.

McPherson, M., Smith-Lovin, L., & Cook, J. (2001). Birds of a feather: Homophily in social networks. *Annual Review of Sociology, 27*, 415–444.

Mandelbaum, R. (2014). There is a salary gap even when women pay themselves. *New York Times*, 18 February 2014. [Blog post]. Retrieved from: http://boss.blogs.nytimes.com/2014/02/18/there-is-a-salary-gap-even-when-women-pay-themselves/?_r=1.

Murphy, T. E. (1970). Female wage discrimination: A study of the equal pay act 1963–1970. *University of Cincinnati Law Review, 39*(4), 615–649.

National Women's Business Council (n.d.). *Women-owned businesses. NWBC analysis of 2012 survey of business owners.* Retrieved from: https://www.nwbc.gov/sites/default/files/FS_Women-Owned_Businesses.pdf.

Ployhart, R. E., Nyberg, A. J., Reilly, G., & Maltarich, M. A. (2014). Human capital is dead: Long live human capital resources! *Journal of Management, 40*(2), 37–398.

Riley, H., & McGinn, K. L. (2002). *When does gender matter in negotiation?* Faculty Research Working Papers Series #RWP02–036, John F. Kennedy School of Government, Harvard University.

Robb, A., & Coleman, S. (2009). *Characteristics of New Firms: A Comparison by Gender.* Third in a Series of Reports Using Kauffman Data. Downloaded from: www.kauffman.org/~/media/kauffman_org/research%20reports%20and%20covers/2009/02/kfs_gender_020209.pdf.

Robb, A. M., & Watson, J. (2012). Gender differences in firm performance: Evidence from new ventures in the United States. *Journal of Business Venturing, 27*(5), 544–558.

Robertson, L. and Kulik, C. T. (2007). Stereotype threat at work. *Academy of Management Perspectives, 21*(2), 24–40.

Slaughter, A. (2015). *Unfinished business.* New York: Random House.

Stuhlmacher, A. F., & Walters, A. E. (1999). Gender differences in negotiation outcome: A meta-analysis. *Personnel Psychology, 52*, 653–677.

Steele, C. M. (1997). A threat in the air: How stereotypes shape intellectual identity and performance, *American Psychologist, 52*(6), 613–629.

Sturm, S. (2001). Second-generation employment discrimination: A structural approach. *Columbia Law Review, 101*(3), 458–568.

Sumner, M. (2015). The social weight of spoken words. *Trends in Cognitive Sciences, 19*(5), 238–239.

Sumner, M., Kim, S. K., King, E., & McGowan, K. B. (2013). The socially weighted encoding of spoken words: A dual-route approach to speech perception. *Frontiers in Psychology, 4*, 1015. Downloaded from: http://doi.org/10.3389/fpsyg.2013.01015.

Swartz, E., Amatucci, F., & Coleman, S. (2016a). Examining women entrepreneurs' negotiating styles: A multiple method and mixed mode research approach. *International Journal of Gender and Entrepreneurship, 8*(1), 48–68.

Swartz, E., Amatucci, F., & Coleman, S. (2016b). Still a man's world? Second-generation gender bias in external equity term sheet negotiations. *Journal of Developmental Entrepreneurship, 21*(3). doi. org/10.1142/S1084946716500151.

Watson, J. (2002). Comparing the performance of male- and female-controlled businesses: Relating outputs to inputs. *Entrepreneurship Theory and Practice, 26*(3), 91–100.

Wilson, F., Kickul, J., & Marlino, D. (2007). Gender, entrepreneurial self-efficacy and entrepreneurial career intentions: Implications for entrepreneurship education, *Entrepreneurship Theory & Practice, 31*(3), 387–406.

Wolfers, J. (2016). Tenure extension policies that put women at a disadvantage. *New York Times*, 24 June. Downloaded from: www.nytimes.com/2016/06/26/business/tenure-extension-policies-that-put-women-at-a-disadvantage.html?_r=0.

Women's Bureau of the U.S. Department of Labor (2016). *Fast Facts: Women in the Labor Force*. Downloaded from: https://www.dol.gov/wb/stats/facts_over_time.htm.

Zolin, R., & Watson, J. (2013). Challenging the female underperformance hypothesis, *Frontiers of Entrepreneurship Research, 33*(8) Article 7. Downloaded from: http://digitalknowledge.babson.edu/fer/vol33/iss8/7.

18 Entrepreneurial passion and social entrepreneurial self-efficacy among Spanish and Moroccan young females

Juan Diego Borrero

Some researchers label women-owned firms as 'under-performing' (Marlow, Shaw, & Carter, 2008). Data that support this hypothesis argue that women constitute approximately one-quarter of the self-employed and only one-tenth of business owners (OECD, 2003). In addition, their firms are concentrated in a low-value-added sector of the service industry (Marlow, Henry, & Carter, 2009; Wilson & Tagg, 2010) and consequently exhibit limited growth in terms of employment, sales, profitability and market share (Carter & Marlow, 2007). On the other hand, other researchers point out that the hypothesis of under-performance is a myth, by positing that women's positioning within self-employment merely reflects and reproduces embedded socio-economic norms; it is not a preference expressed by women business owners which might then be addressed by specific support to encourage them to enter into high-value-added market sectors (Marlow & McAdam, 2013). Clearly, there is limited scope to overcome the performance restrictions associated with these highly competitive sectors per se. Expecting women in particular to do this is both unfeasible and unreasonable. Thus, it appears that women are criticized for not operating.

Although child care and greater hours of housework have a negative effect on female earnings (Hundley, 2001), they cannot be qualified as the result of a basic division of labour by gender; instead, they become an integral part of the complex social identity of contemporary women (Poggesi, Mari, & De Vita, 2015). Women pursue fragmented and flexible working patterns as a response to socially constructed expectations that they will undertake primary responsibility for domestic labour and responsibilities within the family (Bradley, 2007; Rouse & Kitching, 2006). Such responsibilities are socially constructed and historically attributed (Bowden & Mummery, 2009), so women are not exhibiting a choice reflecting restricted entrepreneurial ambitions or limited capital when operating part time or home-based firms but rather responding to social imperatives and ascribed roles. Labelling women entrepreneurs operating in such sectors as under-performing and the suggestions about encouraging women to begin new ventures within higher performing sectors, such as science, engineering and technology (SET) is unfair (Marlow & McAdam, 2013).

In this chapter we suggest that a discussion of the 'under-performance' discourse in the context of social entrepreneurship could provide some answers to this debate. Previous research has shown a higher level of altruism and stronger preferences for redistribution among women and that they are more averse to competition and hence more attracted to the newer markets of social enterprises (Huysentruyt, 2014). Furthermore, in evaluating their firms' performance, women pay attention to other factors such as personal fulfilment, the search for flexibility and the desire to serve the community rather than only economic indicators (Anna, Chandler, Jansen, & Mero, 1999).

In Maghrebi[1] societies women are a key, albeit largely invisible, part of the family (Dris-Aït-Hamadouche, 2008). Overall, women are assigned functions mainly as mothers, wives and educators of their children, while men are the protectors and providers of the family. Although this is in a constant evolutionary process because one of the most important reforms that the new Mudawana[2] brought about in 2004 was the introduction of shared family responsibility for both spouses. Women's involvement in the Moroccan community is closely linked with social structures and values that dominate their society, as well as cultural practices that have been passed down over time (Feliu, 2004). However, today many Muslim women are agents of change in their societies and the profiles of women participating in Islamic society are those of college-educated teachers, writers, etc. (Perez & Rebollo, 2009).

On the other hand, it is suggested that European women have different reasons for taking the step towards entrepreneurship; i.e. women more often claim to do so out of necessity as entrepreneurship offers them the opportunity to combine labour and care tasks, for example for their children or the elderly, and increase their opportunities to work from home (Matera, 2015).

A crucial task for social entrepreneurship researchers is to develop an understanding of the elements that impact the likelihood of social entrepreneurial intention. In doing so, women's social entrepreneurial intention (WSEI) has been guided primarily by Ajzen's (1991) theory of planned behaviour (TPB) and Shapero and Sokol's (1982) model of entrepreneurial event (SEE), using perceived entrepreneurial passion as perceived desirability and perceived social entrepreneurial self-efficacy as perceived feasibility (Hockerts, 2015; Mair & Noboa, 2006) of the social entrepreneurial intentions of females in two different contexts of Spain and Morocco. In considering entrepreneurship as a social change activity with a variety of possible outcomes, we also allow the consideration of new ideas about women's specific perceptions of social entrepreneurship and help to determine whether the level of social entrepreneurial intentions of women is found to be different across Spain and Morocco.

Women and social entrepreneurship in the contexts of Spain and Morocco

In Morocco, as in so many cultural contexts, women have historically been immersed in a situation of inequality. One of the peculiarities of the political regime established in Morocco is the cohabitation of two systems in the same structure: on the one hand, a pluralistic and modern system; on the other, a system of feudal origin – the Makzen – representative of tradition. The coexistence of these two forms of power implies the existence of a contradictory duality of structures of thought that is felt in a special way in reference to the status of women. Following the development of the Family Code in 2004 and in particular the Constitution of 2011, Morocco has removed all forms of discrimination against women, claiming equality between men and women. However, not surprisingly, in Morocco, as in other Arab countries, women still continue to suffer discrimination in access to education – occupying the highest levels of illiteracy – and the political arena, health care, access to basic resources and in gender-based violence.

In terms of entrepreneurial intention (EI), female participation is higher in Spain (51.8%) than in Morocco (26.2%). The difference is still significant to the extent of women's entrepreneurial activity (TEA) (43.80% compared to 11.09% for Moroccan women in activity) (GEM, 2015b).

From a different point of view, the estimate of the TEA index by women notes that the Spanish adult female population is more prone to undertaking entrepreneurial activity than Moroccan adult females. Thus, the Spanish adult female population in 2015 involved in entrepreneurial activity represented 5.00 per cent of the total population, while in the case of Morocco, 2.85 per cent of the total were women. Just as with TEA, Spanish women are generally more likely to start a social venture than Moroccan women. It is clear that despite the emancipation of Moroccan women in recent years and their increased access to civil and social rights, participation in business remains characterized by a relatively low level in comparison with other developed countries such as Spain.

Conceptual development

Entrepreneurship is the process of venture creation. According to Ajzen (1991), intention captures the degree to which people show their motivation and willingness to execute the desired behaviour. Intention has been shown to be the best predictor of planned behaviour, particularly when that behaviour is rare, hard to observe, or involves unpredictable time lags (Krueger & Brazeal, 1994).

Attempts to explain the entrepreneurship process and EI have been approached from different theoretical directions, although most of them are based on Ajzen's (1991) TPB and Shapero and Sokol's (1982) SEE. According to these models perceived desirability, perceived feasibility, and propensity to act are presented as direct antecedents to EI (Shapero & Sokol, 1982). Krueger, Reilly, and Carsrud (2000) tested TPB and SEE, and found support for both models. They demonstrated that attitudes and subjective norms in the TPB model were conceptually related to perceived desirability in the SEE, whereas perceived behavioural control in the TPB corresponded with perceived feasibility in the SEE model. Essentially, it can be concluded that perceived desirability and perceived feasibility could be fundamental elements of EI.

But entrepreneurship is not just about making money. Following Murphy and Coombes (2009), social entrepreneurship is the creation and undertaking of a venture intended to promote a specific social purpose or cause. The idea of social entrepreneurship combines passion (Bornstein, 1998; Boschee, 1995) with an image of business-like discipline (Dees, 1998; Mair & Noboa, 2006).

Social entrepreneurial self-Efficacy

Self-efficacy describes an individual's perceptions of his/her ability to carry out an intended action (Bandura, 1977). In business ethics research self-efficacy has been found to predict the likelihood of entrepreneurial behaviour (Chen, Greene, & Crick, 1998) as well as the likelihood that an individual engages in civic activities (Weber, Weber, Sleeper, & Schneider, 2004). In the context of social entrepreneurship a high level of self-efficacy allows a person

250 *Juan Diego Borrero*

to perceive the creation of a social venture as feasible, which positively affects the formation of the corresponding behavioural intention (Mair & Noboa, 2006; Smith & Woodworth, 2012). In line with Hockerts (2015), we define Women's Social Entrepreneurial Self-Efficacy (WSESE) as the belief in their abilities to generate significant social impact within the context of solving social problems where they act. Thus, social entrepreneurial self-efficacy will places emphasis on a woman's belief in her ability to handle a particular social problem that is appropriate to its needs (Radin & Zaidatol, 2014).

Entrepreneurial passion

A discussion of the entrepreneurial intention process requires rigorous attention to the important aspect of how decision-making is thoroughly intertwined with emotional appraisal. Bagozzi and colleagues' study of effortful decision-making adds emotional appraisal explicitly to the intentions process (Bagozzi, Dholakia, & Basuron, 2003; Dholakia & Bagozzi, 2002). Along the same lines, several social entrepreneurship scholars posit that empathy is a major driver of social entrepreneurial intentions (Mair & Noboa, 2006). Empathy is a well specified construct in psychology (Jolliffe & Farrington, 2006). In management studies empathy has been used in research on stakeholders (Strong, Ringer, & Taylor, 2001), leadership (Holt & Marques, 2012), and business ethics education (Cohen, 2012). Within the context of social entrepreneurship, we are interested not so much in a person's general empathy but rather their empathic concern (Zahn-Waxler & Radke-Yarrow, 1990), or empathy with a very specific group of people or with a social cause (Mair & Noboa, 2006; Niezink et al., 2012).

However, it is not possible to discuss entrepreneurs without discussing entrepreneurial passion (Cardon, Wincent, Singh, & Drnovsek., 2009). It seems a cliché to suggest that social entrepreneurs are even stronger exemplars of entrepreneurial passion. In the present study we aim to illustrate the process through which empathy operates in developing women's social entrepreneurial intentions. We use entrepreneurial passion as a representative of empathy, which in turn creates an altruistic motivation in the social entrepreneur to reduce the pain of others. Thus, we define women's entrepreneurial passion (WEPAS) as the passion they feel about a cause and undertaking a business-like activity that earns money (or provides other resources) to support that cause.

To achieve the aims proposed, and taking the approach of Shapero and Sokol (1982) and Ajzen (1991) as a reference point, a model is put forward in which the construct WSEI is conceptualized as a latent variable depending on two others: the perception of women's social entrepreneurial self-efficacy (WSESE) and WEPAS, in starting up a social firm (see Figure 18.1). Nationality (NAT) is included as a control variable that can have some influence on the factors that predict WSEI.

Following the research model depicted in Figure 18.1, and taking into account that the influence of basic perceptions on intention-model elements should be similar for women from different contexts (Arenius & Minniti, 2005; Minniti & Nardone, 2007), two hypotheses will be tested:

> H1a: women's social entrepreneurial self-efficacy has a positive influence on women's social entrepreneurial intention.
>
> H1b: women's entrepreneurial passion has a positive influence on women's social entrepreneurial intention.

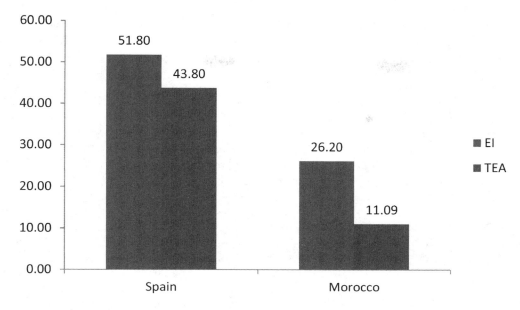

Figure 18.1 Comparison between Entrepreneurial Intention (EI) and Total Entrepreneurial Activity (TEA) levels (% of Female Participation)
Source: GEM 2015a, 2015b

However, the literature also points out that culture and context exert a different influence on people's perceptions and intentions regarding entrepreneurship (Eddleston & Powell, 2008; Gupta et al., 2009; Kickul et al., 2008; Mueller & Dato-On, 2008; Watson & Newby, 2005; Zhao, Siebert, & Hills 2005). This influence tends to be weaker for women from less developed countries (Bertaux & Crabe, 2007; Roomi & Parrot, 2008; Wells, Pfantz, & Byrne, 2003) and for females from regions with low income levels and high female unemployment (García-Cabrera & García-Soto, 2008; Verheul, van Stel, & Thurik, 2006). This therefore leads to the following hypotheses:

> H2a: The impact of social entrepreneurial self-efficacy on social entrepreneurial intention is different between Moroccan women and Spanish women.
> H2b: The impact of entrepreneurial passion on social entrepreneurial intention is different between Moroccan women and Spanish women.

Methodology

WSEI was measured by a single-item from Battilana and Lee (2014). The use of a single-item measure rather than a multiple-item measure is sufficient in exploratory studies if the construct is concrete and it can be reasonably assumed that there is virtually unanimous agreement among respondents as to what characteristic is being measured (see Bergkvist & Rossiter, 2007; Diamantopoulos et al., 2012; Fuchs & Diamantopoulos, 2009; Rossiter, 2002),

252 *Juan Diego Borrero*

as in this study. To measure social entrepreneurial self-efficacy we used Urban's (2013) instrument, which consists of fourteen items. Finally, the questionnaire included six items for measuring entrepreneurial passion related to intense positive feelings (Cardon, Gregoire, Stevens, & Patel, 2013).

Various studies have examined the sociodemographic profile of social entrepreneurs and found the prototype of a social entrepreneur to be female, young and highly educated (Chung, 2014; Cukier, Trenholm, & Gekas, 2011; Global Entrepreneurship Monitor [GEM], 2012; Van Ryzin, Grossman, DiPadova-Stocks, & Bergrud, 2009; Witkamp, Royakkers, & Raven, 2011). In a similar manner, social entrepreneurship is a rapidly growing movement within higher education (Pache & Chowdhury, 2012). With regard to the collection of information, five-point Likert surveys were carried out among university students because many members of this group are also majoring in business and likely to start a business (see Veciana, Aponte, & Urbano, 2005).

Questionnaires were administered in class in the languages of the study's sample population – Spanish and French – with prior permission from the lecturer, in November and December 2015 at the University of Huelva (Spain) and Université Adbelmalek Essaâdi from Tangier (Morocco). A total of 474 valid questionnaires were thus collected, 200 from Spain and 274 from Morocco. The principal methodological details from the research are summarized in Table 18.1.

Given the relationships between different perceptions and social entrepreneurial intention, structural equation modelling (SEM) has been chosen for the analysis. In particular, partial least squares (PLS) was applied (Sanchez, 2013), and the PLS-PM package (Sanchez, Trinchera, & Russolillo, 2015) in R version 3.3.1 software was used for the data analysis (R Core Team 2016). This multivariate statistical technique is suitable when exploratory studies are carried out and relatively small samples are used (Sánchez-Franco & Roldán, 2005).

In order to test H1, a confirmatory factor analysis (CFA) was conducted using data from the full sample (both Tangier and Huelva). Then, with the resulting constructs (WSEI, WSESE and WEPAS) we performed two PLS models: one for Spanish women and the other for the Moroccan sample. Regarding H2, a dichotomous control variable (NAT) was included in the two previous PLS models in order to reflect the influence of the regional environment. Then, a multigroup analysis was performed to look for statistically significant differences in path coefficients (Chin, 1998; Chin & Dibbern, 2010).

Table 18.1 Summary of characteristics of the subsamples

Country	Spain	Morocco
Population	8.424.102	33.170.000
Sample	Female University students	Female University students
Geographic area	Spain (Huelva) (University of Huelva)	Morocco (Tangier) (Université Abdemalek Essaâdi)
Sample design	A stratified random systematic sample of university women	A stratified random systematic sample of university women
Sample size	200 questionnaires	274 questionnaires
Collection of information	Personal questionnaires	Personal questionnaires
Date of field work	End of 2015	End of 2015

Results

The analysis of the measurement model for the full sample found low loadings for a small number of items. They were removed, and the model was run again. Scores regarding item reliability, construct reliability, and convergent and discriminant validity were then satisfactory (see Table 18.2).

Table 18.2 Reliability and convergent validity analysis for the full sample (Tangier and Huelva, N=474).

Construct	Items	Loadings	Communalities	Cronbach	AVE
Social Entr. Self-Efficacy	WSESE2	0.80	0.64	0.94	0.65
	WSESE5	0.78	0.60		
	WSESE6	0.88	0.76		
	WSESE7	0.86	0.74		
	WSESE8	0.83	0.70		
	WSESE9	0.82	0.67		
	WSESE10	0.75	0.56		
	WSESE11	0.83	0.69		
	WSESE12	0.76	0.57		
	WSESE13	0.76	0.58		
Entrepreneurial Passion	WEPAS1	0.76	0.58	0.87	0.65
	WEPAS2	0.82	0.67		
	WEPAS3	0.81	0.66		
	WEPAS5	0.84	0.71		
	WEPAS6	0.79	0.62		
Social Entr. Intention	WSEI	1.00	1.00	1.00	1.00

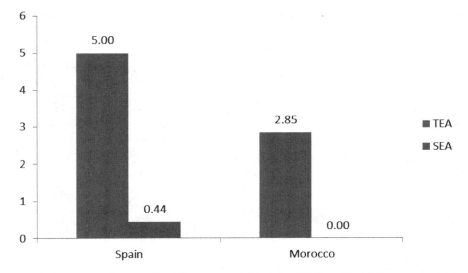

Figure 18.2 Comparison between Total Entrepreneurial Activity (TEA) and Social Entrepreneurial Activity (SEA) levels (% of adult Female Population)

Source: GEM 2015a, 2015b, 2012.

254   Juan Diego Borrero

Table 18.3 t-Tests for multigroup analysis: Women's differences

Links	Spanish women	Moroccan women	Path diff.	p. value	sig.05
WSESE->WSEI	0.06	0.23	0.16	0.07	no
WEPAS->WSEI	0.51	0.39	0.12	0.18	no

The models were tested separately on the subsample for all Moroccan women and the subsample for Spanish women. The model showed 21.9 per cent for Spanish women but only 9.63 per cent for Moroccan women of variance in WSEI (see Figure 18.2). The values reached after running the bootstrapping test (with 5,000 samples) showed that the relationship between WEPAS and women's social entrepreneurial intention were positive and significant for both female groups – stronger for Spanish women – but that the relationship between WSESE and women's social entrepreneurial intention was not significant for Spanish women. Therefore, H1b is supported whereas H1a is not.

To statistically test H2, a permutation test for multigroup analysis (Chin & Dibbern, 2010) was carried out (Table 18.3). As may be seen, there are no significant differences between women from Morocco and Spain. Therefore, this result leads to the rejection of H2a and H2b.

Discussion and conclusions

The phenomenon of female entrepreneurship is observed in many economies; the intensity of it may be higher or lower, depending on the country analysed. The source of this phenomenon comprises to a large extent discrimination against women in the labour market resulting in difficulties in finding employment (high unemployment) and limited access to some occupations (gender-related occupational segregation), including the access to managerial positions (glass ceiling). Difficulties with finding any paid work or a job offering decent earnings and the lack of chances for promotion and obtaining a managerial position push women into self-employment. Social business is undoubtedly one of the forms of economic activation of women who are unemployed or threatened with unemployment.

Cultural factors have a significant impact on the varied levels of the entrepreneurship phenomenon in particular countries, on entrepreneurial intentions, and on the fact that women constitute a definite minority among entrepreneurs. Statistical data clearly show that the intensity of women's entrepreneurship varies from country to country: the rate of female entrepreneurs is lower in Morocco than in Spain (a developed country with a high gender equality index) (EIGE, 2015). Potential women entrepreneurs from Spain have great entrepreneurial passion about SEI but low social entrepreneurial self-efficacy, while women from Morocco have awareness of and confidence in their abilities to handle a particular social problem in the market.

The results of the survey carried out in Morocco and Spain confirm that Spanish women are not so different from Moroccan women in terms of their social entrepreneurial intention. It is true that it has not studied the entire population, only university students, but this sample fits with the social entrepreneurship reality.

The empirical analysis carried out in this chapter has also yielded two main results. First, results show that women's perceived entrepreneurial passion constitutes an antecedent of women's social entrepreneurial intention, although our findings do not demonstrate a significant relationship regarding perceived social entrepreneurial self-efficacy among Spanish women. Thus, this chapter does not confirm the applicability of the TPB theory and entrepreneurial event model to women's social entrepreneurship, irrespective of region. Also, Spanish women were found to exhibit stronger entrepreneurial passion than Moroccan women but, on the other hand Spanish women were found to exhibit weaker social entrepreneurial self-efficacy than Moroccan women. Although Spanish women are more sensitive towards social entrepreneurial intention, they do not feel confident in their abilities to start an entrepreneurial adventure. Spanish women are aware that they need more management skills to develop a social vision and obtain social impact. To do this, it would be advisable to include these skills in academic programmes through courses on entrepreneurship and social innovation. On the other hand, Moroccan women need more education on issues related to innovation, creativity, empowerment and personal development, in order to obtain greater entrepreneurial passion for social entrepreneurship.

Second, regarding their views of the regions around them, both female groups have similar perceptions about their desire (WEPAS) and feasibility (WSESE) regarding the social entrepreneurial activity (WSEI). Thus, our results do not detect significant differences in social entrepreneurial perception among women between developed and developing countries, as the scholars point out (Bertaux & Crabe, 2007; García-Cabrera & García-Soto, 2008; Liñán & Chen, 2009; Roomi & Parrot, 2008; Verheul et al., 2006; Wells et al., 2003).

Acknowledgments

This research was partially supported by the Andalusian International Cooperation Agency (AACID), under 2013DEC010 and 2014DEC010 projects. I am thankful to my colleagues Said Balhadj and Driss Ferhane from Université Abdelmalek Essaâdi who facilitated the data collection process.

Notes

1 The Maghreb is usually defined as much or most of the region of western North Africa or Northwest Africa, west of Egypt (https://en.wikipedia.org/wiki/Maghreb).
2 The Mudawana is the personal status code, also known as the family code, in Moroccan law (https://en.wikipedia.org/wiki/Mudawana).

References

Ajzen, I. (1991). The theory of planned behavior. *Organizational Behavior and Human Decision Processes, 50*(2), 179–211.
Anna, A. L., Chandler, G. N., Jansen, E., & Mero, N. P. (1999). Women business owners in traditional and non-traditional industries. *Journal of Business Venturing, 15*(3), 279–303.
Arenius, P., & Minniti, M. (2005). Perceptual variables and nascent entrepreneurship. *Small Business Economics, 24*(3), 233–247.
Bagozzi, R. P., Dholakia, U., & Basuron, S. (2003). How effortful decisions get enacted: The motivating role of decision processes, desires & anticipated emotions. *Journal of Behavioral Decision Making, 16*, 273–295.
Bandura, A. (1977). Self-efficacy: Towards a unifying theory of behavioural change. *Psychological Review, 84*, 191–215.
Battilana, J., & Lee, M. (2014). Advancing research on hybrid organizing: Insights from the study of social enterprises. *The Academy of Management Annals, 8*(1), 397–441.
Bergkvist, L., & Rossiter, J. R. (2007). The predictive validity of multiple-item versus single-item measures of the same constructs. *Journal of Marketing Research, 44*(2), 175–184.

Bertaux, N., & Crable, E. (2007). Learning about women, economic development, entrepreneurship and the environment in India: A case study. *Journal of Developmental Entrepreneurship, 12*(4), 467–478.

Bornstein, D. (1998).Changing the world on a shoestring. *Atlantic Monthly, 281*(1), 34–39.

Boschee, J. (1995). Social entrepreneurship. *Across the Board, 32*(3), 20–25.

Bowden, J., & Mummery, P. (2009). *Understanding feminism.* New York: Acumen Press.

Bradley, H. (2007). *Gender.* London: Polity Press.

Cardon, M. S., Gregoire, D. A., Stevens, C. E., & Patel, P. C. (2013). Measuring entrepreneurial passion: Conceptual foundations and scale validation. *Journal of Business Venturing, 28*, 373–396.

Cardon, M. S., Wincent, J., Singh, J., & Drnovsek, M. (2009). The nature and experience of entrepreneurial passion. *Academy of Management Review, 34*(3), 511–532.

Carter, S., & Marlow, S. (2007). Female entrepreneurship: Theoretical perspectives and empirical evidence. In N. Carter, C. Henry, & B. O'Cinneide (Eds), *Promoting female entrepreneurs: Implications for education* (pp. 11–37). Training and Policy. London: Routledge.

Chen, C. C., Greene, P. G., & Crick, A. (1998). Does entrepreneurial self-efficacy distinguish entrepreneurs from managers? *Journal of Business Venturing, 13*(4), 295–316.

Chin, W. W. (1998). The partial least squares approach to structural equation modelling. In G.A. Marcoulides (Ed.), *Modern methods for business research* (pp. 295–336). Mahwah, NJ: Lawrence Erlbaum Associates.

Chin, W. W., & Dibbern, J. (2010). An introduction to a permutation based procedures for multi-group PLS analysis: Results tests of differences on simulated data and cross cultural analysis of the sourcing of information system services between Germany and the USA. In E. Vinzi, W. W. Chin, J. Henseler, & H. Wang (Eds), *Handbook of partial least square: Concepts, methods and applications* (pp. 171–193). Springer handbooks of computational statistics series. Heidelberg, Dordrecht, London, New York: Springer.

Chung, C. (2014). *A report on the social enterprise landscape in Morocco: Social enterprise.* London: British Council. Retrieved from https://www.britishcouncil.org/sites/default/files/morocco_report.pdf.

Cohen, M. A. (2012). Empathy in business ethics education. *Journal of Business Ethics Education, 9*, 359–375.

Cukier, W., Trenholm, S., Carl, D., & Gekas, G. (2011). Social entrepreneurship: A content analysis. *Journal of Strategic Innovation and Sustainability, 7*(1), 99–119.

Dees, J.G. (1998). *The meaning of 'social entrepreneurship'.* Kauffman Foundation and Stanford University. Available at: https://entrepreneurship.duke.edu/news-item/the-meaning-of-social-entrepreneurship/.

Dholakia, U., & Bagozzi, R. (2002). Mustering motivation to enact decisions: How decision process characteristics influence goal realizations. *Journal of Behavioral Decision Making, 15*, 167–188.

Diamantopoulos, A., Sarstedt, M., Fuchs, C., Wilczynski, P., & Kaiser, S. (2012). Guidelines for choosing between multi-item and single-item scales for construct measurement: A predictive validity perspective. *Journal of the Acad. Marketing Science, 40*, 434–449. doi:10.1007/s11747-011-0300-3.

Dris-Aït-Hamadouche, L. (2008). La mujer en el Magreb. Estereotipos y realidades. In Y. H. Zoubir & H. Amirah Fernández (Eds), *El Magreb. Realidades nacionales y dinámicas regionales* (pp. 255–282). Madrid: Editorial Síntesis.

Eddleston, K. A., & Powell, G. N. (2008). The role of gender identity in explaining sex differences in business owners' career satisfier preferences. *Journal of Business Venturing, 23*(2), 244–256.

European Institute for Gender Equality (EIGE) (2015). *Promoting Women's Economic Independence and Entrepreneurship: Good Practices.* Retrieved from http://eige.europa.eu/rdc/eige-publications/promoting-womens-economic-independence-and-entrepreneurship-good-practices.

Feliu, L. (2004). *El jardín secreto. Los defensores de los Derechos Humanos en Marruecos.* Madrid: Catarata.

Fuchs, C., & Diamantopoulos, A. (2009). Using single-item measures for construct measurement in management research. *Business Administration Review, 69*(2), 195–210.

García-Cabrera, A.M., & García-Soto, M. G. (2008). Cultural differences and entrepreneurial behavior: An intra-country cross-cultural analysis in Cape Verde. *Entrepreneurship and Regional Development, 20*(5), 451–483.

GEM Consortium (2012). 2009 Report on social entrepreneurship. *Global Entrepreneurship Monitor.*

GEM Consortium (2015a). Informe GEM España 2015. *Global Entrepreneurship Monitor.*

GEM Consortium (2015b). La Dynamique Entrepreneuriale au Maroc 2015. *Global Entrepreneurship Monitor.*

Gupta, V. K., Turban, D. B., Wasti, S. A., & Sikdar, A. (2009). The role of gender stereotypes in perceptions of entrepreneurs and intentions to become an entrepreneur. *Entrepreneurship Theory and Practice, 33*(2), 397–417.

Hockerts, K. (2015). The Social Entrepreneurial Antecedents Scale (SEAS): A validation study. *Social Enterprise Journal,* 11(3), 260–280.

Holt, S., & Marques, J. (2012). Empathy in leadership: Appropriate or misplaced? An empirical study on a topic that is asking for attention. *Journal of Business Ethics, 105*(1), 95–105.

Hundley, G. (2001). Why women earn less than men in self-employment. *Journal of Labour Research, 22,* 817–829.

Huysentruyt, M. (2014). Women's social entrepreneurship and innovation. *OECD Local Economic and Employment Development (LEED)* Working Papers, 2014/01. OECD Publishing. doi:10.1787/5jxzkq2sr7d4-en.

Jolliffe, D., & Farrington, D. P. (2006). Development and validation of the basic empathy scale. *Journal of Adolescence, 29*(4), 589–611.

Kickul, J., Wilson, F., Marlino, D. & Barbosa, S. D. (2008). Are misalignments of perceptions and self-efficacy causing gender gaps in entrepreneurial intentions among our nation's teens? *Journal of Small Business and Enterprise Development, 15*(2), 321–335.

Krueger, N. F., & Brazeal, D. V. (1994). Entrepreneurial potential and potential entrepreneurs. *Entrepreneurship: Theory and Practice, 18,* 91–91.

Krueger, N. F., Reilly, M. D., & Carsrud, A. L. (2000). Competing models of entrepreneurial intentions. *Journal of Business Venturing, 15*(5), 411–432.

Liñán, F., & Chen, Y. W. (2009). Development and cross-cultural application of a specific instrument to measure entrepreneurial intentions. *Entrepreneurship Theory and Practice, 33*(3), 593–617.

Mair, J., & Noboa, E. (2006). Social entrepreneurship: How intentions to create a social venture are formed. In J. Mair, J. Robinson & K. Hockerts (Eds), *Social entrepreneurship* (pp. 121–136). New York: Palgrave Macmillan.

Marlow, S., & McAdam, M. (2013).Gender and entrepreneurship advancing debate and challenging myths: Exploring the mystery of the under-performing female entrepreneur. *International Journal of Entrepreneurial Behavior & Research, 19*(1), 114–124.

Marlow, S., Henry, C., & Carter, S. (2009). Exploring the impact of gender upon women's business ownership. *International Small Business Journal, 27*(2), 139–148.

Marlow, S., Shaw, E. & Carter, S. (2008). Constructing female entrepreneurship policy in the UK: Is the USA a relevant role model? *Environmental Planning C, 26*(1), 335–351.

Matera, B. (2015). *Report on external factors that represent hurdles to European female entrepreneurship (2015/2111(INI)).* European Parliament. Committee of Women's Rights and Gender Equality. doi: A8–0369/2015. 17.12.2015.

Minniti, M., & Nardone, C. (2007). Being in someone else's shoes: Gender and nascent entrepreneurship. *Small Business Economics Journal, 28*(2–3), 223–239.

Mueller, S. L., & Dato-On, M. C. (2008). Gender-role orientation as a determinant of entrepreneurial self-efficacy. *Journal of Developmental Entrepreneurship, 13*(1). 3–20.

Murphy, P. J, & Coombes, S. M. (2009). A model of social entrepreneurial discovery. *Journal of Business Ethics, 87,* 325–336.

Niezink, L. W., Siero, F. W., Dijkstra, P., Buunk, A. P., & Barelds, D. P. H. (2012). Empathic concern: Distinguishing between tenderness and sympathy. *Motivation and Emotion, 36*(4), 544–549.

OECD (2003). *Women's entrepreneurship: Issues and policies.* Working Party on Small and Medium-Sized Enterprises and Entrepreneurship. Paris: OECD.

Pache, A. C., & Chowdhury, I. (2012). Social entrepreneurs as institutionally embedded entrepreneurs: Toward a new model of social entrepreneurship education. *Academy of Management Learning & Education, 11*(3), 494–510.

Poggesi, S., Mari, M., & De Vita L. (2015). Family and work–life balance mechanisms. What is their impact on the performance of Italian female service firms? *Entrepreneurship and Innovation, 16*(1), 43–53. doi:10.5367/ijei.2015.0173.

Pérez, M. A., & Rebollo, M. J. (2009). El Islam en la vida de la mujer a través de los tiempos. *Cauriensia, 4,* 227–247.

R Core Team (2016). *R: A language and enviroment for statistical computing. R foundation for statistical computing*. Vienna. R version 3.3.1. www.r-project.org.

Radin Siti Aishah Radin A Rahman, & Zaidatol Akmaliah Lope Pihie. (2014). Validation of a social entrepreneurial self-efficacy. *IOSR Journal of Business and Management, 16*(11), 133–141.

Roomi, M. A., & Parrot, G. (2008). Barriers to progression of women entrepreneurs in Pakistan. *Journal of Entrepreneurship, 17*(1), 59–72.

Rossiter, J. R. (2002). The C-OAR-SE procedure for scale development in marketing. *International Journal of Research in Marketing, 19*(4), 305–335.

Rouse, J., & Kitching, J. (2006). Do enterprise programmes leave women holding the baby? *Environmental Planning C, 24*(1), 5–19.

Sanchez, G. (2013). *PLS Path Modeling with R*. Berkeley, CA: Trowchez editions.

Sanchez, G., Trinchera, L., & Russolillo, G. (2015). *Partial Least Squares Path Modeling (PLS-PM) Analysis for both Metric and non-Metric Data, as Well as REBUS Analysis*. R package version 0.4.7. Retrieved from https://cran.r-project.org.

Sánchez-Franco, M. J., & Roldán, J. L. (2005). Web acceptance and usage model. *Internet Research-Electronic Networking Applications and Policy, 15*(1), 21–48.

Shapero, A., & Sokol, L. (1982). The social dimensions of entrepreneurship. *Encyclopedia of entrepreneurship* (pp. 72–90). Englewood Cliffs, NJ: Prentice Hall.

Smith, I. H., & Woodworth, W. (2012). Developing social entrepreneurs and social innovators: A social identity and self-efficacy approach. *Academy of Management Learning & Education, 11*, 390–407.

Strong, K. C., Ringer, R. C., & Taylor, S. A. (2001). The rules of stakeholders satisfaction (timeliness, honesty, empathy). *Journal of Business Ethics, 32*(3), 219–230.

Urban, B. (2013). Social entrepreneurship in an emerging economy: A focus on the institutional environment and social entrepreneurial self-efficacy. *Managing Global Transitions, 11*(1), 3–25.

Van Ryzin, G. G., Grossman, S., DiPadova-Stocks, L., & Bergrud, E. (2009). Portrait of the social entrepreneur: Statistical evidence from a US panel. *Voluntas, 20*, 129–140.

Veciana, J. M., Aponte, M., & Urbano, D. (2005). University student's attitudes towards entrepreneurship: A two countries comparison. *International Entrepreneurship and Management Journal, 1*, 165–182.

Verheul, I., van Stel, A., & Thurik, R. (2006). Explaining female and male entrepreneurship at the country level. *Entrepreneurship and Regional Development, 18*(2), 151–183.

Watson, J., & Newby, R. (2005). Biological sex, Stereotypical sex-roles and SME owner characteristics. *International Journal of Entrepreneurial Behavior and Research, 11*(2), 129–143.

Weber, P. S., Weber, J. E., Sleeper, B. R., & Scheider, K. L. (2004). Self-efficacy toward service, civic participation and the business student: Scale development and validation. *Journal of Business Ethics, 49*(4), 359–369. doi:10.1023/B:BUSI.0000020881.58352.ab.

Wells, B., Pfantz, T. J., & Byrne, J. (2003). Russian women business owners: Evidence of entrepreneurship in a transition Economy. *Journal of Developmental Entrepreneurship, 8*(1), 59–73.

Wilson, F., & Tagg, S. (2010). Social constructionism and personal constructivism: Getting the business owner's view on the role of sex and gender. *International Journal of Gender and Entrepreneurship, 2*(1), 68–82.

Witkamp, M. J., Royakkers, L. M., & Raven, R. P. (2011). From cowboys to diplomats: Challenges for social entrepreneurship in the Netherlands. *Voluntas, 22*, 283–310.

Zahn-Waxler, C., & Radke-Yarrow, M. (1990). The origins of empathic concern. *Motivation and Emotion, 14*(2), 107–130.

Zhao, H., Siebert, S. E., & Hills, G. E. (2005). The mediating role of self-efficacy in the development of entrepreneurial intentions. *The Journal of Applied Psychology, 90*(6), 1265–1272.

Section 3

Moving forward

19 The lean scientific canvas method

A proposal to foster women's entrepreneurship in Mexico

Verónica Ilián Baños Monroy, José Manuel Saiz-Álvarez and Edgar Rogelio Ramírez Solís

The business model as a concept is not only part of the academic language but also many practitioners, consultants and entrepreneurs recently use it in their businesses. In this sense, Alexander Osterwalder, founder and consultant of Strategyzer, and Yves Pigneur, a professor at the University of Lausanne (Switzerland), both define the business model canvas (BMC) as the way how an organization creates, delivers, and captures business value (Osterwalder & Pigneur, 2010). This model offers the possibility of fitting a firm's business model in nine boxes or blocks: key partners, key activities, key resources, value proposition, customer relationship, channels, customer segments, cost structure and revenue streams. The BMC is a powerful tool that creates a shared language during the definition of businesses and is an instrument for creating hypotheses using brainstorming combined with an informal way of testing, which is a disadvantage.

The BMC is a gender-neutral conceptual approach, as it does not discriminate between men and women because they are equally treated. During our interactions with under-graduate and graduate entrepreneurship students, we found that both the BMC and the lean business model (LBM) are static planning tools to develop ideas for scientific research, and especially for dissertation proposals using an entrepreneurial mindset. As a result, pro-spective and actual entrepreneurs can plan and validate their ideas keeping in mind users and customers achieved. This planning-based perspective forces them to think how their projects create value for present and future users.

Although the BMC is gender-neutral, our proposed model is female-oriented and based on the 'lean start-up' methodology, seminally developed by Ries (2011) who considers that some business activities create value, while others are considered waste for start-ups. In fact, 'new projects are usually measured and held accountable to milestones and deadlines. When a project is on track, on time, and on a budget, entrepreneurs use well their intuition. But this intuition is dead wrong' (Ries, 2011, p. 45). The novelty of our approach is that women's entrepreneurship is introduced in the analysis, so our proposed model is gender non-neutral. When entrepreneurs present some research ideas, they think these ideas can work if the scientific method is applied. Nevertheless, the truth is they usually do not take into account the final users' needs. Of course, this new gender non-neutral model, barely used in pure research, only appears in applied sciences.

Women's entrepreneurship is of increasing importance in Mexico. But, according to OECD data for 2017, Mexican women face significant obstacles when they desire to participate in the labour market. These obstacles are mainly due to the burden of unpaid work, as Mexican women spend four hours a day more of unpaid work than men. Besides, traditional roles of the genre, especially in rural areas, where women are mainly engaged in the care of children, and the lack of policies to balance work and life family, due to the lack of supply of child care services and flexible working practices, expulse women from the labour market. As a result, traditional family based social structures should be more flexible to foster female entrepreneurs.

The objective of this work is to present a useful framework for women entrepreneurs as a tool to identify problems and solutions focused on better business strategies and market research proposals having into mind women's entrepreneurship. Three out of five small and medium enterprises (SMEs) are female entrepreneurs in Mexico (Secretaría de Hacienda y Crédito Público, 2013), so women's entrepreneurship is of considerable importance in Mexico. We use a lean scientific canvas method (LSCM) to study the importance of female entrepreneurship in Mexico.

The structure of this chapter is as follows. First, we show a brief theoretical approach on the scientific method. Then, we analyse both the lean canvas model (LCM) and the BMC to know their origins, functions and purposes. Due to this, it will be easier to apply the LSCM explained in the last section of this work. Our chapter ends with some conclusions.

A brief approach on the scientific method

According to McLelland (2006), the scientific method consists of the following steps:

1   *Observation*, based on analysing phenomena, events or problems that can start by having curiosity, or by a desire to resolve an issue. In fact, Popper argues that any event or issue must be observable (Midgley, 2008).
2   *Question.* The observation will always cause questions to answer the curiosity generated. As this step has the purpose of narrowing the problem in specific terms (Saiz-Álvarez, Cuervo-Arango, & Coduras, 2013), issues such as: 'why?', 'how?', 'when?', 'who?' and many others will be common, as well as the collection and data measurement.
3   *Hypothesis.* The possible 'educated guess regarding the question's answer' (McLelland, 2006) given to all the issues formulated due to the knowledge previously obtained based on observations are called hypotheses, that must be testable and feasible. Sometimes assumptions can fail after being tested, but they can be correct if context or variables change. In this sense, it is important to remember for proving hypotheses; it is mandatory to identify dependent and independent variables affecting the phenomenon analysed.
4   *Experiment.* Hypotheses must be tested using different statistical and mathematical methods. Depending on the result, experts can consider publishing the analysis. In fact, experimental designs are the most critical stages in the scientific method when exists an interplay between an innate response and calculation focused on generating new discoveries (Hall, 2011). Thus, experimentation leads to eliminate inconsistencies and causes long-term innovation, that it can be in products and services (product innovation), or new strategies used to produce and deliver goods and services (process innovation). Besides, firms can also achieve new ways of thinking (paradigm innovation), and changes in the context how to insert products and services in the market (position innovation) (Mosey, Noke, & Kirkham, 2017; Tidd, Bessant, & Pavitt, 2005).
5   *Evaluation.* After having used quantitative and qualitative methods to analyse data and to interpret results for accepting or rejecting them, as these results define the

path of the research (Schulte, 2003). These evaluations and conclusions must be public in scientific meetings and conferences. Both results and assessments obtained can be the basis for new studies and discoveries. For this reason, it is noteworthy to highlight the importance of their publication, as researchers need a constructive evaluation for their ideas to be accurate, innovative and comprehensive. Although this is the most common way or sequence to implement the scientific method, in some occasions scientific discoveries have been the result of accidents (e.g., penicillin), coincidences (e.g., dynamite) or random. As a result, this sequence is not the 'magic potion' (Spiece & Colosi, 2000).

The scientific method is a tool to decrease uncertainty in the analysis of a phenomenon using critical thinking (McLelland, 2006). In fact, critical thinking is an essential element that researchers need when following their scientific-based processes, where theories are continuously accepted, rejected and suspended (Proulx, 2004). Without critical thinking, the individual is not able to make judgements following the scientific method process to validate (or not) information and new knowledge.

We propose mixing the LSM and a scientific method defined as the systematic and replicable way of research formed by general questions based on experience, testable hypotheses and data to evaluate testable hypotheses for their rejection or acceptance, and able to test predictions (Flowerdew, 2009). According to Vining (2013), the scientific method is a process defined by problems aiming to be solved using general and theoretical factors to generate and analyse data, with the final goal of drawing practical and theoretical conclusions.

Women are increasingly involved in research with the inclusion of the scientific method in their works. In Mexico, 34.9 per cent of the researchers at the National Researchers System (in Spanish, SNI *Sistema Nacional de Investigadores*) are women, especially in fields such as physics, mathematics and engineering (Sánchez, 2016). Women are gradually increasing the number of female scientists in Mexico, so the gender gap in science is slowly decreasing mainly due to the increasing percentage of women studying tertiary education in that country.

Currently, the use of the scientific method and the development of each one of its stages are continuously changing. Social, economic and political contexts where female entrepreneurs develop their skills are always evolving, as female entrepreneurs face new phenomena to solve and explain problems. Hence, researchers develop more theories and resources. Perspectives, information, technology and limitations are changing due to globalization and human diversity, as experts have developed advanced mathematical tools focused on proving theories and strategies (Bisgaard, 2000). Therefore, and due to constant changes and knowledge acceleration, firms have adopted innovations, and has been adapted both to science and to scientific methods (Kelly, 2010). This policy provides the possibility to use it in conjunction with LCM to develop new entrepreneurial strategies.

The lean canvas methodology

As we mentioned early, a hypothesis is an educated guess that provides a possible answer to a phenomenon with the use of predictions and deductive logic (Spiece & Colosi, 2000). In business, when entrepreneurs come up with new ideas, they decide to make it real by creating a vision and a plan of activities to launch (Maurya, 2012). However, most of the time, the business plan does not work, because it is based on untestable hypotheses, and on entrepreneurs who ignore how to draw them.

Based on the plan of activities, female entrepreneurs can draw assumptions, but it has the disadvantage of being static, hard and takes a lot of time. Due to these difficulties, a new way to create a business plan based on BMC has arisen, as the easiest and the simplest representation of a programme of activities (Osterwalder & Pigneur, 2010), because it

> helps organisations to conduct structured, tangible, and strategic conversations around new businesses or existing ones. Leading global companies use BMC to manage strategy or create new growth engines, while start-ups use it in their search for the right business model. The BMC's primary objective is to help companies move beyond product-centric thinking and towards business model thinking.
>
> (Osterwalder, 2013, p. 24)

The BMC is composed of nine blocks: customer segments, value propositions, customer relationships, revenue streams, key resources, key activities, key partnerships and cost structure. In other words, it illustrates the actual business situation, its central value proposition, and its main opportunity areas (Figure 19.1). However, it is a very different story when we talk about entrepreneurship, especially when women manage businesses, due to the unique needs and obstacles that female entrepreneurs face.

Based on the BMC, it created the LCM as a strategic tool. Before exploring the LCM, it is necessary to understand the concept of lean start-up defined by Ries (2011). This idea has its roots on the lean ideology taken from the lean manufacturing revolution pioneered by Taiichi Ohno and Shigeo Shingo from Toyota. This thinking process focuses on making more organizations that are efficient by eliminating non-valued activities, and by reducing cycle times. As a result, profits are increased (Näslund, 2008).

Some successful books popularized the lean start-up methodology. In 2003, Steve Blank wrote *The Four Steps to the Epiphany*, articulating for the first time that start-ups were no smaller versions of large companies. In 2010, Alexander Osterwalder and Yves Pigneur launched *Business Model Generation*. In 2011, Eric Ries published an overview in *The Lean Startup*. Moreover, in 2012 Bob Dorf and Steve Blank summarized the lean techniques in a handbook named *The Startup Owner's Manual*.

When combined with design thinking, LCM has four fundamental principles according to Link (2016): first, rather than engaging in months of planning and research, men and female entrepreneurs accept that all they have is a series of untested hypotheses and strategies. Thus, instead of writing a business plan, entrepreneurs just make their BMC. Second, lean start-ups created by men and female entrepreneurs use an approach called *customer development* to test their products. They go outside and ask potential users, customers and partners for feedback on all elements of the business model. As speed is the name of the game, new ventures rapidly assemble minimum viable products and immediately elicit customer feedback. Third, lean start-ups use *agile development* that works with customer development. This process eliminates wasted time and resources by developing iterative and incremental products. Therefore, the lean start-up is a set of practices that helps entrepreneurs, women included, to increase their odds of building a successful start-up under extreme uncertainty (Ries, 2011) while avoiding waste before full production, and products or services launched to the market. Finally, the combination of design thinking and the lean canvas method develops innovative ideas in start-ups and in existing companies, what strengthens the company.

At this moment, the scientific method gets involved with lean start-up. Any entrepreneur and especially female entrepreneurs, who come up with ideas and decide to make them

The entrepreneurial gender gap in Mexico   265

real, will face uncertainty about business success and challenges to deal with that stress (Grant & Ferris, 2012). Many questions and assumptions arise. The lean start-up method uses experiments as part of the scientific method to test the assumptions made, and know which parts of the business are valuable, and which are not (Ries, 2011).

According to Maurya (2012), the lean start-up embodies the customer into all the process. All experiments have to end in consumer learning, and men and female entrepreneurs must have progressed to demonstrate their customer value. Through a continuous customer feedback, the founder develops the product in a single process to produce services and products that people desire.

One of the biggest benefits that entrepreneurs get by using new business strategies, instead of following market research information, is that they can learn from failure. Before launching the bulk of mass production and selling taking place, low-risk procedures used with samples or prototypes avoid market failure. As a result, both production and commercial risks diminish. In fact, experimentation provides information that is more valuable; hypotheses are accepted or rejected, demanding less time, and satisfying both the new data and customer needs. However, the most significant result is the creation of a sustainable business around the start-up's vision (Ries, 2011). After having analysed results derived from the implemented experimentation, entrepreneurs can decide how, when, where, why and what to do to modify their business ideas to succeed.

All these facts contribute to the development of the LCM proposed by Maurya (2012), with the objective of helping entrepreneurs, mainly women, during their start-up journey. This tool has the characteristics of being a combination between the BMC and the lean start-up which gives place to its name (Maurya, 2012), taking the 'keywords' of both concepts. As a result, the LCM is the sum of the BMC and lean start-up.

Unlike the BMC, the LCM has a scientific/problem approach by being more focused on problem-solving (Joyce & Paquin, 2016). This model mainly focuses on start-ups. To understand the main differences between these two models, we show in Table 19.1 a BMC-lean canvas comparison, based on six elements: target, focus, customers, approach, competition and application.

Table 19.1 BMC *vs.* LCM

—	*Business model canvas*	*Lean canvas model*
Approach	Constructive-oriented	Problem-solution
Competitive advantages	No	Yes
Customer segmentation	Yes	No
Focus	Advisors, consultants, entrepreneurs, investors	Only entrepreneurs
Innovation	Secondary	Primary
Objective	More clients	Better products and services
Quality-based processes	Secondary	Primary
R&D	Secondary	Primary
Target	Start-ups and firms	Start-ups purely
Value proposition	Yes	No

Source: Created by the authors.

When complexity defines women's entrepreneurship, experts use both the BMC and the LCM. An example is the business strategy followed by María Asunción Arámburuzabala, CEO of Tresalia Investment Group, and responsible for the selling of Grupo Modelo by US$20.1 billion to the Belgian beer group Anheuser-Busch InBev S.A. In fact, she is the only Latin American woman on the Forbes list as one of the most powerful 100 women in the world. Another example is Cintia Angulo Leseigneur, president of Alstom Group Mexico, and exCEO of Eléctricité de France (EdF) in Mexico. Both multinationals use BMC and LCM in their daily operations.

- *Problem & customer segments.* These two blocks are joint and are the essential part of the LCM. Entrepreneurs must correctly identify both problems and customer segments to be able to offer a right value proposition. The contractor must identify at least three main difficulties related to women's entrepreneurship that his/her target market needs, find out how these current problems are solved, identify customers and users, and finally, with this information, select the early adopters of products or services. When these problems are not correctly recognized or understood from the very beginning, solutions proposed will not be valid (Maurya, 2015a). As a result, it is always important to determine the root of an issue to offer adequate solutions.
- *Unique value proposition.* The unique value proposition (UVP) is one of the most outstanding parts of the LCM and probably the most challenging, as it is the essence of products and the answer to customers' problems. The key is that goods and services produced and offered by female entrepreneurs have to be different and creative to attract customers. According to Maurya (2012), seven factors are crucial to defining a UVP. First, to identify a significant difference in the product or service offered in the market. Second, to recognize target, early adopters. Third, to have effective communication results on the benefits received by customers when using products or services. Fourth, to pick up keywords to identify products. Fifth, to fully answer threefold questions: what (product), who (customer) and why (usage reason). Sixth, to analyse other UVPs. And finally, seventh, to adopt a high-concept pitch to identify products or services sold quickly.
- *Solution.* It is important to start thinking about possible solutions to the problems identified related to women's entrepreneurship, although they are not the final ones.
- *Channels.* A critical aspect of women's entrepreneurship is to define the path that will follow to reach customers by looking for different options and contacting suppliers and intermediaries.
- *Revenue and cost structure.* Even when products and services were not ready, expenses and incomes must define an accurate price. Setting a price is a difficult task, as it signs product branding or positioning, and determines the customer's segment. The price cannot be too high or low, due to the risk of damaging both product prestige and firm profitability. Therefore, we recommend female entrepreneurs to start applying a pricing plan, when the price is initially set to try establishing the most suitable price for a product or service, with the aim of reducing the risk of failure.
- *Key metrics.* Entrepreneurs measure key activities needed to offer goods and services and are the primary metrics used to measure business performance.
- *Unfair advantage.* This type of strength defined as valuable, rare, costly to imitate and non-substitutive sustains competitive advantages (Porter, 1985). These capabilities are core competencies and allow firms to have success in business competition, and make companies different from competitors, which can be very expensive or difficult to imitate.

The lean canvas model applied to start-ups for women's entrepreneurship is a new tool that helps businesses to deal with the constant disruption to decrease stress on human resources working in any organization. As a result, it will help female entrepreneurs to be adapted to changes, and to turn these changes to have a positive impact on the enterprise.

Examples of the proper use of the LCM by women's entrepreneurs are the cases of Gabriela Hernández, CEO of General Electric, Mexico, with 11,000 workers distributed in twenty plants in Mexico, and Blanca Treviño, chief executive officer of Softek, with 7,000 employees. On this last case, Treviño's sound management won the Women in Technology's Global Impact Award in 2011.

The lean scientific canvas method

The combination of the Scientific method and the LCM forms the LSCM as one of the leading research and business tools for modern corporations. The primary objective of the LSCM is to serve female entrepreneurs as an instrument to identify problems and to propose viable solutions to elaborate better business proposals and strategies. Most of the time, the LCM correctly used for men and female entrepreneurs aim to develop business ideas, while the scientific method is thought exclusively for academic and research purposes. Nevertheless, as we are now combining science and business, experts created a new tool to help more efficiently entrepreneurs to identify problems, and to build viable solutions applied for female entrepreneurship.

We use every section of the LSCM to build solutions to current problems. Based on the literature, female entrepreneurs will be able to generate new knowledge with the purpose of applying it to real social and business problems. We can define this decision tool as composed of:

- *Customer segment & problem.* As the LCM indicates, both sections are critical and are joint. The first step is to assure that is worth to solve customer-related challenges and needs. Depending on the case, entrepreneurs identify and analyse industries, companies and stakeholders. Once information is enough, entrepreneurs observe and question problems following the scientific method. Managers examine every single factor of the problem using observations and the reason for its existence, structure and consequences. 'Even though start-ups are not an exact science, Lean Start-up is a rigorous process or at a minimum a harsh meta-process that requires the same level of objectivity you would demand from a scientific inquiry' (Maurya, 2015b).
- *Unique value proposition.* This factor is one of the most important elements of the LSCM. In this part, products or service value generate solutions. As shown in Table 19.2, the LSCM is the roadmap for men and female entrepreneurs to determine strategic techniques and experiments with the objective of identifying, as soon as possible, the conditions under which accumulated evidence proves or disproves a hypothesis.
- *Channels.* They are the means used to show market research results for men and female entrepreneurs. Depending on the kind of investigation, it will be the way to show results to customers, organizations and stakeholders concerned.
- *Revenue and cost structure.* For men and female entrepreneurs, it is important to know what they need for carrying out market research, and what we will get in exchange. Besides, women entrepreneurs can actively create knowledge and development of new solutions for their business organizations.

- *Key metrics.* After the implementation and the evaluation of the strategic policies carried out by firms, female entrepreneurs try to find solutions to problems defined by using key metrics. As a result, learning is always in progress, as it demonstrates the ability to use what female entrepreneurs have learned to improve their organizations measured with the primary metrics as the common source of evidence. In fact, measuring learning processes requires a shift of attention from the output of models to their inputs.
- *Continuous communication.* When female entrepreneurs receive ongoing feedback, they learn how to modify their goals, or even how to change all business methodology used in the organization. Therefore, women entrepreneurs are sure of frequently reporting the results of their strategies of activities fulfilled. Communicating progress when attracting new clients is the way to stay grounded on learning, reinforced with iterating productive and commercial processes towards a producing and selling products or services. Without this level of rigour and objectivity, there is a danger of creating goods and services that will be out of the market.

Conclusion

Most start-ups fail because they sometimes work on products and services that are out of the market. When start-ups connect to universities, business results tend to be better, and failures diminish. In this sense, Tecnológico de Monterrey in Mexico has a leading role after having created the TEC Lean Accelerator is the first program developed by a university located in Latin America and the Caribbean that is focused on start-ups using the lean start-up methodology based on creating businesses quickly and efficiently. The goal of this accelerator is to contribute to building scalable start-ups with the aim of generating high impact globally and potentiate the enabling environment for firms produced.

One of the keys to having business success is to follow a fast track both in the creation and acceleration processes defined in a four-stage process, with a total duration of twenty weeks. The stages are (1) Lean Training plus Customer and Problem Discovery (three weeks); (2) Customer, Business Model, and Product Validation (three weeks); (3) Sales and Customer Creation (seven weeks); and (4) Excubation and Company Building (seven weeks). Regarding lean training, defined by a mixture of lean management and practical training, it is also widely used in local government units, non-profit organizations, but above all, in various functional units, such as human resources, accountancy, sales and marketing (Podobinski, 2015).

Both business accelerators and incubators help to diminish the gender gap in the labour market. In fact, there is a necessity of a gender-just inclusive growth in Mexico related to women's entrepreneurship, and in this sense, entrepreneurial education has a vital role to play. Although women (21%) have higher graduation rates of tertiary education than men (18%) (OECD, 2017, data from the Mexican Ministry of Labour) show that 34% of women between 15 and 29 years of age, neither study nor works compared with men (10%).

Entrepreneurs must have a strong research capacity to develop their businesses. Following Cintia Angulo de Leseigneur's ideas, CEO of Alstom in Mexico, published in her corporate biography, 'to stand out in business is critical to open gaps and create previously rare opportunities. Business requires seeing, capture, smell and feel new possibilities to make them possible to attain them. Companies need leadership' (Alstom, 2014). In fact, if entrepreneurs were to reduce their entrepreneurial process to a formula, it would be: act, learn, build, repeat, as they start and see how the market responds (Brown, 2016).

Table 19.2 The lean scientific canvas method

Problem	Solution	Unique value proposition	Continuous communication		Customer segments
Problem identification	Research hypotheses	Single Proposal?	Is your business unique and difficult to imitate?		Industries favoured
Observations & Questions	*Experiment & Hypotheses*	What value are you offering?	Contribution to the company		Whose needs are we solving?
	Redefinition	What would be necessary for the case study unit?			Stakeholders favoured
	Key metrics	Why do you think that someone can be interested?	**Channels**		
	Evaluation		Written publications & oral presentations Mass media		
Cost structure			**Revenue structure**		
Resources needed			Funding & financial aid		
			Patents		
			Sales revenues		

Source: Created by the authors.

At the beginning of this chapter, we mentioned that our aim was to propose a useful framework for women's entrepreneurship to identify problems and solutions that can contribute to elaborate better business proposals and strategies. Higher educational levels achieved by women, and their better integration into the labour market, both have helped to reduce both job and educational gender gaps. In this sense, the application of the LSCM methodology tends to accelerate this ameliorating process. The LSCM is still in an embryonic phase and is a useful tool to create wealth in SMEs, so we expect further developments on this issue in the future.

References

Alstom (2014). *Corporate Biography-Cintia Angulo de Leseigneur, CEO Alstom Mexico*. Mexico D.F.

Bisgaard, S. (2000). The role of scientific method in quality management. *Total Quality Management, 11*(3), 295–306.

Brown, P. B. (2016). *Entrepreneurship for the rest of us: How to create innovation and opportunity everywhere*. New York: Bibliomotion – Taylor & Francis Group.

Flowerdew, R. (2009). Scientific method. In R. Kitchin & N. Thrift (Eds), *International encyclopedia of human geography* (pp. 43–45). Oxford: Elsevier.

Grant, S., & Ferris, K. (2012). Identifying sources of occupational stress in entrepreneurs for measurement. *International Journal of Entrepreneurial Venturing, 4*(4), 351–373.

Hall, B. H. (2011). The internationalization of R&D. *MERIT Working Papers, 049*, United Nations University-Maastricht Economic and Social Research Institute on Innovation and Technology (MERIT).

Joyce, A., & Paquin, R. L. (2016). The triple layered business model canvas: A tool to design more sustainable business models. *Journal of Cleaner Production, 135*, 1474–1486.

Kelly, K. (2010). Evolving the scientific method. *The Scientist, 24*(12), 30–31.

Link, P. (2016). How to become a lean entrepreneur by applying lean start-up and lean canvas? *Advances in Digital Education and Lifelong Learning, 2*, 57–71.

McLelland, C. V. (2016). *The nature of science and the scientific method*. Boulder, CO: The Geological Society of America.

Maurya, A. (2012). *Running lean: Iterate from plan A to a plan that works*. Sebastopol, CA: O'Reilly Media.

Maurya, A. (2015a). 'Why lean canvas *vs.* business model canvas?' Author's blog: Practice trumps theory. http://practicetrumpstheory.com/why-lean-canvas/.

Maurya, A. (2015b). 'How to identify a lean startup'. Author's blog: Practice trumps theory. http://practicetrumpstheory.com/how-to-identify-a-lean-startup/.

Midgley, G. (2008). Systems thinking, complexity and the philosophy of science. *Emergence: Complexity & Organization, 10*(4), 55–73.

Mosey, S., Noke, H., & Kirkham, P. (2017). *Building an entrepreneurial organisation*. London and New York: Routledge.

Näslund, D. (2008). Lean, six sigma and lean sigma: Fads or real process improvement methods? *Business Process Management Journal, 14*(3), 269–287.

OECD (2017). *Education at a Glance 2017*. Paris: OECD.

Osterwalder, A., & Pigneur, I. (2010). *Business model generation: A handbook for visionaries, game changers, and challengers*. New York: John Wiley & Sons.

Osterwalder, A. (2013). A better way to think about your business model. *Harvard Business Review*. https://hbr.org/2013/05/a-better-way-to-think-about-yo/.

Podobinski, M. (2015). Application of lean management methods and techniques in non-production departments of selected enterprises-results of the study. In *14th Conference on Business and Non-Profit Organizations Facing Increased Competition and Growing Customers' Demands*, 5–6 October, Muszyna, Poland, pp. 97–109.

Porter, M. (1985). *Competitive advantage: Creating and sustaining superior performance*. New York: The Free Press.

Proulx, G. (2004). Integrating scientific method & critical thinking in classroom debates on environmental issues. *The American Biology Teacher, 66*(1), 26–33.

Ries, E. (2011). *The lean start up: How today's entrepreneurs use continuous innovation to create radically successful business.* New York: Random House.

Saiz-Alvarez, J. M., Cuervo-Arango, C., & Coduras, A. (2013). Entrepreneurial strategy, innovation, and cognitive capabilities: What role for intuitive SMEs? *Journal of Small Business Strategy, 23*(2), 29–40.

Sánchez, V. (2016). *Mujeres en la Ciencia en México* [Women on science in Mexico]. Mexico, D.F.: CONACYT.

Secretaría de Hacienda y Crédito Público (2013). *La situación de la mujer en México* [Female Situation in Mexico], Mexico, D.F.

Schulte, K.-W. (2003). The role of investment and finance in real estate education and research throughout the world. *Property Management, 21*(1), 97–113.

Spiece, K. R., & Colosi, J. (2000). Redefining the scientific method. *The American Biology Teacher, 62*(1), 32–40.

Tidd, J., Bessant, J., & Pavitt, K. (2005). *Managing innovation: Integrating technological, market and organizational change.* Chichester: John Wiley & Sons.

Vining, G. (2013). Technical advice: Scientific method and approaches for collecting data. *Quality Engineering, 25*(2), 194–201.

20 Beyond the gender-neutral approach

Gender and entrepreneurship as an intertwined social practice

Silvia Gherardi and Barbara Poggio

Although the literature on women entrepreneurship has grown rapidly since 1990, its focus on individual women and their businesses does not explain current patterns of women's entrepreneurship because its basic assumptions position women as inadequate and incomplete entrepreneurs, while there is scant empirical evidence of such underperformance (Mirchandani, 1999; Marlow & McAdam, 2013). This literature has been mainly gender blind, positivistic and in danger of reaching a dead end in the absence of a reflexive critical perspective informing the idea of who can be and what might be an entrepreneur (Ahl & Marlow, 2012; Hughes, Jennings, Brush, Carter, & Welter, 2012). At the beginning of the 2000s, feminist/gender studies conducted a fierce critique of the gender-neutral approach in entrepreneurship studies (Bruni, Gherardi & Poggio, 2004a; Wee and Brooks, 2012). The argument centred on the invisible masculinity supported by the concept of entrepreneurship, and on how masculinity was not only a hidden sub-text but also a normative assumption that marginalizes women entrepreneurs and other forms of masculinity and ethnicity, thus establishing a model of entrepreneurialism that appears to be universal and gendered. Since the critiques against a gender-neutral approach and the plea for a gender/feminist approach are widespread, we shall not repeat them here.

Nevertheless, the relationship between gender and entrepreneurship, and the theoretical approach within which both terms become connected, should be made clearer before a 'gender as a social practice approach' is proposed. In broad terms we can distinguish between two conceptions: the gender *in* entrepreneurship approach and the gendering *of* entrepreneurship. To classify these approaches to gender and entrepreneurship, we employ the categories proposed by Calás, Smircich, and Holvino (2014), who use the expression 'gender *in* organization' as opposed to 'gendering *of* organization'.

Within the gender *in* entrepreneurship approach, most of the studies on women entrepreneurs have not assumed a gender perspective and have contributed to perpetuating the notion of women entrepreneurs as 'female' and rendering women's experiences into a homogeneous category, thus gendering and othering a class of entrepreneurialism. Moreover, from a methodological point of view, most comparative studies on female–male firms have methodological weaknesses (De Bruin, Brush, & Welter, 2007) that emphasize women's subordinate role. They thus reproduce the image of a weak entrepreneurialism because women are represented as universally deficient by gendered association. The minority status of women as business owners is therefore used to allege business underperformance (Marlow & McAdam, 2013). As a result, minor performance differences are magnified to fulfil expectations of gender difference, thus masking the broad similarities between the actual performances of male- and female-owned firms. Accordingly, the current debate surrounding gender pivots upon an assumption of difference contradicted by evidence of similarity.

On the contrary, the expression 'gendering *of* entrepreneurship' denotes the approaches that furnish non-positivist and post-structural critical evaluations of entrepreneurial discourses and practices to demonstrate the profoundly gendered nature of entrepreneurship (Henry, Foss, & Ahl, 2015; Calás, Smircich, & Bourne, 2009). In this approach, feminist theorizing is predicated on the assumptions that gender relations are fundamental in the structuring of society, and that a critical and reflexive lens makes it possible to question how gender relations are 'done' and may be 'done' differently.

We position our argument within the gendering of entrepreneurship literature. More specifically, we shall adopt a practice-based approach to illustrate how gendering and entrepreneuring constitute an intertwined practice that should be studied both at the interaction level – as a situated practice – and at the level of the effects produced by such a practising in society. Not only is gender (and not sex) conceived as a socially constructed phenomenon, it is also produced and reproduced as a social practice at the intersections among bodies, discourses and materialities (Bruni, Gherardi, & Poggio, 2004b). Since the gendering of entrepreneurship is conceived as a sociomaterial practice, both gendering and entrepreneuring are defined as material-semiotic processes that require qualitative methodologies for their empirical analysis (Gherardi & Perrotta, 2014).

The chapter therefore consists of an introduction to a practice-based approach to gender and entrepreneurship, followed by two empirical examples that illustrate how the process of gendering is done through material-discursive practices and how entrepreneuring is gendered in the succession process. It concludes by arguing that the co-production of gendering and entrepreneuring is an unstable, discursively enacted, product which arranges human and non-human elements into a situated practice.

A practice-based approach to gender and entrepreneurship

A practice-based approach starts by conceiving entrepreneurship and gender as a conflated practice that sustains gendered relationships and in turn reconstitutes entrepreneurship and gender as social institutions.

Analysing a situated practice requires a shift in focus from 'actors and their actions' to the way in which actors, materialities, discourses, texts, knowledge and activities are connected and performed within an organized nexus of activities (Gherardi, 2012). A practice is therefore rooted in the seeing, saying and doing of organizational actors in connection with a sociomaterial arrangement. Doing business is a social practice, and so too is 'doing gender', but the latter is less evident than the former because common sense attributes gender to the corporeality of persons and therefore to their being rather than their seeing, doing and saying. Yet when men and women set up as entrepreneurs they do not separate the two practices; instead, they reproduce the normative meaning of what it is to be a male or female entrepreneur in a single cultural model framed by a cultural as well as an economic context. Therefore we can say that a practice approach addresses a micro-level of analysis when it is focused on the temporality and situatedness of a single practice in its 'hic et nunc', and at the same time it collapses the micro/macro divide when it is focused on the effects that practising a practice produces on society at large.

The 'doing gender' approach has been the forerunner of a practice-based approach to gender as a situated activity and a cultural practice. Nevertheless, while 'doing gender' positions gender construction mainly in interactional encounters, a practice approach conceives gender as co-produced, processually and relationally performed within a texture of social practices. The concept of 'doing gender' has roots in symbolic interactionism. According to the definition provided by West and Zimmerman (1987, p. 126), doing gender 'is the activity of managing situated conduct, in the light of normative conceptions of attitudes and activities appropriate for one's sex category'. Following the 'doing gender' line, Patricia Martin (2003) explores the implications of a two-sided dynamic – *gendering practices* and the *practising of gender* – for the understanding of gendering processes in formal organizations. She defines practising gender as 'a moving phenomenon that is done quickly, directionally (in time), (often) non-reflexively, informed (often) by liminal awareness, and in concert with others' (Martin, 2003, p. 342). 'Gender practices', 'gendered practices' and 'gendering practices' stand for a class of activities that are available – culturally, socially, narratively, discursively, physically – to be done, asserted and performed in situated contexts.

Gender as a social practice becomes apparent when it is exercised and represented in institutional discourses, material arrangements and interactive practices. For practice-based studies, referring to gender as a situated practice means conceiving language as a discursive activity that performs organizational identities (Diaz-Garcia & Welter, 2013; Bruni & Perrotta, 2014). The practice approach tells us that gender acquires its form as a consequence of the relations in which it is situated, and it also tells us that gender is performed *in*, *by*, and *through* those relations. Gender relations may thus be analysed as the product – unstable and only partly under the individual's control. In focusing on the modes of ordering heterogeneous materials (people, texts, artefacts) into a social practice, we assume that gender is mobilized and situationally enacted (Bruni & Gherardi, 2001) within a texture of social practices (Mathieu, 2009).

Therefore 'doing gender' and 'doing entrepreneurship' may be conceived as an intertwined practice, discursively constructed and situationally performed, thus enriching entrepreneurship studies with a process approach (Hjorth, Holt, & Steyaert, 2015). In fact, there has been an attempt to promote studies and research that consider entrepreneurship as a societal rather than economic phenomenon grounded in social, political, cultural and ecological realities (Steyaert & Katz, 2004; Tedmanson, Verduyng, Essers, & Gartner, 2012). This implies that entrepreneurship is explored as a processual phenomenon, as 'entrepreneuring' (Steyaert 2007; Weiskopf, & Steyaert, 2009), i.e. as a process which can be studied without focusing on economic or managerial logics, but as part of society in its context of production within a texture of entrepreneurial practices. The concept of entrepreneuring inscribes entrepreneurship studies in a social ontology of becoming that is common also to those practice-based studies oriented by an actor-network sensibility (Gherardi, 2012; Law & Singleton, 2013). Moreover, the concept of becoming also has a prominent place in feminist studies.

We have thus developed a 'gender as a social practice approach' (Poggio, 2006) that conceives gender as situated, relational, sociomaterial and discursive, and we shall illustrate it (Table 20.1) with two empirical examples.

Table 20.1 Analytical framework for the study of gendering and entrepreneuring as an intertwined practice

G&E as an accomplishment:	Dimensions to explore	Analytical focus
Situational	How gender is done in the actual doings of entrepreneurship. How situated entrepreneuring modes produce/reproduce gendering.	Activities, as they happen in entrepreneurial contexts and within wider contexts.
Relational	Social relations that are performed in entrepreneuring. How are they gendered and with what power effects. How familiar roles and entrepreneurial ones are intertwined. How networking is done and with whom.	The texture of practices enacted in entrepreneuring and forming a web of social relations in which 'who is the entrepreneur' and 'what is a good entrepreneur' acquire normative meaning.
Sociomaterial	The corporeality in G&E. The sociotechnical web of technological infrastructures sustaining the production process. How bodies, objects and technologies get connected in more or less stable working practices.	Gender inscribed in the bodies, technologies, products and communication devices.
Discursive	Discursive practices and narratives, both at the interactional level and at the level of institutional discourses. What is legitimate in a specific context.	The social and affective process producing meanings and discourses on gender and entrepreneurship.

Authoring as a material–discursive practice

The first example concerns the analysis of a single practice named 'authoring entrepreneuring'. By this is meant the process by which women entrepreneurs construct 'who the female entrepreneur is' when speaking publicly about themselves in relation to their place in the firm and the entrepreneurial project in their life-course. Discursive practices and the materiality of entrepreneurial choices are inextricably intertwined in the same practice linking gendering and entrepreneuring. To illustrate this process we refer to a qualitative study including 70 biographical interviews, conducted in northern Italy, with craftswomen working in the service, manufacturing and artistic sectors, and belonging to an artisan association (for an extensive discussion see Gherardi, 2015).

The expression 'authoring' refers to a material and discursive practice through which a narrative of identity is performed in socially produced activities. The authoring process may also be seen from an organizational perspective, as in the case of Shotter and Cunliffe (2003). They talk about 'organizational authorship', referring to a social constructionist interpretation of work within organizations that provides insights into the sense of authorship developed by the organizational members. They can be considered authors of their own work setting when they 'can play an active role in the daily production, reproduction and transformation of their work processes' (Gorli, Nicolini & Scaratti, 2015, p. 3).

Authoring entrepreneuring as a situated practice of constructing and presenting a life project implies a process of appropriating and enacting behaviours, discourses and competent participation in a local community. It also implies connecting with historical and situated narratives, developing a life project and positioning one's self and one's competences vis-à-vis a community. When entrepreneuring is seen as a lifeworld, an interdependent relationship between entrepreneuring and life is established and both are open and incomplete.

Four different ways of authoring the process of becoming a female entrepreneur can be outlined in relation to gender and life issues: as a business creator, as a co-author of a two-person project, as a responsible wife, as a member of the second generation.

Authoring a life project as a woman business creator

A first way to author the process of becoming an entrepreneur is to position the narrative subject as a 'woman business creator'. In these cases the dominant discourse categories are those of passion, and creativity.

In the testimonies of some of the women in this group, entrepreneurship was recounted as a passion present since childhood, often cultivated within the family, where the craft was learnt, developed by attending a vocational school, and then by gaining work experience as an employee or apprentice or – when possible – by immediately starting one's own business.

> I've always had this passion since I was little, probably because I had two aunts who were hairdressers. So I grew up surrounded by this kind of work and already when I was at middle school my intention was to do this work.
>
> (Giulia, hairdressing)

In these stories entrepreneurship is tied to an urge to express creativity, which is set in relation to the freedom of being an entrepreneur:

> I worked for ten years in a private firm . . . I did the same job as I'm doing now, but obviously as an employee . . . Staying there seemed a bit reductive compared with what I wanted to do. There I did the work, but with the restrictions imposed by the department head. I mean . . . my job is creative, so in the end if I do it, it's because I feel it.
>
> (Chiara, graphic design)

Contrary to the popular representation that depicts entrepreneurship in terms of opportunity-seeking behaviour, in these narratives the main motivation is a passion for a kind of work often inscribed within a female register. This form of authoring seems to substantiate a strong desire to be able to manage one's work free from external constraints, giving full rein to one's creativity. Doing entrepreneurship thus becomes a way to express oneself as the taker of business decisions.

Authoring a life project as co-authoress of a two-person project

A different example can be found in the narratives of the women entrepreneurs who said that they had developed the business idea jointly with their partner. In this case the first person singular (the narrating self) is replaced with a 'we' that includes the wife and the husband. For this reason we can talk of a 'two-person project' and of a practice of co-authoring. The founding of the firm is described as a response to a series of contingent factors usually connected with the husband's previous experience, or at any rate to a business idea of the husband endorsed and supported by his wife.

The relationship between the two members of the couple is described as being based on complementarity whereby the husband is responsible for production – the 'core' dimension of the business – while the wife manages the administrative and accounting side and sometimes customer relations. The two-person project recalls the traditional gender distinction whereby technical matters are male concerns and administration and care are female ones.

> I did administrative studies, and now I work in the administration office. I started working as an administrative clerk at a firm, then I met my husband, and he had just started the business. He said to me: 'Come on, let's get it together' . . . I've never held back [laughs]. I've also done radio and television repairs. If they needed help, I went to lend a hand, I learned all the resistances, you recognize them from the colours, and therefore all the colours, the values. So, now I deal with the administrative part and with the customers, and I know what we sell.
>
> (Luisa, building installations)

The complementarity between roles and activities is here represented as a strength. The co-authoresses performed a narrating self characterized by close synergy with the partner; they claimed the subject position of 'entrepreneur' for themselves – since they shared a common project – but in a relation of complementarity and within a gendered division of labour. In the above excerpt, for example, Luisa describes how she learned the practices of entrepreneurship. At the same time she re-read this experience as useful for the expert performance of the administrative role for which she claims competence.

Authoring a life project as a responsible wife

A third kind of authoring is found in the stories that described women participation in the family business in terms of behaving like a responsible wife. These women usually joined the husband's firm either because they had lost their previous jobs or because they found it impossible to manage them because of the workload imposed by the domestic 'double shift'. Entry into the firm by the responsible wives was attributed to the opportunities stressed by their husbands.

> I started here because I married the owner of the firm. My previous job was different because I'd worked for 20 years at a bank. Yes, completely different. Then my husband needed a hand because the firm had grown. I also had family problems because I had three small children. So I resigned after twenty years, and now I only deal with [her husband's] business.
>
> (Valeria, construction)

Also these authoring processes were framed by the traditional division of labour, which, however, was even more rigid for the co-authoresses because it explicitly referred to (essentially) different gender competences: technical skills, in fact, were regarded as indisputably male, while women had tasks of a more administrative (but partly also strategic) nature.

> There has to be two of you because you can't do it on your own. According to me, it's a very good match: the female part and the male one, at least in this sector, because it's strictly male work. I could learn how to go and take measurements at the construction site, but if I know how to take measurements on site, I must also know how to go with them into the workshop: it's not a female job! The female part of this work is on the other side. It consists in organizing, in seeing, in looking ahead, in discussing.
>
> (Elena, metal joinery)

Moreover, the lack of full identification with the husband's business project was stressed by the prospects that the responsible wives envisaged for the future. These women often foresaw detaching themselves from the business by delegating as much work as possible to a trusted employee or to their sons, even though some of them thought about creating their own businesses in which to put their accumulated experience to good use.

Authoring a live project as the second generation who join the family firm

The fourth type of authoring concerned those women who decided to join the family firm. Here two narratives were identified.

In the first, the women were fully accepted by the firm headed by the father. A common feature in the stories of these women is that, before joining the family firm, they had taken the opportunity to gain experience outside the family context, exploring possible alternatives. But in the end they had decided to take over the firm of their parents. They now represented themselves as fully immersed in the life of the firm, and in relation to the male figure.

> I'd never go into the administrative sector, which my mother runs. At most, my sister will take it on. I'll do what my father did – and so contacts with clients, production. He follows me in that, he's teaching me everything.
>
> (Noemi, graphic design)

In the second group, instead, there was a different positioning of the second-generation entrepreneurs: due to a lack of recognition by their fathers, they had to struggle to gain visibility. The pattern that emerges is therefore that of a pathway to becoming an entrepreneur marked by obstacles and especially the resistance of a 'father master'.

> I wanted to take the computer into the office and do the accounting on my own, but my father didn't want to know about it. So in the end he didn't even give me the satisfaction of having my abilities recognized. But I felt strong; I was determined to go forward.
>
> (Teresa, construction)

In these stories, too, the dimension of entrepreneuring is closely bound up with gendering. What therefore emerges from consideration of these different narratives is, on the one hand, the interplay between entrepreneuring and gendering as intertwined practice, and on other, their situated, discursive and sociomaterial nature. The monolithic category of 'women entrepreneurs' thus fragments into different and situated ways of practising gender and entrepreneurship. In the authoring by the female entrepreneurs of the entrepreneurship process, the condition of entrepreneur cannot be split from the gendering process, in its twofold form of practising gender and gendering practices (Martin, 2006). Entrepreneuring and gendering were two inseparable dimensions co-constituted by discursive practices and materials which fuelled and supported each other.

Gendering and entrepreneuring in the succession process

There is a moment in time when practices for doing gender and doing business become more evident, since the transfer of the firm from one generation to the next adds a further critical dimension to handing over the economic and cultural capital along family and gender lines.

The family business literature stresses that family enterprises form a particular group bound by kinship ties, norms and forms of altruism that are neither financial nor market-based (Astrachan, 2010). However, we cannot consider business, on the one hand, and family on the other as if they were two separate entities, one economic and the other social or psychological. On the contrary, by maintaining the ability to create value over generations, the social capital of the family business is the engine of sustainability (Salvato & Melin, 2008). Nevertheless, in the family business literature, the family is mostly presented as an undifferentiated concept, the outcome of blood or marriage, rather than as a negotiated phenomenon. As a consequence, the potential exploitative effects of family business, the subordination of women, free-riding behaviour within the family, and the politics of value determination that influence the family vision, are treated as intergenerational relationships rather than as gendered processes (Al-Dajani, Bika, Collins, & Swail, 2014).

Previous studies of the succession process in the case of daughters taking over the enterprise (Wang, 2010) show that when a daughter takes over the family business, the legitimacy of her position is under threat: she is the first to perceive that if a son is present, he is the 'natural' successor and she is thus constructed as an 'invisible' successor (Dumas, 1989), often in need of some professional experience outside the company before being considered for the position. The first phase of the succession is the most difficult, since the daughter's credibility, acceptability and legitimacy is at stake not only with her parents or siblings but with stakeholders and customers as well. Moreover, if she is young and the business operates in a male-dominated sector, she will struggle to gain acceptance, and her relationship with her father will directly affect the interactions with stakeholders, since the father can ease the business network or contribute to casting doubt on the daughter's capacity as an entrepreneur (Haberman & Danes, 2007).

We want to illustrate the dual process of gendering and entrepreneuring in the case of daughters taking over the family business by drawing on previous research that we conducted through twenty case studies conducted in northern Italy through repeated visits to the firm and narrative interviews with the daughters in their workplaces. A narrative interview of entrepreneuring as a form of life seeks to obtain descriptions of the interviewee's lived world. This approach works on the assumption that language is creative in giving form to reality, and on the reflexive assumption that narratives are co-created within narrative discourse with others (Cunliffe, 2002).

We became particularly interested in daughters taking over the business both in relation to the gendering of entrepreneuring and the perceived – more or less overt – social injustice involved in the process. Thus, we look at the family business as the locus of the coexistence of competing discourses, where two orders of worth (domestic and industrial) are accommodated or enter into a non-resolvable conflict in the gendered transition from one generation to the next. We rely on a theoretical framework inspired by French pragmatism (Boltanski & Thévenot, 1991) that defines three regimes of engagement: familiar engagement, engagement in a plan, and justifiable action engagement. They are respectively related to three different orders of worth: domestic, industrial and civic.

The regime of familiar engagement involves a dynamic relation with an immediate environment that is experienced as comfortable because it is familiar, and allows the actor to feel at ease. This regime 'configures the person in a kind of personality that is distributed across his/[her] immediate surroundings in accordance with a personal disposition that inclines him [her] to act by turning and making use of familiar, and appropriated things and inhabited places' (Thévenot, 2007, p. 416). The good maintained within this regime has been called the 'domestic worth'. A different kind of engagement is at work within the regime of engagement in a plan; it 'refers to felicitous exercise of the will by an *individual* endowed with *autonomy* and capable of *projecting herself* [himself] successfully into the future' (Thévenot, 2007, p. 417, italics in original). In fact, the good of this engagement relates to plan execution, and reality is grasped with respect to the instrumentality appropriate to the realization of the plan. In this regime, the satisfaction of the accomplished action is very different from the feeling of ease derived from familiar engagement. The order of worth of the regime of engagement in a plan has been called 'industrial', since it adheres to the organizational form of relation to the productive world. Finally, the order of worth is civic, when individuals can only be 'worthy' within a community engaging with qualified things and appropriate discursive language that refers to legitimacy.

We present only two narratives exemplar of two ways in which engagement in the familiar and industrial order of worth are justified in the process of gendering and entrepreneuring succession in the firm. For an extensive discussion of the two case studies see Gherardi and Perrotta (2016).

The justification work in Sara's family business reflects an industrial engagement and a succession process from the father/founder first to the daughter and then to her and her husband:

> I grew up in a family where my father had created his company. He had nothing; he too created his own business. He was a man of great initiative, and he created this good business. So, he was the one who had the flash. Then he had two daughters: me and my sister. We are really different in character: I have a lot of initiative. Even if I hadn't had my father's business, I would have had to find a way to do something on my own; I would have created something.

After having worked in other fields Sara inherited the business, and she worked there with her husband for some years before founding their own company:

> We thought we would stay in the same field which we knew, that is, the medical and pharmaceutical industry, and we stuck to the idea of engineering. Then we conducted a market survey to see what could be done, starting with the network of customers that we had gained from the previous activity. Talking with some of these contacts showed us that there were certain plastic products with special characteristics that were sold or bought at a price much higher than other similar products, because they had a particular performance. And then we said, 'Well, let's see what we can do to produce these types of more sophisticated products with a higher added value.'

Sara's succession story is constructed around the plot of copreneurship amongst married couples in which responsibilities are shared and gender relationships are tendentially egalitarian. Engagement in a plan and engagement in the family are not conflictual.

To illustrate a conflict between the order of worth of familiar and industrial engagement we refer to the story of Emma and her two brothers, where a latent sense of injustice was located in the gender regime of her family, which envisaged different social achievements for the daughter and the sons. Her older brother, who was very close to her in age, had not entered the family business because he was supposed to study and undertake a professional occupation:

> The other brother had to become an engineer; he had to pursue his studies . . . He somewhat decided for the others [children] as well, but we moved him away, since he is an engineer.

In Emma's narrative, the language of the family's engagement in a plan is referred to in the context of her brother, who 'had to become an engineer'. The industrial order of worth is expressed in terms that underline the social status of choosing a professional occupation, versus the implicit gendering of the family business that 'retains' a daughter, but pushes the son towards greater social achievements. In the collective understanding of gender differences, 'having a son who is an engineer' represents a social achievement. Therefore, in Emma's justification work, there is a transition from the logic of familiar engagement that positions her within a gender regime of 'constrained and natural choice' (in her words) to the language of engagement in a plan for her brother. She was working in the family business for a long time, without being paid or having a share in the business:

> We were waiting for him [the younger brother], basically. My father was waiting, and I was too, actually, because I thought that with him, there'll be the two of us . . . My brother joined after I had worked here for years. I was 32 and he was 20. Nevertheless the company was already his own when he joined. Got it?.

Her answer is a sharp criticism of the position of her younger brother in the family business, as he joined a thriving company forthwith as its owner. Emma acknowledges the injustice of this preferential treatment. At the same time, she seems to accept it as an inescapable fact, and she sees her brother as an ally against her father's threat to sell the company. She justifies the gender injustice because she turns it into a possibility to become a legitimate co-entrepreneur in the family business.

In the justification work that the two narrators perform while presenting their succession story, we can explore the fluidity and complexity of the interplay between gendering and entrepreneuring. It would be misleading to think in terms of equilibrium or domination of one type of engagement over the other, since situations are fluid, and it is precisely in analysing how justification work is done as a situated accomplishment that we can appreciate how human beings are able to switch from one order of worth to another according to the situation at hand. Our engagements with the world are complex and fluid, and they also become more visible when we take into account the circuit of reproduction of practices of gendering and entrepreneuring.

Conclusion

With this chapter we have contributed to the debate on gender and entrepreneurship by taking a position different both from the mainstream view of women as failed or reluctant entrepreneurial actors, and from that of studies on women entrepreneurs which, albeit from a different perspective, have treated them as a homogeneous category 'other' than the dominant image of the entrepreneur still restricted to a hegemonic model of masculinity.

Continuing analysis already begun several years ago (Bruni, Gherardi, & Poggio, 2005), we have taken up the invitation of several authors to find interpretative strategies with which to resolve the impasse of the current entrepreneurial research agenda, which still adheres to a notion of entrepreneurship which considers gender to be at most a binary independent variable (Ahl & Nelson, 2010). We have moved in this direction on the one hand by adopting a reflexive critical perspective in order to reframe the idea of who can be an entrepreneur, what entrepreneurship is and how entrepreneuring works, and on the other by making a contribution in terms of methodology in response to the invitation by Henry, Foss, and Ahl (2015) to move towards more innovative methodologies for studying constructions of gender and gendering processes.

We have outlined a methodological approach with which to analyse the interweaving of entrepreneuring and gendering as a situated, relational, sociomaterial and discursive practice. This approach has enabled us to undermine a monolithic view of the constructs of gender and entrepreneurship by showing that the discursive and identitarian construction and sociomaterial practices of women entrepreneurs are in fact fragmented and diversified. At the same time, consideration of justification work with respect to different types of engagement in practice show the fluidity and complexity of the interplay between gendering and entrepreneuring understood as a situated accomplishment.

References

Ahl, H., & Marlow, S. (2012). Exploring the dynamics of gender, feminism and entrepreneurship: Advancing debate to escape a dead end? *Organization, 19*(5), 543–562.

Ahl, H., & Nelson, T. (2010). Moving forward: Institutional perspectives on gender and entrepreneurship. *International Journal of Gender and Entrepreneurship, 2*(1), 5–9.

Al-Dajani, H., Bika, Z., Collins, L., & Swail, J. (2014). Gender and family business: New theoretical directions. *International Journal of Gender and Entrepreneurship, 6*(3), 218–230.

Astrachan, J. (2010). Strategy in family business: Towards a multidimensional research agenda. *Journal of Family Business Strategy, 1*(1), 6–14.

Boltanski, L., & Thévenot, L. (1991). *De la justification. Les économies de la grandeur.* Paris: Gallimard. (Engl. trans. 2006. *On justification: Economies of worth.* Princeton, NJ: Princeton University Press.)

Bruni, A., & Gherardi, S. (2001). Omega's story: The heterogeneous engineering of a gendered professional self. In M. Dent & S. Whitehead (Eds), *Managing professional identities, knowledge, performativity and the new professional* (pp. 174–98). London: Routledge.

Bruni, A., Gherardi, S., & Poggio, B. (2004a). Entrepreneur-mentality, gender and the study of women entrepreneurs. *Organizational Change Management, 17*(3), 256–268.

Bruni, A., Gherardi, S., & Poggio, B. (2004b). Doing gender, doing entrepreneurship: An ethnographic account of intertwined practices. *Gender, Work & Organization, 11*(4), 406–429.

Bruni, A., Gherardi, S., & Poggio, B. (2005). *Gender and entrepreneurship: An ethnographical approach.* London: Routledge.

Bruni, A., & Perrotta, M. (2014). Entrepreneuring together: His and her stories. *International Journal of Entrepreneurial Behaviour and Research, 20,* 108–127.

Calás, M. B., Smircich, L., & Bourne, K. A. (2009). Extending the boundaries: Reframing 'entrepreneurship as social change' through feminist perspectives. *Academy of Management Review, 34*(3), 552–69.

Calás, M., Smircich, L., & Holvino, E. (2014). Theorizing gender-and-organization: Changing times, changing theories. In S. Kumra, R. Simpson, & R. J. Burke (Eds), *The Oxford handbook of gender in organizations* (pp. 17–53). Oxford: Oxford University Press.

Cunliffe, A. (2002). Social poetics as management inquiry: A dialogical approach. *Journal of Management Inquiry, 11*(2), 128–146.

De Bruin, A., Brush C. G., & Welter, F. (2007). Advancing a framework for coherent research on women's entrepreneurship. *Entrepreneurship Theory and Practice, 31*(3), 323–339.

Diaz-Garcia, C., & Welter, F. (2013). Gender identities and practices: Interpreting women entrepreneurs' narratives. *International Small Business Journal, 31*(4), 384–404.

Dumas, C. (1989). Understanding of father–daughter and father–son dyads in family owned business. *Family Business Review, 2*(1), 31–46.

Gherardi, S. (2012). *How to conduct a practice-based study: Problems and methods.* Cheltenham: Edward Elgar Publishing.

Gherardi, S. (2015). Authoring the female entrepreneur while talking the discourse of work–family life balance. *International Small Business Journal, 33*(6), 649–666.

Gherardi, S., & Perrotta, M. (2014). Gender, ethnicity and social entrepreneurship: Qualitative approaches to the study of entrepreneuring. In E. Chell & M. Karataş-Özkan (Eds), *Handbook of research in small business and entrepreneurship* (pp. 130–147). Cheltenham: Edward Elgar Publishing.

Gherardi, S., & Perrotta, M. (2016). Daughters taking over the family business: Their justification work within a dual regime of engagement. *International Journal of Gender and Entrepreneurship, 8*(1), 28–47.

Gorli, M., Nicolini, D., & Scaratti, G. (2015). Reflexivity in practice: Tools and conditions for developing organizational authorship. *Human Relations, 68*(8), 1347–1375.

Haberman, H., & Danes, S. (2007). Father-daughter and father-son family business management transfer comparison: Family FIRO model application. *Family Business Review, 20*(2), 163–184.

Henry, C., Foss, L., & Ahl, H. (2015). Gender and entrepreneurship research: A review of methodological approaches. *International Small Business Journal, 28*(5), 470–486.

Hjorth, D., Holt, R., & Steyaert, C. (2015). Entrepreneurship and process studies. *International Small Business Journal, 33*(6), 599–611.

Hughes, K. D., Jennings, J. E., Brush, C., Carter, S., & Welter, F. (2012). Extending women's entrepreneurship research in new directions. *Entrepreneurship Theory and Practice, 36*(3), 430–442.

Law, J., & Singleton, V. (2013). ANT and politics: Working in and on the world. *Qualitative Sociology, 36,* 485–502.

Marlow, S., & McAdam, M. (2013). Advancing debate and challenging myths: Exploring the alleged case of the under-performing female entrepreneur. *International Journal of Entrepreneurial Behaviour and Research, 19*(1), 114–124.

Martin, P.Y. (2003). 'Said and done' vs. 'Saying and doing'. Gendered practices/practicing gender at work. *Gender & Society, 17*(3), 342–366.

Martin, P.Y. (2006). Practicing gender at work: Further thoughts on reflexivity. *Gender Work and Organization, 13*(3), 254–276.

Mathieu, C. (2009). The (re)production of gender inequality and the gap between deliberate and practical consciousness. *Management Learning, 40*(2), 177–193.

Mirchandani, K. (1999). Feminist insight on gendered work: New directions in research on women and entrepreneurship. *Gender, Work and Organization, 6*(4), 224–235.

Poggio, B. (2006). Editorial: Outline of a theory of gender practices. *Gender Work and Organization, 13*(3), 225–233.

Salvato, C., & Melin, L. (2008). Creating value across generations in family controlled business: The role of family social capital. *Family Business Review, 21*(3), 259–276.

Shotter, J., & Cunliffe, A. L. (2003). Managers as practical authors: Everyday conversations for action. In D. Holman & R. Thorpe (Eds), *Management and language: The manager as a practical author* (pp. 15–37). London: Sage.

Steyaert, C. (2007). Entrepreneuring as a conceptual attractor? A review of process theories in 20 years of entrepreneurship studies. *Entrepreneurship and Regional Development, 19*(6), 453–477.

Steyaert, C., & Katz, J. (2004). Reclaiming the space of entrepreneurship in society: Geographical, discursive and social dimensions. *Entrepreneurship and Regional Development, 16*(3), 179–196.

Tedmanson, D., Verduyng, K., Essers, C., & Gartner W. B. (2012). Critical perspectives in entrepreneurship research. *Organization, 19*(5), 531–541.

Thévenot, L. (2007). The plurality of cognitive formats and engagements: Moving between the familiar and the public. *European Social Theory, 10*(3), 409–423.

Wang, C. (2010). Daughter exclusion in family business succession: A review of the literature. *Journal of Family and Economic Issues, 31*(4), 475–484.

Wee, L., & Brooks, A. (2012). Negotiating gendered subjectivity in the enterprise culture: Metaphor and entrepreneurial discourses. *Gender, Work and Organization, 19*(6), 573–591.

West, C., & Zimmerman, D. (1987). Doing gender. *Gender & Society, 1*(2), 25–51.

Weiskopf, R., & Steyaert, C. (2009). Metamorphoses in entrepreneurship studies: Towards affirmative politics of entrepreneuring. In D. Hjorth & C. Steyaert (Eds), *The politics and aesthetics of entrepreneurship: A fourth movements in entrepreneurship book* (pp. 183–200). Cheltenham, UK, and Northampton, MA: Edward Elgar Publishing.

Index

Abaya design studio (Saudi Arabia) 69
Abdelgawad, S. G. 33
Abdullah, A. 211
Abrahamic religions (Jewish and Christian faiths) 4
access 67, 70, 78–79, 84, 99, 101–2, 110, 112–13, 116; to external sources of capital 78, 113, 160, 176; to finance and networks 116, 177; to jobs 163; to markets xxiv, 99
access to networks 6, 12, 110–11, 211; of business partners 111; and financial support 110; of knowledge and business information 61
Achtenhagen, Leona 18–30
activities 9, 22, 110, 143, 264, 274; agricultural 114; awareness-raising 85; business 27, 111–12, 114–15, 126, 133, 140, 163, 189, 209, 211, 230, 261; civic 249; culture-based 171; entrepreneurial xx–xxi, xxiii–xxvi, 9–10, 18–20, 27–29, 62–63, 76, 78–79, 107–8, 115–16, 125–26, 208–12, 214–15, 249; female entrepreneurial 3, 12, 19, 60–61, 167–68, 170; forest-related 196, 201; home-based 108; non-valued 264; recreational 171; social entrepreneurial 253, 255; social work 156; starting micro-business 25; successful entrepreneurial 19, 60, 251, 253; tourist 171; women's entrepreneurship development 25
ADB 22, 26; see also Asian Development Bank
Ager, B. 198
Agogué, M. 140
agri-businesses 110
agriculture 141, 143, 197–98; based economies 75; and forestry 197
agro-tourism 171; see also tourism
Ahl, H. xx–xxi, 33, 35–36, 46, 74–75, 92–93, 101–2, 201, 206, 208–9, 221, 227, 273, 282
Ahmad, S. Z. 6, 22, 61, 150, 163, 207, 210–13
Ahmed, L. 3–5

Ajzen, I. 248–50
Akdeniz, Aybeniz 119–36, 219, 230
Alsos, G. A. 210
Alstom Group (Mexico) 266, 268
Alvarez, S. A. 120–22
Amatucci, Frances 233–43
AME 33, 35–37, 42, 44, 57; see also Arab Middle East
Anadolu-Okur, N. 8–9
Anatolia 7–8, 82
Anatolian Values Association 83
Andersson, E. 202
Anheuser-Busch InBev S. A. (Belgian beer group) 266
Antecol, H. 233, 241
APEC 91, 95, 101; see also Asia Pacific Economic Cooperation
Appelstrand, Marie xxv, 194–203
Arab countries 43–44, 57, 62, 69, 248
Arab Middle East 33, 35–37, 42, 44, 57
Arab patriarchal culture xxii, 34, 36, 42
Arab societies xxii, 60–61, 70
Arab tribes xxi, 3, 5
Arab women xxii, 34, 42–44, 48, 56–57
Arab women entrepreneurs xxii, 35, 37, 39, 41, 43, 46–47, 56–57; issues concerning 57; in Lebanon 33, 42–43; and understandings of gender 43
Arab world 4, 34–36, 39, 41, 43–44, 56
Arabian Peninsula 4
Arabs 4, 55
architecture 124, 159
Ariffin, J. 212–13
Arora-Jonsson, S. 198, 202
art 159, 171
art galleries 172
arts festivals 171
Asia Pacific Economic Cooperation 91, 95, 101

286   *Index*

Asian Development Bank 22, 26
Ataturk, Mustafa Kemal 8–9
Avnimelech, G. 12
Al-Awadhi, B. A. 46, 50, 57

Bagozzi, R. P. 250
Baig, Y. R. 21, 23
balancing 40–41, 69, 219–20, 222–23, 227, 229;
  work-family responsibilities 186, 222, 228–29,
  262; work-life 68–69, 83, 156–57, 211,
  228–29
Baltic countries 155, 157, 159, 161, 163
Baltic Sea xxi, xxv, 154, 156–57, 159–64
Banaji, M. R. 234, 237
Bangladesh 25, 139, 149
banks 25–26, 41, 53, 63, 80, 113, 142, 175, 226,
  277; for loans 80; microcredit development
  109; and women entrepreneurs 25; and
  women's branches in 63
Al-Banna, Hassan 6
Banu Goktan, Vishal K xxi, 3
Bardasi, E. 106, 112
Barragan, S. 150
Barrett, Mary 139–50
barriers 35–36, 39–40, 64, 91–92, 94, 98–99,
  147–48, 161, 167, 169, 180–83, 185, 187,
  190–91; common 185; critical 176; cultural 155;
  in employment and entrepreneurship 167, 190;
  to export 94; individual 211; structural 211; for
  women's leadership development 208, 242
Basaffar, A. A. 63
Bass, B. M. 35, 40
Baughn, C. C. 19, 47, 78
Baum, J. R. 169
Bedard, K. 233, 241
behaviours 276, 279; assertive 237; and attitudes
  of individuals 116; cultural effects on
  entrepreneurial 121, 211; and expectations
  xxiv, 107; ingrained gender 176; and
  perceptions 110; social 26, 47, 53
Belgian beer groups 21, 266
beliefs 3–4, 6, 81, 128, 134, 160, 241, 243, 250;
  gender-stereotypical 78, 83–84; religious 12,
  84; shared 123, 136; women's 84, 250
Belloc, M. 91, 101
Benazir Income Support Programme 21
benefits 112, 121–23, 127–28, 132, 134, 139,
  142, 177, 182, 185, 188, 220, 227, 265–66;
  delivered direct 177; economic 101; financial
  177; informational 122; insurance 187–88; of
  networks 128; potential 29, 92; rare 9; social
  84, 108; strategic 122
Berends, H. 140

Beypazari (town) 82–83
Bhutto, Benazir 21–22, 25
bias xxi, 206, 237, 241–42; cultural 33; gender-
  based 77; implicit 237–38; unconscious
  241–42
BISP 21; *see also* Benazir Income Support
  Programme
black women 185
BMC xxvi, 261–62, 264–66; *see also* business
  model canvas
Body Works (brand) 124
bonding 97, 128–29
Borrero, Juan Diego 247–55
Al-Botmeh, S. 62, 68
boundaries 27, 35, 171, 227, 242; career 223;
  normative institutional 41
Bowles, H. R. 237
boys 108, 237
"boys network" 184
Bradbury, H. 97
Bradley, H. 208, 212–13, 247
Brahmin upper-castes 108, 110, 114
brands 81, 124, 131, 145
Brandth, B. 202
Braun, Patrice 91–102
Brettel, M. 140–41
Brindley, Clare 206–15
British mumpreneurs 219, 221, 223, 225, 227,
  229; *see also* mumpreneurs
Bruni, A. 180, 194, 200, 272–73, 282
Budak, Gönül 3–13
Bumiputera women entrepreneurs xxvi, 207,
  211–12, 214
Bushell, B. 107–8, 113
business 41, 51, 54–55, 57, 61, 63, 67, 69, 75;
  activities 27, 111–12, 114–15, 126, 133, 140,
  163, 189, 209, 211, 230, 261; area-based 196;
  children toys 189, 222–26; confectionery
  144; content writing and media 128, 132–33;
  decisions xxv, 139, 141, 148–49, 209, 276;
  dressmaking 140, 143–44; e-commerce
  129, 131, 133; enterprises 20, 75, 173; and
  entrepreneurship 27, 63; established 74, 100;
  and family responsibilities for women 222;
  female-run 168, 170, 177; forest 195; goals
  127, 131, 140; growth 129, 167, 187–88,
  210–11; hair products 222, 224, 226, 228; high-
  street 226; home-based xxvi, 221, 228–29;
  international 91, 98, 140; internet 125–27;
  medium-sized 154; mumpreneur 230; new
  38–39, 74, 196, 264; non-traditional 62–63, 70;
  operations 171, 175, 186, 189; ownership xxvi,
  76, 181, 185, 188, 219, 228; performance xxiv,

18, 120, 127, 209; regulations 132; strategies xxvii, 208, 262, 265–66; successful 171–72, 187–88; sustainable 39, 265; training xxvi, 25, 128–29, 170, 175, 210, 214, 227; women 25, 29, 224, 228–29, 234

business development 25, 27–28, 85, 108, 111–12, 126, 140, 154, 196, 210, 228

business model 124, 261, 264, 268; generation 264; new 95; thinking 264

business model canvas xxvi, 261–62, 264–66

business owners 34, 63, 78, 139, 144, 234, 240, 247, 272; established 182; female 78; male 77, 84; successful 5, 229; women's 188

business sectors 20, 66, 180, 196, 230; low-skilled xx; traditional 20

business skills 64, 168, 170–71, 174–75, 188, 211, 225; development of 227; learning key 229; women's 210

business start-ups 140

business support 211, 225; programmes 181, 188; services 76, 183; systems 211

business survival xxvi, 209–12, 214; of Bumiputera women 214; of BWEs 212; influencing women's 210–11; process 214; of women's handicraft businesses 209

businesses xxiii–xxvi, 37–39, 54–55, 119–21, 131–32, 139–40, 148–49, 167–77, 180–81, 187–88, 195–97, 201, 207–15, 226–30; Bumiputera 214; entrepreneurial xxv, 61, 168, 173, 175; fertilizer production 125–27, 129, 131, 134; in Palestine 65; profiles of 57; supporting women's 6, 214; in Wales 120

businesswomen 24, 51, 99

BWEs xxvi, 207, 211–12, 214; see also Bumiputera women entrepreneurs

Calás, M. B. 182, 272–73

Caliendo, M. 12, 163

Caliphate 5, 7–8

capabilities 82, 84–85, 101, 148, 212, 266; business-related 84; perceived 120; social 169; technology absorption 80

capacities 120, 123, 150; entrepreneurial 212; and networks 150; strong research 268; upgrading business 213

capital markets 210

Cardon, M. S. 250, 252

careers xxvi, 63, 69, 219, 228; boundaries of 223; choices of xxii, 36, 39, 42, 52, 55–56, 60, 71, 78, 84, 213, 219–20; entrepreneurial 39, 42–43, 57, 108; options for women 69, 85

caring roles, for women 214, 228–29

Carli, L. L. 237

Carter, N. 94, 191, 208, 210, 247, 272

caste xxiv, 106–10, 113–16; based stratified societal context xxiv; and gender discrimination xxiv, 109, 114; groups 109; and marriage 114; resource-poor lower 110; system 108–9

Cavender, Gray 180–91

CEDAW 9, 22, 76; see also United Nations Convention on the Elimination of All Forms of Discrimination Against Women

Cetindamar, D. 5, 75, 79–80

CFA 252; see also confirmatory factor analysis

Chandler, G. N. 140–41, 248

chemotherapy 222

Chen, M. A. 106, 249

Chettri upper-castes 108, 110

child care services xxvi, 247, 262

child support 188

child tax credits 220, 224–25

childcare 80, 84, 112, 155, 157–58, 163, 182, 186–88, 220, 222–25, 228–29; availability of 227; benefits of 219; centres 229; costs of 219–20, 222–24, 227–28; expense of 182, 187; facilities 220; for families 182; free 223–24; infrastructure 158; institutional 161; local 228; non-subsidized 182; and promotion of 158; providers 13; provisions 220, 229–30; responsibilities 186, 188; subsidized 182; support 223

children 39–40, 51, 63–64, 78–79, 115, 158, 160–61, 171, 182–83, 185–87, 189, 219–25, 227–29, 248; allowances 182; benefits 224; grown-up 114; managing 228; raising of 182; special 224; young 111–12, 115, 187, 227

Chin, W. W. 252, 254

class 82, 183–85, 190, 252, 272, 274; based resources 183, 186, 189; groups 182; middle 185–86; position 184–85, 187

clients 41, 123–24, 135, 175, 213, 265, 278; micro-finance 25; new 268; potential 26, 134, 185; professional 133

Coalition government 220

codebooks 37

Coleman, J. S. 121, 123, 167, 210, 234, 240, 242

Collins, P. H. 180, 182, 279

Collinson, E. 109–10

communication: channels and networks 91, 99; facilities 176; results 266; services 124

communities xxvi, 21, 115, 124, 149–50, 190, 200, 209, 248, 280; disadvantaged Roma 189; entrepreneurial 65; ethnic 191; local 39, 173, 177, 276; Native-American 189; traditional Arab 62

288 *Index*

companies 64, 66, 68, 80–81, 155–56, 160–62, 174, 177, 228, 233–34, 236, 264, 266–69, 279–82; large 124, 264; maintaining of 160; medium-size 160; private 144, 160; registration process for 132; successful 238; thriving 281; transnational 184

competition 136, 141, 169, 247, 265; business 266; and disadvantages for women 214; economic conditions and government policies 175; unfair 66

conditions 21, 66, 70, 79, 154, 163, 177, 197, 267, 279; environmental 167; financial 178; socio-cultural 94; trade ecosystem 102; for women entrepreneurs 50, 177

confirmatory factor analysis 252

conflicts 62, 78, 83, 107, 114–15, 185, 281; earnings/care 187; internal 69; for mothers 185; non-resolvable 280

constraints 27, 43, 48, 66, 71, 113–14, 116, 119, 121, 124, 127, 129, 207, 224–25; budgetary 100; cognitive 27; cultural 102, 126, 197; external 276; gender-based 106, 115; government 126; normative 78; regulative 34; resource 62, 119, 148; social-cultural 47, 69, 113, 139; supply 207; for women 78

consultancy 25, 67, 128–29, 132, 134–35, 176

consultants 131–32, 261, 265

consumers 111, 173

contractors 186, 188, 198, 266

contracts 197–98, 200

corruption 28, 30, 120

cost structures 261, 264, 266–67, 269

costs 65, 68–69, 78, 81, 94, 140, 142, 145, 176, 187, 224; of childcare 219–20, 222–24, 227–28; extra distribution 66; high 127, 222–23; low 148; operational 123

countries xx, 12–13, 18–20, 27–29, 60–62, 66–67, 78–84, 106–10, 154, 156–63, 172–73, 180–84, 186–91, 254; analysis of for business purposes 126, 162; candidate 75; dangerous 23; democratic 75; developed 76, 140, 211, 249, 251, 254; home 69; surveyed 161

courts 241–42; and judges 241; religious 8

Coutinho-Sledge, P. 200, 203

CR xxi, xxv, 180–91; children 182; entrepreneurship support 188; families 186; family policies 182; mothers 186–87, 190; respondents 183, 185–86, 188; Roma women 186; state socialism 181; and US respondent narratives 184; women business owners 182, 184, 186, 188, 190; *see also* Czech Republic

credit 106, 113, 139, 145, 162; cooperatives 109; financing 170; markets 109

Crick, D. and J. 140, 249

cultural xxi, xxiv, 37, 47, 83, 99, 139, 211, 248; challenges 142, 214; conditioning 94; construction of motherhood 229; factors shaping women entrepreneurship xxv, 12, 20, 27, 154–55, 159, 162–63, 208, 211, 254

culture 5, 7, 27, 36, 39, 43–44, 47–48, 126, 160, 168–69, 171, 173, 177, 198–99; collective 37; collectivist 211; gendered 201; individualistic 46; local 61; masculine 41; perceived 126; and previous work experience 70; professional 203; transformed 203

Cunliffe, A. 275, 280

customers 82, 111–12, 121–22, 124, 134–35, 146, 148, 171–73, 226, 261, 264–68, 277, 279, 281; development of 264; foreign 173; international 171; loss of 112; orders 146

Czech Republic xxi, xxv, 180–91

Al-Dajani, H. 33, 35–37, 41, 46–47, 190–91, 207, 212, 279

Dana, L. P. 12, 167

data xxi–xxii, 9–10, 12–13, 18–19, 36–38, 51–52, 79–81, 107, 154, 156, 181–82, 234–40, 252, 261–63; analysis 36–38, 49, 252; collection 37, 235; reliable 18–19, 74; samples 37; statistical 163, 254

databases 13

Daud, F. 209, 212, 214

daughters 65, 110, 139, 183, 186, 188, 197, 221–22, 279–81; elder 65; expectation on women and 197

Davidsson, P. 107, 167

de Bruin, A. xx, 19, 46–47, 50, 55, 57, 106, 108, 180, 208, 233, 272

debt finance 176

definitions xxii, 34–35, 38, 42–44, 92, 121, 159, 195, 261, 274; of entrepreneurial leadership 34–37, 39–40, 42–43; of women entrepreneurs 35

Demir, Zehra Sema 82–83

democracy 7–8, 196–97

democratic government 8; *see also* government

design 23, 109, 124, 135, 150, 159; development 125; graphic 276, 278; and property industries in Wales 124; thinking 264

DeTienne, D. R. 121, 140

developed economies 79, 94, 100

Dew, N. 141, 145, 149

Dholakia, U. 250

Diamantopoulos, A. 251

Diana Project 234

difficulties 68, 112, 136, 146, 157, 160–61, 163, 225, 254, 264, 266; financial 133; finding employment 162 dimensions xxiv, 49, 122, 170, 189, 191, 209, 275, 277, 279; multiple xxv, 180; of SC (structural, relational and cognitive) 120, 122, 129

Disability Living Allowance 224, 227

discrimination 76, 85, 92, 108–9, 157, 159, 162, 184–85, 187, 189, 191, 233–34, 239–41, 248; business type 226; combined gender/race 190; and effect on financial performance indicators on women entrepreneurs 209; ethnic 190; experience of 182, 185; fear of 185; gender-related 157; impacting on women 62; managing 242; pollution theory of 242; prohibiting 157; systemic xxiv, 92–93, 101

Divan (brand) 124

diversity 60–61; cultural 36; of management practices 48

divorce 187–88

DLA 224, 227; see also Disability Living Allowance

Dlouhá, M. 183, 188

Do Maio, M. 91, 101

Dorf, Bob 264

dressmaking 142–43

dynamics 48–49, 115; contextual 107; family 111; group 48; networking of 129; social 213

earnings 114, 157, 182, 184, 187–88, 225, 233, 238; and childcare 187; and mumpreneurs 221; for women 238

economic activities of women 25, 35, 106, 108, 115, 155, 158

economic and financial conditions 178

economic and social contribution in an economy 120

economic crises 191; new 187; recurrent 182

economic development 18, 24, 93, 116, 160, 163, 187; national 25; in Pakistan 24; process of 94; sustainable 28

economic empowerment of women 25, 162

economic growth xxv, 3, 7, 106, 160, 167, 174, 177, 219, 228–29; and employment development xxv; gendered 91; and lower unemployment 174; stimulated 177

economic performance 160

economies 20, 50, 67, 74, 76, 83–84, 91–92, 94–98, 100–102, 120, 160, 174, 196, 233; controlled 69; developed 79, 94, 100; formal 107; local 173; market-oriented 177; prospering 229; service-based 75; transitional 167; weak 62

economists 155, 233, 242

ecosystems xxiv, 92, 94, 101, 119, 125–26, 129, 199; cultural 134; financial 132; forest 199; services 199; in Turkey 125

education xxiii–xxiv, 6, 12–13, 27–29, 70–71, 106–8, 115, 120–21, 123, 155–56, 158, 163, 211, 236; children's 114–15; entrepreneurial 268; formal 111–12, 114; higher 62–63, 159, 252; personal 125; policies 28; post-secondary 159; quality 28; religious 8; secondary level 112; and skills 112; technical 171; tertiary 159, 263, 268; university 157; vocational 157

EES 123, 125–26, 219; see also entrepreneurial eco system

effectuation and causation xxv, 139–41, 143–44, 148; perspectives on entrepreneurship 140; research 150; thinking xxv, 139, 143, 148–49

EIGE 156–57, 162, 254; see also European Institute for Gender Equality

Ekinsmyth, C. 219, 228

Eléctricité de France (Mexico) 266

elements 34, 49, 61, 84, 119, 121, 128, 157, 209, 212, 234, 240–41, 248, 263–65; institutional 206; intention-model 250; normative xxii, 39, 41; of second-generation gender bias 241; weak 126

Elmuti, D. 62

Ely, R. 155, 234, 240, 242

emancipation 191, 249; and approaches to entrepreneurship 189; women's 233

embeddedness xxii, 47, 50, 55, 57, 116, 119; and the approach to studying women entrepreneurship 119; and context specificity of entrepreneurship xxii, 57; entrepreneurial 46, 57; institutional 229; normative 46

emotions 63, 123, 250

employees 40–42, 68, 76, 121–22, 125, 155–56, 160, 171, 175, 182–83, 188, 237, 240, 276; creative 69; female 78; fixed 131; inspired 175; new 131; parental 188; qualified 69; regulations 126, 131; trusted 278

employers 13, 142, 157, 182, 184; female 69; focusing on employing men 157; prohibited 240

employment 55, 60, 63, 156–57, 159, 163, 169–70, 173, 182, 184–91, 194, 219–23, 226, 228; and advancement 191; barriers 184; careers 185, 189; conditions 181, 241; contracts 157; discrimination 185; and entrepreneurship 190; female 106, 156–57; finding 254; full-time 158; influence gender and entrepreneurship 181; mandatory 181; of mothers of small children 191; part-time 187; preferred 186; professional 184; rates of women 187; responsibilities 221; of women 60

empowerment 28–29, 76, 139, 177, 190, 202, 209, 255; economic 3; women's 7, 22, 24

Ennis, C. A. 50, 53

290 *Index*

enterprises xxiii, 75, 80, 83, 91–92, 101, 106, 135, 155, 169, 173, 177, 196–97, 221; female-led 37, 93, 102, 169, 171; home-based 229; independent 79; large 99; male-owned xxiv, 93, 102, 106, 180; medium size 77, 91, 140, 262; small-sized 109, 142; successful 140; women-owned 33, 106, 120, 169

entrepreneurial activities xx–xxi, xxiii–xxvi, 9–10, 18–20, 27–29, 62–63, 76, 78–79, 107–8, 115–16, 125–26, 208–12, 214–15, 249; in Muslim and non-Muslim countries 10; in Pakistan 18, 20, 28; in Turkey 10, 76, 84; of women 163

entrepreneurial behaviour 19, 106–7, 110, 208, 211, 249; and the impact of the normative institution on 47; of women 60, 106

entrepreneurial businesses xxv, 61, 168, 173, 175

entrepreneurial ecosystem xxiv, 119–20, 123, 125–26, 169, 219, 223, 227; characteristics of 173; of different countries 120, 129, 134, 136; distinct 136; domains 171, 173; factors results within life-cycle stage model 174; inclusive 84; models of development 177; and the study of women entrepreneurs in the Polish tourism industry 167; sustainable 169

entrepreneurial environment xx–xxi, xxiv, 3, 119, 121, 131, 209; dynamic 121; for women xxi, 3

entrepreneurial firms xxiii, 71, 92, 167, 174–75; female-run 168; growth and development of xxv

entrepreneurial gender gap xx–xxi, 154, 167, 263, 265, 267

entrepreneurial identities 195, 200–202

entrepreneurial intentions 76, 121, 219, 238, 248–52, 254–55

entrepreneurial leadership xxii, 33–44; behaviour 34; conceptualized 39–40; defining 34, 37; effective 38; perceived 38, 43; studies 34; for women 39

entrepreneurial networks 123, 128–29, 176

entrepreneurial passion 250–51, 254–55; measuring 252; perceived 248, 254; on social entrepreneurial intention 247, 251; stronger 255

entrepreneurial skills 28, 212

entrepreneurial strategies 181, 263

entrepreneurs 33–35, 37–43, 51, 69–71, 77–80, 121–23, 140–41, 148–50, 154, 159–61, 169–70, 234–36, 263–68, 276–79; effective 35, 147; enabled 236; and entrepreneurial leadership behaviour in start-ups 34; expert 149; to finance growth companies 235; in forestry 194; full-time 54; handicraft 211;

high performance 221; male 78–79, 84, 176, 227; potential 169; prospective 169; second-generation 278; social 250, 252; woman 29, 82

entrepreneurship xxv–xxvii, 3, 11–13, 18–20, 33–36, 52–54, 56–57, 74–80, 106–10, 159–63, 180–84, 186–91, 194–97, 272–77; conceptualizing women 150; development 20, 107, 109, 154, 197, 215; and ecosystems xxiii–xxiv, 92–94, 102, 171; and education 160, 163; and institutes 29; and leadership 35; literature xxi, 33, 38, 46, 136, 170, 190, 208, 210, 243, 273; policies 28–29; practices xxvii, 277; rate for women 154; and the rates for women 83, 154, 156, 158–59; and research 35, 42–43, 75, 107; and studies 3, 33, 36, 43, 47, 74, 115, 272; successful 33, 60–61, 169; uniform policy for 94; and women's research xx, xxvi, 47

environment xxi, 60–61, 70, 121, 125, 127, 131, 161, 167, 172–73, 199, 206, 209, 211; competition-minded 155; credit-enabled 140; credit-facilitated 149; enabling 91–92, 102, 109, 268; external 79; high conflict 65; high risk 65; household 112; legal 6, 61; male 198; managerial 184; negative 210; personal 169; regional 102, 252; rural 196; social xxvi, 61, 208–9, 211; supportive 93, 125, 208; women's 206

EPB 24; *see also* Export Promotion Bureau

equal opportunities for women 108

equality 9, 101, 156; enhanced gender 194; implementing gender 200; increased gender 196

equity 91, 234–36; funding 234–36, 242; raising of 235–36

Erogul, M. S. 150

Essers, C. 12, 33–34, 36, 274

Estonia xxv, 154, 156–63; and Latvian women 162; and Sweden 156, 159

ethnic minorities 182

ethnicity 12, 77, 182, 184–85, 189, 237, 241, 272

European Commission 154, 156, 158

European countries 7–8, 76, 81–82, 156, 175, 228

European Institute for Gender Equality 156–57, 162, 254

European Union 156–57

evaluation 22, 100–101, 262–63, 268–69; processes 213; roles 213; of trade support 101

export barriers 94, 101

export knowledge 99

export performance 92

export programmes 95

Export Promotion Bureau 24

exports 20, 24, 91, 93–94, 100, 102; innovation and quality in 24; oil 50
Eyiusta, Ceyda M. 74, 85

failures xx, xxii, 19, 22, 26–27, 61, 64, 120, 126, 159–60, 163, 168, 265–66, 268; of female-run entrepreneurial activities 168; individual's 126; multiple market 91; rates of 120; in Turkish culture 126; venture 126
Fakhro, M. A. 46, 57
family 4–6, 21, 38–39, 55–56, 79–81, 83–84, 106–8, 110–16, 133–34, 157–58, 184–86, 219–23, 228–29, 278–81; businesses 65, 167, 175, 277, 279–82; commitments 94; conflicts 13, 78; constraints 112; duties 98, 160; dynamics 111; entrepreneur's 144; extended 111, 114–15, 144, 148; law 7, 108; life 78, 84, 183, 220, 230; money 64; networks 111–12; obligations 69, 186, 220; parental 111; problems 277; and a prospering economy 229; reconciling of 220; relationships 155; resistance 56; responsibilities 60, 69, 158, 163, 220–22, 227–28; roles 30, 52, 220; status 181, 183, 187, 190; strong supportive 65; support xxiii, xxv, 6, 70, 80; traditional 262; wealthy 6; working 158
family income 158
family members 78, 111, 114, 133, 144, 188; extended 210; female 27
family policies 183, 219, 230; government's 229; institutional 227; regulatory 221; supportive 221
Farid, M. 7
fear 64, 120, 159–60, 163, 176, 228; of discrimination 185; of failure 27
FEI 79; see also Female Entrepreneurship Index
female economic empowerment 62
female employees and managers 78
female employment 106, 156–57
female entrepreneurs xx, xxii–xxvii, 6, 60–61, 70–71, 74–85, 121–23, 139, 160–63, 167–68, 170–71, 173, 177, 262–68; accomplished 62; constraining performance of 61, 71; in Mexico 262; in Poland 177; required to gain business skills 175; successful xxii, 5, 70, 75; in Turkey 76, 78–81, 83–84; young 68
female entrepreneurship xxv, 3, 5–7, 9, 11–13, 60, 74–75, 77, 79–80, 83–84, 155, 157, 161–62, 167; and agency 101; high-potential 79; in Islam 5; in Mexico 262; and secularism 6; successful 60; in Turkey 7, 75, 77
female forest owners 197, 202
female scientists 263

females 6, 62, 128, 141, 168, 171, 175, 233, 242, 248, 251, 272; adult 249; in business 13; hiring of 142; in Palestine 62; Polish 168; young 24
feminism 43
feminist entrepreneurship theories 92
feminist/gender studies 272
feminist theories 36, 74; liberal 74; poststructuralist 74; psychoanalytical 74
feminist values 201
Fernald, L. W. 35, 39
Fernando, W. D. A. 148
fertilizer production businesses 125–27, 129, 131, 134
Fetsch, E. 233, 235
finance 27, 93–94, 99, 102, 113, 116, 119–20, 126, 132, 219, 225, 227, 236, 240; and accounting professions 236; allowances 158; debt 176; growth companies 235; limited 132; and networks 116
financial assistance 168, 170–71, 174–77, 210; higher levels of 176; lack of access to 177; and non-financial assistance 170–71, 177
financial capital 79, 83–84, 214; obtaining 78; training 210
financial constraints 120, 127, 169
financial crises 172
financial institutions 63, 70, 108–9, 113, 121, 127; in Nepal 109; suppliers and employees of 121
financial literacy 80
financial losses 145, 148–49
financial resources 78, 83, 127, 132–33, 169, 225, 238
financial services 109, 120, 188, 236
financing xxiii, xxvi, 18, 23, 27, 63–64, 122, 127, 175–76, 183, 214; business set-up 76; equity xxvi, 234; and execution of women-development issues 23; external 210; first-tier 80; government's 212; securing 78; to support women's businesses 214; women entrepreneurs 139
Finlay, J. L. 56
firms xxvi, 38, 93–94, 168–69, 171, 173, 175–77, 183, 186, 234–36, 247–48, 262–63, 265–66, 268; contract 197; female-owned 247, 273; high-growth 93; home-based 247; male-owned 94, 272; operating 178
Fischer, D. M. 26, 92
Fisher, G. 140–41, 145
flexibility xxvi, 185, 187–88, 221, 223, 248; for mothers 185, 188; temporal 240, 242; in working hours 221, 223; of working time 156–57
Flynn, F. 237

292   *Index*

FOA 202; *see also* forest owners' associations
Fogel, G. 167, 170
Follo, G. 194, 197, 201
forest owners 194, 197, 199, 202–3; associations 202; female 197, 202; private 198; small-scale 196
forest policy 197–98
forest products 195–96
forest research 202
forestry xxv, 194–203; competence 203; contracting 195, 201; culture 197, 199, 201; ecosystems 199; encoding in 'feminine' terms 199; enterprises 194, 196; and forest ownership 202; management 201; organizations 202; in Sweden 196; and technical knowledge 199; traditional 196, 201
forestry businesses 195, 197, 201; and entrepreneurship 195; running traditional 201
forestry sector xxv–xxvi, 194–98, 200–203
forestry work 198–99
forestry workers 199
forests 194–97, 199, 201
formal education and skills 112
Foss, L. 273, 282
Foster, Carley 206–15
framework xxiv, xxvi–xxvii, 22, 48, 61, 100–102, 107, 200, 206, 208–9, 214–15, 241–42, 262, 270; analytical 48, 233–34, 275; applying entrepreneurial leadership 43; gender-responsive 97, 101; informed conceptual xx; institutional 47; integrative 57; intersectional 181; legal 23; multidimensional 206; normative 180; relational perspective 49; second-generation gender 242; socio-cultural 213; for women entrepreneurs 262
funding 64, 67, 111, 113, 120, 127–28, 132, 176, 224–25, 227, 234–36, 269; accessing of 68; in Palestine 67; sources 133, 180

Gabrielsson, M. 140
garment factories 141, 143
Gatewood, E. 208
Gazi, Osman 8
GCC 50; *see also* Gulf Cooperate Council
GEI xxv, 156–57, 162–63, 254; *see also* Gender Equality Index
GEM xx–xxi, 9, 13, 19, 29, 62, 67, 74, 76, 79, 83, 120, 249, 251–53; data 9–10, 12, 19; surveys 19; *see also* Global Entrepreneurship Monitor
gender 21–22, 33, 42–43, 74, 91–94, 101–2, 182–85, 189–90, 198–200, 208, 213–14, 233–37, 239–41, 272–76; analysis 106, 191; based social norms 147; common sense

attributes 273; competences 278; development 21; differences xx, 92, 150, 211, 227, 273, 281; differential 185; embeddedness xxiv, 106; employment influence 181; and entrepreneurship xxi, xxvii, 11, 19, 36, 110, 180, 191, 201, 272–73, 275, 282; practising 274, 279; and religious affiliation in shaping female entrepreneurship 3; and social exclusion 189
gender bias 62, 94, 214, 235, 238, 241–43; deconstructing 233; and discrimination impacting on women 62; implicit 243; interdisciplinary deconstruction of 242; second-generation 234–35, 237, 239–43; and social psychology 236
gender equality xxv, 3, 7, 9, 22–23, 29, 44, 76, 156–57, 181, 190, 194–98, 200, 202–3; in agriculture 197; expectations 187; in forestry 195, 197; policies 195–96, 198; processes 203; ratios 29; strategies 197
Gender Equality Index xxv, 156–57, 162–63, 254
gender gap xxi, xxv–xxvi, 19, 83, 91, 155, 180, 182–83, 187, 190, 195–97, 201, 263, 268; and business practices 180; economic 190; educational xxvii, 270; in entrepreneurship 3, 18–19, 76, 120, 163, 219; in female entrepreneurship 83; global 169; in median wages 242; in science 263; significant 182; widening entrepreneurial 29
gender ideologies 33; prescribed 36; traditional 36
gender-neutral approach 29, 272
gender norms 13, 115, 183, 197
gender parity 91–92
gender policies 22
gender practices 274
Gender Reform Action Plan 22–23
gender-related access barriers 94; converting into opportunities 150; to finance and international trade 94
gender relations 74, 109, 206, 208, 273–74
gender-responsive trade practices 95–97, 101–2; framework 92, 95, 99–102; implementing 92
gender roles 30, 36, 83, 176, 211, 214; associated 77, 84; expectations 13, 181; modern 29; multiple 211; stereotypical 27, 37, 85; traditional 13, 29
gendering xxv, xxvii, 74, 197, 202, 272–73, 279–80, 282; and entrepreneuring 273, 275, 279, 282; of entrepreneurship literature 273; expectations xxii, 33, 36, 39, 41–42; of forestry 195, 198–99; institutions xxiv, 106–7, 110, 115–16; practice linking 275; practices

209, 274, 279; processes 273–74, 279, 282; stereotyping 150, 199; of work 74
Germany 13, 228; and the gender gap in entrepreneurship 163; pro-family policies 228
Gherardi, Silvia 272–82
girls 24, 108, 189, 222, 224, 237; *see also* women
glass ceiling 94, 155, 162, 219, 254
Global Entrepreneurship Monitor xx–xxi, 9, 13, 19, 29, 62, 67, 74, 76, 79, 83, 120, 249, 251–53
Global Gender Gap Report xxii
Gnyawali, D. R. 170
goals xxi, 13, 22, 36–37, 76, 122, 136, 139–41, 144, 150, 175, 190, 200, 268; entrepreneurial 120, 149; micro-entrepreneurs 144; organizational 34; sustainable development 22
Goheer, N. A. 20, 23, 25, 27
Goktan, Banu 3–13
Goldin, Claudia 233–34, 239–40, 242
government xxiv–xxv, 18, 20–21, 23–24, 50–51, 53–57, 63, 66, 68, 98, 167, 210, 223–26, 229; agencies 63, 91, 124; funding 212; grants 132; initiatives 206; institutions 55; interventions xxiv, 91; rules and regulations 6, 174; support 51, 54, 56, 127, 133, 212, 223, 230; and weak entrepreneurship ecosystems 94
government policies 20, 126, 168, 170, 173–75, 177, 180–81; perceived 126; and procedures 168, 170, 173–74, 177; strict 131
Granovetter, M. 107, 122–23
grants 127, 227
GRAP 22–23; *see also* Gender Reform Action Plan
Greene, F. J. 74, 79, 208, 233, 249
Greenwald, A. G. 234, 237
groups 6, 8, 10, 49, 61, 64, 97, 99–100, 108, 113–15, 122, 140, 237, 240; artistic 189; disadvantaged 189; economic 26, 99; educated 6; ethnic 8, 238; female 254–55; heterogeneous 97; homogeneous 46, 180; low-income 25; lower caste 114; marginalized 191; minority 182; networking 122, 127; secular 11; of women 65, 114, 230
growth xxi, xxiv–xxv, 29, 33, 93, 95, 112, 167–71, 173–78, 206, 212, 229, 234–36, 238; capital 234; continuous 177; enterprise 92; entrepreneurial 169, 178; of entrepreneurial ventures 34, 71; experienced 171; exponential 109; inclusive xxi, 94, 102, 268; increased 196, 221; intentions 148; limited 190, 247; of mumpreneurship 229; personal 64, 169; private sector 173; restricting venture 108; sustainable xx, 168; wage 238
growth sector 95, 98, 101–2

Gulf Cooperate Council 50
Gulf countries 55–57
Gunatilaka, R. 141–42
Gunnerud, B. N. 74–75
Gunz, H. P. 57
Gupta, Vishal K. xx–xxi, 3–13, 34–35, 40–41, 75, 77, 95, 167, 251

handicraft industry 206, 212, 214
handicrafts 110, 208
Harrison, P. 33–35, 40, 43, 211
Hašková, H. 181, 184, 186
Hausmann, R. 18
Hayal Kahvesi (brand) 124
health 21, 28, 74, 156, 171–72, 177
health insurance 186, 188
health services 171, 195, 201, 240
Henry, C. 169, 221, 247, 273, 282
Hernández, Gabriela 267
Heslin, P. A. 57
high-growth industries 93, 95
Hindu religion 108
Hispanic women 238
Hjorth, D. 274
Hockerts, K. 248, 250
Hoffmann, A. 163
Hofstede, G. 158
households 25, 27, 60, 68, 98, 108, 110, 114–16, 139, 142, 196, 227; of Pakistan 27; women-headed 109
housewives 78–79
housework xxvi, 78, 155, 224, 228, 247
Hughes, K. D. xx, 162, 272
human capital xxiii–xxiv, 71, 93–94, 119–21, 125–27, 131, 135, 169, 211, 219, 236, 238–40, 242; accumulation of 243; characteristics influence entrepreneurial activities 214; development 92, 102, 242; improving 101; lower 238; recognized 98; resources 125; and social support 120, 219; women 214
human resource development 175
human rights 7
Hung, D. 213
husbands xxii, 25–26, 64–66, 70, 78, 83–84, 111–13, 115, 143–45, 147–48, 186–88, 222, 277, 280–81

Ibarra, H. 234, 240, 242
ideologies xxii, 33, 36; dominant 6; gender 35, 39, 42
IFC 77, 95; *see also* International Finance Corporation
Ilhaamie, A. G. 6

294 *Index*

ILO 9, 106–7, 111; *see also* International Labor
  Organization
immigrants 182–83
immigration process 68
incentives for women to work 201, 220
income 62, 79, 108, 112, 123, 145, 158, 172–73,
  225, 228, 266; discretionary 168; family 158;
  levels 251; limited 190; middle class 185
India 13
individuals 3, 5–6, 43, 47–50, 107, 109, 114,
  116, 122, 155, 202, 206, 210, 280; creative 39;
  and members of multiple social groups 190;
  motivated 6; normalizing of 47; private 196;
  religious 13
industries 25, 51, 121, 128, 134, 136, 142, 196,
  198, 206–7, 238–39, 242, 267, 269; forest 198;
  green 194, 196; textile 81
influences 169; of religion on entrepreneurship
  12; in women's involvement in entrepreneurial
  activities 210
information 91, 95, 121–22, 124, 128, 130, 132,
  134–35, 169–70, 209–10, 225, 252, 263,
  265–67; asymmetric 240; basic 171; constraints
  128–29; core 135; disseminating of 213; early
  access to 122; elicited 170; incomplete 240;
  market research 265; new 122, 127; predictive
  148; processing 19; redundant 122
infrastructure 62, 176–77, 208
innovation 24, 74, 93, 95, 159, 177–78, 255, 265;
  financial sector 149; strategies 172
insecurity 188–89, 191; economic 189; of
  entrepreneurship 188
institutional environment 20, 107, 115, 155,
  208, 215; constrained 228; in Pakistan 20;
  social 110; unfriendly 29; for women's
  entrepreneurship in Nepal 107, 115
institutional support xxvi, 80, 85, 93, 169,
  212–13, 220, 230; for high-growth industries
  and firms 93; limited 80; significant 208
institutional theory 19, 27, 34–35, 47–48, 61,
  154–55, 163
institutions xxv, 3, 6, 9, 18–19, 26, 35, 106–8,
  110, 115–16, 150, 160, 163, 167; academic
  130; cognitive 108; cultural 42; economic
  177; financial 132; formal xxiv, 19, 108;
  international 77; local 77; long-standing social
  113; microfinance 139, 150; in Pakistan 18;
  public 76, 177; regulatory 61, 106; social xxiv,
  106, 108, 110, 113–14, 116, 273
insurance benefits 187–88
interactions xx–xxi, xxiii, 24, 27, 92, 97–98,
  106–8, 113, 123, 199, 208, 214–15, 237, 261;

dynamic 206, 208, 213; frequent 127; social
  149, 237
interests 10, 24, 34, 51, 54, 82, 127, 145, 163,
  175, 194–95, 198, 200, 202; economic 101;
  entrepreneurial 214; group's 212; of women
  entrepreneurs 24
International Finance Corporation 77, 95
International Labor Organization 9, 106–7, 111
international trade 94–95, 100, 177
internationalization 92, 94, 100–101; exposing
  women to 100; influenced by gender-specific
  challenges 94; of women-led enterprises 92,
  102; of women-led SMEs 95
investment 25, 75, 123–24, 133, 139, 176, 210;
  economic 50; initial money/resource 145;
  practices 68
Isenberg, D. J. xxiii, 93–94, 101, 119, 169, 219
Islam xxi, 3–7, 11–13; early 5; essence of 6–7;
  and female entrepreneurship xxi–xxii, 3, 5, 12;
  lobbyists 21; norms and teachings 4; painted as
  incompatible with business and commerce xxi,
  3; societies xxii, 4–5, 12, 248; teachings of 4;
  and women in Turkey 7
Ismail, S. 209, 213–14
Italy xxi, 273, 275, 277, 279, 281
Itani, H. 35–37, 41–42, 56

Jacobsen, J. 240, 242
Jamali, D. 19, 46–48, 60, 70, 74, 77–78, 208, 213
Jayawarna, D. 221, 230
job market 189
Johansson, E. 196, 198–99, 203
Jones, G. 70
Jurik, Nancy 180–91
justice 28, 76, 197, 234

Kantor, P. 106, 111
Karatas-Ozkan, M. 12–13, 77–79
Karim, L. 139–40, 149
Karki, Shova Thapa xxiv, 106, 106–16, 162
Kauffman Foundation xxvi, 234, 237
Kazanjian, R. 170
Khamis, M. 240, 242
Khan, A. 21, 239
Khandker, S. H. 139
Khoury, Grace 60–71
Kolb, D. 234, 240, 242
Krause, A. xxvi, 93, 234, 237, 242
Krieger, L. H. 234, 237, 239, 241–43
Křížková, Alena 180–91
Krueger, N. F. 249
Kuratko, D. F. 34–35, 38–39, 169

labour 50, 106, 109, 181, 194, 200, 228, 247–48, 268, 277–78; domestic 247; economic necessity and shortage of 50; economics xxvi, 233–34; expatriate 61, 68; foreign 50, 66; hired 145; laws 68

labour market xxvi–xxvii, 50, 70, 74, 155–59, 161–63, 186, 189, 233, 236, 254, 261–62, 268, 270; economics 238; and entrepreneurship xxvi; international 109; patriarchal 78; polices 108; problems 183; and quality of work 157; segregation 238; structure 181; time allocation in 240, 242

Lacivert (brand) 124

Lahore 24–25

Lahore Chamber of Commerce and Industry (LCCI) 25

Latvia xxv, 154, 156–61, 163

Latvian women 162

laws xxv, 9, 22, 35, 48, 107, 113, 157, 160, 163, 177, 233–34, 240, 242; anti-discrimination 155; and economic institutions 177; religious 26

LCM 262–67; *see also* lean canvas model

Le-Renard, A. 62–63, 69–70

leaders 35, 39, 41, 43, 53, 167–68, 174, 189; male tribal xxii, 56; relationship with their followers 40

leadership xxii–xxiii, 23, 34–35, 37–39, 41, 43, 53, 57, 93, 169, 250, 268; choices 53; community 38; effective 35; influences 53; organizational 234; political 52; positions 7, 120, 155, 237; studies 35; style xxii, 34, 55–56; theories 43; transformational 34, 40; value-based 38, 41

lean canvas model 262–67

learning 62, 65–66, 221, 224, 229, 268; processes 268; for special children 224

Lebanese culture 36

Lebanese society 39

Lebanese women entrepreneurs 33, 36–37, 39–41, 43

Lebanon xxi–xxii, 33–35, 37–39, 41–43, 48, 70; collective culture of 37; economic conditions of 38; masculine entrepreneurship discourse in 39; unstable 39; women entrepreneurs in 42, 48, 70

lectures, and workshops 131

Ledgerwood, J. 139

Lee, J. H. 208, 211–12, 251

LeFort, A. 70

legal barriers, eliminating 167

legal research 200

legislation 23, 62, 67; civil rights 240–43; federal 241; government 142; Saudi Arabian 63

Leitch, C. 33–34

Lewis, P. 33, 36

Lidestav, Gun 194–203

Lieblich, A. 50–51

Lim, L. 211

Lingelbach, D. 149

Lisowska, Ewa 154–64

Lithuania xxv, 154, 156–63

Living Museum project 82–83

Maden, C. 78–80, 83, 85

Malaysia xxi, xxvi, 96–99, 206–14; government of 208; handicraft industry xxvi, 206–7, 209, 211, 213–15; and Indonesia 98; and the patriarchal system 214; and women entrepreneurs 209, 211–12; and women's handicraft businesses 212

Malaysia Women Exporters Development Program 91

Malaysian Handicraft Development Corporation (MHDC) 206–7

males 53, 114, 128, 141, 167, 176, 212, 233, 240–42, 273; dominated networks 128, 136; experiences of xxvi, 155, 200; family members 26–27, 84; and gender stereotypes 200

management 61, 85, 150, 162, 190, 194, 199, 201, 211, 233–34, 237, 242; active 201; and entrepreneurship 190, 233; experience 169; financial 238; forest 196–97, 203; for micro-entrepreneurs 150; practices 203; recruitment 169; results 155; skills 255; strategic 243; structure 142–43; training 169

managers 74, 78–79, 82, 155, 185, 239, 267

manufacturing 20, 142–43, 206, 275; and artistic sectors 275; firms 140; and industrial sectors 20; sectors 85, 176

market conditions 85, 180–82; entrepreneur analyses 141; historical 180

market economy 158, 162, 174; free 7; transitional 181

market leadership 38–39

market research 267

marketing 85, 133, 207, 212–13, 225, 236, 268; efforts 206, 212; methods 172; practices 172; problems 147; programmes 212; research 37

marketing channels 144

markets 27–29, 81, 93–94, 111–12, 119, 121, 125–26, 130, 140–41, 176–77, 262, 264, 266, 268; domestic 99; established 181; export 94; flexible 28; foreign 94; formal 111; global

296 *Index*

99; new 95, 100, 134, 172; receptive 172;
subsistence 111; target 266
Markin, Erik 3–13
Marlow, S. xx, 33, 35–37, 41, 46–47, 61, 74, 94,
180–81, 190–91, 207, 209, 212, 247
marriage xxiv, 106–7, 110, 113–15, 279
Martin, Patricia 274, 279
Mason, C. 229
Mat Amin, I. 206–7
material-discursive practices 273, 275
material-semiotic processes 273
maternity 131, 142, 157, 186, 188, 219–20, 228
Matysiak, A. 157
Maurya, A. 263, 265–67
Mazzarol, T. 71, 93
McAdam, M. 33, 61
McGowan, P. 121, 208, 210, 212, 237
McLelland, C. V. 262–63
McNally, Beverley 60–71
Mecca 4–5, 7
MEDEP 109; *see also* Micro-Enterprise
Development Program
media xx, 125; businesses 128, 132–33; and
educational institutions 71
median earnings for women 238
Meechan, B. 120–21
Mexico xxi, 96–99, 220, 224–25, 261–63,
265–68
Micro-Enterprise Development Program 109
micro-entrepreneurs 13, 139–40, 143, 145–50;
female 148; low-tech 140
micro-financing 25, 27, 212–13
microcredit development banks 109
microfinance 139, 149; borrowers 150; context of
149; lending mechanisms 149; loans 144, 146,
149–50; schemes 139; specialized 142
Middle East 4, 6, 8, 47, 60, 62
migration 110, 114–15, 180, 194
Ministry of Women Development 21–23, 25
Minniti, M 19, 77, 84
models 35, 48, 124, 128, 167–68, 170, 230, 235,
248–50, 253–54, 261, 265, 268, 272; autocratic
56; contextual 57; hegemonic 282; life-cycle
stage xxv, 167, 174; market-oriented 220;
measurement 253; multiple analysis 48; for
negotiation outcomes for funding 235;
non-neutral 261; normative relational 52; pro-
family 220, 230; single cultural 273; static 169;
underpinning 53
money 64, 68, 78, 81, 115, 133–34, 145, 147, 156,
176, 189, 210, 225–26, 249–50; employer 186;
repaying of 146
Monroy, Verónica Ilián Baños 261–70

Al-Moosa, Hadil 46–58
Moroccan women 249, 254–55; in activity 249;
and Spanish women 251; in terms of their
social entrepreneurial intention 254
Morocco xxi, 248–49, 251–55
Morrison, A. 167, 169
motherhood xxii, 34, 39, 78, 189, 219–21, 223,
226–29, 241
mothers 36–37, 39, 42, 65, 78, 82–83, 112, 177,
185–86, 188–91, 219–21, 224, 228–29, 248;
and babies 82; and entrepreneurs 39; full-time
187–89; good 221, 227–29; lower-class Roma
186; partnered 188; prospective 220; self-
employed 227; single 186–88, 190, 224;
stay-at-home 224
motivations 40, 54–55, 63–64, 66, 79, 84, 128,
134, 162, 169, 183–84, 194, 201, 241; altruistic
250; inspirational 40; internal 79; women's
210
MoWD 21–23, 25; *see also* Ministry of Women
Development
Muffatto, M. 33, 61
mumpreneurs xxvi, 219–21, 223–30; and
challenges 230; motivated 221; narrative
accounts of 229; working to achieve their
aspirations and career objectives xxvi, 229
Murphy, T. E. 241–42, 249
Muslim and non-Muslim nations xxii, 10, 12
Muslim countries xxii, 8–9, 12, 75
Muslim societies xxi, 3, 6–7, 12
Muslims xxi, 4, 6–7, 9–11, 13, 75

narratives 4, 50, 135, 184–85, 188, 223, 225,
229, 275–76, 278–80; of mumpreneurs 229;
respondent 185; of women entrepreneurs 132,
135, 225
National Rural Support Program 25
non-financial assistance 168, 170–71, 174,
176–77
NRSP 25; *see also* National Rural Support
Program

OECD 9, 76, 78, 83, 157, 174, 181–82, 247,
268; *see also* Organization for Economic
Cooperation and Development
Oman xxi–xxii, 46–47, 49–57; culture 49, 52;
families 56; government 50; nationals 51;
people 56; society 55; unemployment rate 50;
and women entrepreneurs xxii, 46, 50, 52–53,
56–57
Organization for Economic Cooperation and
Development 9, 76, 78, 83, 157, 174, 181–82,
247, 268

organizations xxi, 3, 9, 24–25, 49, 54, 77, 82, 202, 261, 264, 267–68, 272, 275; business support 187; corporate 202; economic 198; formal 274; international assistance 177; international women 77; large established 34; local 147; medium development 127; national/international 76; non-governmental 24, 76–77, 80, 85; non-profit 268

Orser, B. 92, 94–95, 101–2

Orthodox Islam 5

Osterwalder, Alexander 261, 264

Ottoman Empire 7–8, 75

Özbilgin, M. 48

Ozdemir, A. A. 78–80

Özkazanç-Pan, B. 7, 9

Pakistan xxi–xxii, 18–30; context for women's entrepreneurship 18; economy 29; micro-financing initiatives 25; parliament 23; and the regions 22; women 21–22; women entrepreneurs 30

Pakistan Association of Women Entrepreneurs 24

Pakistan Association of Women Entrepreneurs (PAWE) 24

Pakistan Federation of Business and Professional Women 25

Pakistan Poverty Alleviation Fund 25

Pakistan Worker Federation 25

Palestinian 62, 66, 68; and Saudi Arabian female entrepreneurs 60; and Saudi women entrepreneurs 61, 63, 65, 67, 69, 71

part-time work 182, 185–87, 220

patriarchal xxiv, 5, 7, 13, 18, 36, 42, 107–8, 158; and caste-based stratified societal context of Nepal xxiv; constraints 21; contexts undergoing institutional change 106; culture 50; economies xxi; nature 71; norms 27, 78–79, 83, 148; practices 143; society xxii, 57, 61, 66–67, 70, 82, 139; values 77, 84, 212

Patton, D. 51–52

PAWE 24; see also Pakistan Association of Women Entrepreneurs

Perrotta, M. 280

Philippines 96–99

Piacentini, M. 155–56, 176

Pigneur, Yves 261, 264

Podobinski, M. 268

Poggio, Barbara xxvii, 180, 272, 272–82

Poland xxi, xxv, 154, 156–61, 163–64, 167–78; culture of 172; economy 167–68, 172, 176–77; and entry to the EU 168; government 177; labour market 157; and Latvia 159; products and services 173; society 159, 171; and Sweden

154; tourism 168–69, 171, 173, 175, 177; tourism industry 168

policies xxii, 18–23, 29, 66–67, 84, 109–10, 113, 149–50, 173–74, 181–82, 219, 228, 230, 262–63; active 7; evidence-based 102; export 91; friendly 142; gender-aware 29; gender-biased 120; gender-neutral 233, 241; gender-oriented 28; gender-related 18; gendered 18; government's 224; institutional 220; naturalization 182; path-dependent 27; public-sector 22; strategic 268

politics 5–6, 19, 74, 155, 279; and public service 5; Swedish 198

PPAF 25; see also Pakistan Poverty Alleviation Fund

PPP 101; see also Public-private partnerships

practices xxv, 5–6, 8–9, 18, 25, 28, 47–49, 240–41, 243, 264, 273–75, 277, 279, 282; adaptive 146; caring leadership 175; coercive loan collection 149; conflated 273; cultural 33, 248, 274; discursive 275, 279, 282; disjoined institutional 149; entrepreneurial 274; flexible working 262; gender-responsive 92; gender-sensitive trade 97; gendered 197, 274; good 102; interactive 274; intertwined xxvii, 273–75, 279; lending 26; sociomaterial 273, 282; traditional 47; unsafe 66

prejudices xxv, 155, 163, 209

private capital markets 210

private childcare 186, 223

problems xxiii, 75, 77–78, 81–84, 112–13, 129, 132, 167–70, 186, 188, 194–95, 197, 262–63, 266–70; bureaucratic 82; common 189; experienced 177; important 175; managerial 173; social 250, 254

production 75, 112, 124, 144, 147, 172, 176, 199, 207, 264–65, 274, 277–78; annual manure 124; daily 275; food 142–43; mass 265; process 275; video 159; worm fertilizer 124

productivity xx, 101, 106; characteristics 240; local 169

productivity sectors, low 141

products 24, 29, 57, 81–82, 135, 146–47, 171, 173, 177, 196, 199, 264–67, 273–75, 281; culture-oriented tourism 173; developing 64; food 111; handicraft 210–11; higher-value niche tourism 168; innovative 172–73; new 169, 172; plastic 281; poor-quality 81; selling 268; unique tourism 173; women's 63

profitability 67, 197, 200, 203, 247, 266

programmes 21–22, 27, 63, 77, 91, 98, 110, 150, 162, 197, 208, 210, 212–15, 264; academic 255; capacity building 62; entrepreneurial 213;

298   *Index*

executive development 63; exporting 210; gender-reform 22; imaginative development 142, 169; launched internship 24; and projects 22; supporting women's export activities 162; trade promotion 95; word processing 97

projects 22, 77, 82–83, 107, 132, 134–35, 147, 261; cultural 83; entrepreneurial 275; individual-centred 190; industrial 25; social sector 22; in Turkey 82

public-private partnerships 101

PWF 25; *see also* Pakistan Worker Federation

Qur'an 4–6

Ramadani, V. 167

Ranabahu, Nadeera 139–50

reforms 8, 75, 85, 177, 220, 248; economic 8, 75; educational 8; labour government 220

religion 3–7, 9–10, 12–13, 77, 237, 241; complex xxi, 4; comprehensive 4; and female entrepreneurship 12–13; official 7, 75; second largest 4; secular societies 7

religious conservatism 78–79

Renko, M. 34–35

research xx–xxi, 12–13, 33–37, 46–47, 50–52, 56–58, 77–78, 94, 157–59, 180, 210–13, 233–34, 236–39, 263–64; agenda for second-generation gender bias 241; and business ethics 249; and business tools for modern corporations 267; designs 80, 92; methodology 34, 75, 80, 96; on women entrepreneurs 106

resources 27, 91–92, 99, 101–2, 109, 122, 148, 150, 160, 188, 191, 224, 228–29, 263–64; accessing 209; available 121, 131; basic 249; deploying 101; economic 113; environmental 177; human 110, 207, 267–68; personal 145; scarce 121; significant 125

Reuben, E. 155

Reuber, R. 92

Reymen, I. 148

Richards, G. 168

Richardson, E. 4

Ries, Eric 261, 264–65

risk profiles of women 62

Rod, M. 150

Roma 182, 184–85, 189; experiencing discrimination 184; women and mothers 189

Romero, Mary 181

Roomi, M. A. 5, 210–13

Rosmawani, C. H. M. 6

Rouse, J. 106

rural development 194–97, 202

Saeed, Saadat 119–36

Saiz-Álvarez, José Manuel 261–70

Sanchez, G. 252

Sarasvathy, S. D. 121, 140–41, 145, 148–49

Saudi Arabia xxi, 4, 61–64, 66–67, 69–71; and Palestine 61, 64; women entrepreneurs 61, 63, 65, 67, 69, 71

SBFC 25; *see also* Small Business Finance Corporation

scholars xx, 5–6, 46–47, 74, 78, 92, 106, 115, 119, 213, 243

school-age children 110, 187

school holidays 223, 227, 229

schools 4, 37, 209, 222, 230

scientists, females 263

Scott, W. R. 19–20, 34–36, 46–48, 61

SEA 253, 255; *see also* Social Entrepreneurial Activity

second-generation gender bias 234–35, 237, 239–43; deconstructing 233; issues concerning 243

secondary education 110–11, 114–15

secularism 4, 6–9

segregation 26, 78, 83, 156–57; gender-related occupational 162, 254; gendered job 181

Selamat, N. H. 211

self-employment 76, 84, 155–56, 158, 160–63, 182, 187, 195, 219, 223, 247, 254; female 182; tried 187; women's 163

Shangri La Bosphorus (brand) 124

Sharabi, E. 12

Sharia law 4, 7–9, 12

Shaw, E. 191, 209, 211, 247

Sheikh, Shandana 219–30

Sidani, Y. 4, 6, 35

Siddiqui, Majid 28

Siemieńska, R. 155

Sikdar, A. 12, 77

Sist, Federica 119–36, 219–30

skills 19–20, 92, 94, 98–99, 101, 109, 111–12, 115, 121–23, 155–56, 160, 163, 210–11, 225–26; and abilities 214; cognitive 121; and export knowlegde 99; good communication 40; interpersonal 175; managerial 25; non-cognitive 239; professional 175; requisite 69, 236; teamwork 64; technical 195, 278; traditional 24, 29; unpaid 111

Small Business Finance Corporation 25

small businesses 51, 93, 120, 131, 167, 187; activity 120; assistance 91

SMEs 20, 23, 29, 77, 80, 91–92, 95, 98–101, 140, 169, 213, 262, 270; and delegates 98–99; development 98; financing schemes 142; listed

99; in Malaysia 213; managed 20; in Pakistan 20; woman-led 100

Smircich, L. 182, 272–73

social behaviour 26, 47, 53

social capital xxiv, 71, 115, 119–23, 125, 127, 129, 135–36, 212, 229, 279; and business resources 212; structural xxiv; of women entrepreneurs 136

Social Entrepreneurial Activity 253, 255

social entrepreneurship 247–50, 252, 255

social media 124, 132, 225

social networks 74, 80, 111, 119, 121, 129, 131–33, 140, 144, 148, 210, 225, 229, 238; informal xxiv, 119; and opportunity creation in business context 131–32; professional 131; small 210; of women entrepreneurs 225; for women's business establishment 80

social networks, for women entrepreneurs 229

social structures xxii, 48, 56, 61, 107, 121, 154, 248

social support 79–80, 119, 125, 133–34, 219; expressed 222; for women 134

social values 13, 56, 60, 121

society xxi–xxii, 3–7, 12–13, 21–22, 26–28, 39–41, 53–57, 83–85, 107–9, 113–16, 154–55, 198, 212–14, 273–74; caste-based 108; heterogeneous 184; masculine 39; modern 196, 202; non-Muslim xxii, 11; polygamous 5; post-socialist 191; secular 7; stratified 107; traditional farming 198; transitioning 61, 67

socio-cultural authenticity 177

socio-cultural constraints 27, 42

socio-cultural framework on women 213

socio-cultural traits 211

socio-cultural values 6, 36–37, 42–43

Solís, Edgar Rogelio Ramírez xxvii, 248–50, 261, 261–70

Soviet regime 168, 171, 174–77

Spain xxi, 248–49, 251–55; and the adult female population 249; and Morocco 248–49, 251, 253, 255; women of 249, 251–52, 254–55

Sri Lanka xxi, xxiv, 139, 141–43, 145, 147, 149; entrepreneurial thinking and behaviour of xxiv, 139, 142, 144

stakeholders 22, 40–41, 78, 198, 200, 237, 250, 267, 269, 279

stereotypes xxv, 68, 155, 157, 162–63, 182; gender roles in society 27, 37, 85; negative 6

Steyaert, C. 274

stock markets 155

Strober, Myra 238

substance misuse training 123, 125, 131

Swartz, Ethné 233–43

Al-Talei, R. 50

Tambunan, T. 20, 208, 213

tax credits 219, 224

tax policies and business policies for women 178, 220

taxes 65, 109, 126, 131

TDAP 24; *see also* Trade Development Authority of Pakistan

TEA 10–11, 19, 76, 141, 147, 249, 251, 253; *see also* total entrepreneurial activity

Thébaud, S. 187–88

theories 33, 74, 248, 263; of entrepreneurship 33, 140; of leadership 43; traditional 46

Thévenot, L. 280

Thomas, G. 120

timber production 195–96, 201

Tlaiss, Hayfaa xxii, 4–5, 33–44, 48, 56–57, 150

Topimin, Salmah xxvi, 206, 206–15

tourism 159, 168, 177, 195, 201; authorities 177; businesses 172; cultural 177; medical 171; in Poland xxv, 168, 172, 178; services 171, 177; sustainability-oriented 177

trade 4, 25, 62, 77, 91, 94–95, 98, 110, 225; barriers 93; ecosystems 91–92, 94, 101; facilitation 95–96

Trade Development Authority of Pakistan 24

trade fairs 109

trade services 91, 95; implementing gender-responsive 102; review 95; women-focused 91

trade support 91–92, 95, 98–99, 101; activities 98; business-women's 98; dispersed 100; gender-neutral 92, 101; gender-responsive 91, 95, 99–101; practices 92, 96; programmes 97; services 91–92, 96–99, 101; for women 91

traditions xxv–xxvi, 6, 26–27, 44, 108, 143, 163, 168, 171–73, 177, 194, 198, 209, 213–14; and caste 108; cultural 61; old Anatolian 8; socio-cultural xxv

training 24–25, 76–77, 98–99, 111, 114–15, 123, 127–29, 143–44, 169–71, 187–89, 210, 212–14, 225, 268; for business xxvi, 25, 128–29, 170, 175, 210, 214, 227; courses 225; for entrepreneurship 225; informal 144; initiatives 127, 210, 225; programmes 77, 85, 127, 135, 143, 150, 212–13; sport-oriented 171; substance misuse 123, 125, 131; and trade support 91, 99; for women entrepreneurs 127, 210, 225; and workshops 177

Treviño, Blanca 267

Turban, D. 12, 77

Turkey xxi, xxiii–xxiv, 3, 6–13, 74–85, 120–21, 123–29, 131, 133–35, 156; culture of 126; and the declining status of women

300 *Index*

under the Persian state structure 8; and experiences of female entrepreneurs in 83; and female entrepreneurs 77, 126–27, 132; and the government's support for high-profile entrepreneurship summits 76; and the problems/challenges faced by female entrepreneurs 83; and the ratification of the Convention on the Elimination of All Forms of Discrimination Against Women 76; society attaches a lower value to women's employment and entrepreneurship due to patriarchal values 77; and women entrepreneurs xxiv, 76, 119–20, 125, 131–32, 136; and women's perception of information sharing within their networks 128
Turkish Industry and Business Association 77

UK 124, 219–21, 227–30; family welfare policies 220, 228; and the government's efforts to reduce the gender gap 219; and the role of institutional family policies on mumpreneurship in the 227
Ul Haque, I. 20, 27
Umaerus, P. 196, 201
underperformance xxvi, 61, 119, 190, 227, 272; female entrepreneurial 60, 70; gender-related 238
UNDP 22, 109, 147, 214; *see also* United Nations Development Program
unemployment 50, 62, 156, 162, 169, 184, 238, 254; high female 251
unemployment rate 50, 62, 156, 159; female 62, 156; increasing national 50, 156
Union of Chambers and Commodity Exchanges of Turkey 77
United Kingdom *see* UK
United Nations Convention on the Elimination of All Forms of Discrimination Against Women 9, 22, 76
United Nations Development Program 22, 109, 147, 214
United States *see* US
university students 252, 254
unpaid care-work 180
unpaid work 228, 261
US 183, 188; business schools 63; and CR family policies 182; and CR mothers 187; and CR women 184; dollars and customers 67; labour discrimination litigation 239; mothers 190; women entrepreneurs 181, 183, 185, 187, 189, 191

Valdez, Z. 180, 182, 188
Valeri, M. 56

values 41, 92, 95, 100–102, 108, 110, 162–63, 195–96, 199, 201, 213–14, 261, 277, 279; business 4, 261; cultural 12, 44, 83, 101, 211; national 211; social 13, 56, 60, 121; and stereotypes 182
Venkataraman, S. 120
venture capital xxvi, 70, 234; accessing 61, 64; assistance 66; assistance for women 66; firms 176
Vietnam 96–99
Vossenberg, Saskia xx–xxi, 18, 77–78, 84, 180–81

Wales xxiv, 119–21, 123–29, 131–35; and multi-country studies xxi; and Turkey xxiv, 120, 125; and Turkish, entrepreneurs 132; and Turkish, markets 126; and Turkish economies 121; and Turkish entrepreneurial ecosystems 119; and Turkish women xxiv, 125–27; and Turkish women, entrepreneurs 119–20, 131–32; and Turkish women, perception of information sharing within their networks 128; women 125–26, 128–29, 131, 135–36; and women entrepreneurs 125, 127
Warnecke, T. 61
WASME 24; *see also* World Assembly of Small and Medium Enterprises
Wasti, S. 12, 77
WBIC 24; *see also* women business-incubation; women business-incubation centre
WEDP 91, 210; *see also* Women Exporters Development Program
Weiss, J. 23
Welter, F. xx, 18–20, 33, 47–48, 60, 107, 119, 180–81, 206, 208, 212, 228, 272
Williams, D. R. 77, 106, 140, 208, 211
Wilson, K. 139, 238
Wiltbank, R. 141, 145, 149
Wingrove-Haugland, Erik 167–78
women xx–xxvii, 5–9, 18–29, 39–44, 60–71, 74–80, 106–16, 154–64, 180–84, 194–203, 206–15, 219–30, 233–42, 247–51; adult 108; better-educated 155; black 185; and children 63, 229; contemporary xxvi, 155, 247; developing 250; disadvantaged 109, 188; divorced 113; educated 6; employed 54, 160; enterprising 12; in entrepreneurial activities 63–64, 84, 119, 154, 236; family capital 80; and the fear of failure 160; forest owning 201; gender inequality subjugates 212; launching businesses by 162; married 113, 141; with multi-tasking ability 229; mumpreneurs balancing their work-family responsibilities 227; networked 65; non-Western 46; privileged 110; programmes targeting 25;

rural 28–29, 200; self-employed 106, 174, 186, 219; single 110, 113; unfair treatment of 23; white 187

women business-incubation 24

women business-incubation centre 24

women entrepreneurs xxi–xxii, xxiv–xxvii, 18–20, 23–29, 42–43, 55–57, 91–94, 96–99, 125–33, 135–36, 159–60, 167–69, 208–15, 234–36; and backstabbing 135; and business network representatives 96; in developing countries 33; in Pakistan 29; in Saudi Arabia 63; small-scale 119; in Spain and Morocco 249, 251, 253, 255; in Wales 126

Women entrepreneurs, in Polish tourism 169, 171, 173, 175, 177

women entrepreneurship 5, 7, 9, 11, 13, 18, 20, 75, 107, 119–21, 123, 125, 155–59, 272–73; in Nepal 107; in Oman 47, 49, 51, 53, 55, 57; in Pakistan 19, 21, 23, 25, 27, 29; in Poland 175; in Sri Lanka 141, 143, 145, 147, 149; in Swedish forestry 195, 197, 199, 201, 203; in Wales and Turkey 120–21, 123, 125, 127, 129, 131, 133, 135

women exporters 24, 91, 94, 98

Women Exporters Development Program 91, 210

women-owned businesses xxiv, 3, 20–21, 74, 84, 106, 119, 180, 187–88, 190, 208–9, 212, 214–15, 234

work 26, 38–40, 63–64, 66, 113–15, 144–46, 155–58, 160–63, 185–89, 220–24, 226–30, 238–40, 261–64, 275–78; duties 158; experience 63, 70, 211, 239, 276

work-family balance 78, 219–21, 227, 229–30

work-family conflict 188–89, 220

workforce 61–63, 66, 106, 220; participation in the 36

working hours 29, 187, 221, 229

workshops 81, 95–99, 131, 177, 278; and lectures 131; and training 177

World Assembly of Small and Medium Enterprises 24

World Bank xxv, 25, 61, 77, 91, 95, 142, 154

Wright, M. 33

Xheneti, Mirela 106–16

Yamani, M. 63

Yavas, Mansur 82–83

Yousafzai, Shumaila 119–36, 219–30

Zahra, S. A. 33, 107, 119

Zapalska, Alina 167–78

Zavella, P. 180, 182

Zehra, Khizran 18–30

Zelekha, Y. 12

Zia-ul Haq regime 21, 28